Mancini

DIARY OF A CHAMPION

BY HARRY HARRIS

EMPIRE
PUBLICATIONS

First published in 2012

EMPIRE PUBLICATIONS
1 Newton Street, Manchester M1 1HW
© Harry Harris 2012

ISBN 1901746 933 - 9781901746938

Printed in Great Britain.

CONTENTS

CREDITS

Thanks to Vicky Kloss, Head of Communications at Manchester City whom I contacted shortly after the season commenced telling her that City would win the title and I was writing a dairy about the season. Vicky was a great source to put into context and sifting out the truth concerning the multitude of rumours surrounding the club.

Thanks too to Empire Publications in Manchester, to John and Ash for having faith in my idea of a Manchester City book a year ahead of publication.

Finally thanks to my wife Linda, a fellow journalist, for putting up with me.

PUBLISHER CREDITS

For John Conway and his late father Jack. Also for Paul Herstell, Colin Evans, Dante Friend and all long suffering blues now enjoying the good times.

Thanks to Phill Gatenby who proofed the book.

DEDICATION

To Roberto Mancini for being City's Special One.

FOREWORD

The number five has been so influential for this club, it isn't true. When I was a Director and this club was at its lowest ebb it came to the rescue - back in 1999 City were 2-0 down to Gillingham at Wembley in the Division Two play offs, and in those five minutes of injury time, we forced the game into extra time and eventually won on penalties and gained promotion. I dread to think what would have happened had City not got back into the second tier and been left in the third tier of English football; carrying the amount of debt and contracts inherited from the previous regime, there would have had to have been a fire sale of the best players. The only way to put it is that City were at their lowest ebb when the fourth official put that number five up. I would hate to think of the club's future had it been any less, if indeed it would have had a future.

No wonder I had flash backs when the same number went up on that Sunday afternoon and another five minutes of injury time produced the winning goals. My executive box is behind the goal where those two goals were scored and I nearly fell off the balcony. I didn't sit down for the last 30 minutes, it was so exciting. It was very, very rewarding to see City win the title, and it was based on so much that the club did right on and off the field. Off the field they showed they are capable of competing at the highest level. I was so pleased on the field that the team came through, especially pleased that it was Agüero who scored that late, late winner, as he was one of the team's leading lights, so reliably consistent when the club had to go through so much with Tévez and Balotelli. It turned the entire season into pure theatre, pure drama.

But I couldn't help thinking back to how David Bernstein, now FA chairman, came in with a new board and sorted out so much, in particular the two year-long negotiations for the new stadium, and has had little acknowledgment because of so much political in-fighting associated with the club at that time.

When the number five went up at Wembley, Kevin Horlock scored in the 90th minute and Paul Dickov scored several minutes into injury time. The crowd erupted just as they did at the Etihad. Many City fans left Wembley before the final whistle thinking it was finished, as they did this time as well, Noel Gallagher was one of them. But they heard on their radio the goals were going in and they came back that day as they came back again as City won the title. It was a 'Groundhog Day' moment.

But what happened at Wembley when the fourth official put up that number five up on 90 minutes will always stay with me, because the victory in that play-off final enabled City to build, it enabled re-growth, it put the heart and soul back and laid the foundations that has taken the club, with its new owners, from the bottom to the pinnacle. The title is a reward for the fans, and it's been a very, very rewarding season. So much is due to the quality of the club's fan base with their patient and loyal support.

The next challenge is to develop the Academy, which this club can now do with the right investment, because, not just City, but every club knows it is of paramount importance to nurture your own youth talent with Uefa's Financial Fair Play rules coming into force. This is the real challenge, and one City is in a position to meet

DENNIS TUEART

INTRODUCTION

"We played the best football. We scored the most goals, we conceded the fewest. We beat United twice. In the history of the club, a final like this does not exist. I am very proud of my players though. To win the championship like this, I think it will be impossible for the next 100 years."

ROBERTO MANCINI

Roberto Mancini became a legend and a Manchester City hero, by delivering the club's first title in 44 years in the most unusual and dramatic circumstances on arguably the most exciting climax to a season for years.

Mancini is the central figure in this book, detailing every team selection, substitution and behind the scenes detail. From the rows that beset the club to the way in which he motivated his players, how he interacted with some of the personalities in his squad such as Carlos Tévez, Mario Balotelli and Yaya Toure. The means of controlling such a diverse and powerful dressing room was not straightforward and only added lustre to the historic achievement.

Mancini knows that City deserved to claim their first league crown since 1968, having established superiority over title rivals United but due to the complexities of life behind the scenes at the world's wealthiest club, where the demands are enormous and failure is unthinkable, it was never likely to be straight forward.

Mancini's men won the crown on an epic final day after injury-time goals from Edin Dzeko and Sergio Agüero secured a 3-2 win over QPR managed by Mark Hughes, who had been replaced by Mancini in incredible circumstances of their own.

Even more remarkable was the way the afternoon unfolded. Reigning champions United had just completed an unremarkable 1-0 win at the Stadium of Light over Sunderland with their players believing they had landed an unlikely title as City trailed 2-1 going into injury time.

Moments later, news came through of a City equaliser, and as Sir Alex applauded at the final whistle like a man who thought the title was his, Sergio Agüero found a route to goal and scored a dramatic 94th minute winner.

It was a devastating way to win and lose a title. Certainly the most dramatic since Arsenal found an injury-time goal to nick the title off Liverpool at

Anfield in 1989.

There's no doubt that on the day itself, City got lucky. Perhaps that luck was deserved. "We deserved it," Mancini said, "we played the best football. We scored the most goals, we conceded the fewest. We beat United twice. I have never seen a final like this though. In the history of the club, a final like this does not exist. I am very proud of my players though. They wanted to win this title until the last second of the last game. The championship like this, I think it will be impossible for the next 100 years. It's probably the best moment for me."

City won on the slenderest of slender margins, goal difference, yet at one stage, the trophy was going back to Old Trafford, with City trailing 2-1 to QPR and United winning 1-0 at Sunderland. "When I saw the time - 89 minutes - I thought it was finished," said Mancini.

Goals in the 92nd and 94th minutes sealed one of, if not THE, greatest finishes to a title ever. "For me, it was really important to win for our supporters. For them, it's an incredible moment."

Mancini, who guided Inter Milan to three consecutive Serie A titles, added, "To win is always difficult. In Italy, in England, in Spain, it's not easy. But, for me, the Premier League is the best championship in Europe. It's very hard to win here."

Captain Vincent Kompany described the title win as a life-defining moment as he led the celebrations following Agüero's winner, a classic goalscorer's goal as Diego Maradona's son-in-law pulled off his shirt and whirled it around his head, as Mancini and his entourage on the bench were hysterical.

"It is one big blur," said Kompany. "I remember jumping on top of Sergio when he scored the goal. He was crying on the floor. All the guys were pouring their eyes out. You don't see strong personalities like that showing their emotion so often. We expected to win the league. The disappointment of being one goal down was incredible. For us to do it was one of the best moments of my life, together with my wedding and the birth of my child."

"On behalf of Manchester United I congratulate Manchester City on winning the Premier League," said Ferguson. "It's not an easy league to win and anyone who wins it deserves it because it is a long haul. They [City] can go on as much as they like. That's what you would expect, but the history of our club stands us aside. We don't need to worry about that. I think we have a rich history, better than anyone, and it will take them a century to get to our level of history. But for us it's still a challenge and we're good at challenges. We'll kick on from here. The players are very disappointed. There's no other way they should be. They conducted themselves brilliantly, played really good football and, but for the Sunderland keeper, it could have been six or seven. So the performance level was good considering the pressure they were under. They never showed that at all and the temperament was terrific. And I'm pleased with their performance this season. With 89 points, it would have been good enough to win most leagues." In the previous 19 seasons, only six Premier League-winning teams beat United's points tally and all of them had won the title.

Ferguson insisted there was "no doubt" he was relishing the challenge provided by City, "Experiences of a good type enthuse people but, when they have a bad one, it brings a sense of determination in you. The players we think we have here, the younger players, they've got a good resolve about them. There should be a good response because they have got the right character. It shouldn't do them any harm. We don't like doing it but, at the end of the day, you have to kick on and take the challenges because we are good at that."

★

When Roberto Mancini arrived at the Etihad Stadium in December 2009, the blue-and-white City scarf he adopted on his arrival symbolised his commitment to the club with the Italian's cool fashion statement, yet he has never been the calm figure he is often portrayed. His touchline spat with David Moyes in March 2010 emphasised the winning mentality wrapped around his volatile personality and there was the now infamous touchline finger wagging with Sir Alex during the pivotal derby game in this season's run in.

What had seemed like a losing hand with 6 games remaining turned into triumph with many saying he won his war of mind games with Sir Alex Ferguson by insisting the title was 'finished' as City staged a stirring late fight back to win their remaining matches.

As well as delving into the details of Mancini's management, the book also looks closely at owner Sheikh Mansour bin Zayed Al Nahyan and the debate about his $1b investment in the club since acquiring it in September 2008. The club posted a £194.5m loss, the biggest ever registered in English football, yet this is the price to be paid for the quest to become England's top team. The size of the loss for 2010-11 raised concerns over City's ability to meet UEFA's strict rules on financial fair play. City's deficit was mainly down to the huge investment in world class players, Dzeko for £27m, Silva £26m, Yaya £24m, Kolarov £19m, Mario £24m, Milner £26m. Total: £156.5m. Since June the previous year, Mansour poured in a further £291m, on top of the £500m already spend up to that period, smashing through the £1b barrier.

Mancini's turning point was the FA Cup triumph that ended the club's 35-year wait for a major trophy, quickly followed by October's stunning 6-1 derby demolition at Old Trafford that signalled the shift in power in Manchester, English football, and throughout Europe. Sir Alex described that defeat as an "embarrassment" and admitted Mancini's team subjected him to his "worst ever day" in management.

Mancini played down the significance at the time, typical of his understated policy.

Former winger and club director Dennis Tueart will be remembered for his acrobatic overhead kick against Newcastle that delivered the 1976 League Cup, the last piece of notable silverware before the FA Cup win that ended that 35-year drought. He became a board member during City's darkest days after relegation to Division Two and the exit of former legend turned controversial chairman Francis Lee.

By helping put City back on a firm footing he has done more than most in leading the club towards the Promised Land. "I think City fans are more grateful for the success because of where they've been," Tueart explains, "I've had some people coming up to me and say 'Things at City aren't the same now', but most supporters are truly thankful for the position the club is in at the moment. For what they've had to put up with over the years, those fans who went to York, Lincoln and Macclesfield in the dark days deserve what's happening now. Without their unwavering support, the club could never have fought its way back up. It's important to remember where you've come from, what we had then and what we have now.'

Tueart, Summerbee, Lee are big names in the club's past. They are big personalities with legendary status among those of a blue persuasion. Now, in a very different era, it is the multi-millionaires, Mario Balotelli, Carlos Tévez and Yaya Toure who are the stars earning over £1m a month apiece.

None come bigger or more newsworthy than Super Mario. He played 86 times for Inter, scoring 28 goals, winning three Serie A titles, a Coppa Italia and the 2010 Champions League, and remains the youngest Inter player to score in European competition – aged 18 years and 85 days – and continued to impress in Italy despite being subjected to horrific and sustained racist abuse from supporters, especially at away games. Mario is a headline writers dream. Mancini was a maverick himself as a player, so recognises those tendencies in his rising star. Mario once said his coach is "like a dad to me". His big break came at Inter, then managed by Mancini, "A trainer should get the best out of his players and Mancini is good at it – he's doing it now!"

It's not easy; throwing darts at youth-team players, wrecking £100,000 cars, trying to break into a women's prison, dressing as Santa and driving around handing out £20 notes over Christmas, and even buying dinner for everyone at a Nando's restaurant in Manchester – you name it and Mario seems to have done it. He insists the stories are "always exaggerated" and he would be happiest if people would stop talking about him and let him get on with his day job. "The most annoying thing is that in Italy those foolish talks are re-used and amplified without checking. If I buy a Fiat Uno, I'll read that for a man like me a Ferrari was more suitable. If instead I buy a Ferrari, you'll write that I should have kept my feet on the ground and bought a Fiat. If I smile, I'm not serious. If I don't smile I'm a rich sulker that doesn't enjoy having the most beautiful job in the world. Someone should explain to adults and elderly people that I'm not the only rich, young footballer. I'm 21 and I've been living far from home for almost two years now. I adapted well, but I don't have real friends here." He was dating 23-year-old Raffaella Fico, who describes him as "family-orientated", and says he loves to read. They spent Christmas together in Manchester. Previously, he dated Big Brother star Sophie Reade and was linked to Miss Italy contestant Melissa Castagnoli.

A terrace chant inspired by his antics goes, "Oh Balotelli he's a striker, he's good at darts, he's allergic to grass, but when he plays he's f★★★ing class. Drives round Moss Side, with a wallet full of cash, can't put on his vest, but when he does he is the best." Mario doesn't seem offended, on the contrary - "I know it, and I like it!" he comments.

City talisman Yaya Toure, comes from a poor African country, at home he has five brothers and two sisters. Shortly after arriving in Manchester, he bought a state-of-the-art 60 inch TV. His wife Gineba told him to take it back. 'My wife is lovely and she does stop me doing things,' Yaya smiled. 'She tells me I don't need things. She is right. Usually.' When City won the FA Cup Yaya was subdued. He scored the winning goal but to him the day was incomplete. His older brother Kolo, the main reason he joined City, had not been part of the team, he was serving a suspension after failing a doping test two months earlier. 'After the game, we were all in the dressing room and he came to me and asked me why I looked so disappointed. I said, "It's because of you. You weren't out there with me. I came here so we could do things together". It was a very big moment for me. My journey with City had begun. But it wasn't the same because he wasn't on the pitch and he wasn't even in his football kit. It didn't feel right and I told him. But Kolo just smiled. He said: "I play with City, I play with you, and I win with you. I may not have been on the pitch with you, but I have still won with you, and it's fine".'

The defender's suspension galvanized the City players aiming to win the FA Cup for their absent colleague. "We have talked about the best way to win this cup, and he is supporting me and the team to win it,"

Yaya added. "He said if we win the cup we will be winning it for him as well." It was Yaya's goal against United that booked a place in the final for Mancini's side. Kolo lost the captaincy to Carlos Tévez, who in turn was stripped of the captaincy in favour of Kompany, and the Tévez saga would make a book all on its own, as indeed would the stories of Mario or Yaya, so this diary is many facets rolled into one, all held together in the dressing room by one man – Mancini.

JULY

CITY PINCH NASRI FROM UNITED...
AS THE BIG SUMMER SIGNINGS ARRIVE

Friday, July 1, 2011

Former City captain Mike Doyle dies after losing his battle with liver disease at the age of 64 at the end of June, a poignant reminder of City's past, Doyle was one of the stars of the last time the club won the title in 1968. Doyle, who won every domestic honour and the European Cup-Winners' Cup during his 16-year career with City, became a legendary figure at Maine Road during the most successful period in the club's history in the 1960s and 1970s a club more steeped in the past, but suddenly with an incredible future.

Manchester City are the only English champions to be relegated following a title winning season, an apt reflection of a club which has lurched between the sublime and the ridiculous, justifying the term 'long suffering'. Thirteen years ago City prepared for Christmas visits to York City and Wrexham in English football's third tier. Now it was a series of summer signings from the top tier competing with the likes of Barcelona and Real Madrid for the game's best talents – in itself it was a measure of the level of talent Mancini was seeking in his insatiable quest for the biggest honours in the game.

Sheikh Mansour's millions had predictably fast tracked City to the elite from the obscure. The FA Cup triumph ended the United mickey taking. The Old Trafford banner 'Linked by geography, separated by success' was folded up and taken down before Mancini turned his sights to the title immediately after his side lifted the FA Cup when Yaya Toure scored a second-half goal as City beat Stoke 1-0 in a one-sided final. United had earlier picked up their record 19th title with a 1-1 draw against Blackburn.

When asked if the cup victory felt devalued, Mancini said: "Absolutely not. In England there are three competitions, the Premier League, Carling Cup and FA Cup. We won the FA Cup. It is an important trophy. We need to improve more to do another step (win the title) but it was important to start to win because when you start to win, afterwards everything will be easier. We want to try (to match United). We have got to the Champions League, that was our first target and we won the FA Cup. It is very important for this club. This night all the people in Manchester are happy. Next year we will see. It is important we finish well this season. We can try to play for the top with the other teams but this Premier League is very difficult because Liverpool and Tottenham are also very strong teams."

Mancini singled out goalscorer Yaya, whose basic pay packet is reported to be the biggest in the Premier League, for special praise. "We bought him for this. He is a fantastic player. He scored in the semi-final and the final. All season he has played very well." Mario Balotelli was named man of the match, also impressed Mancini. "Balotelli played very well. This trophy for him could be important. It can help him to improve like a man and as a player.'

★

Gael Clichy was the first significant signing of the summer. He was on his way from Arsenal in a £7m move to fill the problematic left-back spot filled unconvincingly by Aleksander Kolarov who had struggled since arriving from Lazio for £16m the previous summer. Everton's Leighton Baines was considered but Clichy, who attracted interest from Liverpool and Paris Saint Germain, had a year left on his contract at The Emirates and was soon snapped up.

Partizan Belgrade's Montenegro centre-back Stefan Savic was another transfer target, and the race for Arsenal's Samir Nasri hotted up, as the player once destined for Old Trafford suddenly became a prime target for City.

With doubts over Tévez, Sergio Agüero, one time Chelsea target, became the hot property Mancini planned to bring to the club while hopes of luring Alexis Sanchez diminished following the Chilean wingers' move to Barcelona.

Shaun Wright-Phillips was one of several City players told they could leave, and he was destined for QPR – and a date with destiny in the final game of the season. Adebayor, a £25m signing from Arsenal two years earlier, rejected the chance to move to Paris St Germain less than a week after turning down a transfer to Zenit St Petersburg and he was eventually destined for a loan move to Spurs.

Saturday, July 2, 2011

Clichy signs a four-year deal worth £90,000-a-week in time to participate in the first day of pre-season at the club's Carrington training ground on Tuesday. Two years earlier Clichy had suggested that players who "think only about money could end up at Manchester City". He criticised Emmanuel Adebayor's move in July 2009, saying at the time: "I really believe if you are a player who thinks only about money then you could end up at Manchester

City. You have to think if you want to play for a big club and have your image or if you want to play for a good club and earn big money. When you ask someone to move for something like £300,000 a week it is just crazy." Swallowing his pride, Clichy moved to Eastlands to win silverware after six years without a trophy at Arsenal. "I joined City because I wanted to win a lot of things. Arsenal started well last season and we just collapsed at the end after the [Carling Cup] final."

Tuesday, July 5, 2011

Carlos Tévez issued his second transfer request in eight months only hours before City were due to report back for pre-season training. Tévez, on international duty with Argentina in the Copa America, released a statement revealing his determination to leave, two years after arriving from United in a deal worth £32m. His wage demands and City's £50m valuation was a massive stumbling block to a transfer. The 27-year-old withdrew a transfer request in December when club chairman Khaldoon Al Mubarak told him that he would be allowed to leave only on City's terms. Despite returning from injury to captain City to victory in the FA Cup final, Tévez cited a desire to be closer to his daughters, who live in Buenos Aires, as the motivation for his request.

Tévez said: "It is with great regret that I have to inform Manchester City of my wish to leave the club. I would like to state that I have great respect for the club, its supporters and the owner, Sheikh Mansour, who has been nothing other than respectful to me. I hope that the people understand the difficult circumstances I have been living under the past 12 months, in regards to my family. Living without my children in Manchester has been incredibly challenging. Everything I do, I do for my daughters, Katie and Florencia. I need to be closer to them and to spend more time with them. I need them to be happy because my life is about them now. I need to be in a place where they can adapt."

Tévez endured a strained relationship with Mancini ever since he replaced the sacked Hughes in Dec 2009. Despite the friction, Tévez produced some of the best football of his career at City, scoring 24 goals last season. After the club secured third spot in the Premier League, Mancini claimed that Tévez had made it clear to him that he would remain at the club. The manager's statement surprised the Tévez camp with the player's domestic situation remaining a problem.

The timing of Tévez statement was a surprise given the player's involvement in the Copa America, but Tévez last month revealed his unhappiness in Manchester, regularly flying back to Argentina to spend time with his family.

Yet, Tévez talked of his pride at captaining the club to success last season, "Being captain of Manchester City, qualifying for the Champions League, winning the FA Cup and finishing as top scorer last season has made me very proud. I hope that most of the City fans will understand that I have given them my all on the pitch and that my dedication to the City cause has been one hundred per cent on the pitch. I hope I have done my bit to help City continue their progress towards their ambition to be champions of England and to advance in the Champions League. I have no doubt that the players and management of City will achieve great success in the future."

City responded quickly to Tévez's request by stepping up their pursuit of Agüero.

Wednesday, July 6, 2011

Tévez advisor Kia Joorabchian suggested a deal with Corinthians was "close" and that the player had agreed the move. The Brazilian club tabled a £35m offer, alerted by Tévez's admission that he wished to leave for the sake of his family. A move to a club in Europe had appeared the most likely route until it was confirmed that Corinthians were attempting to re-sign a player who played for them between Jan 2005 and Aug 2006. "Corinthians made the offer, now it depends only on Manchester City. City have to make a decision," Joorabchian told ESPN Brazil. "Everybody is working to make this happen, me, Corinthians, Tévez and Adrian Ruocco (another of Tévez's representatives). It is impossible to determine the situation, but I think it's close." Tévez set his heart on a return to the club he left to join West Ham five years ago - the start of a turbulent spell in England which involved two seasons at both Manchester United and City. Kia commented, "His dream and mine is to see him back with Corinthians. He said he has a job that does not end there. He wants to return because he has the dream of winning the Copa Libertadores."

The massive transfer fee would be funded through sponsorship and money from TV rights. City valued Tévez at £50m, but with potential suitors in Spain and Italy showing no sign of spending that much, it looked like the forward might be at City after all. Joorabchian insisted European sides were also interested as he scored 53 goals in 86 appearances for City since joining them in 2009 and captained the side to FA Cup glory and Champions League qualification. "The priority is Corinthians, but we have other options," Joorabchian said. "Carlos was the best player in the Premier League, he was the scorer of the team for two consecutive years, he won the FA Cup. He has much appeal in the European market. He is no longer a boy, today he is a great player."

A deal with Corinthians was an attractive prospect for City as it would mean Tévez signing for a team who are not their rivals in any competition. The same applied to Argentine outfit Boca Juniors – Tévez's first club – who Joorabchian says the player would also be open to rejoining. "Carlos will not play for any other Brazilian club than Corinthians, that is an absolute certainty. Boca Juniors and Corinthians are in his heart. He would only play for these two clubs if he went back to Brazil and Argentina."

City were forced to deny that Gareth Barry was the bait in a player-plus-cash deal for Napoli's Ezequiel Lavezzi. Mancini's agent Giorgio De Giorgis, suggested it was happening, "Manchester City's interest in Lavezzi could be a reality. (City) has been negotiating for the past few months with Napoli. But 31m euros for Lavezzi, I think it's excessive. However City could include a player in the deal – the only one could be Barry."

Mancini contradicted De Giorgis releasing a statement via a club spokesman, "Mr Giorgis is not mandated by the football club to deal with transfers, in or out, at Manchester City. Furthermore, there is no intention to sell Gareth Barry, who remains a valued member of the team." City continued their pursuit of Lavezzi regardless of Tévez's imminent future.

City ended their bid to sign Aelxis Sanchez, "I have spoken to Sanchez. He said he was open to the idea of coming to City but then we have pulled out. After our last offer, we are out of the race to acquire the Chilean player."

Mancini was confident Tévez would remain at the club, "Tévez is a good player," Mancini added. "I believe he will remain with us."

Thursday, 7 July, 2011

Bellamy laid bare his public feud with Mancini after being left behind when City's first-team squad fly to Los Angeles for pre-season training, delivering a withering criticism of Mancini's management style and refusal to accept the full extent of his fitness requirements. Bellamy's fractious relationship with Mancini resulted in the former Newcastle and Liverpool forward spending last season on loan at home-town club Cardiff. Having returned to Eastlands ahead of the new season, Bellamy had no intention of reducing his £80,000-a-week wages in order to cut short his stay at City, where his contract expires next summer.

"Manchester City is the richest club in the world. They work to a budget that no one else works to, so they can write their own rules. Right now, the club has got itself in a situation where a lot of players have to go on loan." City had no interest in another loan transfer. At present, I expect to go back there and stay the whole year. And if Mancini is still there, I'll do probably very little, obviously I won't be involved with him and the first team."

His career at the club nosedived within days of Mancini installed as Hughes' successor in Dec 2009, according to the player. Bellamy had been allowed to adhere to a personalised training regime under Hughes in order to protect long-term knee problems, but the player's claims Mancini refused to allow it to continue. "It was tough [when Hughes left], it was like losing someone. It was probably as bad as losing a family member in some ways, I even struggled to eat for a few days. It was a totally different structure which affected me completely. Mancini told me to stay with the team all the time. We had longer training sessions, but with no intensity whatsoever. He seemed to know my knee better than I knew it myself. He tried to explain why I had problems with it, and what I should do about it. When I told him that my knee was hurting, he tried to tell me that it wasn't.

"Mancini wanted me to come in another day and do some work, but I told him that I'd finished my work that day, that I was keeping to my own schedule. That was when he started about my programme, that I couldn't follow my own schedule while he was the manager, and that I had to do what he was telling me. He said, 'If you don't, you can go back home now. And don't come in again'. I replied, 'OK, no problem, I'm going home then'. That was a week after he'd arrived, and then he never spoke to me again. When I went into pre-season, the physiotherapist Jamie Murphy spoke to Mancini and told him that I wasn't able to do a lot of the things that Mancini wanted, because it would cause a reaction in my knee. Mancini wants to have it all. I went away to the pre-season tour in America, trained with the squad, but my knee blew up, and it became more swollen than it has ever been. I didn't know what to do. I couldn't have turned around and said, 'Look, I'm not training'. Because then they would have said that I refused to train and that I didn't want to be there. The same old rubbish, so I forced myself to train even more."

Fri, 8 July, 2011

City boosted prospects of meeting Uefa's Financial Fair Play rules, announcing a stadium naming rights deal worth in excess of £10 million a year with Abu Dhabi government-owned airline Etihad. Having posted a loss of £121m in accounts for the financial year ending May 2010, the injection of funds from Etihad - also City's shirt sponsors - enabled the club to move closer to falling in line with the FFP strictures, which could see team's barred from European competition if they post losses in excess of 45 million euros (£40 million) during a three-year monitoring period which commences at the start of the 2011-12 season.

With City owned by Sheikh Mansour bin Zayed al Nahyan of Abu

Dhabi, however, Uefa were likely to look closely at the financial aspects of the naming rights for the City of Manchester Stadium in order to ensure that the monies received as part of the deal are market-value figures in line with similar deals. Uefa made it clear in guidelines for FFP that commercial deals which appear artificially inflated could contravene regulations, but City's deal did not fall into this category. Arsenal's deal with Emirates over the naming of the club's new stadium at Ashburton Grove in Oct 2004 was valued at £100m over 15 years, a figure which also included an eight-year shirt sponsorship worth about £6m a year. The growth of the Premier League since that deal was struck ensure that similar agreements are now potentially much more lucrative.

Alongside Etihad, City have commercial deals with other Abu Dhabi-based companies such as Etisalat, Aaabar Investments and the Abu Dhabi Tourism Authority.

Chief executive Garry Cook insisted that the club will maintain a "very open dialogue" with Uefa over their attempts to comply with incoming Financial Fair Play regulations. The agreement increased City's portfolio of Abu Dhabi-based commercial partners to five. A Uefa spokesman said: "We are aware of the situation and our experts will make assessments of fair value of any sponsorship deals using benchmarks."

Incorporated into the naming rights deal is an upgrade of the current shirt sponsorship agreement – worth just £3.2m-a-year when struck in 2009 – and a substantial investment into the area surrounding the stadium in east Manchester, which includes Sportcity, retail outlets, car parks and a proposed new academy and sports science facility. That area will come under the umbrella of the Etihad Campus and, with infrastructure development exempt from FFP regulations, the wide-ranging make-up of City's deal with Etihad leaves Uefa with no obvious benchmark to measure against when reviewing the club's lucrative agreement.

City needed to deliver a clear breakdown of the deal to Uefa, but Cook insisted that discussions have already taken place and will continue to do so. "We already have a very open dialogue with Uefa and have had several meetings with their people. They are very supportive of our plans. All clubs have to comply to meet regulations and we are no different, but we are looking to grow, on and off the pitch. The backdrop, of course, is Uefa's Financial Fair Play and this [deal] helps to continue to make significant progress in that area. It would be very fair to say this is a real deal. Financial Fair Play isn't the driver, commercial growth is the driver."

Despite Etihad being owned by an Abu Dhabi government headed by Sheikh Mansour's half-brother, Sheikh Khalifa bin Zayed bin Sultan Al

Nahyan, the airline's chief executive, James Hogan, insisted the sponsorship arrangement is purely business-driven. "If this deal didn't add up, I would not be doing it. We are a stand-alone business owned by the Emiracy, but we are responsible for our own activities."

City rented the stadium from Manchester city council, Sir Richard Leese, the council leader, revealed that a new rental agreement between the two parties which enabled the club to secure a naming rights deal, was struck earlier this year, with the council receiving £20m over the next five years from the club.

But while the financial fillip of the Etihad deal will go a long way towards helping City break even, comparisons with individual deals struck by the world's major clubs suggests that the naming rights deal is not likely to fall into the category of artificially-inflated rates. Barcelona secured a five-year shirt deal worth £125 million with the Qatar Foundation earlier this year, while United are expected to replace their £302.9m kit deal with Nike – struck in 2002 – with a deal in excess of £500m in the next year. In contrast, City have reached their impressive figure by packaging the stadium name together with shirt space and surrounding real estate.

Sir Bobby Charlton ruled out the prospect of United selling the naming rights to Old Trafford by insisting that the club's heritage is "too important". Liverpool's managing director Ian Ayre wanted Uefa to investigate whether City's sponsorship was an illegal deal under its financial fair play regulations. Speaking in Kuala Lumpur, where Wenger accused City of "financial doping", Ayre suggested that the ten year sponsorship may be an illegal 'related-party' deal, which financial fair play specifically outlaws.

City's first-team squad flew to Los Angeles for pre-season preparations with several out-of-favour players left at home by Mancini. Shay Given, who was on his way to Aston Villa, remained in Manchester, along with Craig Bellamy, Emmanuel Adebayor, Wayne Bridge and Jo, who was a loan target for CSKA Moscow.

Saturday, July 9, 2011

Patrick Vieira, the former Arsenal captain, was in talks over a coaching role at Eastlands following the expiry of his playing contract. Vieira rejected a similar offer from Arsenal in order to consider City's offer, which also includes an ambassadorial role. Vieira said: "This role is a fantastic new challenge for me and I am very grateful to Manchester City for offering me this opportunity. I have a lot to learn about the non-playing areas of the business, but there are many very experienced people here for me to learn from, and I am confident that I can make a significant contribution to the club's ongoing success."Vieira was Mancini's first signing when he left Inter Milan to return to the Premier League in January 2010. Not a regular starter, he made 47 appearances, scoring six goals, with his final run-out in a City shirt coming as a late substitute in the FA Cup final victory over Stoke in May.

As well as working in the youth set-up, Vieira will also help to deliver the club's social responsibility programme and help with the commercial side of the business in an ambassadorial role.

Tuesday, 12 July 2011

City rejected a 40m euros offer from Corinthians, a club-record bid from his former employers. City valued last season's leading scorer closer to £50m and dismissed Corinthians' opening offer within 24 hours, confirming Joorabchian's view that getting his clients' potential move back to Brazil "will not be simple". City's wealthy hierarchy felt under no pressure to sell a key figure in Mancini's team who was under contract until 2014. City also recognised the destabilising effect of Tévez's frequent claims of disillusionment and a compromise fee, plus encouragement in their own search for a replacement, made a deal possible. President of Corinthians, Andrés Sánchez, claimed that no official response had been received from City but on being told by ESPN Brasil that his offer had been rejected, he said: "In that case it's over, we'll never have Tévez back at Corinthians." Recognising that Tévez is the highest-paid player in the Premier League on £198,000-a-week, Sánchez added: "If he comes, he will be earning less. Because it's his wish to return here. If they want £50m, then he's going to stay in England. Corinthians are not going to raise their bid," although ESPN Brasil noted this response was "in the heat of the moment after being told the news". Although time was running out for the deal to be agreed – the Brazilian transfer window closed on 20 July – Tévez and his representatives were hopeful the pending arrival of Agüero would facilitate the sale of Tévez.

Joorabchian said prior to City's rejection: "It is a big deal and a tough deal, because it is one of a very big nature and it might not be simple. We wait to see. If they do accept, then everyone will be running to make it happen. If they don't we will have to see what other options would be available for him."

Jose Mourinho wished to sign another forward but Joorabchian added: "It is very difficult to start speculating – the reality is that Corinthians have made an offer. We have never spoken to Real Madrid and they have made no offer."

Corinthians' ability to fund a deal for Tévez came as a surprise but with a new training centre and 68,000-capacity stadium costing £140m due to open in 2013, they soon expect to become the biggest club in South America. The club reportedly bring in £40m every year from their TV rights and £23m from main shirt sponsors Neo Química.

Tévez originally joined Corinthians from Boca Juniors for £13.7m in 2005 and scored 25 goals in 38 league games before signing for West Ham in 2007. "His dream and mine is to see him back with Corinthians." Tévez said: "An offer arrived and I would have no problem returning. They got in contact with me, sent an offer to the club and in eight to ten days the transfer market in Brazil closes."

Wednesday, 13 July, 2011

Emmanuel Adebayor effectively goes on strike by failing to appear for training. He had been due to take part in a practice session at the club's Carrington headquarters. But he did not appear and faced being docked two weeks' wages by the club, £330,000. Adebayor claimed he received an email from the club informing him he would not be part of their pre-season tour. "I don't know what I have done wrong. I get an email, out of the blue, on my holidays telling me I wasn't going on the tour and they told me I am not going to train with the first team. It's an insult to me to tell me I am now only fit to train with the reserves. I will return to training but I feel I've been let down and disrespected."

Thursday, 14 July, 2011

City players try out planking, the internet craze for lying facedown in odd places, to kill the time during their pre-season tour. Shaun Wright-Phillips was the first to tweet a picture of himself planking, a pose on the side of a door frame. Micah Richards responded with an imaginative but poorly-executed effort on top of a tactics whiteboard, Hart's contribution looked impressive enough, but his team-mates were holding his legs. Shaun Wright-Phillips later posted a video of himself attempting a moving plank.

Jerome Boateng joined Bayern Munich on a four-year deal. The 22 year-old joined City last summer from Hamburg but struggled to make an impact due to a succession of injuries. Boateng left City's training camp in Los Angeles to fly to Germany, to sign for 13.5m euros. Boateng was upset at being played at right-back at Eastlands. "I told Roberto Mancini that I want to play in central defence and not at full-back. Bayern have indicated I will play in the centre. To play there regularly is important for me because I will have a better chance of playing in the national team."

Fri, 15 July 2011

Corinthians make an improved offer of £40m in the hope of concluding a deal before the Brazilian club's self-imposed deadline. Corinthians described their latest bid as final. No clubs in Europe made a formal offer although Real retained an interest, but Mourinho favoured a permanent move for Adebayor, who spent five months on loan at the Bernabéu from City last season.

Corinthian president Andres Sanchez claims Juventus had entered the race by lodging a £45m bid, although that was denied by City. The South American side increased their offer despite saying last week that they would not go above £35m and Tévez, the Premier League's highest-paid player, accepted a cut to his wages to return there. City would not countenance a loan deal – similar to the one that allowed Robinho to join Santos in 2010. Sheikh Mansour was content to retain the unsettled Tévez for another season if his valuation was not met but was mindful that Mancini preferred to sell.

City's move for Agüero, viewed by Mancini as the best replacement for Tévez, although he had a release clause of £38m. Mancini confirmed his interest in Agüero, though admitted a deal for Nasri was "difficult". Mancini added: "Samir is under contract with Arsenal. Also for Samir it depends on many things." Asked if an offer has been made for Nasri, Mancini continued: "I don't know in this moment, I don't know the situation but for Nasri it is difficult. I hope that we can buy because we need other players, and I hope that this player can arrive before the end of the month."

Mancini was already giving thought to the role Agüero could play at City, "Agüero is a player that can play for Manchester City because he is young and he is a good player like Carlos. He can score a lot of goals and can play with Mario, with Edin ... it could be."

Saturday, 16, July, 2011

Yaya Toure expects to win the title, "The new season will be very, very hard and we need to improve, because this season the club will play in the Champions League. We expect to stay in the top four of the Premier League and we expect to win the Premier League because now we are coming with more confidence, the players know each other better. I think this year will be fantastic for us." Yaya, who scored the winning goals in the semi-final and final of the FA Cup, expects his brother, to make a successful return, "Kolo's well. He's in New York with the family. We hope September will come quickly and we hope to help the club win something again next year."

Arsene Wenger claims Roberto Mancini was "out of order" for publicly declaring his wish to sign Nasri. Wenger was furious at the way other clubs were openly talking about players who are under contract at his club. Wenger called Barcelona "disrespectful" for their repeated public pursuit of Fabregas and he accused Mancini of breaking football's code of conduct. "I think the comments are not allowed. They are against the basic rules of football and he should be informed. What we want is respect and we don't make these comments about players who are under contract at other clubs. It's time football in England came back to these basic rules." Asked if Mancini was also disrespectful, Wenger said: "I cannot say otherwise. This comment is absolutely out of order but I don't give it more importance than that."

City received a second bid for Tévez, 40m euros plus 4.5m euros in add-ons, still short of City's 45m euro asking price, but gave both clubs a basis for a deal.

Tévez was owed significant sums in bonuses by City and if he decided not to take them up it could help get closer to City's asking price. Another factor was that City will accept a lower bid from Corinthians than they would from a European club, partly as the player wants to be closer to his family but also because they are not a Champions League rival.

Sunday, 17, July, 2011

Mancini confirmed an agreement had been reached with Corinthians for the sale of Tévez. Mancini said: "We have an agreement with Corinthians but Carlos now is still a City player." Asked whether Tévez would now be discussing personal terms, Mancini replied: "I don't know this. I repeat, at the moment, Carlos is still a City player. I want to wait. At the moment we are here, we are working with the other guys. We should think about this." Joleon Lescott would be disappointed to see his team-mate depart, "We'll be disappointed if Carlos leaves but it was down to the club and Carlos what was best for each other and they have come to an agreement so I wish both parties all the best. Carlos is his own man. Last season he played to 110% every game so none of us will be holding any grudges towards him and we'll wish him all the best if he does leave."

Mancini moved to defuse his feud with Arsene Wenger, "I said only that Nasri, Agüero are two good players and I said also that Nasri is under contract with Arsenal. I don't know why he's upset. Because the question was about some good players, I say it like this. I said also that Nasri is under contract with Arsenal and it's difficult. Only this."

Tévez's miserable summer took another turn for the worse, as his missed penalty sealed an ignominious exit for Argentina in the Copa America quarter-finals. The competition hosts were beaten 5-4 in a shoot-out by Uruguay, with Tévez's decisive effort saved by goalkeeper Fernando Muslera after the teams had been locked at 1-1 in normal time.

Monday 18, July 2011

Roberto Mancini is clattered by new signing Savic during preparations for the friendly with Vancouver Whitecaps. Hart observed, "It was awesome, I was watching it. Brilliant. The gaffer was training and Stefan properly did him. I think that's a statement of intent. The gaffer took it well, I think he'd love all that. If the boss wants to get involved in training I think he should realise he will get the treatment off the players. Everyone had a laugh about it, I was roaring with laughter. I liked it. You train as you want to play."

Hart noticed how the new acquisitions had their eyes opened by the competitiveness of Mancini's training sessions, "Gael Clichy didn't know what had hit him with people flying in. There was no malice in it but if the ball is there, you want it. We're all men and sometimes there's a bit of bad blood, but obviously everyone respects each other. We're a football team, not a bunch of idiots who just go around fighting each other, and we just want to keep proving that we're winners." Mancini gingerly iced his bruises and had vivid evidence on his ankle.

Meanwhile, Corinthians denied Mancini's claim that the club accepted a bid for Tévez. Mancini said there was an "agreement" pending Tévez securing personal terms. President Andres Sanchez denied a deal had been reached. "Regarding the news published during the early hours of today stating an agreement between Corinthians and striker Carlos Tévez, the (club) president Andres Sanchez would like to clarify to the public that Manchester City did not accept the Corinthians offer for the player. The truth is that the club sent Corinthians a counter-proposal in the early hours, that due to the time difference only was noticed by the Alvinegra (white and blacks) management this morning. In the counter-proposal, the English club have asked for changes in the form of payment and on the value of the transfer. In addition, Manchester City has also insisted that Tévez would have to give up a pending amount with the English club. Lastly, president Andres Sanchez informs that for the time being there does not exists anything concrete for Tévez and the counter-proposal will be analysed by him and by his management."

Tuesday, 19, July, 2011

After City's 2-1 win over Vancouver Whitecaps, the post-match discussion soon turned to Tévez's on-off move to Corinthians, "I slept last night and I had a game to prepare for today so I don't know any more," Mancini said. "The clubs are talking. They only have one number and it does not work at the moment."

Nevertheless it appeared that Sergio Agüero was on his way to replace Tévez "Maybe in the next days," Mancini said. "I have not spoken to anyone about it, but probably. I think so."

There was dressing room discussion about Tévez, "There has obviously been the odd chat about Carlos," revealed Gareth Barry. "He has made it clear he is ready to leave and the players will respect his decision. It is down to the club to decide what fee they want for Carlos. We would be sad to lose him because he is a class player who has worked really hard for the club. If you believe what you read, then yes, he has played his last game. But he has been great for Manchester City. He has helped the club win its first trophy and he has always given 100 per cent. We are grateful for that."

The loss of one top player just heralds the arrival of another. "Agüero is a very exciting player from what I have seen on TV," said Barry. "He is a class act. Names like that will excite fans and the players."

There was also praise for John Guidetti, who equalised for City before Wright-Phillips slammed home a late winner. "John is young. He is a good player and I think he can have a good future at Manchester City," said Barry. "He is strong. He is a typical English striker, even though he is Swedish. He has a good technique. He wants to improve. He will have time here. It is important that he continues to work well and continues to improve. Today he scored a good goal but when you are a young player, you need to improve every day. This year is important. He has a chance."

Wednesday 20 July, 2011

Tévez faced returning to City against his wishes, following the official announcement from Corinthians that it was "impossible" for them to conclude what would have been by far the biggest transfer in the history of Brazilian football before Wednesday night's transfer deadline in Brazil. "While acknowledging the efforts of Manchester City, and everyone involved in the negotiations, there wasn't enough time for the transfer to be completed," a Corinthians statement said. "We are aware our fans wanted Tévez to join our club again and we hope we can have the player with us in the future"

City accepted Corinthians' valuation of the player, with another £4m in potential add-ons, but the deal first ran into trouble because they could not agree a payment schedule that was acceptable to both parties. City made allowances to help facilitate the move, lowering their original £50m asking price, but their suspicion over the last few days was that Corinthians had badly over stretched themselves. The Brazilians' previous transfer record was £9.35m, when they first signed Tévez as a 20-year-old from Boca Juniors in 2004, and they were heavily reliant on sponsorship money to bring the player back to São Paulo. They were unable to afford the first payment of £8.7m, asking City if they could delay settling it until next year. City were willing to accept four different payments over four years but Corinthians were unable to provide the bank assurances regarded as fundamental to signing off the deal.

The collapse of the deal left Tévez required to return to City for the start of the new season, resuming life in Manchester, the city he has openly admitted disliking. Tévez was still looking to leave, but was not "overly worried" about his proposed transfer to Corinthians falling through. Joorabchian, expected other clubs to come in for his client. "This is Carlos Tévez we are talking about, one of the best players in the world. We are not overly worried. He wants to leave but is still a City player at the moment and we will of course respect that. We've just got to wait and see who comes in next for him. This deal was always going to be difficult because of the timing. In the end, this came down to small details, to haggling over a relatively small amount of money, and it couldn't be done in time."

Joorabchian played down suggestions that the deal had collapsed because Corinthians were unable to provide a bank guarantee. "To say that Corinthians could not provide guarantees for the money is nonsense. Firstly, they are the biggest club in Brazil. Secondly, any club that makes an offer and cannot pay will get suspended by Fifa and have points deducted."

Thursday, 21, July 2011

David Beckham faced Manchester City in a friendly and then United as part of a Major League Soccer All-Stars team. Still a United man he could not resist taking a swipe at City, describing the game against them as "small" telling them that even their lavish spending cannot buy United's history, "This game on Sunday is just a small game. I am looking forward more to the All-Stars game against the best team in Manchester. The best team in England. That's going to be a great game. The money that has been pumped into the club has been incredible. Players have been bought and that does a lot but United have that history and its not all about paying fortunes for players. It's important that the players get along with each other, for example. That makes team spirit. As much as they have got the money to bring players in, sometimes that doesn't work.

"If they continue they will be a threat but there are no guarantees. I don't know. I haven't been around their team and their squad and I wouldn't want to be around Man City. If they continue to bring players in then who knows? You saw it with Chelsea when Roman arrived. They won two leagues and they won them on the trot. It works sometimes, but hopefully it won't work at City." Despite his enjoyment at the chance to goad City a little, Beckham added, "There is no extra motivation because it's Man City. It's just another game. It's not special to me because its Man City. I am a Man United fan. They may have some great players and be a threat against teams but Manchester United have the history and the silverware. I am a United fan so I will always say there's only one team in Manchester."

Fri 22 July, 2011

Roberto Mancini wanted greater control over team affairs, being more hands-on in matters of transfers, especially, will make him and his club more successful, as well as shaping his own destiny as he prepares for the double challenge of going for title and a first assault on the Champions League.

He admitted there had been tensions between him, the then chief executive Garry Cook and Brian Marwood, the football administration officer. Having wanted to bring in five new players this summer he welcomed only two so far, although Agüero's £38m transfer was a done deal. Mancini played down talk of a rift between Cook and Marwood, saying all three are thinking the same way: "All of us want to win. Maybe we had a different way but now we have a good relationship. Maybe because I think this way and Garry another way but this is normal when you work with other people. We have all the same targets – we want to win and we work for this. For me it's difficult because I have only been here for 18 months or so. Maybe I need to have more control of the team and the other situations. For a manager that's very important.

"Maybe if I win the Premier League this season it will be different. It's important for the manager to have control over the players and the medical staff and the other situations. It is different from Italy where managers do not have this control and I prefer the English style because if the manager loses, the manager is sacked, and for this I think the manager needs to take every decision. If he makes a mistake he pays for it."

Sir Alex Ferguson earlier described City as a 'thorn in the flesh' of United but Mancini would like to copy the all-powerful Scotsman at Old Trafford. "I agree with him but he has been at United for a long time so for him it is easy, but yes, he has to be in control of everything."

Mancini was perturbed that his desire to recruit more new players sooner rather than later so that they could bed down during City's North American tour had not happened, "For a team like us it's important to move quickly and to move before the end of the season. Then you have no problem in June and July. You have the players for pre-season.'

Mancini believed Agüero could become a big star in England. "Agüero is a good player, like Samir Nasri, like Cesc Fabregas, like Robin van Persie.

Agüero is young and can score a lot of goals. For me he will become a top striker. He is 23 and it is his time." Mancini still believed the unhappy Tévez and Agüero can become a potent partnership. In other news, Pablo Zabaleta signed a new three-year contract.

Sunday, 24 Jul 2011

Mario Balotelli was embarrassingly substituted by an enraged Mancini after performing a pirouette and back-heeling wide when clean through on goal. Mario enraged his manager and team-mates 29 minutes into the final game of his club's North American tour, having already scored with a penalty kick, only needed to touch the ball to Dzeko to allow the Bosnian the easiest of strikes from no more than two yards. Instead he attempted an outrageous back-heel after turning full circle that also involved a drag back, the only problem that he missed the target. His circus trick brought a furious verbal assault from team-mate Nigel de Jong and much worse from manager Mancini, who immediately signalled James Milner to come on. Three minutes later, as Milner replaced him, Mario made a petulant gesture to his boss indicating his surprise and annoyance that he was substituted, not having occurred to him that his action was viewed as selfish and disrespectful. In response Mancini gave him a mouthful, pointing to the Galaxy goal as he did so, and when the tempestuous 20 year old tried to answer back as he headed for a seat on the bench, Mancini followed him, shouting all the way.

Last season Mario had found himself in hot water for throwing darts at some of his club's youth team players and he impressed neither the club nor its supporters by failing to turn up for City's FA Cup victory parade through Manchester, heading for his home in Italy instead.

Mancini commented, "I have spoken to Mario and told him that every game, no matter who we play against or in what tournament, that players must be professional and that they must always be serious. Mario is young and sometimes he makes mistakes but I want to help him as much as I can and I think that can be a lesson to him. I hope he sees what I did was a lesson and that he understands that. By taking Mario off after 30 minutes I think I am sending an important message. That is that any player, if plays serious, then he can stay on the pitch for 90 minutes. Mario knows that he made a mistake and he knows that he has always to be serious, that when he has a chance to score a goal he should try and score. But for me now, the matter is finished."

Mancini wanted to start bedding down his team for the forthcoming season, but in a game in which Beckham never figured, 18-year-old Swede John Guidetti missed an open goal with almost the last kick of the match.

In the shoot-out that followed with the scored level at 6 – 6, Hart stepped up himself to fire the ball past his opposite number Josh Saunders. That kick gave City the third successive win of their tour, having already beaten Club America and Vancouver Whitecaps.

Monday, July 25, 2011

Edin Dzeko was looking forward to his first full season with City, after a disappointing first five months that followed his £24m transfer from VfL Wolfsburg in early January. He had scored only two goals in 15 League games, managed just six in a total of 21 games in all competitions and the nickname of The Lamp Post, that haunted him from early in his career, seemed to be accurate. "I was sick of it, all about this transfer. For my head, it was a little bit difficult. I was new in the team and it was a hard season. It's always difficult to come to a new club midway through a hard season like that although I still think I had some good games, but that's passed now. Now is my second season and I want to do better. I will do my best."

Dzeko was talking at a beach soccer event held by City down the Pacific coast from their Marina del Rey HQ before their final game of their North American tour against LA Galaxy, relaxed about the wealth of talent at the club, yet he insisted: "I don't think about that. Manchester City didn't pay money for me because they saw me once on YouTube or something like that. They saw me scoring good goals. I haven't forgotten how to score goals and I will show that next season. I think the fans have helped me a lot. Sometimes when a striker hasn't scored and they're still singing your name, it's something special and the manager, he's telling me all the time, 'I believe in you and just work hard' and that's what I'm doing. So I want the new season to have started already. I've had a pre-season with the team now, which I think is the most important thing for every player, and I think I'm working hard and well and so we'll see. But I know this season will be much better. City hadn't won anything for 35 years and then we won the FA Cup and I was in the team. I think that could be a beginning for me. I'm not thinking about what has happened in the past or what may happen in the future. It's important what I do now. I've trained well and we'll see what happens when the season starts."

Fri, July 29, 2011

Mancini hailed Sergio Agüero as the man to help fill the City trophy cabinet. Mancini splashed more than £50m on Agüero, Clichy and Savic, but if his team were to make an impact, Agüero can't be the last new arrival, "Agüero is here because we think he is a top player and he can have a big future at the club. Sergio is a really top player because he is young, but he has also scored a lot of goals. I think he can score more goals for us and help us win trophies. If we want to compete with all the other top teams in the Champions League we need other players. We need one midfielder and one winger."

That could change if Tévez engineered a move. Mancini believed he had the strike force to challenge at home and abroad – if Tévez stays. "At the moment Carlos is a City player. Carlos is an important player for us but I don't know what can happen. A top squad needs to have four good strikers because this season we will play in the Champions League, FA Cup, Carling Cup and the Premier League. Agüero can play with Edin Dzeko, he can play with Mario Balotelli and he can play with Carlos. We need to have four strikers and at the moment we do. If Carlos stays, I'm happy."

Agüero spoke to Tévez before making the move, but he doesn't care if he stays or goes. "I spoke to Carlos. He's a good friend. I will adapt to the team either way. If he's here, I'll adapt and play with him. We are good friends and we have played together in the national team. Of course it is down to him, whatever he wants to do. I just want to concentrate on playing here. I'm very happy to be here." Agüero canvassed opinion from father-in-law Diego Maradona, "I'm enjoying my time with my colleagues. I'm looking forward to starting playing and moving forward, that's what we all want to do. They are a great team with great players and I think I am playing with one of the best English teams. There are many things that can be achieved. I always play to win titles and hopefully I can do that here."

Meanwhile Tévez's hopes of escaping Manchester for Milan were dealt a blow after Inter manager Gian Piero Gasperini dismissed suggestions the Nerazzurri would look to discuss a move when the two teams meet in the Dublin Cup. "The transfer window is still open but what is important is the reality of things, and the reality is that Carlos Tévez is with Manchester City."

Agüero was ready for English football, "I believe so. There is no doubt in my mind that my football education has been rounded off at Atletico as I'm more team-orientated than before. I am much more aware of what is going on around me and tactically sharper. I've become a more versatile attacker and more aware in my movement. However, there is still so much more for me to improve on."

Agüero first met his prospective father-in-law back in 2007, as 19-year-old he was invited to Diego Maradona's home as the new man in his daughter Giannina's life.

As for City, he commented, "I'm sure I'll settle in well to the team. I don't think I'll need to change my style. I'll obviously be doing my best to do what the manager says, and try to work the way he wants me to, and of course he will know how he wants to use me. Obviously I can't say for sure because I haven't even made my debut yet, but I'm sure everything will be fine. I'll be relaxed about it. I think I'll adapt to life in England – I don't like hot weather, so I'll be fine there. I'm sure I'm going to enjoy myself there and life will be fine."

The new No.16 believed his team can upset their rivals at Wembley. "I think it's a classico, a derby that every fan wants to see. People count down the days to the match. Of course there has to be a winner, but you have to be happy and enjoy it as well as focusing because you know it's an important game. Someone has to win, and all the better if it's us. They're always difficult games, they are great to play in, and let's hope people enjoy them.

I saw the FA Cup victory [over Stoke in May], and it's clear that from now on this is a team that will be competing for important things every year. Let's hope that there will be quite a few trophies. Pablo Zabaleta has told me a lot about the squad. He's told me everyone is happy, so when I get a chance to meet up with my team-mates, I'll be able to see exactly what they're like. But I've only heard good things about them and can't wait to get to know them. After talking to Zabaleta, I asked my agents to do everything possible because this was a good club, a club I like, and I'd always wanted to play in the Premier League." Agüero linked up with his new team-mates ahead of the Dublin Super Cup.

"Tévez is our player and I am happy with him," Mancini said after City's victory over an Airtricity XI. On the potential signing of Samuel Eto'o, the manager said, "Eto'o is a fantastic player, but he plays for Inter Milan. It's not true [about a potential swap deal]. Tévez will return on August 4. It depends on how he arrives, if he's in good form. He has a programme of training. He can play in this team, he can play in the Champions League. There's a chance he might go, but then there's a chance he might stay here with us now and, if so, we are happy."

Even Mario Balotelli experienced redemption for his show boating. "Mario should play like today, always, because he has class, he has everything. If his concentration is in his head, he can play like this. This week for Sergio will be recovery. He did the Copa America and finished only two weeks ago. He will be ready to come on the bench next week."

Yaya Toure believed City would prove they were worthy of a place in the European elite. "Last season I was asked to compare City to my former club Barcelona. I responded by saying that I thought City could be as good as Barca one day. When I said City could be as good, I truly believed it and I still do. We have a way to go to match those teams but it is our aim. With the ambition that the club has shown in the last few seasons and the way we are improving as a group, I think other clubs are now starting to take notice of the new Manchester City. We have shown we can match and beat the best in the Premier League and the next step is to do that in Europe too."

AUGUST

Monday, August 1, 2011

The pursuit of the title and to take on Europe's elite were the priorities for Roberto Mancini. Key to these ideals would be retaining the talents of the temperamental Carlos Tévez, 20 League goals the previous season, but he caused acute headaches for Mancini, and how he handled them would be pivotal to the entire season.

The Corinthians deal collapsed, but Inter were on the prowl to ensure the Tévez saga showed no sign of abating. Corinthians marketing director Luis Paulo Rosenberg stated that the club would make another bid too in January, while Inter met with Tévez and his advisors to see if something could be done before the summer transfer window expired. "You can expect us to go after him again," the Corinthians chief told Bloomberg . "I think [our offer] was 5 million euros (£4.4m) [too low]. But we would still have to deal with Tévez; we did not [get] to because we still needed to reach a settlement with the City," he concluded. Inter technical director Marco Branca had a casual meeting with Tévez, "There was one meeting and it was casual and very nice, it happened on a beach [in Sardinia]," Branca told Il Corriere dello Sport.

Inter were waiting for United to bid for Sneijder. Inter demanded a straight cash bid of £35 million, but it was the Dutchman's lavish wage demands of £200,000-a-week put off Sir Alex. The Italians could not afford the Argentine without first offloading Sneijder.

The arrival of Agüero, earmarked as Tévez replacement, though, was a big boost to Mancini, after the exits of Jo, Caicedo, Bellamy, Adebayor and Santa Cruz, and the inconsistency of Dzeko keen to prove himself in his first full season in England, and the unpredictable Mario, with his fiery relationship with his boss. Hopes rested with the son-in-law of the great Diego Maradona. Agüero signed a five year-contract for a record £35m fee including add-ons, lured to the Eastlands side by the opportunity of winning trophies. "I think they [City players] are great players and a great team. I think I am playing with one of the best English teams so I'm really happy. There are many things that can be achieved. I always play to win many titles and hopefully it will be a trophy year and hopefully get some titles. I'm very happy to be here. I'm enjoying my time with my colleagues here today. I'm just looking forward to playing and moving forward. Playing in the Copa America I wasn't thinking about playing for different clubs, my agents were doing all the work. I'm very interested in playing here it's a growing club and I hope it will help me grow as well and that we can grow together."

Mancini still relied on Vincent Kompany. Making the Belgian captain was just reward for his ability to lead from the back. Hart was part of the backbone of the team along with Yaya. With two defensive midfielders and Yaya flexible enough to give an advanced role on occasions, a title challenge was a distinct possibility.

Mancini had plenty of creativity but Spaniard David Silva remained pivotal in that department Adam Johnson had been tricky but would need to convince Mancini with greater consistency. A season long loan approach from Everton for him was rejected and would have only been considered seriously had City clinched the signing of Sanchez. Mancini wanted to keep Johnson but would not stand in the way of Shaun Wright-Phillips if he wanted to leave in search of regular football. "Adam Johnson, sure one hundred per cent," Mancini answered when asked if he, Barry and Wright-Phillips are an important part of the first-team squad. "Gareth is the same, but Shaun is a different question. He was born in Man City, he is an important player for Man City. For me, it's difficult to put him on the bench. A player like Shaun deserves to play every game because he's a strong player. But now, we have so many players it's not easy for him. I need to speak with him in the next days. It's difficult because Shaun is a good guy." Mancini replied "no" when asked if former Middlesbrough star Johnson would be allowed to leave the club.

Mancini was under no illusions, this was always going to be a landmark season in the club's history. Mancini went into the Community Shield believing United were "five yards" ahead of City and they can forget about winning the League unless they sign at least two more players. "They are on the top," Mancini said. "They're a strong team, they won the last Premier League, they have bought good players and at the moment they are over us. We are very close but United have maybe five yards more than us. We want to improve on last season and we'll try to win the Premier League but we need two or three more players and, if we can do that, I think we will be very close. But look at United – they have 29 senior players whereas we have 20. To be competitive, we need more. We're missing players, we don't have enough for the whole season and it's a problem. We haven't managed to get all the players we want and it is important we get them now in the next seven days."

Mancini's top target was Samir Nasri and Arsenal's position appeared to be softening. Mancini upset Wenger earlier in the summer by discussing his pursuit of the player so he was careful not to inflame the situation again. "It's better we don't talk about this," he said.

Costel Pantilimon, a 6ft 8in Romania goalkeeper, became City's fourth signing of the summer, £1.6m from Timisoara, subject to a work permit, to become Hart's understudy. Alessio Cerci, the Fiorentina winger, was another target. Mancini also wanted a central midfielder. "We had five last year but Patrick Vieira has retired now."

City had a senior squad of 24 players, even excluding Adebayor, Bridge, Bellamy, Santa Cruz and Onuoha, all of whom were training away from the main group because they do not fit into the manager's plans. Mancini made it clear he would not change his mind – "They are good players but not part of our plans," even though he believed City, with their current squad size, may find it difficult to adapt to the rigours of competing for the title as well as playing in Europe. "We need a good list of players because when you are playing in the Champions League for the first time it is very hard, totally different from the Europa League, and you need to change five, six, even seven players after every Champions League game. Tottenham struggled with this last season and we don't want to have the same problem. It's different for Manchester United, they needed only three [new] players. For them, it is easier."

City had to clear up Tévez's position. Mancini could not be certain whether he would remain at the club with Inter keen on a player-plus-cash exchange involving Eto'o or Sneijder. Mancini believed Tévez will return to training on Monday after being given a three-week break to recuperate from the Copa América. "He's still a City player at the moment. He's a professional and, if he doesn't get another team, he'll play for us and he'll play seriously like last year." The manager spoke to Tévez for the first time in the entire summer on Monday – "His telephone is working again" – and reported that the club captain was "happy" and "told me he would come back".

Mancini believed his side will have to score "10 to 15 more goals than last season" if they want to win the league, an indication that he will be more attack-minded in the new campaign. Agüero, who, was also involved in the Copa América, will be given his debut as a substitute at Wembley, and Ferguson believed Mancini's men could provide the most credible challenge to United in the title race. "We accept that challenge and it's good for us, as it keeps complacency away from the door," Fergie said.

Tuesday, Aug. 2, 2011

The collapse of Carlos Tévez' move to Corinthians left Inter as the only remaining suitors. Mancini, though, was sure Tévez could remain at City, despite recently adding Agüero, "When Carlos comes back to training on Thursday we will have four strikers fighting for the shirts. That's good for us. When you are playing in four competitions, we need that competition, we need those players. Players fighting for the shirt is a good thing."

Mancini confirmed Craig Bellamy could be heading for Celtic, after spending last season on loan at Cardiff. "It is possible that there have been conversations about Craig Bellamy between us and Celtic. I met Craig two days ago at Carrington. I spoke with him for 10 minutes. It was a friendly conversation – everything was normal. He told me something I want to keep to myself. What I said two days ago was that if Celtic want Craig, he is a good player and I think he can go. He is a good striker and needs to be playing. Celtic are a good team. I would let him go on loan, because Craig deserves to play and he deserved to play for a good team. If they want him, sure."

Emmanuel Adebayor meanwhile made no secret of his desire to return to Real Madrid. Mancini welcomed it, "It is the same with Adebayor. Manu is in Carrington. He wants to go to Real Madrid and if they want to take him, they can. We have four top strikers and it is really difficult. Manu is a good striker. We can't carry six strikers. He needs to play and I would be happy for him to go back to Real Madrid. I hope he can go back there. It is like with Craig. We have a lot of strikers, but I can't play six in the same strikers. It's important we find a good solution for them. I understand their situations."

Friday, 5 Aug, 2011

Mancini believed the increased physical strength, speed and stamina of modern footballers was matched by a decline in their mental robustness, which might explain why he was so patient with Mario. "When I was a player 15 or 20 years ago we were mentally stronger than they are now. Why are they less strong? We were hungry then, we had less money and we wanted to become top players. We were prepared to give up everything for this. We were serious. When I was young, 17 or 18, I made mistakes like all of you. But when you are 20 it is time that you change because a player's career is not long – 10 or 12 years. It is important that Mario [incidentally, aged 20] understands this. But I have more patience with players that are young. I understand Mario is homesick and I am patient with him although sometimes I am really disappointed with him but he needs experience and he understands that he needs to improve his behaviour. When I spoke to him last time he said: 'Boss, I want to be here.' I have known him since he was at Inter. Mario's a fantastic guy and I don't say that because I bought him or because I'm his manager, it's because he is a fantastic guy. He sometimes does incredible behaviour on the pitch, sometimes he doesn't think but, off the field, Mario is often very kind to people. He's fantastic. I trust him because I know him very well and off the pitch he's an incredible man. I also think Mario is one of the top players in the world." Mancini needed Mario to be at his best this season.

Meanwhile Sir Alex Ferguson regarded Liverpool as potential dark horses because they were not in Europe. "It's a bonus for Liverpool that they don't have that distraction. It's difficult having those European nights and then you come home and have an early kick off on a Saturday which is absolutely ridiculous. The Champions League is not easy. It's a fantastic league but it's the game after it that's difficult to prepare for because the Premier League is just as important. I always look at the fixtures right away and see whether we're home or away after the European games and what time we kick off. It's not fair, for every club. No team in Europe should have an early kick off on a Saturday after a Champions League game; it's ridiculous but Sky dominate that. Sky are running the game now. What do you do? Sacrifice the points?"

Ferguson believed there was a downside to the game's lucrative television deal with Sky. "France are the best at protecting their teams because they have Friday games. We played Lille and Lyon over the years and they always played their games on Friday before we met them. We can't do that because of the control of Sky and they are going to pick the best [Premier League] games aren't they? That's the problem."

Whether Carlos Tévez would feature in City's opening League at against Swansea was doubtful as he had not played since the Copa America last month. David Silva commented, "Carlos has to return and that's great. He's a very important player for us. I don't think we'll have a problem. We know Carlos well. If he stays, great. There are a lot of competitions and we hope to play well in all of them. He would help that."

Saturday, 6 Aug, 2011

Dzeko wanted the fans to get behind City in their first clash with United. "Of course it is a big game for us and our fans. I think we are fit and hopefully we can we can win the game but you never know and Wembley will be full again and I hope to win another cup before the season starts."

United were holders of the Community Shield after beating Chelsea last year and Rooney wanted revenge following his side's 1-0 defeat to City in the FA Cup semi-final at Wembley last season. "Playing City in the Community Shield is the best way to start. I hadn't even thought about it until I turned on the telly the other night and someone was talking about potentially the best Community Shield ever. It's a great way to start pre-season training, knowing that at the end of the hard work, before the games begin, there's a Manchester derby. You couldn't get better motivation to start the season with a bang." Rooney was confident of retaining the title despite City adding more big-name players such as Agüero to their squad. "The names are obvious, but we can't concentrate on them. We've got to concentrate on our job. But saying that, you know City, Chelsea, Arsenal, Liverpool and maybe Spurs will go into it with winning the title in mind. All we can do is keep improving and try to retain it. When you're at a club like Man United you pretty much know what the goals are. We want to win the league, the Champions League and both the cups. It's pretty simple. Obviously, sometimes you fall short of that, but at Man United you've got to keep striving for it."

Mike Summerbee anticipated the Community Shield would kick-start the season. He twice won the then-titled Charity Shield in 1968 and 1972, and says the trophy is still important. "Every footballer wants to be involved in winning something, and the Community Shield as it is now known is something very special. It means you can kick the season off with a trophy in the bag before even starting the league programme, and that's what it's all about, and if you can get one trophy early on then it can give you the confidence to go on and win more. Winning the derby at Wembley would act as a major boost ahead of the season." Summerbee now an ambassador for the club says the atmosphere created by City's overhauling United in last season's FA Cup semi-final and subsequent victory in the final was a driving force for the team. "I honestly believe that if we'd had a couple more games last season then we could have gone on to win the Premier League. We looked brighter, fitter, and more confident, and it all seemed to come together in those last few games. To start the season in that way would be huge for us. The Cup Final showed what real football support is all about. The atmosphere was unbelievable, and Stoke's fans really contributed to that. Our fans will turn up to the Community Shield in the same spirit as they did the FA Cup and they'll re-create that atmosphere. Hopefully we'll show people just how important the Shield is.

Another old boy Paul Lake, who had just published his autobiography, observed the changes in the 20 years since he had been City's golden boy before injury prematurely ended his career, "I suppose it is like being on a different planet now as far as City are concerned. If you look at the number of staff for instance you are talking about having four or five physiotherapists and four or five masseurs that are all highly qualified. Plus you have sports scientists and fitness and conditioning coaches as well as a sports psychologist and a full-time doctor and a part-time doctor and the list goes on. Whereas when I played there was literally one physio and that was it. That person did all the pre-season training, all the medical checks. He organised the pre-season tour with one of the coaches. It was almost like having a skeleton staff by comparison and you wonder how the job was done at all. But I suppose that in those days the expectations were far lower with regards to what was expected to be done for each individual player.

"A lot of the time you fended for yourself. I suppose there is a lot more attention to detail for players to make them focus on just the football hence the reason there is so many more staff. It is the way it should be but because football has moved on so much over the last 20 or 30 years it beggars belief." Lake, who starred in City's 5-1 humiliation of Sir Alex's side at Maine Road, successfully battled against depression following his premature retirement and has rebuilt his life, "I am back working at City so my life has turned full circle. I'm back being a fan again and really enjoying be part of it and being made to feel part of it as well, which is lovely. Now I really enjoy going to games and being a fan, just as I was before I signed for City as an apprentice. So it is nice to have rekindled those feelings and going to games with my children and really enjoying City's success which has been a long time coming, and we are making the most of it."

As the new Premier League season beckoned, Lake was bullish about the prospects for his club, "We won our first major silverware in 35 years so the monkey is off our back now and we can express ourselves and there is no reason we can't reach for the stars. There is no reason we can't go for everything just as Chelsea, Manchester United and, to a certain extent, Arsenal will. We finished the season on an absolute high. Gone are the days of conceding goals in the last five minutes and using the expression: 'That's the old City'. Those days have gone. You look at the team on the pitch and you get a sense of what it is like off the pitch because that team spirit was there for all to see in the FA Cup semi-final and final. They will develop a siege mentality over the next season or so. We have a real bite to our game now and will add strength in depth. Coming to the Etihad Stadium will not be easy for anyone next season."

Sunday, 7 August 2011

The Community Shield was billed as setting the tone for the entire season, the prospect of a personal Manchester duel for the big honours. Yet it was United who quietened their noisy neighbours by rallying from 2-0 down to prevail 3-2 in injury time. Nani capitalised on the uncharacteristic hesitancy of captain Vincent Kompany, to run clear, evade Hart, and tuck the ball into the net for his second. When City played this same fixture here in last season's FA Cup semi-final, they won 1-0. The outcome might not be a sure guide to the outcome of the Premier League, but it left Mancini with much to ponder. His talk of the need for further signings was justified, although Tévez was recovering from the Copa América and Agüero stayed on the bench while Adam Johnson came off the bench to replace Milner. City had five men booked; United two.

David De Gea, promising successor to the retired Edwin van der Sar, was all but motionless as Dzeko's shot went past him in first-half stoppage time to send City into a 2-0 lead, after Lescott headed in from a Silva free-kick after 38 minutes. Despite this, United had dominated the opening period.

Ferguson made three substitutions at the interval. The first United goal, after 52 minutes was too simple for Mancini's liking as Smalling turned in a Young set piece. United's leveller six minutes later was reminiscent of the Barcelona team that humiliated United in the Champions League final just three months earlier. Following an intricate exchange of passes between Rooney, substitute Cleverley and Nani before the Portuguese clipped the ball into the net for the first of his goals in the 58th minute.

A rare lapse by Kompany stopped City from having the opportunity of a penalty shoot-out, but it still felt as if his team will need a more expansive style in some fixtures. A hopeful ball forward was watched rather than played by the Belgian stopper who was caught and then passed by Nani who streaked on to score the decisive goal.

Rooney said that United had shown their neighbours who was boss, handing them what he described as a "footballing lesson" which set down a marker for their title defence. The striker, who was central to Nani's wonderful equaliser as a youthful United turned round a 2-0 half-time deficit, revelled in his team's superiority and the bragging rights that accompanied the result. Nani, the man of the match, scored the winning goal in the third minute of injury time. "This shows who the best team is," Rooney said. "All game we dominated. The difference the young lads made was outstanding. We never know when a game is finished. We took them apart. The scoreline is deserved. We're champions and we're the team to beat. We want to prove that."

Rooney was asked whether the victory tasted sweeter because it had come against City, who defeated United at Wembley in last season's FA Cup semi-final, a tie that the striker missed through a controversial suspension. "Of course," he replied. "Obviously they are wanting to try to fight for that title and today I think there was only one team that was going to win. We dominated the first half and they had five minutes when they scored two goals from nowhere but we showed our character to come back and win."

Rooney later tweeted to his million-plus followers: "Have to say. I think today was a footballing lesson. Great win for the champions."

Sir Alex felt that the most pleasing aspect of the game was the way that his young players showed their mettle. "For us I think it just confirms what I've thought. People were saying that we're not the best United squad and things like that but you've got to remember a lot of young players will improve. We are very confident with this group of young players."

The blot on United's afternoon was provided by de Gea. He might have come for the Silva free-kick from which Lescott glanced City ahead while he was horribly slow to get down and across to Dzeko's 25-yard blast that made the scoreline 2-0. "City are a big team and the delivery of the ball [for the first goal] was good ... goalkeeper no chance with that," Ferguson said. "The second goal I thought we could have closed them down but the shot swerved a bit and just caught the goalkeeper on the wrong foot. But I think that you have to cope with these things and he's [got] no problem."

Mancini, who made his players watch and applaud as United lifted the trophy, faced more questions after the game about Mario Balotelli, who walked straight off down the tunnel when he was substituted in the 59th minute, although he did return to the bench. Gary Neville, in the Sky Sports studio, called him an "embarrassment" to City.

"None of my staff told Mario to come back," Mancini said. "Every time he does something, people read things into it. He can play better than he did today."

City needed to show a "strong mentality", Mancini said. "I think that they played better than us but, when you go 2-0 up, you need to control the game. Maybe at the end the correct result would have been 2-2 but this is football. United is a top squad ... it's better than any other team. But we can win the title."

He denied an interest in Sneijder, coveted at United, but hoped to make further signings. Nasri was prominent on his wish list. "We need to complete our squad. We have the targets we had at the start of pre-season. Sneijder said yesterday: "All I know is that Inter need money and apparently I'm for sale for the right amount. I have spoken with neither City nor United so I cannot say anything about my future."

Asked if the result gave United a psychological edge, Kompany said: "No, nothing. I'm sure if we would have won United would have said the same. We are very confident. We have seen here that even when we do not play our best game we can still be very dangerous. It was really close regardless. We have got a lot of potential and much to improve. Come the league, the Champions League and the FA Cup we will be ready. We are a strong team, an organised team. It would have been nice to win it but the fact we didn't isn't going to change anything for how we have worked towards the Swansea game. It is good we have another important 90 minutes in the legs. It wasn't our best performance but when we start next Monday, that is going to be the big one. We are going to be ready."

Kompany captained the team and was expected to be handed the role full time in place of Tévez, made the error for the vital goal. "It happens," said Kompany. "You play centre-half, that is a lot of responsibility. Sometimes it goes your way and sometimes it doesn't. It's part of what football is about. I'll move on now to the next game. That's what I've always done."

The season promised to be an exciting one, Kompany said: "Every competition we start this season will be a priority for us. We are excited because it's a big season ahead we have been working hard. Come Monday it will be a big kick-off for us. But now is not the time to give big talk. We have to be ready for the Swansea game."

Micah Richards believed defeat served as a wake-up call. "As much as it pains me to say it, United were the better team. It was a bit of a wake-up call for us, people know what we can do but maybe we got a little bit ahead of ourselves. We just didn't seem to get going. We didn't really seem to create much even though we went 2-0 up before half-time. I didn't think it was like a usual derby. There were no flying tackles."

Monday, 8 Aug 2011

Mancini leapt to the defence of Mario Balotelli after Gary Neville had labelled him an "embarrassment". Mario was not pleased to be substituted midway through the second half after an ineffectual performance, walking straight down the tunnel before later rejoining the City bench. Neville, now a full-time pundit for Sky, believed Mario should be ashamed of his latest behaviour, but Mancini insisted the situation was blown out of proportion. "None of my staff told him to come back. I was concentrating on the game. Every time Mario does something people read things into it. I think he can do his job better. He can play better than he did today. But it's important he works for the team like the other players. Sometimes it's possible to play not very well. I am disappointed because we were in the dressing room after 45 minutes leading 2-0."

Mancini was aware of the strength of feeling among the supporters, as well as in the dressing room, for Kompany to take over as captain. Mancini regarded Kompany as a more deserving candidate and his only reservation was the potential for more problems with Tévez given that there was still the possibility he may be heavily reliant on him.

Tévez took part in a 20-minute training session, in the rain that he says he detests so much, before driving off without comment. Carrington was largely deserted otherwise because the players who had taken part in the Community Shield defeat had the day off.

While Tévez continued to seek a way out, Hart was "very privileged" after signing a new contract that committed him for the next five years. "I can't think of myself being anywhere other than City. When I signed from Shrewsbury it was always my aim to be the No. 1 here and I was prepared to do anything to achieve that."

City held more talks with Nigel de Jong after their first round of contract discussions ended him rejecting the terms on offer.

Thursday, 11 Aug, 2011

Arsene Wenger confirmed the futures of Fabregas and Nasri were to be resolved "very quickly". Asked whether either could already be considered a done deal, he replied: "No". With Fabregas on his way to Barca, Wenger focused his attentions on keeping hold of Nasri, with City offering £22m, for a player could leave on a free next summer. Although included in Arsenal's Champions League squad, Nasri was unlikely to stay. Le Parisien reported that a move to City was "nearly completed", while France Football claimed it's "just a matter of hours" before the deal is done. The transfer speculation had an effect on the midfielder, who was substituted midway through the second half of Les Bleus 1-1 friendly draw with Chile after a below-par performance.

The Gunners included both Nasri and Fabregas in their squad for their Champions League play-off against Udinese. Should either player take any part in the game, they will not be eligible to play for another club for the rest of the competition.

Saturday. Aug, 13, 2011

Mancini believed City were capable of winning the title if they "complete" the squad. "Last year was the same too. I don't understand this. I thought we could get all the players we needed three or four weeks ago, but here we are and the deals aren't closed. We need this player. I asked for this player two months ago. I'm worried because I don't have this player today and I probably won't have him tomorrow. We play three games in August and I am worried. If we complete our squad, we can fight for the title this year, but that is a problem at the moment because we play our first match. It is not important whether you are the richest club or not. The market is difficult – I understand that – but when you have your targets, it is important to go very hard. It was important to have these players for pre-season because it is there that you prepare for the season. At the moment, we don't have these players. I asked and I hope we can have them this week."

Fiorentina winger Alessio Cerci was among the other players Mancini is looking to sign, "Cerci is a good player. He is young and he could be an option but there are other players."

Everton, Blackburn and QPR bid to sign Nedum Onuoha, the 24-year-old was not in City manager Mancini's plans. "I'm not surprised at this level of interest, because Nedum has proven that he's a very good player," remarked Joorabchian. Onuoha came through City's academy and played 94 games. The centre-back won 21 caps for the England Under-21s and played 31 games on loan for Sunderland last season. He was behind Kompany, Kolo, Lescott and even Boyata in the reckoning at City.

Sunday, Aug, 14, 2011

Mancini anticipated a tough evening of Monday night football to open their League campaign against newly promoted Swansea, "When you start the season and you play against a team that comes from the Championship, it is really difficult. Last year, with all the teams that came from the Championship, it was very hard to play against them in the first 10 games and it will be the same this year. But this is why the Premier League is difficult. Every game is hard."

Mancini was well aware of the kind of challenge posed by Brendan Rodgers' side, "I have watched many of their games. Swansea play good football. They don't play long ball and they have good players. The manager is good – last year, he played really good football and got promoted."

Record signing Sergio Agüero was still some way short of full fitness, while Tévez only came back to training on Monday.

Micah Richards meanwhile believed the club were genuine challengers, "The title is possible, definitely, I do believe we're title challengers. United are obviously a very good team and there's Arsenal, Chelsea and Spurs. I do believe on our day we can beat anyone so why can't we win the title?" While expectations raised following the signings of Agüero and Clichy, Richards felt the team cannot afford to take their opening game of the season anything less than seriously. "We'll look to improve in the first game against Swansea. They're going to be up for it so it's going to be a good game. We know of their threat but we don't want to focus on them, we want to focus on us. We'll go into it all guns blazing."

Monday, Aug 15, 2011

Sergio Agüero scored twice as City hammered new-boys Swansea. What a spectacular start for Agüero, who had been struggling with blisters and only began the game on the bench. Clichy started, one of three changes from the side beaten by United in the Community Shield. There are few better Premier League debuts; Alan Shearers' two goals for Blackburn v Crystal Palace 15 August 1992, Jurgen Klinsmann's goal and celebratory dive for Tottenham v Sheffield Wednesday 20 August 1994, Fabrizio Ravanelli's hat-trick for Middlesbrough v Liverpool 17 August 1996 and Alan Smith scoring with first touch for Leeds v Liverpool 14 November 1998.

Yet, remarkably Agüero was not quite at his best, needing more time to produce his best form as Mancini observed, "He is not tired, I think that he needs to recover because he only finished the Copa America three weeks ago, but in the last week he worked with the team. He needs another two or three weeks to be 100% maybe. For me he is a fantastic striker, he is young, I think for us he will be a fantastic player in the future."

David Silva and Gareth Barry both struck the woodwork before Dzeko prodded home after Vorm parried a Johnson shot. Agüero slotted home unmarked at the far post shortly after his introduction. The second-half substitute then audaciously flicked the ball for Silva to volley home before scoring with a long-range late strike. City's second-half blitz, with Silva and Dzeko shining, showed their intentions for the new season.

Mancini paid tribute to his other two goalscorers, it was important for the team to get off to a strong start. "We played only the first match, the season will be very long. It was very important to start the season like this," he added. Dzeko is a different player to Sergio, it's important for him, that he scored. For him it's important to work for the team."

Swansea - the first Welsh side to play in the Premier League - finally cracked on 57 minutes when Dzeko pounced from close range after Vorm had only parried Johnson's effort. It started a spell of three goals in 14 minutes, the second coming when Agüero, who replaced de Jong and almost immediately scored with a shot from the edge of the box, tapped in a low cross from Richards. Agüero's next contribution was even better, drifting past Vorm and acrobatically hooking the ball back for Silva to fire home. Agüero crowned a memorable debut with a sublime strike from 25 yards.

"Yes I'm delighted after this performance," commented Mancini, "But I think in the first half, Swansea played very well, and for 15-20 minutes we had some problems. After that we started to press, and then we had many chances to score but in the end I am very happy."

Wednesday, Aug 17, 2011

Samir Nasri used Twitter to deny earlier comments posted on a Facebook account suggesting he was set to leave the Gunners on less than amicable terms. The Facebook page, masquerading as part of Nasri's personal account, said his Arsenal exit was imminent and that he would "certainly leave very soon" with "bitterness and anger in my heart". The quotes attributed to Nasri were in relation to what he earlier described as "disrespectful" chants aimed at him by fans during Arsenal's Premier League opener against Newcastle – despite the France international not appearing on the pitch. "I was very disappointed by the supporters last weekend," the message read. "I am still an Arsenal player but I will certainly leave very soon. It's nearly done. But I will leave with bitterness and anger in my heart." To which the Frenchman later replied via Twitter: "Just to make things clear I don't have a facebook so I never said I was leaving with bitterness the guy who said that used a fake account."

Fri, Aug 19, 2011

Roberto Mancini was expected to finalise Nasri's move "this week", with a deal almost complete. Nasri was ready to undergo a medical at Eastlands, ahead of signing a five-year deal. No official word had been given on the potential transfer, but Mancini addressed the press ahead of City's game against Bolton this weekend. "I hope that we can close very quickly now," Mancini said when asked about the Nasri situation during Friday's press conference. "I don't know the latest because my concentration is on the game." Asked if there was progress, Mancini said: "I hope. I hope we can complete our target. The season is long, it's hard, and we need him."

Mancini added that, due to the failure to offload squad players such as Adebayor and Bellamy, it has been difficult to complete their transfer business. "The market is finished in ten days. We have a problem because we haven't sold other players, but we need players to complete the squad. Until we sell the players that are here, it's a problem."

Spurs boss Harry Redknapp indicated that he expected Adebayor to join on loan, but Mancini was coy. "I don't know," he said. "It's possible." Redknapp was reticent to be drawn but suggested a deal was imminent. "I honestly don't know. The chairman deals with that, I have never spoke to the player or Manchester City or anybody there. I think it has been progressing along. It seems like it probably will happen."

Arsene Wenger intended to carry on selecting Nasri. Asked if he would hesitate to play him, Wenger replied: "Not at all, because one thing I don't question is his commitment to this club. Every day since he has arrived here, every day in pre-season, he has worked with a fantastic spirit in training."

Reacting to the fact a number of supports sang offensive songs about Nasri at Newcastle, he added: "You have to be careful. We live in a modern democracy where everybody has a right to have their opinion, but it does not mean always that a few opinions represent the majority. The unfortunate thing is that the extreme opinions get more media attention than people who have normal common sense and intelligence. Because a few people have a bad opinion of one person, it does not necessarily represent the majority of our fans. The majority of our fans are behind our players and I think they will show that tomorrow."

Sunday, Aug, 21, 2011

City continued their superb start to the league season with a 3-2 win at Bolton. City were one of only two teams with 100 per cent records and scored seven in two games. David Silva gave City the lead from the edge of the box when Jaaskelainen got his positioning all wrong. Barry then smashed a shot into the top corner before Klasnic swept home Petrov's cross. Back in the lead when Dzeko fired in and despite Kevin Davies' late header, City held on for the win.

With Tévez on the bench, City looked impressive, Agüero could easily have scored twice before the break after good work by Dzeko, but he missed the target on both occasions. Tévez came on after 68 minutes, but the way in which Dzeko, Agüero and Silva combined gave City Mancini plenty of encouragement for the season ahead, whatever Tévez's long-term ambitions.

Bolton came back twice to reduce a two-goal advantage, even though at certain moments they were outplayed. Silva began to dictate play, so it was no surprise that City extended their lead on 37 minutes. Barry collected a short corner from the right, and with time and space to shoot, he fired superbly into the top corner. Out of nowhere Coyle's side recovered through Klasnic. Dzeko re-established a two-goal lead when he fired in two minutes after the break.

Milner began to orchestrate proceedings in the second. Bolton's second goal came against the run of play when Robinson swung in a free-kick deep on the right and Davies rose to head expertly past Hart. Mancini had stated his intention to take more risks this season, and by naming two strikers from the start his side produced a performance that was as entertaining for the neutral as it would have been for the watching City fans.

"Last year we played many games very well, this year we want to improve. All the players that come from another country, they need to know very well the English Premier League because it is really different from other championships,' commented Mancini, "Dzeko arrived in January with new team-mates and a new manager and now I think he can continue to score."

Mancini hoped to complete the signing of Nasri before Arsenal's Champions League match on Wednesday. Mancini said, "It's a big problem [if he plays] but I'm sure we can close in 24 hours, maybe 48. It's vital he's free for all games."

Earlier on Sunday, Wenger told French media outlet TF1 the deal was "far, far, far from being done". "He is happy here," Wenger told the television station. "There is no departure of Nasri at the moment."

The hold-up led to Nasri playing in Arsenal's 2-0 home defeat by Liverpool on Saturday. The framework of a deal was in place, as were Nasri's personal terms, but other financial details remained to be ironed out before the switch can be finalised.

Meanwhile, Mancini no longer expected Tévez to leave. "Carlos is here, I don't think the situation will change. Carlos is an important player, a top player for us and at the moment we haven't received any offers for him."

Emmanuel Adebayor was still on course to complete his loan move to Tottenham. Dialogue continued between the two clubs about the structure of the deal.

Monday, Aug, 22, 2011

Mancini knew it would be a "big problem" if Nasri played against Udinese, while on the verge of a £25m move. He had hoped to sign Nasri by the end of the weekend, only for the deal to be delayed by the reported demands of the player's agent. Wenger started Nasri against Liverpool, and he was not worried about picking him again for the Champions League qualifier in Italy.

Mancini remained convinced the deal could be tied up imminently, but he did warn Arsenal and Nasri to seriously consider the consequences of playing in Udinese. "I think we can close in the next two days, but if he plays in the Champions League, it will be a big problem. It's a big problem because we have followed Nasri for 40 days and I have hoped it [would be completed] in two days or in three days. I am sure we can close this in 24 or 48 hours, but I don't know why it hasn't been closed."

Asked if he could look elsewhere if Nasri becomes cup-tied, Mancini replied: "It could be possible, yes."

Sunday Aug 28, 2011

Edin Dzeko scored an incredible four times as City maintained their 100% start with an awesome display at Spurs. Tévez looked a grumpy, isolated figure on the bench. Surely it could only be a matter of time before he gets frustrated as a bench warmer. Dzeko felt City were still evolving and growing stronger with Nasri making his long awaited debut, 'I think we're getting better and better. I hope we can improve in the next game and try to win every game.'

Dzeko hit a hat-trick inside 55 minutes to put City in a commanding position before Agüero added a fourth. Dzeko prodded in from close range from a left-wing cross from Nasri, who was outstanding on his City debut. From another Nasri cross Dzeko headed in by Dzeko. In the second half Dzeko tapped in his third, Agüero fired in after a mazy run, Younis Kaboul headed one back for Spurs but Dzeko curled a sublime fifth.

Having lost 3-1 at United on Monday, Spurs found City even more formidable opponents. Harry Redknapp was not allowed to include new recruit Emmanuel Adebayor under the terms of his loan from City while Gareth Bale was kept largely quiet by the returning Zabaleta. Nasri, Agüero and Silva provided some mesmerising moments going forward.

Redknapp revealed Chelsea target Modric requested not to play, "He came to see me at 12pm, probably 11.30am, and he told me he didn't feel his head was right. I told him he needed to play. I had injuries in midfield. He's our main man." Modric remained largely anonymous figure as Spurs were thrashed.

Mancini always had faith that Dzeko would come good. "We played a really good game against what is a fantastic team. I was always sure Dzeko would score a lot of goals for us, he always scored in Wolfsburg. The only thing I'm disappointed with is that we conceded. I think we need to pay more attention in this situation. This is a very long season and it's important that we started well. The next games will be very hard because now everyone thinks we will score three or four goals, but that is impossible."

Tévez looked a grumpy, isolated figure on the bench. Fifteen months earlier, Peter Crouch scored at Eastlands as Spurs reached the Champions League at the expense of City and a year ago, Mancini was rightly criticised for fielding a defensive team at White Hart Lane with only a terrific performance from Hart securing a goalless draw. How times had changed.

As if to not be outdone Manchester United spanked Arsenal 8-2 in the other Sunday game to complete a disastrous double for the North London clubs.

SEPTEMBER

*"Do you think a Bayern Munich a player would ever behave like this.
At Milan? At Manchester United?"*
ROBERTO MANCINI

Fri, Sept 2, 2011

Kolo Toure's six month ban came to an end. On Saturday, he watched from the bench as Ivory Coast beat Rwanda 5-0 in an Africa Cup of Nations qualifier. "I have gained a lot of strength from this hard time and I just need to focus on the future. For me it is really important to get back to what I love to do - which is football. When you can't do what you love to do it's always difficult but I am a strong man - I have learned from [my ban] and now I am back." He received huge support from his team mates at his club and in Ivory Coast. "People know I am not someone to try and cheat. I was really unlucky, all the people at the club and in Ivory Coast a lot of support – and the most important thing is that now I am back. I hope to be back next week but there are lots of games to go and I just want to be ready when the manager calls me."

Monday, Sept 5, 2011

City investigated reports that chief executive Garry Cook emailed defender Nedum Onuoha's cancer-afflicted mother mocking her illness. Dr Anthonia Onuoha received an offensive email which was intended for the club's football administrator Brian Marwood, in regard to a contract dispute her son was having with City.

Cook denied he sent the message, claiming his account was hacked. Dr Onuoha told The Sun the email had left her "humiliated and devastated".

Onuoha's mother, who acts as his agent, had previously sent a message to Marwood and Cook, explaining that while she was "ravaged with cancer" it would not prevent her negotiating on behalf of her son. Dr Onuoha then received an email, allegedly from Cook and addressed "Brian", which apparently ridiculed her use of language in describing her illness. The email read: "Ravaged with it!!...I don't know how you sleep at night. You used to be such a nice man when I worked with you at Nike. G". City have responded to the allegations by releasing a statement promising a full investigation.

Following allegations made to the football club by Dr Anthonia Onuoha, subsequently reported in today's media, the club can confirm that a board-led review has been launched into the matter," said the statement.

Dr Onuoha told The Sun, "When I opened my emails and saw the message, it was the worst day of my life, even worse than being diagnosed with cancer. I couldn't understand how anybody could behave like that. I just cried and cried for hours. I'm critically ill and at that point I was undergoing chemotherapy. I was just so shocked but I couldn't tell Nedum or any of my family because I didn't know how they would react."

Dr Onuoha said she replied to Cook the following day, writing: "Thanks very much for your insightful email." She told The Sun: "The illness I have is very stressful, I'm having chemotherapy and radiotherapy, including having radiotherapy on my brain and this year has been traumatic. I didn't want anybody adding to my stress but that is what they've done. The feeling of humiliation still persists. Now I just want the FA and the Premier League to see what's happened and to take the appropriate action. Treating people like this is completely abominable."

Cook apologised for "any hurt or embarrassment this may have caused" as well as denying sending the email. He told Dr Onuoha: "I cannot and will not condone this unacceptable behaviour. I can confirm Brian did not receive this email and disciplinary action is currently under way regarding one of our employees."

Tuesday, Sept 6. 2011

Carlos Tévez was stripped of the City captaincy and although fit to start his first match of the season against Wigan, Vincent Kompany would continue in the role he filled for the last three games. "The reasons are simple," said Mancini "Carlos wanted to leave for family reasons. I respected his opinion but Carlos is still here because we didn't find a solution for him. He's a fantastic player for us, someone who can score 20 goals a season, but I decided in the summer that Vinnie was the captain."

Tévez accepted the decision, according to Mancini – "He's a clever man" – and Kompany's promotion was well received in the changing room. Mancini put off telling Tévez and announcing his decision publicly until a couple of days later, because he did not want to risk any more damage to his relationship with the striker. Tévez recently spoke of a "love-hate language and a love-hate relationship" with Mancini. He did not seem prepared for his demotion saying he expected to regain his starting place once he was fit "because I'm captain and the symbol of a big club".

His chance was likely to come against Wigan because Edin Dzeko played two recent games for Bosnia. Mancini said it was "probable" Tévez would start but there was also a warning that he was no longer an automatic first-team selection.

Gary Neville, a former team-mate at United, wrote in his autobiography of how Tévez could not tolerate being in and out of the team. "He'd been upset by the signing of Berba, and Carlos is a player who needs to feel the love. He's not someone who can play one game in three and be happy."

Mancini maintained Tévez had no choice now Agüero had signed and the Premier League's player of the month, Dzeko, was starting to justify his £27m price tag. "This season it could be like that. In the first three games we played Agüero and Edin and the team played very well, and I can't change a team that plays very well."

Mancini picked his team mindful that Napoli visit City in the Champions League on Wednesday. His options were reduced in midfield because Nigel de Jong was still troubled by a foot injury and was out for at least two weeks, and Gareth Barry returned from England duty on crutches, wearing a protective cast on the ankle that he twisted against Wales.

Mancini made it clear he would not rush free-agent signing Hargreaves. "I think Hargreaves will be fit in maybe two or three weeks and, after that, he can play for us always. He's 30 – that's young – and he's been very unlucky with injuries. He's been training with us but needs another two weeks for his confidence."

Meanwhile, Kolo Toure would not be involved while Samir Nasri was wearing a cast to protect a broken bone in his left hand but Mancini said it was "not a problem because he's not a goalkeeper".

Thur, Sept 8, 2011

Roberto Mancini believed a more mature mindset would help Mario Balotelli stay out of the headlines. Mario courted more controversy for playing on his iPad from the Italian substitutes bench in the Faeroe Islands.

Anti-mafia investigators in Italy wanted to interview Mario over possible contacts he may have had unwittingly with the Neapolitan mafia, the Camorra, last year, as part of a wider investigation into money laundering. There was no suggestion Mario committed any crime. He was photographed in the company of a couple of known Camorra gangsters as he toured one of the most deprived, violent and crime-ridden parts of Naples. Maradona was well-known for his allegedly close relationship with several Camorra godfathers during his time playing for Napoli in the 1980s. Earlier this week Mario was given a hero's welcome when he visited a prison in Florence with other members of the Italy squad.

"I am disappointed because everything that Mario does is a big situation," said Mancini. "I think that Mario played well for Italy on Tuesday, this is important, it is important that on Saturday he can play [against Wigan]. The other situation is not important." Asked if Mario should moderate his behaviour, Mancini replied: "I hope. But Mario is 21 years old, he can change in two months, three months or six months. I think that you are right, the moment he changes his mind, he changes everything."

Ahead of the clash with Wigan, Mancini said that Kolo Toure was two weeks away from peak fitness.

Fri, Sept 9, 2011

The club issued a statement confirming the board had accepted Garry Cook's resignation and that chairman Khaldoon Al-Mubarak had apologised to Dr Onuoha. In the statement, Khaldoon said: "Garry has made a remarkable contribution to Manchester City Football Club over the past three years. His judgement in this matter should in no way lead to his accomplishments being overlooked. On every level, the club is unrecognisable from the organisation which he inherited and our staff and supporter services, community outreach and commercial activity have seen unparalleled growth under his direction with yet more projects to be realised on the horizon. On behalf of Sheikh Mansour and the Board, I would like to thank him for his energy and tireless commitment to serving all those connected with the football club. He will always be welcome at Manchester City."

Cook said: "I am privileged to have held my position at Manchester City Football Club and to have experienced the opportunities that it has presented. The privilege is in part offset however by the significant personal focus which has at times, detracted from the magnificent achievements of those working at the football club. It is that factor, together with my error of judgement in this matter that has prompted me to reach this decision, which I believe is in the best interests of the football club." City director John MacBeath will fill the role of temporary chief executive officer while a replacement is sought. Cook was recruited by previous City owner Shinawatra as chief executive in May 2008. He appointed Hughes as manager after Sven-Goran Eriksson was sacked. The club was taken over by Abu Dhabi United Group, with Cook heading up player recruitment in September 2008. Brazilian Robinho signed for a record £32.5m deal. City brought in Bridge, Bellamy, Given and de Jong but failed in an infamous bid for Kaka. City kept spending under Cook as Tévez, Santa Cruz, Barry and Adebayor all joined. Cook mistakenly welcomed City legend Uwe Rosler to "the Manchester United hall of fame" at a club gala. Hughes was sacked by City and replaced by

Mancini after Cook courted Mourinho. Cook infamously jotted down a list of player targets on a napkin at a meal with Oasis singer Noel Gallagher in South Africa. There was little doubt that the gaffe prone Chief Executive would leave behind a memorable legacy.

Saturday, Sept 10, 2011

Roberto Mancini insisted there was still room for improvement after City's 3-0 win over Wigan extended their winning run to four league games, as United won 5-0 at Bolton and so were top on goal difference 15-12.

Mancini described Agüero as "fantastic" after he scored the first hat-trick of his City career but "feels sorry" for Tévez after he missed a first-half penalty, but the striker was still not "100%". City were well on top and had chances before Agüero opened the scoring on 13 minutes by shooting into the corner from Silva's cutback. Tévez had a tame penalty saved and Richards and Kompany hit the woodwork.

But after the hour mark Agüero tucked in twice to seal victory. Both his second-half goals looked simple in their execution, after he was put clear by Nasri and Silva, but in scoring his fifth and sixth goals of the season, Agüero again underlined his class. He also signalled that any continued problems with Tévez would have little impact.

Tévez, who was making his first League start this season, was at the heart of much of City's endeavour, despite being stripped of the captaincy. Mancini's side now having scored 15 goals in four games, the display was the perfect way to put football back on the agenda.

On a balmy afternoon with Tévez replacing Dzeko in attack, City were into their stride from the beginning and should have been out of sight by half-time. Johnson and Silva both went close early on and even Lescott inadvertently deflected Kompany's header over, before Tévez helped create City's opener, feeding Silva, who in turn cut the ball back to Agüero, with City's newest South American striker tucking into the bottom corner. Tévez could then have capped his return to the side with a goal after Silva was upended in the penalty box, but his spot-kick was poor and Ali Al-Habsi saved to his right.

It was not long until City finally yielded the rewards their superiority deserved. Tévez was replaced by Nasri just after the hour and within two minutes the former Arsenal midfielder had set up City's second goal. Silva was involved again, as his drag-back teed up Nasri, and the Frenchman's poke set Agüero through for his fifth of the season. That became six when Silva had acres of space to watch his team-mates' angled run, and Agüero slotted past a helpless Al-Habsi to seal the points.

Coming into the game Wigan had an unbeaten run of seven games going back to last season, but they had little chance of maintaining that record.

Monday, Sept 12, 2011

Roberto Mancini believed Silva is one of the best players in the world, on a par with Barcelona duo Xavi Hernandez and Andres Iniesta. Mancini expressed his surprise that Spain's biggest clubs overlooked him when he joined City from Valencia in 2010. "Silva is a top player. I don't know why he didn't go to Barca or Real Madrid as he's Spanish. I think he's at the same level as Xavi and Iniesta."

City prepared for their debut in the Champions League and Mancini hoped to benefit from his large squad – even if some players were unhappy with his rotation policy. "They may not be happy because every player wants to play always, but I'm the manager and I need to take this decision. Now we have a difficult match coming up, we play every three days and players like Samir Nasri, Aleksander Kolarov, Stefan Savic and Dzeko have played two games in four days and they need to recover."

Mancini expected a special atmosphere at the Etihad when Napoli returned to Europe's top competition for the first time since 1990, shortly after the end of Maradona's time as club captain. "For Napoli it will be the first time in the European Cup after many years, after Maradona, and for them, like us, the first night will be very exciting.'

Tuesday, Sept 13, 2011

The build up was enormous, "It's an exciting day for the club because to play in the Champions League after many years is a very important and special day," said Mancini. "Napoli are a good team and did very well in the Italian championship."

City went into the game full of confidence after making a perfect start to their league campaign and Mancini believed the match practice will be an advantage against a team only one game into their season, with the start of Serie A delayed because of a players' striker and Napoli only started their campaign on Saturday with a 3–1 victory at Cesena. "Probably [it will help] because we have played five games (including the Community Shield). Napoli have played only one game, Wednesday is exciting for us but also for them."

Milner suffered concussion after a clash of heads in the win over Wigan, de Jong remained on the sidelines while Mario was suspended after being sent off against Dynamo Kiev in last season's Europa League.

Clichy rubbished the idea that Napoli are the weakest team in Group B with German side Bayern Munich and Spanish outfit Villarreal. "It's not only me who has played in it before - Yaya has won it. For us it may be one more game, like many we have played in the past, but we have to be aware it's a big part of City's season this year."

Wednesday, Sep 14 2011

City needed Aleksander Kolarov's free-kick to rescue a point as they suffered a disappointing Champions League debut. Mancini's men found it tough against the Italian side on their return to elite European football after a 43-year absence.

Cavani finished off a swift counter-attack to give Napoli the lead after 69 minutes. Kolarov spared his side's blushes with a wicked, curling strike into the corner of the net six minutes later but, with Bayern and Villarreal to come, Group A was not going to get any easier.

With Mancini demanding a "fast start" in his programme notes, expectations had been high but City's bid to become the first side to win the Champions League on their debut did not begin with a damaging defeat, but Mancini admitted his side were "nervous and naive". Mancini said: "For us, this game was very important. And because of this I think maybe the players were nervous."

He said he was confident his side could win their next match in Munich. "It was our first Champions League game, and because of that all our players wanted to win it, and maybe all of them wanted to score. Was I surprised by that? Just how we played in the second half. But maybe it was just down to their desire and the pressure to perform well. We will do better in Munich. We will be calm, more than tonight and we can win there. They are a fantastic side but we have a team that can win anywhere."

Mancini was unhappy that his side over-elaborated when they went forward and that led to Napoli's breakaway goal. "We need to understand how important it is to play easier, simpler football. A team like us should not concede a goal like that. When we lost the ball we didn't have any midfielders in front of the defenders. For 10 minutes in the second half we left a lot of space for the Napoli players and they were very dangerous. This cannot happen. It is down to naivety. We need to improve as a team. We have got some fantastic players but every game in the Champions League is difficult, and different."

Mancini did not blame Dzeko or Agüero for failing to find the net. "It is impossible for a striker to score three or four goals every game. Napoli defended very well with three central defenders. It was difficult. It is important to play the ball around quickly up-front. We did this in the first half, and in the second less so, but I am still happy with their performance."

Fri, Sept 16, 2011

Mancini believed City's trip to Fulham would examine his squad's ability to cope with challenging in the League and Europe. City headed into the weekend second in the table behind United after four wins from their opening four matches. With United hosting Chelsea the next day, the game at Craven Cottage offered the chance to take control of the title race. "It is important when you play like us — like all the teams playing Premier League and Champions League — you have time to recover between one game and another," Mancini said. "It is important to recover very well. It is hard but this is football in 2011. I don't think it will be possible to win always, but we want to try to win. We know against Fulham it will be a very tough game because at home they are strong."

City had scored 15 goals in their opening four Premier League matches but Mancini believes his team could be even more prolific. United, who have managed 18 goals, played after City in each round of matches so far this season.

But Mancini, whose team put in one of their most impressive performances of last season with a 4-1 victory at Craven Cottage, maintained that his players were not frustrated at being pegged back by United. "Man United are a top team, they have been used to winning for a long time. They have strong players. When they played against Arsenal, when they scored two or three goals, they continued trying to score. We need to have this mentality. If we have a game like Tottenham where we can score, we need to continue to try to play."

Saturday, 17, Sept 2011

Martin Jol pledged to go at City despite Fulham only registering two points from their first four matches and drawing three of their past four home games. "They play attacking football but still with two defensive midfielders and four players at the back. They don't take a lot of initiative but they've got four quality players that try to get behind your midfield. They have a lot of quality. We have to come up with something to stop that and still get goals." Danny Murphy insisted that Fulham can still beat the League's best despite the two Manchester clubs' blistering start to the season. "We believe we can win the game because we've shown before that we can perform against good quality opposition, especially at the Cottage where there's always a good atmosphere. So I say 'bring it on'. Everybody thinks the likes of United and City go out and win every week but the Premier League always throws up a few shocks and hopefully we can cause one." Fulham's defence, which had not kept a clean sheet in the League since the opening day, would have to be on form to contain City's incisive forwards. "We know we're going to have to defend very well to get a result, because the one thing City have in real quantity is attacking flair. Sometimes you see players go out against the big teams and they're finished before they even get onto the pitch."

Sunday, 18 Sept 2011

City dropped points for the first time. Roberto Mancini felt letting a two-goal lead slip would serve as a lesson for the rest of the season. Agüero struck twice to give City a healthy lead but Fulham drew level following a goal by Zamora and Murphy's deflected shot.

Mancini commented, "It's incredible, we lost two points after we scored two goals and dominated the game. But I think this can be a lesson for us. When we have the chances we should score."

It was the first time City had played a league game after a Champions League fixture but Fulham had also played a day later in midweek, hosting FC Twente in the Europa League. Mancini bemoaned his side's concentration, with Fulham's first goal coming from a Micah Richards foul throw, while Dzeko was fouled in the build-up to Fulham's equaliser. "For 10 or 15 minutes after Fulham scored, they played very well, but a football match is 95 minutes and a top team like us needs to have more control of the game. I'm not angry. I'm just disappointed because we conceded two stupid goals."

Mancini defended his decision to withdraw Silva, replaced by Zabaleta before Murphy struck. "In the middle I didn't have any players because we have James Milner and Nigel de Jong out injured. So I didn't have a chance to change it in the middle."

Yaya Toure had started every match, while Barry only missed one game. Now with Milner, de Jong injured and Owen Hargreaves not yet match-fit, Mancini said: "We are lacking at this moment because we lost two midfielders. I don't have players. I can only change the full-backs." Short of holding midfielders, Mancini handed a debut to trainee Abdul Razak, 18, in the win over Wigan. He added: "I have only two midfielders, because James and De Jong have injuries."

Wednesday, Sept 21, 2011

Kolo Toure captained City in a 2-0 Carling Cup win over holders Birmingham, his full return to competitive football. "I feel great - it was a special time for me to be back on the pitch. Having been out for six months, it's been really difficult - not doing what I love."

"It was the correct decision to choose him as captain," Mancini commented. "It's great for him to be back after a year."

Kolo played the full 90 minutes, made his mark as he cleared Davies's overhead kick off the line in the first half. He paid tribute to those who gave him moral support during his ban, including Wenger and the Gunners' former vice-chairman David Dein. "I just want to thank all the people who have supported me during this really hard time. This football club showed they really liked me. I also want to thank David Dein and Mr Wenger because they have been supporting me and have never let me down." He played under Wenger for seven years at Arsenal, before joining City in 2009.

Meanwhile Owen Hargreaves hogged the headlines as he made a dream debut for City, scoring the opener, then coming through almost an hour unscathed. "It has been three years and four months," he said. "That is frightening in itself. I am not surprised how quickly I was in contention. There was a bit of a misconception and I don't think people would believe me if I said everything that went on. I would never have anticipated all these setbacks in my worst nightmare. You are left to pick up the pieces. That has been the biggest obstacle. It was a pretty humbling experience but I knew this day would come.'

When Hargreaves was posting a video on YouTube showing himself being pushed through a bizarre exercise routine that at one point had him tied to a running machine, it appeared like the last act of a desperate man. It triggered interest, first from West Brom manager Roy Hodgson, then Mancini, who needed midfield reinforcements and the day before the deadline closed, took a punt on a player Sir Alex Ferguson had deemed not reliable enough to offer another contract to.

Snapping up a loose ball 25 yards out, the former Bayern Munich man rasped a shot past Doyle which flew straight into the top corner. "I don't score a ton of goals because I play a bit deeper in midfield," said Hargreaves, who found the net only twice during his entire time at United, "But when I do score they tend to be decent ones because they are from a distance." Hargreaves departed to a standing ovation.

Saturday, Sept 24, 2011

Everton had won on their last four visits to Eastlands but home turf was rapidly becoming the lynchpin of City's title bid even though for an hour Everton frustrated Mancini's team, but patience was also becoming a hallmark of the quest for points in this 2-0 home win.

The introduction of Mario Balotelli on the hour led to the breakthrough as he scored with a deflected shot after 68 minutes. Milner, another second-half substitute, added the second with two minutes left from Silva's sublime pass to allow City to move top ahead of United's visit to Stoke.

Everton's dour approach was likely to be mirrored by sides attempting to suppress City's wide range of attacking options at Etihad Stadium. Everton failed to offer anything in attack, although substitute Saha - and his manager - were rightly infuriated when referee Howard Webb failed to award a free-kick when he was blatantly fouled on the edge of the area by Kompany with the game still in the balance. Moyes also believed Everton had been the victims of injustice in the build-up to Mario's crucial goal, claiming City were wrongly awarded a throw in.

Mancini relished this 'ground out' win as much as victories earned in style. Moyes earmarked Silva as central to City's threat, deploying Rodwell to man-mark him. When he received a yellow card for a foul on Silva responsibility briefly switched to Phil Neville, until he drew similar punishment after a clash with Silva.

When Mario Balotelli replaced Edin Dzeko on the hour, City made serious inroads before the Italian broke the deadlock seven minutes after his introduction. His finish from the edge of the area was measured and also took a decisive touch off Jagielka to send the ball out of Howard's reach into the bottom corner.

City were playing with renewed confidence and Silva hit the woodwork with Howard beaten. Mario was then narrowly off target before setting up Silva for a tap-in, only for the goal to be ruled out for offside. Silva was at his creative best as City wrapped up the win with one minute left. Everton substitute Drenthe lost possession in midfield and Silva threaded through a perfect invitation for Milner to slide his finish past Howard. Another City substitute Savic made a timely intervention in injury time to clear Fellaini's shot off the line.

Mancini was delighted with Mario's attitude, "Mario didn't start for three or four games but he has worked well, did not say anything and he was waiting for this moment. He scored an important goal and now it is important that he can continue." Mario rushed to embrace his manager, who has often appeared frustrated with the striker, after he scored and Mancini said: "Mario is a good guy. Sometimes his behaviour has been so-so but he's a good guy. He likes Manchester City and he likes English football. He was really happy. Sometimes when he scores he is unhappy but he knew this was a very big goal for us."

David Moyes was unhappy about City's first goal and a tackle by Kompany that forced Cahill off injured, although it was the Everton man who was booked by Webb after the clash. Moyes said: "I thought the crowd influenced the decisions. I thought the referee was taken by the crowd." Moyes was defiant about his team's approach, "I wasn't going to come here for the enjoyment of Manchester City. I was going to come here to do my best for Everton and try to get a result."

Moyes believed City would mount a serious challenge for the title after watching them at close quarters, "They have got a really talented, excellent team. They can change how they play and I think they will be contenders, no doubt about that."

Tuesday, Sept 27, 2011

Mario Gomez scored twice as City were given a rude awakening by Bayern in Munich. City had two penalty appeals in the first half but could not deal with Bayern's swift attacking play. But this match will forever be remembered for the antics of Carlos Tévez than the brilliance of Bayern and the capitulation of City, clearly still someway short at the highest level of European football.

Gomez poked in on 38 minutes after Hart saved Ribery's fierce shot and the forward reacted quickest to another Hart stop before half-time. City were outclassed thereafter but the bombshell came when Mancini said that substitute Tévez refused to play, staying on the bench after he planned to introduce the Argentine in the second half.

That startling admission capped a miserable night for City as they arrived in Germany following an unbeaten start to the season. They came up against an impressive force in Bayern, who extended their run to 10 wins in a row, scoring 28 goals, conceding none. Gomez hit his 10th and 11th of the season but only Hart's excellence prevented that total being extended, as the four-time European Cup winners flexed their muscles.

Although it was only City's second appearance in the Champions League, they had plenty of European experience in their ranks. They had two decent penalty appeals in the first period, when former City defender Boateng caught Silva in the first minute when he cut back from the by-line, and then blocked a surging run by Richards.

Roberto Mancini named an attacking line-up and once he altered it in the second half by introducing de Jong in place of Dzeko it seemed to make the situation worse, but Tévez's refusal to play cast the biggest shadow over his future at the club.

Mancini also had to contend with a strop from Dzeko, who took exception to being replaced by de Jong 10 minutes into the second half, "I should be unhappy with this performance, not Edin," said Mancini, "but he played a poor game. If you play every three days, it is impossible that one player can always play well and that he can always stay on the pitch for 90 minutes." There was a stern warning for the giant Bosnian.

"This is the last time one player leaves the pitch and moves his head like this," Mancini continued. "I can understand a player is disappointed. I can understand inside he can be upset if he thinks he has played well. But I am the manager. I decide everything."

Tévez was angered by Mancini telling him to warm up on the touchline after being overlooked in favour of de Jong as a 55th-minute replacement for Dzeko, who left the field shaking his head and threw his boots to the floor. Mancini then clashed with Zabaleta, sat alongside Tévez in the dugout, after the defender was unable to warm up due to a delay in tying his boot laces. Tévez is seen saying the words: "Por que?" Why?

Mancini was adamant. "This can never happen at a top club that one player can refuse to help his team-mates in an important match like tonight. In the next day I'm sure I will speak with Khaldoon [al-Mubarak] because he is the chairman and he will decide everything but let me ask a question: Do you think at Bayern Munich a player would ever behave like this. At Milan? At Manchester United? No. That is the answer. It is the same for everyone."

Tévez did not look particularly perturbed by the situation he had landed himself in when he left the stadium. He emerged from the dressing room and made it clear he wanted to offer his version of events, denying that he had done anything wrong. "I didn't feel right to play, so I didn't," he said.

Informed that Mancini had said he would never wear City's colours again, he replied: "I was top goalscorer here last season, I always act professionally so it is up to him."

There was extra security at the airport to ensure angry City fans did not encroach beyond acceptable levels.

Wednesday, Sept 28, 2011

On his return from Germany, City and Greater Manchester Police were taking no chances with three police cars providing an escort for Carlos Tévez's Hummer as it left the airport. Police chiefs said the cost of the protection from irate fans would be charged to City after officers from seven divisions were rushed to Manchester Airport to help protect the wayward star. Special Greater Manchester Police 'spotters' were alerted to a number of threatening messages posted by Blues' supporters on the internet. Hundreds of City fans had been due to land at the airport just four minutes after the team's plane. A dozen officers from across Greater Manchester were diverted to the airport to meet Tévez as he landed at Terminal Three. He was whisked by the police to a waiting Hummer SUV, driven by a friend, before being escorted back to his home in Alderley Edge.

Cash-strapped GMP bosses now planned to write to City asking them to 'contribute' towards the cost of the operation, which is believed to have cost thousands of pounds. The force is already having to spread its resources more thinly as it sheds 3,000 jobs in the face of a £134m five-year budget cut. Supt Bob Lomas said: "We received intelligence suggesting fans travelling back from Munich were planning to stage a protest on their arrival at Manchester Airport. A small number of officers attended for less than an hour and assisted our airport staff in ensuring that the safety of the public as well as that of airport staff and general security was not compromised. It is the job of GMP to prepare for any potential threat to public order and our response was appropriate and proportional." One lone protestor greeted Tévez's arrival at Manchester Airport at 2am!

Following a day of talks involving Mancini, senior figures from the club's hierarchy and City's legal advisers, Tévez was told to stay away from the Carrington training ground as an internal investigation was launched that resulted in Mancini claiming that Tévez was "finished" and would "never" play for the club again.

Tévez was also facing the possibility of the ultimate sanction of dismissal for gross misconduct after a telephone conference involving senior staff, including chairman Khaldoon al-Mubarak. "Manchester City can confirm that striker Carlos Tévez has been suspended until further notice for a maximum period of two weeks," said a short statement released by City that evening. "The player's suspension is pending a full review into his alleged conduct during Tuesday evening's 2-0 defeat to Bayern Munich. The player will not be considered for selection or take part in training whilst the review is under way."

Tévez grew up in a town called Apache, known as one of Argentina's most dangerous places to live due to its violence, drugs, poverty and high crime rate. After a series of big-money moves, football has earned him a fortune.

Fans placed a small flag reading 'you are a disgrace Tévez' on the gate of his home in Alderley Edge, Cheshire, and one even tried to speak to him via the intercom system. Further indignity was heaped on Tévez when he set off for a round of golf with his wife but was turned away. Strolling through the car park at Tytherington GC in Cheshire, he did not seem to care about the uproar he has caused around Britain with his behaviour. However somebody certainly cared about his lack of golf etiquette – as the Argentine and his wife were not allowed to play after not booking a tee time, and the course was full.

Comedian Pete Sinclair tweeted: "What's the difference between Carlos Tévez and a tramp? £150k a week. What's the similarity? They both refuse to get off the bench."

Media mogul Piers Morgan added: "I think Carlos Tévez needs an urgent chat with Michael Owen to learn how to stay happy on the bench."

Tévez was unrepentant after the match, but denied that he had simply not bothered to save City from defeat. He said it had been a 'misunderstanding' – but an irate Mancini said that the forward was 'finished' at the club.

"I would like to apologise to all Manchester City fans, with whom I have always had a strong relationship, for any misunderstanding that occurred in Munich. They understand that when I am on the pitch I have always given my best for the club. In Munich on Tuesday I had warmed up and was ready to play. This is not the right time to get into specific details as to why this did not happen. But I wish to state that I never refused to play. There was some confusion on the bench and I believe my position may have been misunderstood. Going forward I am ready to play when required and to fulfil my obligations."

The player's attempt to dodge responsibility was mocked almost immediately as #Tévezexcuses began to trend on Twitter. Tévez later offered a statement denying that he had refused to appear as a substitute, but he said could not go into 'specific details' as to his reasons. PFA chief Gordon Taylor suggested on the radio that Tévez should be compensated if his contract at City was terminated.

Mancini commented, "In the next days, we will speak with Khaldoon. It is normal. He is the chairman. He decides everything. If I decided, yes (he would leave). He wanted to leave last year. I helped him for two years every time. He refused to play. I cannot accept this behaviour from him. I decide the substitutions, not Carlos."

City were determined to seek 'evidence', with players and coaching staff present on the substitutes' bench at the time of the incident likely to be asked to provide observations, with television interviews also set to be reviewed. Despite the prospect of writing off a playing asset valued at £50 million, the Abu Dhabi power brokers had not discounted the prospect of sacking Tévez, although such an extreme measure was highly unlikely, despite the anger and thirst for retribution.

Chelsea's decision to sack the Romanian forward Adrian Mutu in October 2004 for testing positive for cocaine offered City a precedent; it also illustrated the problems connected to such action as the west London club were still chasing the player for compensation due. Mutu was ordered to pay £14.6 million in compensation to Chelsea in July 2009 for breach of contract, although there is no suggestion that Tévez's refusal to play for City is comparable to Mutu testing positive for cocaine. Sacking Tévez was regarded as an option of last resort. Mancini made it clear to Khaldoon al-

Mubarak that he does not want the player at the club's training ground, but opposed a sacking.

Suggestions that Mancini told Tévez to "---- off to Argentina", and also urged Dzeko to "---- off back to Bosnia", during the touchline row were put to City, who declined to respond.

Asked if he will ever pick Tévez again, Mancini replied: "No. If we want to improve like a team, like a squad, Carlos cannot play with us. With me, no – it is finished. It may not be my decision but if I'm deciding then, yes, he goes. For me, if a player earns a lot of money playing for Manchester City in the Champions League and he behaves like this – he cannot play again. Never. He has wanted to leave for the last two years. For two years I have helped him, and now he has refused to play. Never again."

The controversy erupted after Mancini made his first substitution, replacing Dzeko with Nigel de Jong. Dzeko reacted badly to the decision and Mancini was fiercely critical of him, too, saying the Bosnian would be dropped from Saturday's game at Blackburn Rovers.

The plan, according to Mancini, was to introduce Tévez "three or four minutes later" but he refused to leave the dugout for his warm-up. "I make the decision [about substitutions], not Carlos. I think he was disappointed because he didn't go out for the first change – maybe. But when I said 'Carlos, go, for 35 minutes to the end,' he refused. I think that in 35 minutes we can change every result. For me, it's a bad situation because it's impossible if a player decides he will not help the team. It's impossible. We have 11 players and I can't accept that one player refused to go on to the pitch. I can't accept this."

Mancini was asked whether a club with City's immense wealth could effectively sack Tévez by terminating his contract. "I don't know," he replied.

Dzeko directed a sarcastic thumbs-up at Mancini after his 55th-minute substitution before exchanging angry words with his manager and throwing down his tracksuit top. "He played a bad game, a poor game," Mancini said. "Next time, maybe if he plays better he can stay on the pitch. He needs to improve his behaviour. I should be unhappy with his performance – not Edin."

The manager continued: "This is the last time that one of our players leaves the pitch and moves his head like this [shaking head]. I can understand why a player is disappointed but I am furious with Dzeko and he will sit the next game next to me. This is the last time he has this behaviour. He is disappointed. But the manager can do what he thinks. We play every three days and one player can't play in every game."

Mancini had also confronted Zabaleta in the dugout after mistakenly believing that he heard him say something in Tévez's favour. "With Pablo, I made a mistake. I have spoken with Pablo now and it's nothing."

Mancini's anger extended to the rest of his team. "We played well for only 30 minutes and we conceded stupid goals. We have another four games and in my opinion we can still go into the second stage. If we win the next three games we will go through. But a situation like tonight? Never."

City had the support of Fifa should they wish to terminate Tévez's contract, with Fifa vice-president Jim Boyce claiming that the player's behaviour was "despicable". Boyce said: "If City write to Fifa and state the exact circumstances, then I believe Fifa should have the power, as they do for drugs-related and other cases, to ban the player from taking an active part in football." Northern Irishman Boyce, speaking in a personal capacity, said: "It hasn't occurred before but I think what happened was despicable. If this player did what he has been accused of doing, then if Manchester City were to release him I don't think it would be right if he could go and earn a considerable amount of money somewhere else next week. I would have no problems if some sanctions were imposed by Fifa in that respect. People within the clubs and within the top level of Fifa have to consider that if Carlos Tévez does it, who's to stop someone else doing it the next week or the week after?"

Stefan Effenberg, who captained Bayern to their last Champions League triumph in 2001, said Tévez behaviour was unacceptable and that he, like Mancini, would never consider the player again. "That player would never play in the same club as me again – that goes without saying. There is a clear order from the coach and he disregards it. That is poor behaviour and the club has got to come down hard on it. Other clubs are going to have to consider whether they want to sign a player with such a character. It is disrespectful to your team-mates and is not just in spite of the coach, but in spite of the whole team."

Tévez's actions drew a scathing response from TV pundit, former Liverpool manager Graeme Souness commenting, "He is one bad apple. He can undo all the good work that has been done. He's a disgrace to football. He epitomises what most people think is wrong with modern football. It is totally unacceptable. He's a football player and he is paid to play. He is refusing to help his team-mates. It's all about him, him, him. How can you deal with players acting like that?"

Tévez thought he should have started the tie, he didn't and that added to a simmering sense of resentment which has grown through the early part of this season after an initial acceptance that having been given extra time off this summer and with Agüero signed and doing so well, Tévez could not expect to be an automatic starter for City. Tévez accepted his place among the substitutes but, also, warmed up along the touchline virtually throughout the second-half in readiness to come on. He felt like he was getting ready for an eternity and when it was clear that, with City 2-0 down, and Dzeko set to be replaced, Tévez thought he would be coming on, especially as he felt he had been asked to get ready. Instead Mancini introduced a holding midfielder, de Jong, and Tévez carried on warming up — albeit bemused by that decision. Eventually Tévez took his seat back in the dug-out only for Mancini to send over a member of his medical staff to tell the player to go back out and warm-up again. Tévez replied that he was ready, now, to go on and that message was relayed to Mancini. Again the manager told him to warm up and again Tévez said he was ready. Finally Mancini snapped.

Tévez felt the victim of vendetta against him ever since he handed in a transfer request last December. Tévez believed he was treated in a heavy-handed way by Mancini, comparing his treatment to Sir Alex, Wenger and Redknapp, who have taken a more sympathetic approach to players at their clubs – Rooney, Fabregas and Modric – who all pushed to leave at one stage or another.

Tévez reached a breaking point. His relationship with Mancini improved last season but there was still no great feeling between the pair especially as the player had been awarded a handful of minutes and only featured for longer in less high-profile matches, not what Tévez, the former captain, the top-scorer, talisman and main player, was used to and mentally and emotionally he has struggled with it. City refute this. Mancini awarded him more time off than other players and did not have an agenda to freeze him out of the club.

Thursday, Sept 29, 2011

Edin Dzeko refused to speak to reporters as he left the stadium. Having had a chance to consider, he apologised to Mancini and his team-mates. ''I know my reaction was bad. I have spoken to the guys and to the coach as well. I have apologised for the reaction and Roberto has accepted it and said that everything is OK and that we have to be positive for the next game.'' Dzeko was extra motivated to win the game because of the time he spent with Wolfsburg. ''I was unhappy because we were 2-0 down and I wanted to win the game. It was something special for me to go back to Germany where I played for a long time. I wanted to do well and wanted the team to do well. Things didn't go well for us. That is why I was extra frustrated.''

City took such a stringent approach of obtaining all the evidence that journalists attending scheduled pre-match press conference looking ahead to

Saturday's trip to Blackburn were warned that Mancini will not speak about Tévez. Dzeko recalled it was at Ewood Park where he broke his League duck at the 10th attempt in City's single-goal triumph back in March. "I remember last year when I scored there and we won. We had great support from thousands of City fans and we hope to make then cheer again on Saturday."

City were urged to 'get rid' of Tévez by supporters. An online poll by the Manchester Evening News asking whether Tévez should play for City again resulted in 90 per cent of respondents voting for the player to be sold. Various fans websites were flooded with calls wanting Tévez out. Andy Savage, editor of mcfc-forum.com, said: "I posted an online survey immediately after the game giving supporters three options to choose in terms of how they would deal with Tévez. The choices were sack him, let him rot or 'other' and, by Wednesday evening, the vast majority had voted for the club to let him rot. After what happened at Bayern Munich, the club should get rid of him as quickly as possible. All of the fans I have spoken to want Tévez out on the grounds of gross misconduct. If I had been Roberto Mancini in the Allianz Arena, I would have told the fourth official to raise his board with Tévez's number on it when he substituted Samir Nasri. Had he done that, he would have hung Tévez out to dry in front of the watching world. If somebody is willing to pay £20-25m for him, then the club should take it because the effect Tévez is having risks becoming cancerous within the dressing room."

Kevin Parker, chairman of the City Supporters' Club, said: "When I was speaking to people in the airport after the game, everybody wanted Tévez out of the club. They never want him to wear a City shirt again. His relationship with the fans is in tatters. I can't see how this can be repaired. Nobody is going to believe his story that he didn't refuse to come on. We just want to move on without Carlos Tévez. No single person is bigger than any football club and certainly not Carlos Tévez."

Fri, Sept 30, 2011

Tévez training-ground parking space was promptly occupied on by another well-known employee as Mancini looked to draw a line under the fall out, insisting dealing with Tévez was "not my problem".

Tévez was absent from training as the first-team squad prepared for the trip to Blackburn. With direct questions relating to Tévez off limits at the press conference, Mancini reiterated his stance that Tévez was no longer in his thoughts. "It's finished. I'm the manager. Our focus now is on the Premier League and Blackburn – other things are finished. Not my problem."

Unlike with Tévez, that issue with Dzeko was quickly resolved. "We didn't have any problem with Dzeko. That was finished on Thursday morning (when the players returned to training). Our focus now is on Blackburn." Mancini, criticised for his strict discipline, forgave Dzeko. As an expert goalscorer during his distinguished playing days, Mancini appreciates the frustration of being substituted. "In this situation, I'm not disappointed because I can understand every player. We have blood inside, we don't have water." In noting Dzeko's apology, Mancini admitted: "Sometimes I can make a mistake and I can apologise to the players. When you work every day you can have some problems but it is important to resolve them very quickly."

Mancini bore the confident look of a manager who enjoyed the backing of his club's owners. Rival managers such as Sir Alex voiced support, Mancini held court at Carrington, expressing his conviction that he was "in control" and that he had the "good men" in his dressing room to make City successful. "With good men you can build a strong team for the future. This is very important. When you have good men, you can lose some games and it is not important because in the end you can take [achieve] your target – one hundred per cent. I have good men. I am sure of this." Mancini never once mentioned the name of Tévez. "I have control. For the manager it is important to have things under control. I have this. I don't have any problems."

Mancini rejected widespread jealousy of City's wealth, "I don't think we are in a difficult moment. I don't feel this. We lost only one game. Manchester United drew with Basle at home. The Champions League is very difficult for every club, even for those with big experience. With four games left we have many chances to go to the next stage. I don't think we will have a problem."

He was thinking long term. "I have a contract for this year and another year. I try to work always hard. When I finish my contract if the club is happy we can talk about this. I would like to stay here until we have built the new training facility [the Etihad Campus is due to open in 2015]. I would like to see it. I would like to stay. When you start to build a new team like Manchester City, you have many chances to win trophies over the next years. To manage a club like City is fantastic for me. It's good. Both me and the club should be happy."

When questions strayed back towards the state of dressing-room morale, Mancini responded with a smile. "I thought we were on the top of the table, not on the bottom! I think. I don't know. I think we have the same points with United." Asked whether he hoped the Tévez situation will be finished quickly, Mancini replied calmly: "It is finished."

Mancini had endured more difficult weeks — "at Fiorentina we had no money". He was a tough individual. "I left my home when I was 13 years-old so what do you think?"

As Mancini talked, investigators were at work inside Carrington, interviewing a few players before they rush off on international duty after Saturday's game. "I work focused on the Premier League, Champions League and the FA Cup," continued Mancini. "The other things are finished in my mind."

Photographs emerged from training of Mancini and Agüero, appearing to have strong words but City dismissed the suggestion of any more dissent towards the manager. City were far less reliant on Tévez since the arrival of Agüero and Nasri and the improvement in Dzeko's form.

Sir Alex Ferguson would not speak directly about Tévez but said Mancini handled the incident well, "I think that Roberto Mancini has come out showing his strength of character, the strength of management and the strength of support for his management. We have all had our own difficulties in management. You cope with it as best you can, and in my own experience, strong management is important. There is nobody more important than the manager."

Informed of the support of Ferguson and other managers, Mancini concluded: "I know if I'm doing my job well or not. I'm happy because our season has started very well."

Meanwhile, Paul Scholes sought to understand the player. "I can see his point of view, yeah. His state of mind will be that he's being messed around by the manager. And you could say he's got a case. He was far and away City's best player last year, and he hasn't featured this season. He'll look at the Napoli game when they were struggling and he's only been brought on with ten minutes to go, he'll see he's been left out of the Everton game, he'll watch Balotelli coming in to the team instead of him and all that will rile him. He'd have thought he should be playing against Bayern Munich after the Manchester City forwards didn't play well against Everton. He is someone who wants to be playing. He'll think the manager's taking the ---- out of him and he'll reckon this is the only way he has of making a point. The state of mind he's in he'll think what he's done is the only way to get his manager back, to eff him off if you like. I'm not saying it's right, of course it isn't. But I understand it." After being left out of a couple of Premier League games, Scholes refused to play for a second-string United line-up in a Worthington Cup tie at Arsenal. "I regretted it immediately. It was a stupid thing to do. And I'm sure over time Carlos will come to regret what he did. Sure, there are some players these days quite happy to sit there on the bench. But Carlos wants to play every week. I remember when he was at this club, when there were four of the top forwards in Europe here, he still thought he should be playing every week. He wants to be involved every second of every game and it will be absolutely killing him sitting on the bench."

The then QPR manager Neil Warnock weighed into the Tévez debate by declaring: "The sooner he leaves the country, the better." Warnock called for Fifa to allow clubs to slap long bans on players who show the kind of disobedience towards their managers. Warnock has no love for Tévez, who was at the centre of the third-party ownership saga four years ago that saw West Ham keep their Premier League status at the expense of his own Sheffield United. Warnock suspected Tévez would ultimately escape serious punishment, "When somebody's paid such a large amount, to even think about what he did, it's so disrespectful, irrespective of the problems you have with managers. Because every manager has problems with players. It's like having 35 kids to look after and have a party outside. Unfortunately, I think players hold all the aces. When you're paying a player up to a quarter of a million pounds per week, it's difficult to say, 'We'll pay him for a couple of years and make him stew in the reserves'. It sounds good for the press. But, in reality, you're not going to chuck all those millions of pounds away when you're running a business. He'll come out with a two-week fine, two-week ban, and that's all, irrespective of the campaign to do this, to do that."

Gordon Taylor, the chief executive of the PFA, offered to mediate, "It's not good for Man City, the manager or the player. It is not giving the right image across the world. Any conflict is capable of resolving if it's for the best for all parties." He believed that Tévez can come in from the cold, working with Mancini again. "In the same way you don't want a player humiliated neither do you want the manager undermined. It's about trying to achieve that balance with a full apology, a very serious fine and then 100 per cent application by the player, see how it goes for three months and then review the situation in January. Clubs do have that potential to impose a very heavy fine and a warning. That preserves the discipline of the manager. There is a potential for six weeks. Sometimes a transgression, if substantiated, brings a two-week fine which looks nominal but up to six weeks is not meagre at all. If it is substantiated that he refused to play that goes to the very heart of the contract.

"Everybody is quick to condemn Tévez, but he's a world-class player. He might not be a favourite with the fans now but he certainly has been last season. When he's pulling his weight, he chases lost causes. City paid a lot of money for him, is it necessarily the best thing for him or the club that he is put out to grass? Or to talk about 'stay away from the club'? Or have him playing in the reserves? You can't treat people like that. At the moment,

I don't see a lot of good of having Tévez out of the game for three months. They have an asset that is going to be declining. It would be cutting off their nose to spite their faces. I am looking to mitigate. Rather this than what could be a very protracted legal business of perhaps sacking the player, seeking compensation and not having him at the club – particularly when we have two contrasting views of what happened. Part of the problem is that 'players only love you when they're playing'. It is about the pride of the individual, the respect they feel.

"There is a strong feeling amongst the players that Tévez was feeling he was getting humiliated by the manager. People will say for the money he is on, that's what he has got to do but we are talking about human beings. It's like Nureyev the ballet dancer would have his tantrums. Top people can throw tantrums. It's about human emotions. At the moment the club are minded to support the manager but appreciate that maybe it is the Italian culture of 'no messing about, this is it', of not being soft in handling some of these big stars. The public like that. It got the same [positive] reaction when Fabio Capello came in after Sven-Goran Eriksson. In reality, it's stick and carrot. On the other side of the city, Alex manages to keep quite a few big-name stars within the fold and make sure they are all pulling for him."

Taylor pointed to that rapprochement between Rooney and United as a reminder that peace can break out. "You remember what it was like with Wayne Rooney. We can retrieve the situation. I hope for the sake of English football that it will be sorted."

Alan Hansen and pundits like him were sure Tévez would never play again for City. "There can be no doubt that Carlos Tévez is finished as a Manchester City player after his refusal to play against Bayern Munich on Tuesday, but his actions have also left the club and Roberto Mancini in an impossible situation," Hansen wrote in his Telegraph column. He added, "Mancini is correct in taking strong action by saying Tévez will never play for him again and the only possible outcome at the end of the sorry saga will be City deciding to get rid of the player."

Few would have guessed that Tévez would indeed be back!

Hansen worried that the players absence would cost City the title, "…. aside from the unwanted distraction that Tévez has caused and the disharmony that his actions could lead to, he has also left City worryingly reliant on three forwards, none of whom can match the 27 year-old's proven credentials in the Premier League….Even if Agüero's injury proves, as expected, to be a short-term problem, Mancini must negotiate the next few months with only three strikers – or two strikers and a maybe when you consider Balotelli's reliability. City have to be lucky with injuries, loss of form and suspensions, but those things affect every club." Hansen blamed Tévez, "...whichever way you look at the situation, it is Tévez's fault. He is the only one who is culpable for what happened in Munich. How can a player misunderstand that the manager wants him to go on as a substitute? It just does not ring true. It was an idiotic thing to do and I have no sympathy for Tévez. The whole episode seemed almost pre-conceived and anything but a spur-of-the-moment thing."

OCTOBER

City scored more goals in the opening 10 games than any team since Preston's
38 in the Football League's inaugural season in 1888-89.

Saturday, Oct 1, 2011

Roberto Mancini name was chanted by City fans prior to kick off at Ewood Park and by the end Blackburn Rovers fans were baying for manager Steve Kean's blood as a convincing 4-0 away win ensured the City manager had the fans backing in his stance with Tévez, and the general up lift in the challenge for the title. "It was the result we were looking for to put Bayern Munich to bed," said the first-team coach, David Platt, on media duty as Mancini had to catch a flight to Italy straight after the game, and speaking on condition that the subject of Tévez was off limits.

City had made six changes and lost Agüero in the first half, so the winning margin was all the more impressive. "We know what we're blessed with here," Platt said. "We have a talented squad and one of the hardest things is just to pick 11 players. Most weeks we have to send very good players to the stands to watch the game." Under siege Kean commented, "City played a freshened team and it took a very good goal to put them in front."

Agüero limped off with a groin strain after half an hour, with Blackburn playing a containing game and refusing to commit too many players to attack. Mario Balotelli, making his first Premier League start of the season, struck a post at the start of the second half as he was about to prove there was life after Tévez.

City soon took control with two excellent goals in two minutes. A partially cleared corner landed at Johnson's feet in the 55th minute, controlling with his left foot and then using minimal back lift the shot found Robinson's top corner from outside the area. City scored a second before Blackburn had a chance to compose themselves, Mario finally proving his finishing ability by guiding Nasri's cross past Robinson. Nasri added an easy looking third after exchanging passes with Silva. Ewood echoed to "Kean Out" and "You're getting sacked in the morning". Savic's headed goal from Nasri's free-kick was the defender's first in the Premier League. At the final whistle fans at one end of the stadium sang in praise of their manager, at the opposite end several hundred stayed on to demand a sacking.

Sunday, Oct 2, 2011

The dirty tricks were in full swing when it was leaked that Mancini was furious with his son Filippo for refusing to play for City's reserve team, two months before Tévez's refusal to take the field as a substitute. Filippo, a non-contract, unpaid player, refused to appear as a substitute in the closing stages of a friendly for the club's Elite Development Squad against Liverpool in August after he was instructed to prepare to take the field by EDS coaching staff, but instead declined to play for the team, a mixture of reserves and youth players, managed by Andy Welsh. The emergence of Mancini jnr's behaviour was an embarrassment for City and Mancini. The timing of its emergence hardly coincidental. With Filippo not tied to a contract, the club was unable to apply a disciplinary procedure beyond a verbal rebuke.

A City spokesperson said: "Filippo is a non-contracted, unpaid player who was on the substitutes' bench for the non competitive game in question. In these circumstances, a disciplinary procedure would have been invoked, however, as he was not an employee of the club, this was not a viable option. The matter has been dealt with internally. Roberto Mancini was not aware of this incident." Since his refusal to play, Filippo, who was with his father as a junior at Inter Milan, appeared for the EDS team, making an hour-long appearance last month.

Monday, Oct 3, 2011

City's human resources and legal teams interviewed Tévez, giving him the chance to formally state his version of events. The club kept the location and time of the meeting secret. City needed to conduct a thorough investigation to ensure their position is legally watertight. After meeting club officials, Tévez would not be expected back at City until his suspension ended on October 12 and could therefore return to Argentina should he wish. He was suspended on full pay. An eventual fine of six weeks' wages, which would cost Tévez £1.2m

Tuesday, Oct 4, 2011

Tévez landed in Buenos Aires with his advisors keen for a swift conclusion but while City had pledged to complete the investigation within seven working days of the player receiving official notice of his suspension and the investigation, the club were determined not to be rushed into a hasty decision.

Mario Balotelli picked up a back injury on international duty. Italy's team doctor Enrico Castellacci told a press conference, ''We have decided, having spoken to Manchester City, to send him home."

Savic's England squad team-mates teased him about his country's diminutive size. "They keep asking me: 'Where are we going?' and saying they don't know where Montenegro is, because we are such a small country. We have only 800,000 people in our country but everyone is proud of what the football team means, and of the results this team has had in this qualification campaign. It should be a good game for both teams, but I expect a good result for us." Fabio Capello's men headed for Montenegro after the Group G minnows walked away from Wembley with a goalless draw in October last year and were currently second in the group with a game in hand.

Sergio Agüero could yet play for Argentina against Chile, despite being ruled out for 2-3 weeks by the club after suffering a groin injury against Blackburn. Agüero was examined by Argentina FA doctor Daniel Martinez before being confirmed in the squad by manager Alex Sabella. City's medical staff were in regular contact with their Argentine counterparts. Agüero was expected to be sidelined until the trip to Manchester United, a game described by Sir Alex as bigger than ever before. Fergie said: "All derbies are big now, that is the nature of the landscape. But the impetus City now have – they have a huge squad of players and the financial power to attract some of the best footballers in the world – actually changes the focus of the derby these days."

Wednesday, Oct 5, 2011

Kia Joorabchian maintained that City's performance analyst, Pedro Marques, who translated the television interview with Tévez broadcast immediately after the game, had misunderstood the forward's words. Sky Sports released this transcript of the Tévez: interview, translating Tévez. Marques, a Portuguese member of the City staff, is not a club interpreter and only assisted in what the club considered an unauthorised interview at Tévez's request. After seeing new footage on Sky, Tévez's advisors believed there was evidence the interpreter was distracted as the first question was asked, which added to the confusion.

Geoff Shreeves: "An extraordinary situation this evening, Roberto Mancini has said Carlos refused to come off the bench. What is the truth?"

Carlos Tévez: "I didn't want to warm up because I wasn't feeling very well so I thought it was better not to (interrupted). So I didn't think I was in a good situation to come on, because my head wasn't in the right place."

Translation: "Just was not feeling very good inimically/anaemically [sic] and mentally, so I put my opinion to just that."

Shreeves: "Roberto has also said in a press conference that you will never play for him again. Do you think your future lies elsewhere now? Are you finished at this club for refusing to play?"

Tévez: "Those are decisions which he makes and I agree with that. It's just that I have been professional up until now. I was the top goalscorer last season so I don't think I deserve this treatment. Yes I wanted to leave. I asked to leave because I had family problems but now my family is here and I'm happy, but I don't have the manager's backing."

Translation: "Yeah, I think it's his decision. I have been a professional during all the time in here. Last season I was also the best scorer. And I put my opinion through that I want to leave because of family reasons but I keep trying to do my best."

Speaking as a late addition to the Leaders in Football conference held at Stamford Bridge, Joorabchian said he did not believe Tévez refused to play. "After a game, questions are asked and if you do not have a very professional interpreter you have a problem. I listened to the questions in English and the answer in Spanish and the interpretation is incorrect. Both questions were interpreted incorrectly and then both answers misinterpreted. Geoff Shreeves asks if Carlos is finished and he says the truth is how can I be fit to play? In the second question he is asked about the situation being finished and Carlos says it is a well-known fact that since his family was not here he has asked the club if he could leave to be closer to his family, but now his family is in Manchester he is comfortable again. The interpreter says something different. Carlos does speak English but it is not good enough for a full-blown interview. There is an ongoing internal investigation so this is all my opinion, not what I have spoken about with Carlos. The main issue is what happened caused a lot of confusion as shown by the TV footage. While I do not think it is correct for any player to refuse to play, the events of Munich have been judged prior to the real outcome. We did not see what really happened, just the TV footage. There is a lot of arguing going on when Edin Dzeko comes off. You could see Carlos warming up in the first half and in the second half I saw Carlos warming up and as he returned to the bench there was a row between Dzeko and Roberto Mancini. Then Carlos stood up and sat down. The next thing we hear is what Roberto says."

Joorabchian reiterated that Tévez refused only to warm up, "he feels he has been judged and condemned before the case has really been looked in to." Tévez blamed "confusion on the bench" for the "misunderstanding" and so there was no reason why he should apologise to Mancini.

Mark Hughes - who is also represented by Joorabchian - struggled to see a way for Tévez to return to the City side. "I think it would be very,

very difficult. The assumption is that Carlos refused to come on to the field of play. Let's hope it is - one way or the other - because it's damaging to Man City, to their manager and to Carlos Tévez. A lot of things were said but there are not too many options if things are proved to be correct. It's a shame because we don't want top players to leave the Premier League, but if it's borne out that the things suggested are correct, it will be very hard to see any other outcome."

Joorabchian commented, "You can criticise Carlos for anything but one thing you can't criticise him for is his commitment when he's on the pitch and you can never criticise him for wanting to play. There have been several times at Manchester City throughout his two-year career where he is taking injections, playing with swollen ankles, where he has played in situations when maybe even doctors have told him not to play. My opinion is that Carlos throughout his career has been one that fights to play. If there is any issues it's because he's always so eager to play. You have to remember Carlos joined Manchester City when he had an official offer from Real Madrid and Manchester United on the table. He was one of the first players to join Manchester City's new vision. It's a great vision and Carlos was brought in to help start that vision. So he feels very differently towards the club, he has a very intense feeling."

Joorabchian said other managers handled similar cases in a more harmonious fashion. "We have seen Fabregas, Nasri and Modric hand in transfer requests. The situations were handled very differently by their managers and clubs. Cesc had a big problem through the summer and Modric did not play in the first European game when it was reported he did not want to play. Carlos has been unfairly judged and condemned before the case has been looked into. You can criticise Carlos for anything but not his commitment on the pitch. Carlos has stated it was a misunderstanding and apologised to the City fans for that misunderstanding. We should wait until the investigation has run its course and then both parties can sit down and decide what they will do."

Fri, Oct 7, 2011

Corinthians general manager Edu insisted that the club had no intention of returning to the race for Tévez, "We are always interested in world-class players like Carlos, but you need to analyse if it's right for you at that time to try to sign him or not. We have not spoken to him or his agent. On Wednesday, I spoke to our club president to see if he wanted me to make contact and start negotiations while I'm over in Europe but he said 'no'. I was talking to Manchester City in July and we tried to buy him for £40m, but the negotiations were not easy. We needed to arrange bank guarantees and other things. To organise all of that in two or three days was very difficult. That's why we lost him." Wealthy Russian club Anzhi Makhachkala were mooted as a possible buyer but their interest was unconfirmed. West Ham were keen to sign him on loan, yet funding such a transfer was likely to be prove impossible.

Wednesday, Oct 12, 2011

City announce that Tévez faced disciplinary proceedings, over alleged breach of contract. A senior City figure who had not been part of the initial investigation would chair the hearing. Tévez can request that club captain Vincent Kompany or a member of the PFA be present. If the ruling goes against him, he could then appeal – with that hearing to involve a representative of the Abu Dhabi-based owners. If he is again unsuccessful, Tévez would be able take his case to the Premier League, meaning the dispute may not be settled until mid-December.

The club statement said: "There is a case for Carlos Tévez to answer of alleged breaches of contract. He will face disciplinary proceedings. The hearing will be convened shortly. Carlos will be required to report for training on Thursday."

PFA Chief Executive Gordon Taylor said: "Manchester City have conducted things in a proper manner and they feel the evidence, as far as I am aware of, justifies a charge. There are a number of options to consider but ideally I would like a situation where both parties can walk away from it. The transfer window is not open until January. We've got the position of the manager and the position of the player to consider when trying to make sure both sides of the dispute can keep their heads up high. The most extreme option could be termination [of Tévez's contract] if the evidence justifies that or it could be a suspension without pay, or a fine. That fine could be anything from two weeks up to six weeks, with the approval of the PFA."

Thursday, Oct 13, 2011

Tévez arrived at the Carrington complex at 12.10 pm and was put through his paces by a club physio. Tévez had not been expected to train with City's first-team squad and instead underwent a fitness session and assessment. Sam Allardyce believed Tévez's best chance of playing again before the January transfer window was in the Championship with West Ham. City had already rejected such a move.

Saturday, Oct 15, 2011

With a comfortable 4-1 win over Villa, City climbed ahead of United before the first Manchester league derby of the season gave them a chance to display their title credentials. "We started the season well but we knew this would be a hard week because we play Aston Villa, we play Villarreal, which is a crucial game in the Champions League for us," said Mancini when asked if his team had been distracted by off-field matters. "So our minds are very busy. Our confidence is high because we started the season well, but we need to improve."

Mancini looked ahead to Old Trafford, "Sir Alex Ferguson has more experience than me. He knows he has a fantastic team on his hands and he has respect for every team he plays against but I hope we are earning more respect."

City were unconvincing in the opening 20 minutes, yet a goal appeared inevitable, arriving after 28 minutes when Bent could only flick on Johnson's corner and Richards controlled the ball with his chest. The rebound sat up invitingly for Balotelli, whose overhead kick gave Given no chance from six yards and Villa had little hope of preserving their unbeaten start to the League season. Then Yaya's hanging ball over the Villa defence, Warnock miskicked allowing Johnson to beat Given from just inside the penalty area. Warnock lashed in a consolation goal. Former Villa midfielder Milner claimed the game's most impressive goal, starting the move with a deep pass to Johnson and meeting a short, square ball from Barry with a shot into the top corner. Substitute Silva might have made it all the more painful for McLeish who commented, "They have got to be contenders with the squad they have."

Tuesday, Oct 18, 2011

Villarreal took the lead after only four minutes and City's only response was an own goal from Marchena just before the interval. Deep into stoppage time, and with what turned out to be almost the final kick of the game, substitute Agüero arrived at the far post to turn Zabaleta's cross past Lopez to revive City's hopes of reaching the knockout phase with City's first win in the Champions League.

Roberto Mancini replaced Johnson with Barry after only 39 minutes, much to the player's obvious displeasure, and another substitution that tested the manager's powers of man-management. As the home fans grew impatient, Mancini illustrated the scale of his concern by making the tactical substitution six minutes before the interval – a decision that saw the England winger depart shaking his head.

Mancini spoke to Johnson to explain the move and there was no problem between the pair, "We were conceding four or five counter-attacks. We needed to have more players in the middle and I wanted to move Yaya Toure behind Edin Dzeko. It was not because Adam was playing badly, he was playing very well, but it was a tactical decision. I spoke with him and he understands this. Sometimes every manager takes these decisions or feels the team needs a tactical substitution and unfortunately a player has to leave the pitch. I can understand every player leaving the pitch after only 38 minutes is unhappy but Adam is an important player for us."

Mancini made another change after 62 minutes when Agüero, now recovered from a groin injury, came on for de Jong. Zabaleta's cross was touched on by Silva and Agüero arrived to score. There was barely time to kick-off and a scene of total frustration had been instantly transformed into one of celebration at the final whistle in the hope that this dramatic finale would see their campaign back on track.

Mancini made it clear before kick-off that victory was the only priority – no matter how it was achieved after picking up only one point from their opening two games. "We were lucky because you need luck to score in the last seconds but we deserved to win."

Roberto Mancini believed the meeting with Napoli held the key, "This game will be very important – 100%. We play Villarreal before Napoli. It will be a crucial game in Italy but I don't know for which position in the group. It is still open for the first or second place. I hope Sergio's goal will prove to be very important for us. It was really important to win our first game in the Champions League. At this moment everything can happen in the group but we also know when we go to Villarreal in 15 days it will be a hard game because they are a very good team who played really well."

Thursday, Oct 20, 2011

Mario Balotelli promised to do his talking on the pitch, after a run-in with the Villa fans, determined to keep his cool against a side he has had run-ins with before. During the FA Cup semi-final last April he clashed with Rio Ferdinand. "They can say what they want. I won't say anything to them. I will be focused on the game. All that matters is the result, nothing else. After the game I might think about the supporters but not during it or before. I don't have anything against them. He is a great player. I didn't ever speak to him. I was just celebrating, but not against them. I showed him the shirt of City and obviously he got angry with me. For me, what happened on the pitch stayed on the pitch and now we are friends like before. Or we respect each other anyway. I'm going to give him the handshake before the game like I give to everyone."

Ryan Giggs lavished praise on Mario but admitted the Italian is "strange". Mario was reportedly playing with his iPad on the subs bench during an Italy match, and confronting school bullies of young fans. Giggs remarked, "He is very good, but also a little strange. In England all but the City fans hate him. But trust me, he is very talented."

Mario was confident his side can beat their rivals, "I think we can beat them. I think it will be a lot of fun – and soon United v City will be the biggest derby in the world." Mario collected four goals in his last four games, improving under Mancini. "With Mancini I feel very comfortable. I've known him a long time and he's a good manager. He believes in me. Even when no one in England believed in me, he did. And he kept on believing. I want to do something important here with him."

City fans were surprised to answer the phone to Roberto Mancini during the build-up to the clash with Villarreal. He recorded a message asking supporters to attend the must-win game. It was then used for a telephone marketing campaign directed at club members who had not bought tickets. Fans who received the calls heard: 'Hi, this is Roberto Mancini. As you know we have a very important match coming up against Villarreal in the Champions League. I hope we can count on your passion and support for this match. It makes a huge difference to the players. I hope to see you there. Ciao.' A club spokesman said the 'fun' marketing exercise may be repeated, but with players recording the messages.

Saturday, Oct 22, 2011

Cheshire Fire Service were called to extinguish a blaze at Mario's mansion in the early hours of Saturday morning after his friends attempted to release fireworks from the bathroom window. His latest controversy came just days after he moved from his apartment in Manchester city centre to the countryside for a quiet life.

Sunday Oct 23, 2011

City fans serenaded Sir Alex with "getting sacked in the morning" with thoughts of designing their "Six and the City" T-shirts. Sir Alex described United's 6-1 defeat as an "embarrassment" and admitted Mancini's team subjected him to his "worst ever day" in management.

Mario Balotelli, having almost burned down his upstairs bathroom in the early hours of Saturday, celebrated his first goal by lifting his shirt to reveal a T-shirt that asked: "Why Always Me?" Cue another idea for a range of t-shirts.

United's worst home defeat since Anthony Eden succeeded Winston Churchill as PM, Clement Attlee resigned as Labour leader and Hammer

Film Productions released The Quatermass Experiment. Fifty-six years on. Yet another t-shirt!

Mancini brought a bottle of wine, but Fergie was seeing red, red mists of anger, as City delighted in United's remarkable demise. Ferguson was outwitted by Mancini, who celebrated his 100th game in charge of City in style.

Mario provided the fireworks with the opening two goals, while Silva was the outstanding individual. Ferdinand was so sick, he declined the Glazers' offer of a helicopter ride to the NFL road-game at Wembley later in the day. Micah Richards was named man of the match but it could easily have been Milner, a force defensively and creatively, or Silva. City's depth of quality was highlighted when Mario was replaced by Dzeko and Agüero by Nasri.

Fergie's decision to start only two in the central midfield, Fletcher and Anderson, was a failure swiftly exposed by Silva, Yaya and Barry. Roberto Mancini was constantly in his technical area, having a word with Mario after 20 minutes. Mario rewarded his manager within a minute of the pep talk. From Milner's throw-in, Touré and Silva combined to release Milner, whose cutback was aimed perfectly for the Italian. As Evans slipped, Mario placed his shot expertly past David de Gea.

As the injured Nemanja Vidic watched from the stands, Evans was dismissed within a minute of the second half for pulling back Mario as he strode through on goal. City failed to capitalise then but Balotelli's second arrived on the hour. Milner and Silva played a one-two, Young failed to track back, and Milner crossed for Mario to score. United fans sought to lift their 10 men, chanting "stand up for the champions". As it happened City took United apart, the ball flowing from Silva to Touré to Balotelli to Milner and then Richards, whose cross was turned in by Agüero for the third.

By way of consolation Darren Fletcher scored from long range to give United a glimmer of hope but City responded with three breakaway goals in the last four minutes to stun United fans into silence and, as would prove crucial, radically alter the goal difference at the top in City's favour. When Barry flicked a corner on and Lescott turned the ball back, Dzeko pounced to make it 4-1. Then Dzeko sent Silva down the inside-right channel, he slipped the ball under his compatriot De Gea. City fans partied like it was 1989, the year of a famous 5-1 thrashing of United at Maine Road before Silva flicked the ball up and then guided it through to Dzeko, who completed the humbling of the champions.

Sir Alex Ferguson, who celebrates his 25th anniversary as United manager on Nov 6, witnessed his club's biggest derby defeat since another 6-1 loss to City in January 1926 — just one short of United's record home defeat, a 7-1 loss to Newcastle in September 1927.

Playing with 10 men following the 47th-minute dismissal of Evans, United capitulated in the dying stages as City ran in three late goals. But with City moving five points clear of United with their emphatic victory, Ferguson admitted he had never experienced such a dark day as a manager. "It was our worst ever day. It's the worst result in my history, ever. Even as a player I don't think I ever lost 6-1. I can't believe the scoreline. The first goal was a blow for sure, but it was retrievable at 1-0. I'm shattered, I can't believe it. It was an incredible disappointment, but we will react, no question about that. It's a perfect result for us to react to because there is a lot of embarrassment in the dressing room — and quite rightly so — and that will make an impact. You have to recover. The history of Manchester United is 'another day' and we will recover."

The humiliation of United's defeat resulted in the club's American owners, the Glazer family, being barracked and jostled by home supporters as they travelled from the players' tunnel to a awaiting helicopter. Sources in the tunnel reported angry chanting outside as the Glazers left the stadium for their transport to Wembley for the NFL fixture between their Tampa Bay Buccaneers team and the Chicago Bears. Rio Ferdinand cancelled his plan to travel to the game for a guest appearance on the pitch.

With three City goals coming in the final minutes, however, Ferguson insisted that United contributed to their downfall. "The sending off was the killer blow. After that, we kept attacking. I thought with the experience we've got – Rio Ferdinand, Patrice Evra – they would have [defended more] but we just kept attacking. It's all right playing the history books [United's reputation for fighting back] but common sense has to come into it. When we went to 3-1, 4-1 we should have settled for that. We kept attacking when we went 4-1 down and we should have just said: 'We've had our day'. They were attacking three versus two. It was crazy football and it was a bad day. But we'll come back. By January, we'll be OK. We usually get the show on the road in the second half of the season and that will have to be the case. Over the years we have always enjoyed a better goal difference than our rivals but after today, we are 10 goals short."

Mancini played down the significance. "I'm satisfied because we beat United away and I don't think there are a lot of teams that could win here. But I'm not satisfied for the 6-1 — it's because this is important for our supporters and maybe for the goals in the table. I am happy with the three points. Against Tottenham we played very well and against Bolton, but this is different because we played against a strong team like United. In the end there are three points, finished, we don't take six points for this game. I think the season will be very long and probably four or five teams that can win the title. This is important for our confidence, it's important because we showed that we are a good team, but we should appreciate the mentality United had because after 1-0 and the sending off, they continued to play to score. I think that's a very important mentality."

Mancini, who shared a post-match drink with the United manager, claimed he took no satisfaction from humiliating the Scot. "No, because I have big respect for him. I have big respect for United because we are talking a top manager and a top squad. I still think United are one yard above us. I think we can only change this after we win the title in the end. After, maybe it will be different, but now United are better than us."

★ *It may be no consolation to Sir Alex, but he was wrong to claim that the 6-1 defeat was the worst he had experienced since beginning his senior career with Queen's Park in 1957. He was on the receiving end of an even bigger hiding 40 years ago, when playing for Falkirk against Airdrieonians, on April 26, 1971. It was the final First Division game of the campaign and Airdrie needed to score six goals to overtake Rangers and win a place in the following season's short-lived Drybrough Cup. Goals from Billy Wilson (2), Drew Busby (2), Derek Whiteford, Drew Jarvie and Sam Goodwin gave Airdrie a 7-1 win.*

Monday Oct 24, 2011

The question was on everyone's lips. Had the balance of power finally shifted in Manchester? Alan Hansen wondered in his Telegraph column, 'Manchester United have been written off many times before and proved their doubters wrong, but Manchester City genuinely now have absolutely everything in place to win the Premier League and that was always the reality even before their incredible 6-1 win at Old Trafford. The title is now City's to lose. They have the squad, their manager is no longer quite so cautious as he was last season and they obviously have the financial power. If City do win the title this season, then the worry for the rest of the league is that the rest will never get a look-in again. That was the fear when Jose Mourinho arrived at Chelsea and won the title in his first two seasons and it is the same again with City.'

Hansen also argued, 'At some point, they will hit a bad patch and that will be when their progress and togetherness will be truly judged, but we always knew that their time would come at some stage and maybe that time is now. In a strange kind of way, City's defeat against United in the Community Shield earlier this season now appears to have been a crucial result for both clubs. From City's point of view, after conceding a 2-0 lead to lose 3-2, it gave Roberto Mancini and his players an early reality check and now looks like a blessing in disguise for them.'

Tuesday, Oct 25, 2011

Mario Balotelli does not care about his reputation. He produced his best performance for City as United were destroyed. After being billed as 'Rocket Man' and 'Mad Mario' following the firework episode, Mario insisted he had nothing to do with the fire and was not concerned by how he is perceived by others. "I don't care what people say about me. People are interested in my private life, but the thing at the weekend didn't come from me, it came from one of my friends and one of my brother's friends. Maybe I should be more careful about who I let in my house. But it wasn't about me, I didn't do anything. People got the story wrong about me and the fire at my house. I didn't set any fireworks off, it was a friend of mine – I didn't know anything about it until I heard the shouting coming from the bathroom. Luckily, nobody was injured, and my friend apologised to me for the damage to my house. It was a really stupid thing for him to do, someone could have been really hurt, and I was really, really angry with him about it."

After seeing his bathroom set alight after fireworks had landed on towels, Mario urged children not to play with fireworks as youngsters prepare for Guy Fawkes Night, and he was fronting a safe firework campaign, "It is an important message that children should not mess with fireworks. They can be very dangerous if they are not used in the right way. People should follow the firework code."

The furore prompted his 'Why Always Me?' "I did it for many reasons. But I'll leave it for other people to figure out what it means! I'm sure people can work it out. Chappy [Les Chapman], our kitman did it for me, I told him the words and he printed them. He is a good guy Chappy, one of the best! But no [I won't do it again], because otherwise I'll get booked every week, so it was a one-off for United! In a bad period, people can talk about you and say what they want, but I am focused on my football, my team-mates and my manager, girlfriends and my family, and what they say to me. What anyone else says is not important."

Mario stressed that the Old Trafford result underlined City's title-winning credentials, "I think this win and the performance showed everyone that we can be the best. I think the United game was one of the best we have ever played together for sure. At the moment, we play well every week, but the United win was special. The most important thing was the result, then the score and the performance. All of them were good for us against United, so we are happy. It was brilliant. It was a great atmosphere and my first goal was a good goal. I'm a striker and sometimes you don't think about what you will do. Those types of goal, sometimes they go inside and sometimes they don't. It was on target and it was a good goal, so I was happy. The feeling was great. To win a derby away at Old Trafford is one thing, but to win it 6-1, none of us knew what to say. We were really happy."

Mancini believed he could become one of the greatest players of all time, if he can learn to behave. "I don't know what happened about the fireworks. The important thing is Mario and his friend were okay. If we want to talk about Mario as a player, I put him in the first five in the world." Lack of maturity was the problem, according to Mancini. "The problem is his age. He is young and he can make mistakes. I hope for him we arrive at the day when Mario has changed completely his mind because after this he becomes one of the best three players in the world."

Mario Balotelli might have been asking "Why Always Me?" when he was caught laughing at a porn magazine while shopping with his girlfriend Raffaella Fico in Manchester City Centre. He was pictured picking up the XXX rated mag, and couldn't resist sneaking a quick peek inside and sharing a joke with the gorgeous Raffaella, who had been out shopping with him.

Some Twitter gossip suggested he was driving around Manchester in a convertible Bentley high-fiving City fans the day after bagging his famous brace against United.

Wednesday, Oct 26, 2011

Mancini was seen chewing Fruit Pastilles during his team's 5- 2 Carling Cup victory over Wolves. Managers have quirks while on the touchline; Sir Alex chewing gum and Andre Villas Boas enjoys squatting during matches. Mancini was pictured smiling has he handed out the sweets, which come in several fruity flavours.

City were being dubbed The Great Entertainers' rattling in the goals, with a 5-2 Carling Cup win at Wolves. Mancini's fruit pastels add to the fun that City were bringing to English football. Mancini's side scored 45 goals in 15 matches this term and registered 21 in their last 450 minutes of football; impressive statistics by anyone's standards. Well that was Mancini's second string, Wolves now faced the real thing three days later and away from home. Good luck.

Milijas put Wolves ahead here, City scored three in four minutes before the interval. Mancini left out the entire starting XI from Sunday, yet Dzeko scored twice to take his tally for the season to 11. Johnson was outstanding in a £100m reserve team, scoring City's equaliser and having a hand in the two other goals before the interval, an impressive response considering that he did not even make the substitutes' bench against United. Mancini continued to demand more from the winger. "I think sometimes he thinks: 'OK, this game I scored one goal, I did one assist and that's enough. He needs to think in a different way: 'OK, I scored one goal, I did one assist, I shall try to score another goal and another assist and after I run back to defend.' Because he can do this if he wants. My opinion is that he has everything to become one of the top wingers. I think you can improve when you are 30 or 31 years old. Adam is young, this is his third season in the Premier League, he has everything and it disappoints me when Adam plays every game and doesn't put everything on the pitch. Tonight he played well but, for example, on the second goal that Wolves scored, he didn't follow his opponent."

City played "maybe a different style", according to Mancini alluding to changing the emphasis to attacking football, given his profusion of attacking options. Mario Balotelli, an unused substitute, reacted unhappily when one of the City backroom staff asked him to do some running after the game. "Mario? No, no, no," said Mancini, denying there had been an incident.

Thursday, Oct, 27, 2011

City refused to sell Tévez for a cut-price fee despite claims to the contrary from Corinthians and the threat of legal action by the player against Mancini for defamation. Tévez's representatives considered their options after the striker was hit with a record four-week fine of £1.2m and warned as to his future conduct having been found guilty of misconduct. The Corinthians president, responded to the deterioration in Tévez's already poor relationship with City by telling the Brazilian media that Tévez will be available for less than half his summer value when the transfer window reopened in January. Sánchez said: "Although many people do not believe it, Tévez is much closer to the Corinthians than you can imagine. The initial offer was 40m and that is now 18m (£16m) because of all the problems he has faced back in England."

City were adamant this was not the case and that, given Sheikh Mansour's wealth and his belief that Tévez had shown frequent disrespect towards him and the club, the owner was prepared to hold Tévez to the remaining three years of his contract – even if Mancini chooses not to select him – or until a club meets the player's market value. They gave their complete backing to Mancini. Mancini did not discuss the situation after the cup tie. A spokesperson for the club explained that was due to the legal process.

Lawyers for Carlos Tévez were assessing whether to sue manager Mancini over the City manager's comments that the striker refused to play but the Argentinian's camp will not rush to a decision on their next move. Tévez had 14 days to appeal and was certain he will do so, with the player expected to present his case first to City's board of directors and, should they rule against him, then to the Premier League.

City's exhaustive disciplinary hearing found Tévez guilty of five breaches of contract. Tévez's representatives insisted City's charge relates to a failure to resume warming up rather than a refusal to play. City suspected Tévez's actions may have been premeditated after he had been told six days before the game that his requests to leave the club had cost him £6m in loyalty bonuses due over the course of his contract. They also believed his anger at being demoted to fourth-choice striker by Mancini, and confirmation that his contract would not be renegotiated following the breakdown of a transfer to Corinthians, may also have been factors. Tévez could apologise to Mancini, who said the striker was "finished" with the club on the night, although that was highly unlikely.

Kolo Toure was planning to contest any potential punishment he was given for his six-month suspension for a failed drugs test. The former City captain was due to appear before an internal disciplinary panel, chaired by Brian Marwood when the club would, no doubt, fine the player. Kolo's agent, Saif Rubie, said: "Kolo is disappointed the club have decided to take this stance and he will contest any planned action against him."

Fri Oct 28, 2011

The 18-year-old attacking midfielder Abdul Razak, born in the Ivory Coast, who made four appearances for City joined Portsmouth on a month's loan. Pompey joint caretaker manager Guy Whittingham commented: "Abdul is a gifted midfield player who Manchester City think very highly of. It's a great opportunity for him to come here and get some experience." Mancini said: "He's a talented footballer and a very good young man. I believe he has the ability to become a very important player for Manchester City."

Saturday, Oct 29, 2011

Only three goals this time and it was possible to feel let down. Ten league games, 36 goals, including six against United and five against Tottenham, so three against lowly Wolves three days after rattling in five against the same opposition in the Carling Cup, was bordered on a 'disappointment'. Nothing of the sort. City could have scored eight but for keeper Wayne Hennessey's first-half heroics.

Hunt's 84th-minute penalty, following a Kompany foul on Doyle which saw the captain dismissed, ensured a nervous end to the game for the home side, until an injury-time strike from substitute Johnson restored City's two-goal advantage. The mark of City's progress under Mancini was evident in the manager's programme notes for this game, warning that the club must not "dwell on what we have done", and instead focus on using last Sunday's derby win as a platform for greater success.

Mancini stressed the need to keep expectations sensible. "It is impossible to always score four or five goals every game. I don't know how many chances we had today, but their keeper saved everything in the first-half. In football, we need to be patient some time. Sometimes it is difficult to score, but it was important to beat Wolves today. After Man United, I don't want everybody to think every game will be easy. Football is not like that."

Hennessey's 51st-minute clearance was charged down by Agüero and the ball dropped to Dzeko, who was gifted an open goal from 18 yards, then 15 minutes later his failure to hold on to Silva's 20-yard strike enabled Aleksander Kolarov to convert the rebound from six yards. Hunt's penalty gave Wolves hope of a point but City strengthened their grip on top spot with Johnson scoring their third in stoppage time.

Monday Oct 31, 2011

City launched a bid to recoup £1.5m of Kolo's image rights in a bitter battle over his failed drugs test. Toure considered leaving in January if the club succeed at a hearing, chaired by club executive Brian Marwood with a lawyer present. City first tried to fine the £120,000-a-week star around £500,000, but decided to go for his image rights, which were worth 20-25 per cent of his earnings. His brother Yaya was naturally angry. City supported the player during the legal process during the disciplinary hearings, which ended with a six-month ban in May from the World Anti-Doping agency. No disciplinary action was taken by City at the time and he received his image rights payment as normal in August.

PFA Chairman Gordon Taylor described the decision as "strange". Taylor attended the hearing into the gross misconduct charge. Taylor felt the six-month ban was punishment enough, but City insisted the PFA knew about the charge as far back as July. Taylor commented: "We have had the hearing today and we presented the fact that the FA could have given him two years but only gave him six months because they took into account that it was a genuine mistake and not performance-enhancing or a diuretic to mask drug-taking. He also had excellent character references from Arsenal and a number of other players. It just seems strange that after being welcomed back to the club, reinstated as captain for Carling Cup matches, that someone has come up with this hearing. Instead of sending out a message that this is someone who has made a mistake and served his punishment already, they are now taking action against him again. It seems very strange against someone who is acknowledged by all concerned to have a top-class character." Kolo was shocked to find out City were to hold a disciplinary hearing, as Taylor commented, "He trained every day while he was off and maintained a very positive attitude so he was shocked to find they were looking to take action against him."

City's chief communications officer Vicky Kloss commented: "It is not a new decision – we had consultations with the PFA about this in July." The hearing had been postponed on a number of occasions due to people involved being unavailable – Kolo himself was in Ivory Coast during the close season.

Roberto Mancini was named Barclays Manager of the Month, leading the club to four straight wins with his team averaging over four goals a game, netting an incredible 17 goals during October. City scored more goals in the opening ten games than any team since Preston's 38 in the Football League's inaugural season in 1888-89. City, labelled a defensive team last season, had become Europe's great entertainers, topping the continent's goal charts; all that with the man who has borne the burden of goalscoring for the previous two seasons persona non grata. Thirteen different players had scored this term, something of a contrast with the last two years when it felt was that if Tévez didn't score, the Blues would struggle. Agüero was named on the 23-man shortlist for the 2011 FIFA Ballon d'Or after netting ten since his move from Atletico Madrid.

NOVEMBER

"We all want to create history for this club"
James Milner

Tuesday November 1 2011

David Silva, with six top flight assists and scoring three helped propel City to the summit and ignited dreams of lifting the title. "Our win over United showed we are the team to beat in England. We have shown we can become champions. In the summer, Mancini promised us a bigger attacking system and is fulfilling what he said. I think we are creating many openings because of this strategy. Roberto Mancini insists I improve my performances even more and that's my challenge. I am a winner. I dream of winning the Premier League." Such was the quality of the Spaniard's displays that rumour suggested Spain's big two could target him. Silva, nicknamed Merlin the Magician by his team-mates, reacted: "City believed in me and I'm very well here. Real Madrid and Barcelona are definitely two great clubs, but I hope to stay in Manchester for many years.

"Money has never been my motivation and that was not the reason I joined City. I came here because this club wanted me more than any other and, in the end, they convinced me this was the right move. I liked the ideas the club had and, obviously, their financial strength means they are capable of carrying out the plan. However, it was never my ambition to be the biggest star at City, more to be part of a winning team, so even though I'm happy with the contribution I have made so far, the success we have enjoyed is not just down to me. Team unity is the secret to success, as one man can never make the total difference on his own. We have some big personalities at City and this is always going to be the situation when the club is investing such big finances in top players, but the manager keeps telling us that we need to come together to achieve our goals and this is what we did last season. Our 6-1 win at Manchester United showed we should believe in ourselves."

The Spanish wizard shunned controversy, "It rains a lot in Manchester, but I have got use to that now and this is the same for so many things in England. I live away from the city in a quiet place and the people are so welcoming and allow me to have a life away from football. In Spain, you are talked about and followed everywhere you go, but this is not the case in

England. I can stay in my quiet area, or go into Manchester and it is not such a big ordeal for me or my family. I like the English people as they have a nice sense of humour and they are respectful as well.'

A 30 foot tall effigy of Mario Balotelli, was unveiled in Kent, the latest sports star to go up in flames at Edenbridge - with Rooney the centre-piece the previous year. Each year the Edenbridge Bonfire Society picks a celebrity who has been in the news. Jon Mitchell, from Edenbridge Bonfire Society, said: "We were all quite worried a few days ago because no celebrities had done anything quite silly enough to be celebrated on Nov 5. We thought about the politicians and the other usual suspects - but Super Mario earned a unanimous vote among the committee." Mario was living in a hotel while repairs were made to his house. It was reported that he had built a race track in the garden.

Mancini insisted that his talented striker was not mad; football is the better for having such characters. Mario was in jovial mood in training, ripping Agüero's hat off his head before jokingly tossing it in the air. Although tough to manage, Mancini feels he is good for the game. "Mario is a special player, someone who can break open any match. Yes, he's different. But he understands his football and has given us some lovely moments. Mad? No. Mario is different, unpredictable. Some days he arrives in a very serious mood and other times he is joking. But these types of player are needed in football."

City arrived in Valencia to face Villarreal for a Champions League tie they dare not lose. Mancini identified the penultimate tie against Napoli in the Stadio San Paolo as the most significant assignment of Group A and, by then, Tévez could conceivably be involved. "Sorry is a little word, an easy word. Everything depends on Carlos. But I think these are easy words – very, very easy. If he apologises then everything will be like before. If not, then we look at January. This is what I've told him: all of us can make a mistake. The important thing is to apologise and then it's finished. And he can finish it. It is easy. These are crucial words. But these are easy words."

Mancini explained that this was why he had invited Tévez to his house. "But this was 20 days ago. It wasn't yesterday. I told Carlos 20 days ago to apologise, and he said no. I don't know his agent but I think the people around Carlos are giving him bad advice." A reference to Tévez's agent Kia Joorabchian, whose dealings with City had been strained for some time. Mancini reflected on his own playing days and occasional controversies. "Every time I made a mistake, I apologised. It's a very easy word to say." And Tévez would definitely play for City again if he did likewise? "We'll see. He needs to do it first."

Meanwhile, the Argentine's camp were mulling over Mancini's remarks, as well as an interview in Corriere della Sera in which Mancini reiterated his complaints about Joorabchian saying, "He is totally unprepared and being badly advised. I don't want it to be like this and I would be the first to forgive him."

Clearly City had now moved on from when Tévez was integral to winning. Yet the defeat in Munich disguised the fact it was City's least distinguished performance of the season. "For example, we talked for four days about the way Ribéry likes to do this," he said, referring to the way Bayern's French attacker instigated their second goal by cutting inside from the left wing to shoot on his right foot. Mancini was confident they could learn. "It was a lesson for us. I am sure if we make the second stage and meet Bayern again in the quarter or semi-finals the outcome could be different."

Perhaps Tévez might find a Premier League club? "His family are now living in England, so he's quite happy and settled," commented Joorabchian. "He had some problems about being away from them before, but they are with him now and everything is fine. He'd be happy to move to another Premier League club.

"This week, the Professional Footballers' Association rejected the claim that he had refused to come on as a substitute. That has changed everything and clarified what actually happened. Carlos was desperate to play. He loves to play the game and always wants to play. Having to sit on the sidelines is very tough for him. It's not easy for him at the moment, but, in the January transfer window, City will want to get him out either on a permanent basis or on loan. We'll have to wait and see what happens."

Joorabchian insisted a loan move to West Ham was not on the cards. "He loves West Ham - but that's not going to happen."

Agüero's stoppage-time winner against Villarreal two weeks earlier had led to angry clashes in the tunnel, with the Spanish players accusing him of goading them. "He did nothing," Mancini argued. "I'm sure there will be no problem." Pablo Zabaleta, who spent three years at Spanish side Espanyol, knows some of the Villarreal players, and hoped to use his contacts to request Agüero was not targeted. "I don't know what happened in the tunnel but I know some of their players, including their captain, so I will try to speak to him and tell him what happened in the last game is finished." Mancini added, "If he plays, he will be OK. He is experienced and has played at Villarreal many times with Atletico Madrid. It's a difficult place to go to, but we want to try and do well. He will cope with it."

Wednesday Nov 2, 2011

ITV pundit Roy Keane and former arch enemy Vieira enjoyed a pitchside reunion at El Madrigal, before City's match. The two Premier League greats, who clashed whenever Keane's United took on Vieira's Arsenal back in 2005, had nothing but kind words to say about each other, in stark contrast with the intense competitive heat of their playing days. These days Vieira works for City as their Football Development Executive. "I always tried to nail him", said Roy, but they both talked about their deep respect for each other. Talking prior to the game Patrick thought de Jong was the closest to the style of himself and Roy. Patrick predicted that City were "strong enough to win the game."

There were more headaches for Mancini on the bench! He banged his head on the low roof as he leapt from the dug out and needed ice treatment for the top of his flowing locks. But his pain was eased with a 3-0 win. City, whose performances in Europe had not matched the standard of their League form, claimed back-to-back wins to move up to second in Group A after becoming the first English team to win away to the Yellow Submarine. Mancini remarked, "It's sore, so sore. I did the same thing here with Inter and I think they need to change the dugouts. But I am very happy as we are in a good position now."

With Napoli losing to Bayern, City travelled to Italy in three weeks knowing that victory will ensure they qualify. Mancini added: "It will be incredible to go there and it will be difficult. It will be a fantastic atmosphere with 70,000 people."

After taking one point from their first two games in the group, City recovered to the extent that Mancini has not ruled out lifting the trophy. "There are lots of teams with more experience but with my team anything could happen, if we make the knockout stages because we're a good team. We are going very well and want to improve if possible."

City had won seven games in a row in all competitions since Munich and were never troubled as they swept past Villarreal. "I enjoyed this performance," added Mancini. "Villarreal were missing four or five key players but it's still difficult to win away. We had 65 per cent possession and scored three good goals, which is good for confidence. The team have improved in this competition since the first group match."

Mancini said that Silva's injury was not serious after the midfielder was forced to come off with a back problem in the 65th minute. "In 60 hours we play QPR. I think he'll recover in that time."

Mario Balotelli's penalty in first-half stoppage time was greeted by home fans with noises that briefly resembled monkey chants. Spanish football has been troubled in the past by racist abuse but City officials stressed that Mancini's players had reported nothing. Yaya Toure, who had not scored since the FA Cup final, scored a timely goal to fire City ahead on the half-hour before sealing the win with 20 minutes remaining.

Yaya believed the club are taking giant strides in the right direction. "We have made a quantum leap this season compared to last in terms of our winning mentality. The arrival of important players like Samir Nasri and Sergio Agüero is the key factor in that. We also have top quality footballers like Edin Dzeko and David Silva in impressive form right now." He also reckoned City were developing Barcelona's winning mentality, "That's what we want – to have the same mentality as Barcelona. And everybody is getting that winning mentality. The mentality we have in the squad is fantastic and if you want to win things, you need that. The team is evolving. Everyone enjoys themselves on the pitch and if we continue like this, it will be a fantastic year for us." The free-scoring attacking football drew comparisons with the European Champions however Yaya did not think his current club are at the same level yet. "It is a big difference because Barcelona have been a big team for a long time. In Manchester to be like them we have to win some Premier Leagues, some Champions Leagues.'

Meanwhile, Sir Alex Ferguson spoke in depth for the first time about the pain caused by the humiliating 6–1 derby defeat. In his programme notes for United's Champions League clash against Otelul Galati, he reflected, "It's painful even to think about it. But I don't want the players to forget it totally because it must serve as a reminder of the necessity of keeping our concentration levels high and thinking all the time. The score against us only reached such high proportions because of our own stupidity. The game was a lost cause when City went three up; a man down following the dismissal of Jonny Evans, we should have contained the game. Instead, we continued in our usual cavalier way to bomb into attack. You have to be sensible though and we left hardly anyone minding the shop, allowing City to pick us off with ease. It was a recipe for disaster. We were left with an embarrassing scoreline, the butt of many a joke I know."

Ferguson admitted the score would cast a shadow over the club for years, but insisted that his players would respond, "There is no progress in life without failure. For one thing, it means you think about how you got to the top in the first place. It's another day in our history, one that will be talked about for a long time to come. We have certainly had better days, but there is no time for tears. Our players are eager not to make that kind of mistake again, or at least not for a very long time."

Thursday, Nov 3, 2011

Roberto Mancini's son Andreas joined Oldham on loan along with Luca Scapuzzi. Midfielder Mancini, 19, agreed a one-month loan while striker Scapuzzi, 20, stays for two months.

Adam Johnson signed a new five-year contract to underline his status as a key member of Mancini's squad, he would no longer be the lowest-paid player in City's first-team squad with his wages doubled to an estimated £80,000-a-week. The £7m winger had a testing relationship with his manager, who has admitted to being extra hard on the 24 year-old. Johnson was angry at being left out of the 6-1 win at Old Trafford and was upset after Mancini criticised him following a match-winning performance in the Carling Cup at Wolves a few days later. Mancini said: "If he were not a good player, I wouldn't waste my time on him. But, because he has everything, I don't want him stopping at this level." Johnson was enjoying his best spell at the club with four goals in his last six games. '

The Napoli fixture was regarded as high-risk for both players and supporters. City asked United's advice about how they prepared for trips to Rome, Milan and Turin and, following the lead of their neighbours, they will supply detailed safety information to the 3,000 fans heading to Italy. Security staff had been out to Naples to learn more about the issues with the notorious "Ultras" and the club planned to advise their supporters about parts of the city to avoid, the importance of not becoming isolated and of being aware about what has happened in the past. They also intended to speak to Bayern and Liverpool.

Fri Nov 4, 2011

Having seen off the threat from Dalglish, Wenger and Mourinho over a quarter of a century in charge of United, Alex McLeish knew Sir Alex Ferguson wanted to put Mancini in his place. McLeish spent eight years under him at Aberdeen in the late Seventies and early Eighties and then remained friends over the last two decades. McLeish believed the threat to United's domination of English football from nouveau riche City means he will be around a few more years yet. "That 6-1 defeat by Manchester City, he'll want to react to that, without a doubt," said McLeish. "That has got Sir Alex going again. Mancini has thrown down the gauntlet and he'll be rearing up at that one. Absolutely. No danger that he will want to put that right. He sees City as a genuine threat and I think they are the real deal. Mancini is Sir Alex's challenge now, he'll want to see him off like all the others. He has seen a million managers come and go – his adversaries – and it's almost like when he sees a new manager talking a good game, he has got to hang around and see him off as well."

Meanwhile Carlos Tévez's guru Kia Joorabchian told me that they were unhappy with comments made by Graeme Souness on television. Kia consulted with media expert lawyers. Legal soundings always take time, and this seemed unlikely to result in legal action.

Roberto Mancini knew only too well the main danger posed by his former player Shaun Wright-Phillips. The winger had shone at Loftus Road since leaving City in August in the hope of getting more first-team opportunities after Mancini admitted he could not offer any guarantees over appearances. The manager commented, "I am sure Shaun will want to play very well against us, but I am happy because now he plays in every game – and he deserves that because he is a good guy and a good player. We need to pay attention to him on Saturday."

City headed to London with a five-point lead with Mancini making a number of changes once again to keep his side fresh. Mancini, whose side dropped just two points in the league and scored 36 goals in their 10 games, said: "Now we need to recover very well because we play just 60 hours after Villarreal. I need to change some players because it is impossible, but at least there is a break after Saturday. We want to continue to play well if it's possible, but we know that every game is hard. They are a different team at home, a very strong team at home and we need to play very well if we want to win there. We will try to attack but it's not all down to us – there is always another team, and we need to play very well. They also have some very good, experienced players and they beat Chelsea in their last home game, so they deserve respect and have made a very good start this season. Loftus Road is a tight, compact ground and it will be hard if we are not at our very best."

City were top because of a goal glut, but Mancini played down any target of trying to beat Chelsea's record of 103 Premier League goals, set two seasons earlier. "That's impossible. Records are there so that one team can beat them, but this one is impossible. We have good players. I hope we can continue to score but sometimes I hope we can do a 1-0. Sometimes, we need to win the Italian way."

Under Stuart Pearce in 2006/07, the club managed only 10 league goals at home all season, the lowest home goals tally in the 123-year history of English top-flight football. This season it took four home games to pass that figure! Mancini wanted to tighten defence again, conceding only 33 Premier League goals the previous season, the fewest they had ever conceded in a top-flight campaign. Mancini wanted to ensure that City's attack does not come at the expense of defence. He also wanted to be as dangerous on their travels as they were at home, unbeaten at home in all competitions in 2011. But their ability to pick up big results away had perked up in their last three away matches too – a 6-1 thumping of United, a 5-2 Carling Cup hammering of Wolves and a convincing 3-0 at Villarreal. "I think that we have totally changed our mentality from that of a year or two years ago," Mancini said. "Now, for us, playing away or at home is the same. We don't change. This is important if we want to be a top team. The pitch is always the same, whether you are at home or away. Sometimes, when you go to play away, the game is different. We know that we can lose every game if we don't always play well, if we don't always play at one hundred per cent, if we don't focus."

"I'm happy about the number of goals we have scored," said Mancini. "Sometimes, winning 1-0 would probably be good too. I don't prefer 1-0 to 4-0, but I do know it's impossible to always win by three or four. There will be some moments during the season when winning 1-0 will be good. If you keep a clean sheet every time, that is good."

Mancini puts their red-hot scoring form down to different options. "Maybe it is a surprise we have scored so many goals, but we have Sergio, Edin, Mario, Samir, David and Yaya – all of these players can score in every game. It's important to have three different strikers with different attitudes. Edin, Mario and Sergio are totally different as strikers, but we also have a lot of players in behind the strikers who can score. What other team has all these resources? I think this is very important."

Mancini recalled Dzeko and Agüero to his starting line-up as he freshened up his frontline after beating Villarreal in midweek, flew directly from Spain to London to prepare for QPR wary of Warnock's side. He noted their win over Chelsea and knew Wright-Phillips was fired up. "They beat Chelsea and did well against Tottenham last Sunday so we know it will be a tough game. I have a big respect for them. We need to play very well. I'm sure Shaun will want to play very well and I am happy because now he plays in every game.'

QPR manager Neil Warnock advised City not to book their open-top bus tour and "parade the cup" after just ten games, "We're talking about a side that scored six at Old Trafford and five at Tottenham - a phenomenal team. We've got to find a way of giving them a game, but if we play like we did at Fulham it could be double figures. At this stage, I would have to pick City for the title because of their squad, how they play and they will probably strengthen it again in January. But I'm a bit too old in the tooth to know that you can start parading the cup when you're five points clear after ten games. You've got to give the old man - I think I can call Sir Alex that - a bit more credit. He's seen and done it all, he's seen these young whippersnappers around his ankles before but he's seen them all off and gets on with his job.

You can never write him off, especially as it's his 25th anniversary at United. It's difficult for Man City to keep all the players happy, but you still need top players to be as good as they are, and it hasn't all been a bed of roses for Mancini over the last 18 months because he has signed positive players, flair players to excite the crowd.

"To start off with it was just about getting in defensive players, not getting beat, the Italian way. But now he's signed people like David Silva, City have two or three players you would pay to go and watch. I like the way Balotelli goes about it, and Mancini deserves a lot of credit for the way he has dealt with him. If you watch him, he works a lot harder than a lot of people think. To get a player like that, who works that hard with all the ability he has got, it is like winning the pools. And he might only be on the bench - that's how good they are. What they have done probably seems unfair to clubs who don't have as much money, but I can remember when Kenny Dalglish was at Blackburn with Sir Jack Walker's backing, but you still have to sign the right players and get the right blend. When it is an open pot, as City seem to have got, the sky is the limit. There is no-one they can't sign and good luck to them. The best thing for them was qualifying for the Champions League because he has been able to keep all the egos happy."

Steve McManaman, who played 44 games for City after leaving Madrid in 2003, was convinced it wasn't so bad behind the scenes in the dressing room, "Not only that, despite what people say about City, I know that it is a happy camp. I know a few of the City lads, and there is not a problem. The City players are all professional footballers, and whether you play for Crawley Town or Manchester City, you just want to win games. Regardless of whether you dislike one of your teammates or not, something that brings you together is that you all want to win the Premier League. None of the stuff off the field would ever have bothered me. You can have players hating each other but it doesn't matter if you go out together on a Saturday and win. But when you look at City's results and the celebrations, talk of it being an unhappy camp is clearly a long way from the truth."

McManaman was part of the Liverpool team which was famously 'knocked off their perch', in Sir Alex's words, by United in the early '90s. Now McManaman feels it could be City's turn to ruffle Fergie's feathers. "City are now favourites to win the league, especially after the mauling they gave United at Old Trafford. They have a five-point gap at the top of the league, have arguably the best squad in the league and could still invest further in January if they need to. It's only two months into the season but City are the biggest and best around. But the thing about Liverpool, and then United, is the solidity of their past. They didn't just win the league

– they won it again and again. City's target has to be to emulate that, not be a Leeds or a Blackburn, who both won it and then drifted away again. As long as Sheikh Mansour stays involved I am sure they can do that."

McManaman singled out Silva as the league's outstanding player this season, "Goalscorers tend to get all the credit, so people talk about Sergio Agüero or Wayne Rooney but, for me, Silva is the best around at the minute. He is a star among stars, an extra special player who makes the team tick. He was making things happen for City last season but they were a more defence-minded team then. With the introduction of Agüero and Samir Nasri, they have added a bit more creativity and it has freed up Silva , allowing him to become the stand-out player in the Premier League."

Saturday, Nov 5, 2011

Behind in a league game for the first time since they lost at Everton the previous season, City hit back with determination to win 3-2 at Loftus Road to extend their unbeaten run to 15 games, their best sequence since 1947. Edin Dzeko called QPR the "best team we have played this season". Helguson's header struck the bar right at the end as City were hanging on grimly, sorely missing suspended centre-half and captain, Kompany. "There have been games when you're winning 5-1 and you're sat there with that Ready Brek glow around you," said assistant manager David Platt, "but we didn't have that luxury here. In the cold light of day that's a great performance for us to look back on because it shows we can win games without being at our best."

Yaya Toure headed the winner that restored the five point lead over United, and when Micah Richards, sporting the captain's armband for the day, was asked how the club would cope when their match winner goes off with Ivory Coast at the Africa Cup of Nations in Gabon and Equatorial Guinea early next year he said, "We'll just go and buy someone else."

Goals continue in abundance; 11 league games, 39 goals. Should they continue at the same rate they would score 133 times this season. Stefan Savic, on his first Premier League start, could not stop Jay Bothroyd heading home a Barton free-kick after 28 minutes, the first time City had trailed this season - and after goals from Dzeko and Silva turned it around, Helguson brought the hosts level before that late Yaya Toure winner.

Mancini was delighted to take the points from a tough encounter. "When you play every three days, it is impossible, every game can be hard. QPR played very well but in the end it was important that we won. We had some problems with Samir before the game - his knee - and we can't take any more risks with him after so many games so it is better we did not need him because his knee is not good. It was hard in the second half, even though we played better and scored to make it 2-1. We had three or four chances to close the game, but when you don't close the game you take a risk because anything can happen. David for me is one of the best players in the world, but not only him, all the other players - Yaya, Edin, for sure. It was really important to win. In the last two weeks we have played six games, which is very, very hard, we have won always and it is very important to go into the international break with the five-point gap." QPR manager Neil Warnock commented, "It is results like that that make them champions elect."

Meanwhile Micah Richards observed, "Maybe we found more out about ourselves. Everyone expects us to win four or five nil, but you have to give credit to QPR. They are a tough team to break down and scored some good goals, and that meant we had to fight back. We had to grind and give one hundred per cent to get the victory. Our players are known for flair and scoring goals but we worked hard for the team." Further evidence Mancini succeeded in changing the mind-set of his team. Richards observed, "There is a different mentality about us now. We have great players who go right to the end and give 100 per cent. It was a great honour to lead out a team of such stars and quality players. Sometimes I just watch and admire. David Silva is one of my favourite players – some of the stuff he does is amazing and he is a very humble guy. I think all the best players are humble. I think on current form he is the best player in the country.'

Monday, Nov 7, 2011

Despite international week, there was huge anticipation in facing surprise package Newcastle with the best defensive record in the top flight, eight conceded in 10, facing a City attack whose 39 goals is the best in the first 11 games since Tottenham bagged 40 at the start of the 1963-64 season.

City's demolition of United proved Mancini's men were destined to finish top. Yaya commented, "After the game at Old Trafford some people at home asked me 'Is it real? You beat United 6-1?' People understand now City are becoming a big team. A great team. We get fantastic players and we want to beat strong teams like Manchester United and Chelsea. Everybody understands City are coming to the top and we wait until the end of the season because we know the Premier League is not easy to win."

Tuesday, Nov 8 2011

Kolo Toure was fined six weeks wages, approximately £540,000, following a tribunal. City's case was that his absence from first-team duty cost them in the region of £3 million in wages and legal fees. A City statement said: "Kolo accepts the decision and he and the club now wish to draw a line under this matter and focus on the season ahead." Mancini commented that Kolo would remain in contention for selection because it had been an unintentional error. "Kolo is a different situation. It was a mistake - a totally different situation. In the other case I think that every player should have good behaviour, always."

Carlos Tévez opted not to contest his misconduct charge. The deadline for lodging an appeal passed, but he faced a new disciplinary charge after defying Mancini again by flying home to Argentina without permission and faced another fine of a further two weeks' wages unless he turned up for training at 10.30 on Wednesday morning. The striker's representatives asked City's temporary chief executive John MacBeath at the weekend if the striker could spend a week in Argentina but the request was denied as Mancini wanted him to continue working on his fitness. Tévez then asked Mancini's assistant Fausto Salsano on Monday and was again turned down after the second request had been relayed to the manager. Tévez ignored these instructions and flew to South America anyway. On arriving at Buenos Aires airport with his daughter Florencia, Tévez said, "I am here to get some rest." Tévez was on a day off on Tuesday so had not breached his contract. But unless the former club captain turned up at Carrington on Wednesday morning he would once again find himself facing a misconduct charge. In order for him to be back in Manchester, Tévez will have had only a matter of hours on the ground in South America. Tévez missed at least some of his training in recent weeks with mystery injuries.

On two occasions, he did not train because of non-football related injuries and as a result Mancini's staff believe he made relatively poor progress as they tried to get him in a condition in which he could theoretically play a competitive game. "Carlos returned from his recent trip to Argentina and was not match-fit," a City spokesman said. "The coaches therefore devised a training plan to return him to full fitness. Carlos is part way through that plan and is due to resume his training on Wednesday morning at Carrington following a rest day on Tuesday."

Gordon Taylor expressed concern at Tévez's latest indiscretion as he failed to show up for training. "To say the least, I am very disappointed and extremely concerned now. To go out to Argentina when - as I have been informed - he was clearly told not to because they (City) needed to work on his fitness, and to blatantly ignore that instruction starts to affect any chance of any reconciliation now. The whole relationship between clubs and players is one where there has to be clear understanding of what is to be expected and what is not expected. From that point of view, he is making it virtually impossible to have a reconciliation and leaving himself very vulnerable to strong action by the club. If he is determined to leave the club, which may well be apparent, then his money value is being diminished by his actions and can affect another club's interest. As such, he could be held responsible for that, so it is getting to be a situation that I am not at all happy about. Neither are the club of course, and it is one that we will have to deal with."

The PFA fought Tévez's corner to get the first sanctions reduced, but Taylor added, "I have been accused at times of defending the indefensible. It is very difficult to now be in a situation where we put our heads on the block. I do feel very disappointed to say the least that when I was hoping things could move on, it has gone into reverse and now he is left in a position that becomes very vulnerable. The lad is digging himself a hole and it is going deeper. It is a worry to me how we can now get out of this. He is a human being and a top-quality footballer, but his actions are not what we could possibly recommend to any other player in the game. It goes to the heart of the contract and that could be gross misconduct in anybody's language. I don't want to predetermine, but I am very concerned because it is a serious situation and one that the PFA are not happy about."

Meanwhile, Corinthians marketing director Luis Paulo Rosenberg believed the club would be making a mistake if they re-signed Tévez. "Enough with signing old players. In marketing terms it would be successful, but financially, and for the morale of the team, it would not be a good idea." Boca Juniors Juan Roman Riquelme was hopeful a deal can be reached. "I have spoken with Carlitos about the situation and I told him: if they are not going to take him into account in Manchester he should come here. I think that all of us Boca fans should put money in to be able to bring him back. Either that, or the club should make the effort to bring Carlitos back to Boca."

Wednesday, Nov 9, 2011

A team of ex-footballers and F1 drivers including Vitaly Petrov, Felipe Massa and Sergio Perez are undone by a UAE XI featuring City chairman Khaldoon Al-Mubarak.

Nasri withdrew from the France squad diagnosed with tendonitis in his knee. French coach Laurent Blanc said, "It is a tricky one that he picked up while playing for Arsenal." Nasri told French television: "I've had a problem in my knee since the Villarreal match. It's an old issue which is resurfacing."

Sergio Agüero was a doubt for Argentina's World Cup 2014 qualifiers against Bolivia and Colombia after he pulled up in training with a groin problem. He missed City's win over Aston Villa last month after suffering a similar injury in the first half of the win at Blackburn.

Speaking ahead of Italy's friendlies against Poland and Uruguay, Mario Balotelli commented, "They tend to talk more about my private life than what I do on the field. This is normal, but I get tired of it. And if I didn't do the things I do, I would be bored. I'm not mad, not at all – even if sometimes I do things that are a bit strange. English newspapers like The Sun are worse than the Italian ones. A newspaper that puts naked ladies on the front cover…" He claims to have improved since moving to England, citing the influences of Mancini, and Italy's Cesare Prandelli. "They brought me calmness and helped me from a tactical perspective. I feel like a centre-forward, but I can also play on the wings. English football taught me the pressing game and to chase opponents when I lose the ball. I don't miss Italian football, the level there has fallen a long way, while English football is beautiful and enjoyable." However he refused to rule out an eventual return to Serie A. "If the conditions were right I would even return to Inter. For now, though, I am happy in England. We have a great team at City."

Meanwhile, Mario Balotelli told prosecutors in Italy that he saw a 'table full of drugs' at a Mafia boss's HQ in Naples. The Italian media reported that he said in evidence: "I saw, from ten metres, a table full of drugs." The striker was due in Naples on Champions League duty, but claimed his testimony is "nothing to worry about."

Fri, Nov 11, 2011

Vincent Kompany, speaking about another famous Belgian, insisted, "I'm not more famous than Tin Tin - I don't think I'll ever top him!" He looked back on that famous victory at Old Trafford, "I didn't dream that scoreline was possible. You don't go into that game thinking you're going to win 6-1, you just try to win and hope that's enough. It was a special game and seeing the fans celebrating afterwards was incredible. I looked at the score at 3-0 but then we conceded so I didn't look after that. We were buzzing in the dressing room after that - everybody was over the moon."

"We will hit a bad patch, like with every team, but you don't necessarily have to lose just because you're playing badly. Let's just keep playing well for as long as possible. We've got many players here who have won titles at different levels, so that's not a problem. The club hasn't won the title for a long time but we showed in the FA Cup final that we won't let that affect us."

Balotelli and Pazzini struck either side of half-time to give Italy a 2-0 friendly win in Poland. Italy coach Cesare praised Mancini when he spoke to the press at La Borghesiana in Rome, almost all the questions were about man of the match Mario, perhaps partly because Mario didn't speak after the game. Prandelli stuck by Mario even when he was being attacked from all sides, "Well done, both to him and to Roberto Mancini, who has been working with him on that at club level. Is this the turning point for Mario? I hope he's now on the path towards maturity. After that you need a bit of madness, a touch of quality and complete freedom. What sort of a player can Balotelli become? He's not your typical forward. He's a modern-day forward whose movement leaves the opposition no reference points. He can play as a centre forward or wide with good vision for the game."

Inter coach Claudio Ranieri would welcome Mario back to the San Siro "with open arms", describing the City forward as a "formidable talent". Mario insisted last week that he had no desire to return, though he did say that he "could return to Inter one day if certain things were in place". Ranieri would be happy to work with Mario if he felt the time was right to play for Inter again. Ranieri said in an interview with Corriere dello Sport. "He is a formidable talent ... He can become one of the best players in the world but it's all down to him." Former AC Milan coach Carlo Ancelotti believed Balotelli's progress can be attributed to Mancini's handling of him, and congratulated his compatriot on ensuring the flamboyant frontman has "found the right path". "Balotelli has matured," Ancelotti told Gazzetta dello Sport. "Now on the pitch he shows seriousness and gives an added value to the national team. Mario has found the right path thanks to Mancini."

Meanwhile, the striker faced a £400,000 bill for the repair of his bathroom. His landlord wanted him to pay himself for the damages rather than go through insurance. Two fire crews using breathing apparatus put out the blaze at the £7,500-a-month house. There was nothing left of the designer bathroom but charred and melted remains. Thick smoke made the whole place uninhabitable, sending the damage costs spiralling.

City were still waiting for Tévez to make contact and the club gave him until Monday to report back. A club spokesperson said: "We have asked Carlos to get in touch today but have not yet heard from him." The club were concerned that he could apply to use Article 15 of the FIFA regulations, which allows a player who has been banished from the first team to terminate his contract under 'sporting just cause' if he appears in fewer than ten per cent of his club's games in a season. To avoid that, City could be forced to pick Tévez for another four full games if they are not to lose him for nothing. City will defend themselves with the contention that, by being absent from training without permission after flying to Argentina, as well as missing other sessions, the striker has left himself short of the fitness required for him to be considered for selection. Gordon Taylor indicated that the player is making more problems for himself. "He is in danger of burning bridges rather than reconciliation. This now leaves him very vulnerable. He's diminishing his value by his actions at the moment. You just hope he will soon try to get to a place of reality, otherwise he's on a self-destruct route. It could be a very difficult and complex legal situation."

Fresh reports Boca were planning to offer Tévez a route out of City were denied. President Jorge Amor Ameal admitted the club had contact with Tévez, but there was no chance they will be able to match his valuation. "Carlos is deservedly a very important figure here," Ameal told local radio. "But from the economic point it is impossible. I did talk to him, and I lent him our support.

Fabio Capello called up Glenn Johnson and Kyle Walker to fight it out for the right-back berth against Spain and Sweden, leaving Richards out in the cold. Hart could not hide his disappointment, "Micah's been absolutely fantastic. He's given everything. I'm really proud of how he's played for Manchester City — he captained us against QPR. It's just unfortunate he's not in the squad but I'm sure he won't take it to heart. He'll just keep on training well like he is and pushing to be in that squad."

Joe Hart admitted to his "hurt" every time Silva doesn't make the Spain starting line-up, 'David's a big part of our team, on the field and off. We get on really well with him. He's a fantastic player. You'd have thought Silva would struggle — that he would get eaten alive in the Premier League — but he finds a way out. Jack Rodwell at Everton tried to play a man-marking role against him and I said to David, "get used to it mate because the way you are playing, that's how sides are going to try to deal with you". And he does deal with it. He comes in with kicks and bumps and just dusts himself down and gets on with it. Nine times out of ten if you try and kick him, you'll miss."

Saturday, Nov 12 2011

Patrick Vieira was looking to follow the model of Barcelona at Eastlands, but City fans need to be patient, "You have to remember that City is a new club among the elite. In fact, this is the first time we've played in the Champions League. If we take the example of Barca, this team got where it is after many years among the elite and a youth policy means several years of patience. When you see a team win the Champions League with six or seven of its youth players in the side, you know they're doing the right job. It is an example Manchester City should follow."

Roberto Mancini believed England were good enough to win the European Championship, though he still believes Spain are the team to beat. After watching Capello's side record a confidence-boosting victory over reigning world and European champions Spain, Mancini tipped his compatriot to mount a serious challenge at Euro 2012.

Harry Redknapp and Milan Mandaric faced trial on 23 January relating to allegations of cheating the public revenue. Redknapp denies any wrongdoing but would have good reason for his mind to be on other matters when Spurs take on City at the Etihad Stadium the day before the proceedings begin.

Sunday, Nov 13 2011

There were a profusion of names thrown around by the media as City are linked with an entire new team! Mancini was keeping tabs on Daniele De Rossi's contract situation at Roma. City had regularly been linked with a bid for the 28-year-old Italy international and Mancini opened the door to a move, "It's always difficult to get your hands on a Romanista who plays for Roma. As a result, I wouldn't be surprised if he renewed his contract. But, if De Rossi is one day available on the market then Manchester City will be ready, as will Real Madrid, Chelsea and all the big clubs. He's a top player, one of those few players who can get into the very best teams in the world. He's a complete midfielder, with class and experience." City technical director Mike Rigg confirmed interest in Borussia Monchengladbach winger Marco Reus, City were expected to go head to head with Barcelona for the signature of AC Milan defender Thiago Silva and had sounded out Athletic Bilbao over Spain Under 21 captain Javi Martinez, also coveted by United, Liverpool and Chelsea. Patrick Vieira revealed the Blues are keen on Rennes midfielder Yann M'Vila, dubbed by many as 'the new Vieira', but he was also high on Wenger's hit list. City were linked with Valencia's defensive midfielder Mehmet Topal. City expressed an interest in signing United youngster Paul Pogba, another who has been likened to a young Vieira.

Meanwhile Carlos Tévez was pictured playing golf on a course in Argentina and Inter captain Javier Zanetti hinted the club will try to sign Tévez.

Monday, Nov 14, 2011

Another day of Tévez meyhem, more 'leaks' despite both sides agreeing a shut down of briefings to the media. The afternoon began with Press Association Sport putting out an article based on a briefing with Tévez "representative". The article stated that Tévez remained in Argentina and did not attend a meeting with the club but discussions have taken place between the two parties. "Over the weekend there have been a series of meetings and conference calls," Tévez's representative said, "Carlos is still in Argentina, however, both sides are kind of in agreement that they want a resolution as quickly and as smoothly as possible. Discussions will probably be ongoing for the foreseeable future." It was reported that the meeting with City officials formed part of a disciplinary process but Tévez's representatives say they were not aware that was the case. They rejected claims coming from South America that the striker had obtained a medical certificate which excused his absence. "The meeting that Carlos was asked to attend today and subsequently didn't does not, from our view, form part of any ongoing disciplinary procedure," added Tévez's representative, "From our side we are not aware of any disciplinary procedure being invoked by City." City declined to comment, according to the Press Association article.

Kia Joorabchian was insistent that there would be no comments from him, when I spoke to him earlier in the day so he was shocked that 'a representative' had made such comments. When I checked with Kia, he was none too pleased, and told me he planned to contact PA Sport and have references to comments from Tévez's representative removed from the article, and not long afterwards, the media received this notice......

ATTENTION SPORTS EDITORS - story removes references to quotes from Tévez's representatives at their request) TÉVEZ WANTS SWIFT CITY RESOLUTION.

After the PA fiasco, Gordon Taylor felt the situation between club and player was irretrievable. "It's another week and there are more problems really. The situation continues and the longer it goes with him being away, the more impossible it becomes to reconcile the situation. January is coming up soon, but before then I want it to be satisfactorily resolved. He's a footballer and, like the Fleetwood Mac song, players only love you when they're playing and he needs to be playing. To be playing he needs to be fit and to be fit he needs to be training. I thought we were making some progress, but it's gone backwards. I don't want him to leave the club. He's had so many problems at other clubs, with West Ham then the problems with third party ownership, with United when he left them. I don't want him to leave with a bad taste in the mouth with City supporters and the club. He's been too good a player for that. I think it's time now that changed and try to get his mindset changed to a better place. I'm worrying about him now because it's a self-destruct pattern."

Tuesday, Nov 15 2011

Manchester United striker Michael Owen questioned whether City would sustain their impressive form for the entire campaign as the Red Devils were ready to capitalise on any slip-ups. Owen expected City to be United's main title rivals, but while Owen recognised that City were "a force to be reckoned with", he was confident that they will not experience an uncontested title.

"They are top of the league, playing great - as well as they've performed in years. They obviously beat us quite well in the league and deserved to win that game but it was only a few weeks earlier that we played really well and beat them in the Community Shield - everyone was taking a step back then and saying 'it might be a year too soon for Man City' and it just shows how quickly things can change. They're on a crest of a wave at the minute - but every team will go through a sticky patch at some point and we're still early on in the season.'

England beat Sweden at Wembley with Barry's deflected headed winner. Zlatan Ibrahimovic revealed he turned down City in the summer of 2010 but he eventually went on loan to AC Milan from Barcelona. Edinson Cavani believed he and Mario "would make a good partnership" and said he would be happy for the striker to join him at the Stadio San Paolo. Italy lost 1-0 to Cavani's Uruguay. When being questioned by reporters, Mario said of Napoli, "I have said that I like the town", and Cavani believes he would be a great addition for the Partenopei in the future. "He said he would like me to come to Napoli. I would love to play with him, we would make a good partnership." Cavani and Mario meet again when City visit Napoli.

Wednesday, Nov 16 2011

Dennis Tueart entered club folklore scoring the overhead kick that beat Newcastle to win the 1976 League Cup Final. Now he was convinced Mancini would take the title from United, "They have what it takes to win the title. The likes of Mario Balotelli, Edin Dzeko and David Silva have taken us to the next level. But it is the English players who give the team its heart. To have five or six Englishmen — our own people — galvanises the fans who identify more with the team. It underlines the bond between supporters and players. I am going on a book tour and meeting lots of City fans who are very excited about the season. It's a bit surreal. It's like winning the pools. Not only can we win the title, I think we can do well in the Champions League — at least get through to the quarter-final stages."

On Tévez, he commented: "With the Tévez situation, having the full support of the owners was critical. Tévez has insulted the fans and his team-mates. I can't believe what he is doing. What's he trying to achieve? I wasn't surprised something like this happened, but I was surprised it was him. It was inevitable that when you throw money at a team one player behaves like this — although I thought it would be maybe Balotelli or Adebayor, not him."

His Wembley winner was voted the greatest moment in League Cup history. Tueart added: "Like now, we had great individual players but they did it for the team not themselves. I can't imagine any of us refusing to play or to warm-up. It was just not in our make-up. I admire the way Mancini has handled this, and other issues, by being very cool, calm and collected — but very firm. He put out an olive branch to Tévez after the last incident, so what has happened is just astonishing. But City are bigger than this. They are not only winning matches, they are playing some cracking football."

Mancini has followed the example of Ferguson in handling the dressing room egos, as Tueart commented, "Sir Alex Ferguson is the past master at handling egos, Cantona, Ronaldo and Rooney; handling people like that is a skill. Roberto spent 18 years at the top level as a player for club and country. He then spent four years at the most politically soccer sensitive club in the world, Inter Milan, and delivered them seven trophies. That shows he accepts responsibility and is used to dealing with egos. He has one himself, which is not a bad thing. This was always going to be his challenge and he has come through it."

A director before his dismissal by Shinawatra in 2007, he added, "Manchester City have lagged behind for the last 35 years. We nearly made it with Kevin Keegan but we didn't have the investment. We were treading water near the end. Everything else was in place but we couldn't invest in the top end. We were buying bits-and-pieces players. Obviously, how long this present situation goes on for depends upon the owners sustaining their investment. The thing is, we have been buying young players. They will be there for three or four years, so we shouldn't have to buy an awful lot unless he wants to replace Tévez, if he goes. They have thrown money at it to get to a certain level, which is similar to how Roman Abramovich started at Chelsea. We can go further than them, but the second phase will be challenging Manchester United off the field. That will take a long time because we are not global yet. Our turnover is just over £100 million, theirs is £300 million. It will take time but that has to be the aim."

Thursday, Nov 17 2011

Adam Johnson and Pablo Zabaleta signed new long-term contracts. Johnson penned a new four-year deal until 2016, Zabaleta extended his stay until 2015.

In a letter to the 800 fans who bought tickets for Napoli, officials urged them to avoid no-go areas, including the railway station and the city centre. It is the first time City have issued such advice. No alcohol will be served inside the ground and City supporters would be locked in after the final whistle for 45 minutes.

Ossie Ardiles moved from Argentina to England to became one of the best-loved players in the country. Ardiles popularity in England endured beyond the Falklands War when he temporarily went on loan to Paris Saint-Germain. In contrast, Tévez finds his reputation in tatters. Ardiles commented, "I am really sympathetic to Carlos. Not because we are both from Argentina, but because I like him. Some people say he is a bad apple but he's not a bad apple at all. In May [after winning the FA Cup] he gave huge plasma televisions to the cleaning ladies and people who working the canteens at Manchester City. About 45 people, a television each."

Ardiles remembers how homesick his 'other half', Ricky Villa, felt when the pair of them joined Spurs in 1978, having just won the World Cup with Argentina. "Ricky wanted to go home from the moment he got here," says Ardiles. "The irony is that he loves England now, but back then he just wanted to get away. He wouldn't even buy a mirror for his house. He didn't see the point in buying anything that was going to be too big and awkward to take back to Argentina when his contract ended. He told me he was going to leave Spurs and play in Florida. It was only two years before his famous winning goal in the 1981 FA Cup final but he said he wasn't enjoying his football, he was sick of the weather and wanted some sun. But I know later on he regretted it. Tévez will regret it, too, if it ends like this at Manchester City. I'd tell him to come back to England immediately. Just say "for whatever I did, I apologise". It might be a bit difficult for a couple of games but score two or three goals and it will change. Last season Wayne Rooney came out at Manchester United and basically said "All my team-mates are crap. I am brilliant, but they are crap". But he scores a few goals and everything is forgiven. Carlos lives for football and as a footballer, Manchester City is the place to be. They will win all kinds of trophies and they still need him as well. It will be a mistake for everybody for him to go. He was adored at City but things started to change when he wasn't No 1. Sergio Agüero and Edin Dzeko were picked for the easy games and Carlos would have been thinking "I bet to my last dollar when Manchester City need something, I will be asked to rescue them". It is exactly what happened against Bayern Munich."

Ardiles believed Tévez's mood of resentment in Munich was heightened by Mancini sending one of his assistants over to ask the player to warm up. "I didn't recognise the young guy who went to speak to Tévez but when this guy touched Zabaleta in a friendly gesture, Zabaleta pushed him away as well. It came out that Carlos complained about Manchester. He appeared on a lunchtime TV show and said it was always raining in Manchester. Well, it's true but it was also clearly a joke. Even in his worst game for City, he has never stopped working for the team."

Meanwhile, Gabriel Batistuta, the country's all-time leading scorer, criticised his conduct. "I would never do what Carlitos is doing. I would return to Manchester City to work. I do not know all the reasons but I would not do that. The club pay his wages and must be respected."

Friday, Nov 18 2011

Manchester City announced the biggest losses in English football history, £197m for the most recent financial year. The loss on that huge scale, bankrolled by the club's oil-rich owner, Sheikh Mansour bin Zayed al-Nahyan during the third year since he bought City in 2008, eclipses the previous biggest loss ever, £141m by Chelsea in 2005, the second year of their ownership by the oil oligarch Roman Abramovich. City's loss was made principally by buying players to make Mancini's squad strong enough to top the League, paying wages of £174m, £21m higher than the club's entire turnover. During the 2010-11 financial year City signed Boateng for £10.5m, Dzeko for £27m, Silva for £26m, Yaya for £24m, Kolarov for £19m, Mario for £24m and Milner for £26m, totalling £156.5m.

Mansour made it clear when he took over that he would spend the fortunes necessary to make City successful, and since June 2010 he personally poured a further £291m into the club. Added to the £500m he invested up to May 31 2010, he had spent an unprecedented £800m on the football club, to bankroll the expenditure on transfer fees and wages. All the money has gone in as equity, in new shares, making it permanent, not as loans. The net loss City made on their operations, £160.5m, was increased by £34.4m writing off the value of several players signed previously, including the Brazilian striker, Jô.

A loss on such scale raised concerns about whether City have any chance of complying with Uefa's "financial fair play" rules. City acknowledged the looming enforcement of financial fair play when releasing their figures, restating that despite this record loss close, they will attempt to comply. Graham Wallace, the club's chief operating office, said the 2010-11 financial year, in which those signings of top players added to the mountainous wage bill already accumulated, will be City's worst. "Our losses, which we predicted as part of our accelerated investment strategy, will not be repeated on this scale in the future. These financial results represent the bottoming out of financial losses at Manchester City before the club is able to move towards a more sustainable position in all aspects of its operations in the years ahead. As we undertake the club's commercial transformation, we are cognisant of the incoming Uefa financial fair play regulations and consequently we continue to maintain positive and ongoing dialogue with all appropriate football authorities."

Chairman, Khaldoon al-Mubarak, a senior adviser to Mansour's al-Nahyan ruling family and the Abu Dhabi government, acknowledged City's need not to depend on such huge subsidy from Mansour in coming years: "Now that we are witnessing progress, both on and off the pitch, it is more important than ever to work towards achieving our ambition to establish Manchester City as a more successful, sustainable and internationally competitive football club, which remains rooted in the heart of the community it serves."

City are confident that with income having risen 22.5% to £153m during 2010-11, the boost of Champions League football, increased TV and commercial earnings from being successful, the £350m ten-year shirt sponsorship and stadium naming rights deal with Etihad airline and the shedding of players no longer part of Mancini's plans, will draw income and spending closer together. They hope to show Uefa a "trend" towards breaking even by 2014-15 even if the losses have not been sufficiently staunched.

In contrast to all the negativity about the finances, City point out that they have broken no rules and in fact should be credited for investing fortunes in England, and in economically blighted east Manchester, at a time of economic meltdown here and in Europe.

Meanwhile the Tévez saga rumbled on with Mancini asked if he could play for the club again. "I don't think so," commented the manager, "I know he is in Argentina. I don't know what he is doing." Before adding, "Why are we continuing to talk about Carlos? We have an important game." Mancini, speaking at a regular pre-match press conference, was also asked if the club had managed to make contact with the player. "No," he said. "It is not important at this moment. We have this problem and we hope it can be resolved." The long-running affair had not affected the mood among the rest of the squad, "I think this is important. The squad is good and the players are positive at this moment. It is important that we start (back in) the Barclays Premier League with a result."

Mancini told Micah Richards that he must improve his mental approach if he wants to be an England player. "Micah is young. In the last year he improved a lot as a player but I think he needs to improve more. He has good quality but sometimes Micah is too strong and he thinks he can play at 50 per cent. If Micah plays to one hundred per cent, for me he can become one of the top full-backs in Europe. With Micah, his body is on the pitch but his mind is left at home sometimes. For this, he can improve - if he can remember to pick up his brain. I say this because I love Micah, like all the players do, and I don't think Micah can lose time because he has everything." Asked if he had discussed the issue with Capello, Mancini answered, "We have spoken about Micah only once, about six months ago. My opinion is he has improved a lot since then, but he can improve more. For Capello, it's not easy to choose because there are a lot of good players. It's clear some will have to stay at home but I hope Micah can go." Mancini finished by making a remarkable assessment of the club's progress, "I don't think we are playing better than Real Madrid and Barcelona but we are probably the same level now. We are very close to these teams."

With a tough run of games Mancini observed, 'I think the crucial moments are now, December, January and February, these three months. I think it will be very hard because in January we will play every three days if we win against Arsenal in the Carling Cup and we will probably lose Kolo and Yaya Toure, two very important players, for the Africa Cup of Nations. So I think December and January will be crucial. But I don't think the players feel pressure. They are confident at this moment. We have played only 11 games but we played good games against top teams like Tottenham and Manchester United. This confidence is important. After winning the FA Cup last season I think they know they are good players and we have a good team. We have started the season very, very well. But if we want to stay at the top we have to continue to work very well every week because the season is long and hard. Until now we have been lucky because we didn't have any problems with injuries."

Newcastle manager Alan Pardew said: "City have the luxury of full internationals going up to squad number 30. We don't have 11. We have to play at our best and I hope we come back with our pride intact. City are top of the league and the biggest scalp. Outside of Barcelona and Real Madrid, they look like being one of the three best teams in Europe. I'm sure Sir Alex Ferguson won't like me saying that and he'll probably ring me, but they are. We have to knock them off their perch. That's what we're all trying to do."

Saturday, Nov 19, 2011

City fans sang "We'll score when we want" as the leaders continued their record-equalling start with a 3-1 victory over previously unbeaten Newcastle, even with David Silva rested. Silva was on the bench until the 70th minute as he recovered from a long flight from Costa Rica, where he had played in a mid-week friendly for Spain. Mancini commented, "I am glad we are scoring goals and winning many games in a row because we will have difficult moments during the season. I hope we can continue like this but we have 26 games left and there will be a time we will lose a game.'

City fans had little to moan about, but the club's catering department elicited boos when they announced there would be no more chips, just before the break. An announcement over the tannoy said, 'We are very sorry, but there are no chips available in the concourse at half-time today.' A separate message on the scoreboard shortly afterwards: 'Due to unforeseen circumstances, there are no chips available during half-time today' but it was Newcastle who had their chips when it came to City on the pitch.

A penalty either side of half-time and a strike by Micah Richards saw City pierce the league's meanest defence to maintain their own unbeaten run. Mario Balotelli scored from the spot on 41 minutes after Ryan Taylor handled, and Richards seized on the Newcastle full-back's error to double the lead before half-time. Richards was also instrumental in the final City goal, Agüero scoring from the spot on 72 minutes, after Richards was brought down by Ben Arfa.

It is more than a decade since Newcastle's last won at City when Shearer scored the only goal at Maine Road in September 2000. This defeat ended Newcastle's 14-match unbeaten run in the League – which had equalled their all-time top-flight record set in 1950.

Mario dummied the keeper then toe-poked the ball hard into the bottom corner, before another distinctive celebration, walking towards keeper Krul stern-faced and with his arms folded across his chest. "Mario is fabulous with penalties. It is impossible for him to miss," said Mancini, "he is very important to the team. I have tried to help him but he deserves credit because he has done the work. Mario is a great player; he's becoming better and better and taking on more responsibility for the team. He is relaxed and confident. I am pleased at the way he has improved because all the work is down to him. I am just helping him become the best player he can be because I don't want him to waste his talent. He feels the same and that's why he has been working so hard."

Mario allowed himself a rare smile minutes later when Ryan Taylor failed to collect Nasri's through-ball and Richards was on hand to steal in and score from 10 yards.

City had not secured a clean sheet in the league since a 4-0 victory at Blackburn at the start of October and Hart feared their impressive attacking play could be undermined unless they become meaner in defence. "It's leaky goals we don't like to concede, but there have been some nice goals, too," said Hart, who kept a clean sheet in both England matches against Spain and Sweden the previous week. Hart produced a superb save to deny Demba Ba with the scores locked at 0-0, and was thankful when the post denied Ben Arfa from reducing the deficit at 2-0 early in the second half, before substitute Gosling claimed a consolation goal with a minute remaining.

Alan Pardew commented, "City are the best team we've played by a distance but we still had our moments in the game. City have so many players with flair it makes it difficult for your defenders."

It is hard to believe Mancini's side were booed off the pitch earlier in the year when they were held 0-0 by Birmingham City. But they had now registered 42 goals in 12 League games, the best by any team for 50 years. Mancini added: "Since the Birmingham game, from that moment, the team have improved a lot. We play as a team. We are a very strong team now."

Sunday, Nov 20 2011

Carlos Tévez spent his time in Argentina winning golf tournaments, including a Buenos Aires Grand Prix for professionals and amateurs, partnering golfers Sebastian Fernandez and Andres Romero. Fernandez said: "He did not say anything about his problems with his club, but I was struck by the peace he had... He plays golf very well."

Roberto Mancini warned Tévez's potential suitors that the £40m-rated forward will not be sold on the cheap. "Tévez is strong regardless of what has happened," Mancini told Italian television station Rai Due. "And great players have a price that is rather high." AC Milan stepped up their interest after assistant boss Mauro Tassotti would be happy to accommodate Tévez at the San Siro but only until they assess the 27-year-old physically and mentally.

Chief scout Carlo Cancellieri admitted City's interest in Napoli's attacking trio Hamsik, Lavezzi and Cavani. Cavani scored Napoli's goal in the 1-1 Champions League draw at the Etihad, four days before scoring a hat-trick against AC Milan. When asked about City's reported interest in the Uruguay international, Mancini said: "The good players are all interesting but there's nothing. We can't buy every player."

Sergio Agüero wanted to inspire City in the manner his father-in-law did for Napoli. Maradona will forever be revered in Naples after inspiring the Italian club to two Serie A titles and a Uefa Cup win between 1987 and 1990. Agüero made a fine start, scoring 11 times in 15 appearances, but dreamed of reaching his compatriot's heights. "It is my dream, doing what Maradona did for Napoli, doing the same for Manchester City." Maradona would not be at the game following the recent death of his mother. Agüero said: "I couldn't speak to him because of the situation, the loss of his mother. I just want to send the best wishes to him at this moment."

Monday, Nov 21 2011

Harry Redknapp warned City and United they faced more than just a two-horse race for the title. An Emmanuel Adebayor double helped Spurs beat Villa 2-0, the North Londoners' eighth victory in nine games after initially beginning the campaign with successive defeats against United and City.

The result moved Tottenham into third, four points behind second-placed United but with a game in hand over the reigning champions. He admitted pipping City and United to the post to bring a first league title to White Hart Lane in more than half a century "will be very difficult".

City had drawn most of the plaudits so far, but Redknapp insisted they were "not on a different planet to everyone else", predicting that the current league leaders would not go through the whole season undefeated. "You saw them at QPR and QPR could have beaten them," Redknapp said. "Man City did very little and came away with a victory. I would not say that they are on a different planet to everyone else. They had a great result at Man United and here against us. They will not go through the season unbeaten. I don't think they are that good. They are a very good team and worthy favourites, they are above Man United at the moment but I would not say that they are certainties to win the league. City beat us by five but that wouldn't happen again.'

Napoli coach Walter Mazzarri elevated City to the level of Barcelona and Real Madrid. "They are in a great period of form, but we have to play without fear. No matter who they put on the field, they have the same strength as Barcelona or Real Madrid. City are doing well in their championship - they scored six goals at United - but we have the weapons to hurt them."

David Silva was the standout performer in the opening months of City's campaign, even with fierce competition from a number of team-mates in a star-studded squad. ''It took me a while to settle in and get going because it had been a long summer with the World Cup. I wasn't in the best shape without a regular pre-season. Then there were trips to Mexico and Argentina that messed up the programme a little bit - making it hard to settle and find my rhythm. But, bit by bit, I found my rhythm and started to feel a whole lot better. One of the reasons we're working better is because this group has settled as well. The team are coming together really well, players have been developing an understanding.'

Fabio Capello would be in Naples, presenting a chance for Micah Richards to state his case for a place in his squad for Euro 2012. Richards was ready for the challenge, tweeting: "Just arrived in Naples. Hostile isn't the word!" The squad had their first taste of what to expect from a group of Napoli supporters at the airport as the team set off to train in the stadium.

Mancini was considering whether to select Richards or Zabaleta in the right-back position. Mancini has expressed doubts over Richards' ability to concentrate for 90 minutes.

"If we win, it is finished," Mancini said. "If not, it will go to the last game and we know that it will very difficult for us because Bayern Munich are a top team and even if they are already through they will make sure to play a good game. We know Napoli can be dangerous and put us under a lot of pressure. They are a strong team and, playing at night, in their own stadium, they normally beat everyone. So it will be a hard game. But we also know we can do everything if we play well."

The manager was aware of overplaying the effect of the Neapolitan crowd. "Look at me. I played there for 13 years and I'm still alive and here. The Napoli fans are very passionate but these are the kind of matches the players should want to play. If we play our football and don't think about all the other issues, I don't think it will affect us." He hoped the game could take place without the knife-related incidents, "I don't think it will be a big problem. This kind of thing can happen in every stadium in every city, everywhere. But I'm sure our fans will be able to support the team and see the city. I think Naples is beautiful. Our supporters have the opportunity to see a beautiful match and a beautiful city."

City were concerned Mario would face abuse, possibly with a racial element, but Mancini would not let it prevent him starting with the Italian. "It's possible he will play, but I don't think about the crowd reaction. Mario has played in Naples maybe 10 times. For him every game for Manchester City is important. Now it's different because he plays for us for the first time in Italy in Naples, but I think the fans in Italy understand Mario can be an important player for the national team."

Mancini needed to avoid the complication of Thursday night football by dropping down into the Europa League. "It's clear we want to win in Naples for this reason. We know it will be difficult. We know also that we play every three days and it is difficult to play every three days at one hundred per cent. But we also want to go through in the Champions League because, as a team, we want to play in this competition. We will go there to win, always. I think for us it is important to have this mentality. We can't change the mentality for one game. In football, you can lose sometimes. This can happen. But we want to go there and play our football and show that Manchester City is a very good football team. If we do not win in Naples then the last game will be very important. But if we win, it is finished. If not, it will go to the last games, although I don't think it will be easy for Napoli against Villarreal, either. In the Champions League every team tries to play well to the last game. Our target for our first year in the Champions League is to get to the second stage and now we have a chance with two games to go. I think we should be quiet, we should play football. Only this. It is not easy when this is the worst group. But at the moment we are in a good position. Even if we lose we are not finished."

Mancini's mother Marianna and wife Federica come from the historic city in southern Italy and 21 years ago, almost to the day, he starred in a Sampdoria win over Napoli, a victory that put his team on course for the 1990 Serie A title. Mancini said: "It is one of my favourite cities and one of my favourite Italian grounds. It was in Naples, as a player for Sampdoria in the year we won Serie A, that we started our run to the title. It was 4-1 against a team that included Diego Maradona. I scored two and Gianluca Vialli scored the other two. I always found it fantastic to play there because the stadium is big, the pitch is good and atmosphere good. It is important to me going back to Italy because I had 20 years there as a player and six as a manager, and now this is a very big game for Manchester City. But our focus should only be to play football. If we concentrate only on the game then I think we can do well."

Mancini knew his side had improved since he clashed with Naples at Eastlands, "In the home game with Napoli we left a lot of space for them to counter-attack us and they are fantastic at that. So we know they are dangerous. But we learned a lot from that game. It was our first game in the Champions League and we were nervous. I think we have improved since then."

Mrs Mancini was backing him all the way despite her hometown loyalties. "Who will she be supporting? Manchester City of course!'

Tuesday Nov 22 2011

Mancini refused to give up despite a shattering defeat in Naples. City now had to beat Bayern in their final game and hope for a favour from winless Villarreal to progress to the knockout stage after losing 2-1 in the San Paola Stadium. Cavani struck both goals either side of a Balotelli equaliser. Mancini said: "I am disappointed about the result and I am sorry for the lads. I think we lost undeservedly. We played a very good match and we conceded two goals we shouldn't have done. There is nothing to explain, we are a strong team and we always play well, we always play to win. But occasionally you can lose matches, especially in the Champions League. I am not too disappointed. We have still got another match to play and if we don't qualify we will play Europa League. Our target was to go into the second stage and at this moment we are depending on other teams. But in football anything can happen. If Villarreal play a serious match they can get a result. It is important we play our game against Bayern Munich."

Mancini admitted the chances of progress were probably a "70% to Napoli and 30% to us". He started with Dzeko alongside Mario with Agüero on the bench. He rotated his full-backs, so no place for in-form Richards on the right as Zabaleta came in. Kolarov and Silva were the others to return and both were prominent as City probed. As well as scoring, Mario had a number of other chances and was also sick on the field. Mancini rubbished suggestions Mario might have been ill after being spotted in a pizzeria in Naples with his girlfriend on the eve of the match. Mancini said: "He was sick but he didn't have many problems. He has a small fever, it was nothing serious. He had my permission to see his girlfriend for half an hour - it was only to say hello to his girlfriend in a pizzeria. He did not have a pizza."

Mancini added, "We knew how Napoli play, they wait behind and counter-attack. We conceded too much space to them, but I am happy with ball possession and the chances we created. I am disappointed about the result but not about the performance. I think both teams are excellent teams, they are improving at the moment. We need to accept the result. We made mistakes. When you are against players like Hamsik, Lavezzi and Cavani they can put you under pressure."

City supporters were greatly outnumbered but did their best to contribute to the atmosphere by setting off a number of firecrackers themselves. Napoli president Aurelio De Laurentiis provocatively stated that the defeat of City demonstrates money cannot guarantee you success in football. "Our success proves two things: the first is that perhaps money isn't everything, as even with the budgets in order you can still go far. It also means that this Napoli side has a strong fibre and can give us great moments." De Laurentiis also suggested that Sheik Mansour might walk away from his £1b investment, "I think Mansour just wanted a toy. He says that he doesn't want immediate success but if they don't win something quickly, he could just go somewhere else and buy another toy."

Bayern's 3-1 win over Villarreal secured top spot and their place in the last 16. It was suggested that Bayern's already assured progression could work in City's favour, but Rummenigge insisted his club will be seeking victory when they head to Manchester, "We are still going to try and win in Manchester. First of all, there are points for the five-year ranking at stake, and then there are 800,000 euros to the winner. We are not going to give anything away. After winning such a tough group, all you can do is pay a compliment to the team and the coach. The team did what we expected in that they won again."

Wednesday, Nov 23 2011

Samir Nasri's multi-coloured underpants caused an internet stir, after he was caught on camera stripping off in front of his bemused team-mates when he was gearing up to replace Nigel de Jong in the 70th minute as he whipped down his shorts in front of Clichy and Pantilimon to adjust his curious choice of undies. Clichy seemed unmoved, Pantilimon gave Nasri a sympathetic smile and pat on the rear. Internet users passed comment on the undergarment via social networks after it was posted on YouTube.

Mario Balotelli was given permission to stay in Italy after the game while his team-mates flew home as the pizza mystery gathered pace and how he met his girlfriend despite being advised not to by Mancini's coaching staff. Mario went on to score but vomited on the pitch at half-time and he told the local media he 'had been sick for two days'. Yet, Mario did not have any noticeable illness when the team arrived and that he left the hotel at around 9pm having been told it was a bad idea. He had a slight cold and that Mancini's attempts to explain that were lost in translation in the press conference that followed the defeat. Mancini has a relaxed attitude to his players leaving the team base on foreign trips, as long as they are sensible and obey usual curfews. Mario was not in breach of any instructions, nor benefiting from any preferential treatment. Mancini did not know about Mario's excursion and the player was told by one member of the manager's coaching staff that a walk round a town where he has such a high profile the night before such a big game was not a great idea. He went out anyway. Mario was picked ahead of Agüero as Mancini wished to use the forward's pace down the left with a view to opening up space for full back Kolarov to exploit on the overlap. Mancini felt Mario had a decent night, scoring a goal late in the first half and coming close with two other efforts in the second period.

On the team plane earlier that day Mario ranted at a member of the club's PR staff after being informed that he would not be the player chosen to speak at the pre-match press conference. Informal talks had taken place with Cavani's representatives but Mancini said: 'Another striker? No. I have three strikers and that's enough. I'm satisfied. We have another three or four players who can play as a second striker. I think Cavani and Lavezzi are strong players but they play for Napoli at the moment. I don't know what can happen in the future.'

Besides Mancini's disappointment, a demotion to the Europa League would also have financial implications as City looked to maximise revenues ahead of the implementation of UEFA's fair play rules. City could lose out on £15m in TV cash, prize money and gate revenues by being relegated to Europa League. Mancini commented, "We hope we can beat Bayern Munich and Napoli can lose a point at Villarreal but I think we should be realistic. I don't think we have a team to win the Champions League because Real Madrid, Barcelona, Bayern Munich, (AC) Milan are maybe better and they have more experience than us in the Champions League. I hope we can stay in the Champions League but if we go into the Europa League we will try to win it. It is not like the Champions League but for us it is an important trophy. I hope we can stay, because after the Champions League (group stage) it is strange. If you go into the second stage maybe you can meet APOEL Nicosia or Bayer Leverkusen and you can go through – but I don't know what can happen. We did everything and I think we did a good game."

Arsene Wenger feared UEFA will not be able to force through new financial fair play regulations. The likes of Manchester City and Paris St Germain have risen to the top of their respective domestic leagues on the back of the vast wealth of their Middle Eastern owners. Wenger commented: "When I see the numbers announced by Manchester City, do you really think it will work in 2013? I cannot see it when the wage bill is bigger than the turnover. Frankly, that cannot happen in one year. Secondly, with what happened with Sion challenging UEFA, they have lost a lot of power. There is also the statement of [European Club Association chairman] Rummenigge against UEFA, representing the hundred clubs who are in there. We live in a world where any decision made is challenged. Europe has created that and we see how far Europe has gone. The authority of the legal affairs is challengeable everywhere."

City had the joint best defensive record in the top flight but looked suspect at the back against talented Napoli. Joleon Lescott said: "It was explained to us by the manager that we can't expect to always score three or four goals to win every game. Sometimes we need to be hard to beat. At Napoli we were disappointed with the two goals we conceded." Next up, Anfield. Lescott observed, "It's the way this season is going: Tuesday was Lavezzi, Sunday it is Suárez. Before it was Wayne Rooney. It just doesn't stop. Giuseppe Rossi for Villarreal. Mario Gómez for Bayern Munich. I love playing against these players. I measure myself against them."

Thursday, Nov 24, 2011

AC Milan refused to comment on widespread reports that they began negotiations to sign Tévez on loan in January. Tévez's agent Joorabchian met with Milan vice-president Adriano Galliani and transfer director Ariedo Braida at the Italian club's head office to discuss a deal of 5m to secure a temporary deal ahead of a potential permanent switch in the summer with City demanding £4.3m for Tévez to join a club on a six-month loan, another £18m to make the deal permanent at the end of the season. However, my City sources told me that they would not consider any offers below 'market value'. The source revealed that the two clubs had yet to talk directly, while

City made it clear that their stance hadn't changed from a year ago - in that a loan deal won't be acceptable, nor would they consider any cut price deal. My insider told me that the club "won't take the hit because of his behaviour" and that they want "the fair market value" for Tévez, around £25m. Tévez was still in Argentina, still defying orders to return and faced disciplinary proceedings, while City were considering legal action, but will wait until the situation is resolved until they make a decision over how to deal with him.

Kia Joorabchian acknowledged Milan fitted the criteria of club Tévez would like to join. "Milan is a great city. I have spoken to Tévez but we have not discussed anything for the time being. In Italy, they play great football. You have great clubs. (Milan and Juventus) are top clubs. Milan are one of the top clubs in the world with a long history and there is a possibility that Carlito will go to a top club. I spoke to Carlos and he is happy to move to Italy. We have spoken to Milan and the big Italian clubs are good options. Tévez wants to play at an important club."

Mancini again refused to discuss Tévez at his weekly press briefing. "I do not want to speak about Carlos Tévez," said Mancini. "I will answer no questions about him."

Fri, Nov 25, 2011

Roberto Mancini turns 47 on Sunday and hoped to celebrate by seeing his side consolidate their place at the top of the table by kicking off a difficult run of games with a victory at Liverpool. He was set to face Bellamy for the first time since their clash of personalities led to his acrimonious departure. "If he plays against us he'll want to play well and that's normal," said Mancini. "If he's happy, I'm happy for him."

The Blues had not won at Anfield since 2003 but travelled there with a five-point lead after winning 11 of their 12 games. City won nine games in succession in all competitions after losing at Bayern and were hoping to make a similar recovery after another Champions League defeat, although Mancini was taking nothing for granted, "Liverpool will be a very hard game on Sunday. Liverpool are a strong team. In my opinion - they are 12 points under us but I think they have a team that can win the Premier League. The Barclays Premier League is difficult, it is long and hard. We have played only 12 games. The squads now at Liverpool, Arsenal, Chelsea are why they can fight for the title. We have started the Barclays Premier League very well but the season is long and every two or three games can change the situation. I am satisfied but, as I said, I don't think we can win all the games. Everyone thinks we can win all the games but this is difficult."

Along with Liverpool City share the best defensive record in the division despite their free-scoring performances. But Mancini was alarmed by some of the goals conceded in the Champions League, while they have also managed just one clean sheet away from home in the league, "We can't score three or four goals in every game because if you do score three or four goals, then you will win all your matches; but sometimes we need to pay more attention and not concede a goal. We have the best defence in the Premier League but we need to improve. In the Champions League we've conceded six goals in five games and this is too much. But we can't think that the problem is only the defenders, it's the midfielders and strikers as well."

Mancini admitted that his back line may be strengthened in the new year, although any incomings would depend on him being able to move Carlos Tévez, Wayne Bridge and Nedum Onuoha out. "It depends what happens with him," Mancini added. "If Carlos leaves we can probably try, but we may also lose Yaya and Kolo for a month and this could be a problem."

Kenny Dalglish suggested clubs have got to stop moaning about their opponent's riches and start worrying about how to stop them on the field. Dalglish won the title with Blackburn in the mid-1990s, when they were bankrolled by Jack Walker, but believes there are other ways to compete. "If you're a football club in the fortunate position Manchester City are in, everyone is going to be delighted," he explained. "Nobody wouldn't want the financial strength they have got. We have to accept that, not worry about it. They are exactly the same. They are in a position where they can compete financially for any player in the world, whether it's wages or transfer fee. You tell me a fan who wouldn't like their club to be doing that. It may make the transfer market skewed, but hasn't that always been the case? It's always been harder for some than for others. Nobody wouldn't want the financial strength they have got. We have to accept that, not worry about it."

Dalglish insisted City were not unbeatable, but were better off without Tévez, "City have got a lot more points than they had at the same stage last season. The fact that they are top of the league means they must be better now than they were then. I remember when we beat them last season at Anfield when they lost Tévez to an injury after about 20 minutes. Tévez was a big miss for them that night, but they didn't have Agüero to replace him. Losing Tévez is a blow, but Agüero has come in and done well so they have just replaced one with the other. I think the number of points they have got, the start they have had, tells you that they are for real. But at the start of the season they were one of the teams mentioned anyway. It's not a surprise they are up there but it might be a surprise that they have got a few points gap. Eleven wins out of 12 isn't a bad start is it? There will not be too many teams who go past that record."

Saturday Nov 26, 2011

Mario Balotelli was at the centre of yet another chaotic drama after police rushed to his home following reports that his luxurious pad was being ransacked only to find the 'burglar' was the star himself. He had returned to his home with a friend to collect electrical goods following a blaze there. Since then he has been living away. On returning to his luxury property neighbours failed to recognise him and called the police, thinking that the home was being burgled. The report was of two men running down a road carrying stuff and loading up a 4x4.

Manchester United defender Phil Jones believed City could feel the pace as they enter a crucial stage of the season. "City have done fantastically this season,'" Jones said. "I am not taking anything away from them. But they do have some tough games coming up. I don't care how good you are, teams can be put under pressure. This is a difficult league to be in. It would be nice to reach top spot by Christmas. But it is not essential. Don't be writing us off if we are not there by January.'"

United dropped points at home to Newcastle suffering a dodgy penalty decision against them, something of a rarity at Old Trafford. Sir Alex was fuming after referee Mike Jones was persuaded by assistant John Flynn to award a penalty against Ferdinand for what seemed a clean tackle on Ben Arfa, it helped Newcastle to a point despite having Gutierrez sent off. Ferguson said: 'Two years ago when the linesman gave the offside goal against Chelsea it cost us the League, so hopefully we're not saying that at the end of May."

There would be a fresh batch of transfer speculation being prepared for the Sunday papers ahead of the clash at Anfield with speculation growing that City would go for Robin van Persie in the summer, while City were seeking to sell as many as 20 players in the next two transfer windows to reduce their wage bill to try and meet Uefa's Financial Fair Play regulations. The club employed 63 professionals and wanted to get that down to the low 40s by next summer. City had 23 players out on loan, some to aid their development, others in the hope that they can attract buyers.

Meanwhile Juventus ruled themselves out of the running for Tévez. Sporting director Giuseppe Marotta said: "Tévez doesn't interest us. Absolutely not."

Sunday, Nov 27, 2011

Kenny Dalglish sent Bellamy home to grieve following Gary Speed's sudden death. Dalglish, who signed Speed for Newcastle in 1998, said, "Gary was like a mentor to Bellers. He was upset and I took the decision to leave him out. There are more important things than playing a football match."

A draw at Anfield, reinstating their five-point lead over United, was an acceptable outcome, as Dalglish's side were unbeaten at Anfield this season, a sequence of four draws and two wins before this game. The point was hard fought especially after the sending-off of substitute Balotelli, who soon gathered a second caution after leading with his elbow in the 83rd minute and hitting Skrtel.

Yet during the first half, City had appeared in total control, taking the lead in the 31st minute as Vincent Kompany got away from markers at the near post to meet Silva's corner kick with a firm header. Moments later a long-range effort by Adam was miscued, destined to go well wide until Lescott stuck out a leg and diverted it past Joe Hart. The England keeper made amends with a remarkable save from a header by substitute Andy Carroll in stoppage time.

Mancini felt Mario was unlucky to have been sent off, questioning the second booking, "For me the second was not a yellow card." Mario stopped and had words with his boss on the touchline after the sending off but Mancini remained tight-lipped when asked what had been said, "I don't remember, nothing." He also denied there were any issues with Mario, who was heard kicking the dressing room door following his third red card of his City career. Mario banged the visitors' dressing room door so hard the handle broke, he then charged off to find a TV monitor to see the clash with Skrtel. Aleksander Kolarov went to calm him down and took the City star back to the dressing room, while the handle was easily replaced without apparent need for repair. "No, we don't have any problems. He is young, I think he was disappointed for the yellow card," commented Mancini.

Mancini later accused the Liverpool players of getting Mario sent off. He was booked twice in seven minutes. The first was for a needless pull back on Glen Johnson, the second came after he clumsily collided with Skrtel. Mancini claimed referee Martin Atkinson was influenced by Skrtel's reaction, "Mario moved his arm and Skrtel reacted like a young player. I don't think it was good. The referee gave the free-kick but he didn't want to give the yellow card. When the Liverpool players saw this, they went there and said "Yellow card! Yellow card!" Mario should pay attention because he knows many players provoke him. This is not correct. I am disappointed with him for the first yellow card but not for the second. He did not deserve it. The last three months Mario has played well and scored a lot of goals."

Kenny Dalglish insisted that Balotelli had only himself to blame, "The reaction of our players? I think Balotelli got himself sent-off. His actions spoke louder than anyone else, didn't they? Sometimes when you look in the mirror, you get the answer. Sometimes he doesn't help himself. If you help yourself, you don't get in that position. I don't think our boys did anything."

Liverpool were the better side in an entertaining second half and but for an inspired display from Hart they would have won all three points. "Joe saved an important point," said Mancini. "We played five days ago in Naples. There was a difference between us. Liverpool had freshness. We were not one hundred per cent. We tried to win but it is not easy. Liverpool are a good team."

Mancini rotated his full-backs and Gael Clichy was restored to the side at after making way for Kolarov in Naples. Clichy said: "As a player you always want to play as many games as possible and for me it is a big change because I was used to playing week-in, week-out with Arsenal. Of course you are disappointed but I am not the only one and so far we have been playing some amazing games against Manchester United, Tottenham and now Liverpool. I believe in February we will have the fresh legs to go all the way. We need a big squad to go all the way and hopefully we can carry on like this because I think the atmosphere is good and the way we are playing is okay."

Monday, Nov 28, 2011

Police investigated reports of racist abuse towards Micah Richards. Angry fans contacted the police following a comment posted on the defender's Twitter page. The Twitter user WillMadine94 tweeted: "You big fat n★★★★★ u r s★★★. Martin Kelly over u all day for England. Play for Africa!!!" on the footballer's page. Richards later replied: "Love the racist abuse. Keep it coming."

David Beckham's loyalty towards United was pretty transparent after the former England captain declared that City have 'no chance' of winning the title. Remember the 6-1 thrashing. Obviously not! Becks said: "I don't think Manchester City have a chance. This season they have got a good team and have some good players, but Manchester United have more experience and know how to win a championship."

City had the potential to emulate Arsenal's legendary 'Invincibles' of 2004-5, according to Wenger who says they will need luck as well as exceptional stamina to complete a League season unbeaten. The Carling Cup quarter-final was the Gunners first meeting with City this season as Wenger commented. "I hope Samir gets a good reception." Wenger admitting that he thought about signing Owen Hargreaves after he became a free agent.

Roberto Mancini complained about an "impossible" fixture schedule taking on Arsenal, just 50 hours after the final whistle in their league draw with Liverpool. Mancini replaced all 11 players accusing the authorities of killing the national team. "I think this is the reason why the national team arrive for European Championships, World Cups and they are dying. The players don't have time to recover. We'll change all the team, because this is an incredible situation. Arsenal played on Saturday, we play Sunday evening. Monday, travel to London, and we play Tuesday night. Incredible. To play again in two days like this so soon after the Champions League is incredible."

Liverpool faced a similar situation with a trip to Chelsea in the same competition on the same evening. Mancini believed the Premier League should have made a stand to protect their players. Dalglish warned he may be forced to field a team of kids for the quarter-final at Stamford Bridge, and Mancini suggested he could do the same - to teach the authorities a painful lesson. "I know Kenny is upset also, and I agree with him. It's incredible. It's a quarter-final. We should play with 11 young players - maybe 14 or 15 years old. I maybe should do that to make a statement, because it's not correct. Not so much for us, but for the players. It's not right. I don't know who is to blame, but the Premier League should have said something. It's important to play, but it's also important to recover. You need three days between one game and the other. We'll have the same in January when we play Sunderland (on New Year's Day) and then Liverpool in two days. Liverpool play three days before us. Is this correct? I don't think so." Mancini has a powerful squad, which allowed him to bring in an entirely new side. Meanwhile the manager maintained his support of Mario Balotelli, "There's a lesson for Mario. He gets booked when he does not deserve to be booked. For this reason he must pay attention, always."

Tuesday, Nov 29, 2011

City won at Arsenal for the first time in 36 years with a late Agüero goal to seal a place in the semi-finals. City had not won in 28 trips to the Gunners stretching back to 1975, the same season they last won the League Cup.

Edin Dzeko helped create the winner on 83 minutes. After an Arsenal corner, his pass set Johnson free and he teed up Agüero to score his 12th goal of the season, a cruel blow to the Gunners, who for much of the game looked the more likely winners.

Samir Nasri was the only player to remain in the side from the trip to Anfield and he was given a torrid time from the start by the home supporters. The former Gunners midfielder's first touch was resoundingly booed, before chants of "you only left for the money" rang out around Emirates Stadium before being involved in a post-match spat with Emmanuel Frimpong. Frimpong - who made clear his unhappiness with Nasri's exit for City in

August on Twitter – hassled and harried his opponent throughout the game, with words being exchanged at various points. Matters escalated after the final whistle, with the two players seen in a heated exchange as they headed down the tunnel. Reports that Nasri subsequently aimed a punch at the Ghanaian were immediately denied. "Words were exchanged – that was that," an Arsenal spokesman who saw the incident said. "There were no punches thrown, but there was a lot of noise. Sami was speaking in French and Mani wasn't. It was handbags, they didn't even touch."

Mancini commented on his players performance and reaction of the crowd, "Samir Nasri can play better because he is a top player. Tonight is the first night he came back to Arsenal and it is not easy for a player that played here for four or five years. I think that he can improve a lot but it was the same situation with those who arrived last year, like Edin and David. It (the win) is not important for him, it is important for the team. For him it is better than he played tonight so, when he comes back to play here in the league, he knows what will happen."

City's 6 foot 8 inch tall keeper Costel Pantilimon was in outstanding form. Pantilimon had to be patient at City during a season-long loan from Timisoara, but his attitude and his display against Arsenal enhanced his chances of a permanent deal as the club had an option to buy, for a fee of £3m, in the summer. Pantilimon received a text from Joe Hart, rested from the squad, before the game wishing him luck. Mancini switched formation during the first half as Agüero was introduced in place of Kolarov, who looked miffed by the decision when he took his place on the bench, Owen Hargreaves was making his third appearance of the season.

The manager was happy with the result, "We had a chance seven minutes from the end and we scored. It was a great goal. A great counter-attack. I don't think that Arsenal had a lot of chances, I think we played well. It will be better to win here in the Premier League but it is a good feeling because we are into the semi-finals of the competition. We have a strong squad – all of the top teams have a good squad and can change eight, nine or ten players. It is normal for the Carling Cup to change. December and January will be crucial months because we play tough games and we play every three days. After January we can talk about whether we can win things or not."

Wednesday, Nov 30, 2011

The latest crazy video featuring Mario Balotelli giving a lady working at City the fright of her life when she opened a door as he shouted at her as he walked through it, causing her and another lady in a chair to jump out of their skins as he strolled off smiling. The joke was taken in the good-natured way it was delivered. For a third lady behind a computer she looked like she had seen similar practical jokes from the striker.

Joe Hart was filmed belting out the indie anthem 'Wonderwall' by Oasis during a City training session, and complemented his off-key tones by mimicking Liam Gallagher's famous swagger. A City TV cameraman encouraged him with calls of: 'It's good, it's good! You should be on X-Factor.'

It was revealed that City had spent more than any other Premier League club on agents' fees over the past year with £9.66m going to player representatives. Tottenham spent the second-highest amount, committing £7.57m to agents with Liverpool third on £7m. United spent £4.46m, the seventh-highest amount. The £71.87m total spent by the clubs between 1 October 2010 and 30 September 2011 is the highest since the Premier League first published the figures in 2008, a rise of £4.73m on the £67.14 million.

Manchester United crashed out of the Carling Cup at home to Crystal Palace, Sir Alex apologised to the fans, "That was not a Manchester United performance, and I have to apologise to our supporters. I don't want to take anything away from Palace, because it was a fantastic, mammoth effort from their players." City were drawn against Liverpool in the semi-finals of the League Cup with the first leg at home. Crystal Palace will play Cardiff.

DECEMBER

"In my opinion, his plans are on the right path..... our main objective is to win the English Premier League and if we achieve that, then it will have an impact on the team and the club as a whole and will show we can achieve anything."

SHEIK MANSOUR ON UNDER PRESSURE MANCINI...

When it was pointed out City could be top at Christmas for the first time since 1929, Mancini said: 'We want to stay at the top for a long time, not only Christmas.'

Thursday, Dec 1, 2011

City owner Sheik Mansour promised to support Roberto Mancini even if he failed to deliver the title this season. Mancini guided unbeaten City to a five-point lead over United after ending their 35-year wait for a trophy by lifting the FA Cup the previous season. Mansour admitted that the former Inter Milan boss still has his critics, but pledged to give Mancini time to achieve even greater success. The Sheik ploughed more than £1b into the club since taking over in August 2008 but his only visit to the Etihad Stadium came 15 months ago.

In a rare interview he said: "We are satisfied with the progress that is being achieved - the success and development at this level of football, but we must also continue to have patience. Sometimes I meet City supporters who criticise the work of the manager Roberto Mancini. In my opinion, his plans are on the right path. We need to reflect upon where the club has been and what we have achieved so far, and realise that what we have accomplished to date is formidable, but hard work is still required and it needs to be delivered with patience."

Defeat to Napoli meant they were unlikely to reach the knockout stages of the Champions League, but the Sheik reminded Mancini that his first target should be the title. He added: "We must not forget that our main objective is to win the English Premier League and if we achieve that, then it will have an impact on the team and the club as a whole and will show we can achieve anything."

Mancini responded, "I think Sheikh Mansour understands we have worked well. I think we have built a good team in a year and a half but we need to continue to work harder. If we win the Barclays Premier League, for us that would be an incredible moment. But from now until the end, we have 25 games. It is very difficult to say now if we can win the title. Five points is a good gap but the season is long." Mancini was happy with the job he had done in the near two years since his appointment but he was aiming much higher over the next two years, "City have improved a lot. I think we have a good mentality – we want to play to win always, away or at home. But we understand also in this process there will be mistakes. This is normal. I think in two years we can be in the four top teams in the world."

Napoli president Aurelio De Laurentiis launched another outspoken attack on the Abu Dhabi owners by suggesting that they might try underhand tactics to influence the Spaniards. The Italian movie mogul had already branded City 'money wasters' and accused Mansour of using the club as 'a play thing'. De Laurentiis went a step further, saying: "I can feel strange things going on surrounding the Villarreal game – princes and sheiks are getting agitated. To think about it would be evil but sometimes you can guess what is happening."

Mancini reckoned City became the new club everyone loves to hate, but he couldn't care less. He knew he had little sympathy for the punishing schedule his team faced over the next two months, because he has such an expensive, successful squad. He had to adopt the siege mentality that served the likes of Sir Alex so well over the years. "Every team that wins things doesn't get sympathy. Do United get sympathy from other teams? No, because United win always. When Arsenal won Leagues and Cups was there sympathy? No. Because every team knows that when they win they do not get sympathy. I hope we don't get sympathy for the next games either."

Mancini believed City's chances of silverware depended on the way they coped with the games that were coming thick and fast over the next two months. "The season is hard now. We have two months, December and January, that I think will be crucial months because we play tough games and we play every three days. I think that, after January, we can start talking about whether we can win something or not."

AC Milan believed they were close to a breakthrough on signing Tévez, who brushed off the drama by taking in another round of golf in Buenos Aires. Corinthians president Andres Sanchez wanted to make a blockbuster signing. Sanchez said: "I want to sign Tévez. We are going to hire a top-class player for 2012 and I hope it will be Tévez. I don't know how much we would pay but if Tévez decides to move, I'm sure he will play for us."

Fri, Dec 2, 2011

As City prepared for their home game with Norwich, the manager said: "I think that now we are starting an important two months because we play hard games every three days. December is hard and January will be incredible. We will lose Yaya and Kolo for the African Nations Cup and I hope we are lucky with injuries to players. If not we could have a serious problem."

Norwich had made a good impression since returning to the top flight and were 10th, Mancini said: "I think this is one of the good things in England, that all the teams try to play and want to win. I have watched Norwich and up until now they have done very well. Tomorrow we will need to do a good job. We play every three days, Norwich have time to prepare for these games every week."

Mancini feared Mario Balotelli could become a target for streetwise opponents, "Mario should pay attention and he should be clever. I can do nothing – only he is on the pitch. He should pay attention and think only about football and not other things. I think he made a mistake only for the first foul when he took the first yellow card [in the Liverpool game]. Then he should not take any risks. He is more mature, this is clear. But in my opinion, if Mario was on the pitch in the last 20 minutes we could have won the game. It is important Mario understands we need him as a player on the pitch."

While chopping and changing the starting line-up might be tough for players to accept, it's a necessary evil, according to Richards. "It can be frustrating but if you want to be part of the squad you have just got to grin and bear it. This is a team that is going places and if you want to be part of it you have just got to get used to that." Mancini's rotation policy would continue throughout a busy Christmas schedule of 14 games in 56 days in all competitions, the period to decide City's fate this season, "The season is hard now. We have two months, December and January, that I think will be crucial months because we play tough games and we play every three days. After January, we can start talking about whether we can win something or not."

Kolo became frustrated as he wanted to win back his place after only three League appearances from the bench since returning from his drug ban. The former captain, who joined from Arsenal for £16m in 2009, and who was being linked to PSG, told France Football: "It is a delicate situation for me and I know that it is going to be very difficult for me to regain my place because the team is doing well and getting good results. But I am patient and the African Nations Cup is nearly here. For now, I don't see a departure in the January window as an option. It is difficult to think that when you are at a club like Manchester City. But, in football, everything can change very quickly and you never know. That will depend on the game time I get before the window."

Kolo criticised team-mate Stefan Savic, "I know my qualities and I have got nothing to prove here in England. They know me here. When you look at the performance of Savic against QPR, excuse me but I am relaxed." Kolo's comments about African players would cause a stir, "To compete in the Africa Cup of Nations is catastrophic for a player these days. Coaches no longer want to sign players because of it. I feel it's going to be more difficult for the Africans in football in the future. I'm convinced that, if I'm not playing for City, then it's not only for football reasons. If it was only about that then I would be playing every week. I'm a victim of that and it has to be said. When I was in Angola for the Africa Cup of Nations in 2010 the club hired a plane so that I could get back quickly to play in a game against Manchester United. I could not get back in time and we lost. I believe the club have not got past that and I'm paying for it now." Toure believed African footballers in general are being discriminated against because of their obligations to the Africa Cup of Nations, "'Clubs at this level always have big squads. It goes one way and then the other. I was captain here and so was Carlos Tévez. He is no longer here and who would have thought that would have happened? African players are the victim of discrimination."

In contrast his brother Yaya had started every game. Along with Hart, Kompany and Silva they were the backbone of Mancini's team. Yaya helped Barcelona beat United in a Champions League final while playing at centre half, a position he had occupied just twice before, but he badly wanted to win the English title. "Here at City we have different challenges and to me the Premier League means everything. You have to understand that I mean that. One time when I was still in Spain I saw Kolo and Drogba when I was with the national team. A few months earlier Drogba had won the Premier League. I said, "Didier I saw you on the TV and you were so happy. I have never seen you like that. Why was that?" He told me it was because it's just so hard to win the Premier League that the happiness is like nothing before. Even when you go to Blackburn and Stoke and Blackpool… it is so hard every week.

"He said I wouldn't understand until I played here. He was right. He told me that here you play Boxing Day, New Year's Day . . . you never get a break. I had not experienced it before. So when you win you are so happy. When I signed for City I called my brother and told him if we won any cup I would be so happy. We won the FA Cup last season and that was great. But the big target now is the Premier League. If I win the Premier League, I will go crazy. Playing United and winning the Champions League was great but maybe not so great. We won everything that year. We kind of expected to win it. But to beat United 6-1 this season was amazing. No team does that! That, to me, was a bigger story than the Champions League. After the game I arrived home and I took the team sheet home and recorded 6-1 on it. Sorry, I should say 1-6. I took that and put that in my home. It will always be there at home. Later I spoke to my friends in Paris on the phone and I told them we had beaten United 6-1. They said, "What? On the Play- Station?" They said I was crazy and that sums it up. It was crazy."

Saturday, Dec 3, 2011

City kept their 100% home league record, with a Jimmy Greaves style opener from Agüero, surrounded by five defenders, he still managed to stabbed his 13th goal of the season through a crowd of legs to put the league leaders in front. The breakthrough didn't come until the 32nd minute. Nasri, making his third successive start, was surprised himself when his 35-yard free-kick evaded everyone to double the lead before Yaya curled in a third.

Mario, on as a substitute for Agüero, cheekily scored with his shoulder virtually on the goal line after his close range effort had been saved and bobbled up into the air, reacting with his now familiar straight face. Johnson's precise finish made it five. The stand out moment was Agüero's solo goal. Assistant manager David Platt said, "It was always going to take a little brilliance in a tight area to open up the game." Yaya's third ensured City scored at least three at home for the sixth time this season. Platt tried to keep City's supporters grounded. "The goals are irrelevant. We'll happily take just one if there is no reply."

Hopes of keeping a clean sheet for the first time in seven games were ruined by Morison who climbed above Clichy at the back post to head in Tierney's cross. Johnson rounded off City's seventh successive home win in the League as Mancini observed, "It was not easy because it was only 1-0 in the first half and if you don't score the game can change. Norwich defended with all their players behind the ball. [Agüero] scored a fantastic goal because it was not easy to score and the goal Mario scored today was fantastic because it was the only way he could score. It is not important now [to be top of the table], it is important to be there at the end of the season."

Norwich manager Paul Lambert commented, "Manchester City deserved to win. Whether by five is a bit harsh, we tried to keep going and at 3-1 the goal gave us a bit of confidence but we were beaten by a better side. How much did Balotelli cost … £24million? How do you compete with that, or with a player like Johnson to come off the bench? More established Premier League teams than us will come to Manchester City and have a hard time."

Barry and Yaya, whose 124 passes were the most by any Premier League player since Xabi Alonso three years ago, provided the foundation. "When you come here you are pitting your wits against some of the best players in the world," said Lambert.

Gareth Barry warned fans not to start expecting too many goals after taking their goal tally to a remarkable 48 in just 14 league games – just 12 behind their total for the whole of last season – well on course to smash Chelsea's record of 103 from the 2009-10 campaign, "It is an unbelievable record and at times people were getting frustrated because we were finding it hard to break them down in the first half hour. But if people are patient they will realise we are going to create chances and eventually get the goals. When people start expecting 5-1 wins at home it can become very dangerous. It is important the players keep trying to create as many chances and score as many goals as possible, but most importantly keep playing as a team and keep winning football matches. That is what we have got to try to do until the end of the season."

Barry was awarded the fans' man-of-the-match award but felt the accolade should really have been shared around for another superb team display. "I am playing in a fantastic team. The squad is fantastic in terms of the attacking ability. You pick up the ball and you're looking at the four or five players ahead who you can give the ball to and let them create chances. Obviously with these players your confidence keeps growing and growing. The squad is fantastic and the manager has got great options. If we are going to achieve stuff the squad is going to be more important than the team. Everyone has had to wait their turn all season, including myself."

City were too reliant on Tévez for goals last season. But with five different scorers against Norwich, Barry claimed that was now a thing of the past. "It's definitely a different case. Everyone is stepping up to the plate. We're not just relying on one player, which may have been the case last season. Everyone used to look at Carlos when things weren't going to plan. But it's different now."

The midfielder admitted it would be a huge blow to exit the Champions League, "It would be a massive disappointment. We're not going to lie and just say that we could concentrate on the Premier League, because it would be a big disappointment. But it's the first time the club has been in the Champions League and, although we feel we've got the quality to progress, it's another learning curve. If we go out we'll just concentrate on the rest of the games, the Premier League and the other competitions.'

Meanwhile Mancini would keep juggling his players, "Always it is difficult to choose a team sheet because I am very sorry when I leave out players. But now we play every three days. In three days we have an important match in the Champions League and then we play Chelsea and Arsenal. We have a lot of games."

Sunday, Dec 4, 2011

Roberto Mancini refused to rule out any of his rivals for the title, "I think for the title race it will be a number of teams. Chelsea, Arsenal, Liverpool, Tottenham, United and us. I think Tottenham are having a good season - they have started very well. I hope my team continue to play well, score goals and continue to win."

Mancini expressed his delight at City's start, "I'm very satisfied and very happy for my players. They deserve to stay at the top at this moment. But we know the season is very long and very hard."

He will not change the attacking style but they could have been more defensive when they first faced Bayern. "The first game away in Champions League maybe we should have defended better, with one striker less. That would have been good for us. But we started the season with this mentality. We scored a lot of goals in this way but sometimes it's important to defend very well, like we did against Liverpool. When we've played in the Champions League we have been more offensive. At this moment there are several teams in the Champions League who are better than us. If Chelsea didn't win it in 10 years this says something. We won't change anything [for this game]. We want to get to second stage but if that's not possible will go into the Europa League and we will try to win it."

Dutch legend Ruud Gullit, who lifted the European Cup in successive seasons when he was playing for AC Milan and who managed Chelsea to FA Cup glory in 1997, said of City, "In Europe there has been no sign of their class. I find that amazing. Almost all of their players have experience at Champions League level. They can't use that as an excuse. They are so much better than their form in Europe suggests."

The FA Cup holders were drawn at home to rivals Manchester United, the draw taking place with Franco Zola at Wembley. The clash of City and 11-time FA Cup winners United was the stand out tie with the teams sitting first and second, respectively in the League. Rio Ferdinand wrote on Twitter, "3rd round FA cup game vs mancity..great game to kick off this yrs FA cup, can't wait." The clubs had only met once in the FA Cup at Manchester City's home ground - back in 1954/55 when the home side won 2-0 in a fourth-round tie at Maine Road.

Monday, Dec 5, 2011

Mancini started a City Santa Stroll charity event, but couldn't work the air horn!

Roberto Mancini was joined on stage by City's football development executive Patrick Vieira, who couldn't save him from the embarrassment of a failing horn. Mancini battled with an aerosol-powered starter horn for five minutes before a replacement was found, and the run could finally begin. The event was a collaborative effort between United and City fans in aid of Sport Relief. Sets of fans from both teams dressed as Santa and took part in special dash events at Old Trafford and the Etihad Stadium, including a 5km race. Over 1,000 Father Christmases ran the SportCity route, all dressed in a blue Santa suits. Similarly an army of red St Nicholas's ran the United course, marshalled by Red Devils fan Eamonn Holmes.

City put on a cake class for their players, and Mario stole the headlines, botching his attempt to craft a star out of marzipan (using a stencil!), then manhandling a Father Christmas toy. Nigel de Jong and Owen Hargreaves managed it. Agüero passed judgement on Zabaleta's effort. 'Very bad,' he observed, sporting a dashing City-coloured Santa hat.

Stoke handed Mario Balotelli's younger brother Enoch a trial at the Britannia Stadium. Enoch had been training with the Stoke youth team, making his debut this week for the Potters' reserves in a 0-0 draw at Burton Albion, where he showed some neat touches and the family penchant for showboating. The 19-year-old forward, who was born in Ghana before moving to Italy with Mario, played 82 minutes before coming off with cramp. Stoke academy coach Dave Kevan commented, "He's a good boy but a little bit raw at the moment." If Enoch signed for Stoke, the Balotelli's will join Rio and Anton, Fabio and Rafael as brothers playing in the Premier League.

Mario had a school named after him after striking up a friendship with a former child soldier of the civil war in Sudan. The striker had donated money to help build a secondary school in the South Sudanese village of Cuey Machar, to be named the 'Mario Balotelli Wing' in his honour. Mario helped the project after meeting John Kon Kelei in Milan in the summer of 2010. Mario watched a film about Kon Kelei's life called 'The Silent Army' and was so touched by his story that he offered to help finance a project to build a secondary school. Now aged 29, Kon Kelei was kidnapped by rebels of the Sudan's People Liberation Army at the age of four and forced to fight in the country's civil war. He managed to escape the conflict and after arriving in Holland as a refugee he graduated in law before returning to his homeland when South Sudan declared its independence. Mario said: "Kon told me that he was forced by the rebels to use a rifle that was bigger and heavier than he was. He wasn't even able to hold it properly. But he managed to run away and save himself. He could have built a new life but he wanted to help his country, so I have helped him."

Mario also helped himself to a brand new Maserati and had it seized by police just 24 hours later. He picked up his new 187mph, £100,000 Italian supercar on Monday, but was pulled over by police on Tuesday on suspicion of speeding. The car was confiscated, by police who thought it had not been legally registered. He produced the appropriate paperwork, and he was allowed to get back on the road. His previous Maserati was impounded 27 times for non-payment of parking tickets, damaged by thugs wielding crowbars, and written off when team-mates left a bag full of rotting fish in it for several days as part of a tit-for-tat prank war at Eastlands. After that, he resorted to two wheels instead and bought a brand new motorbike only to be immediately banned from riding it.

Vincent Kompany's limousine company faced police prosecution, accused of failing to have insurance. Kompany owns a third of the 900 shares in Elite Limousines VIP Protection Services, a firm who chauffeur City players and officials around town. The company signed a contract with Garry Cook during his time in charge of day-to-day operations but were accused by Greater Manchester Police of failing to have their cars appropriately insured. Police pulled over five Elite vehicles on the way to City's ground for their final home Premier League game last season against Stoke. Shares in the company were divided equally between Alyas Hussain, Mohammed Fayaz Hussain and Kompany. Although City have a sponsorship deal with Jaguar/Land Rover, City players and staff often used Elite, while Cook used the firm to take him to his home in Alderley Edge. Kompany has been a director of Elite since October 14, 2010. Elite, who also have a contract with Manchester United, took promotional photographs of their fleet outside the Etihad Stadium.

Meanwhile, City were ordered to pay Norwich just £250,000 for England youth keeper Angus Gunn. Gunn - son of former Scotland keeper and Norwich legend Bryan Gunn - quit the Canaries for the Etihad Stadium in the summer. Norwich wanted £1m plus add-ons for the 15-year-old, but an independent panel ordered City to pay just a quarter of that. Gunn is a regular in England's youth side and chose to advance his career at City. City will have to pay some extras for Gunn if he becomes a first-team player and ultimately succeeds Hart.

City were in talks to sign Mateo Kovacic, the 'new Luka Modric', beating competition from Spurs, Arsenal and United for the 17-year-old Dinamo Zagreb midfielder who had a year of first-team football under his belt. City chiefs held a meeting the player's agent. Dinamo were asking £10m.

Edin Dzeko's agent denied reports in the Italian media suggesting that the Bosnian forward had been in contact with Juve defender Andrea Barzagli to research the club. The pair were team-mates at Wolfsburg and Dzeko was said to have been asking about the Turin club's pay structure and goal-bonus scheme. Irfan Redzepagic, the striker's advisor, told Italian news agency Ansa that the story was false.

Roberto Mancini supported Kolo after quotes attributed to him in So Foot magazine also included a damning assessment of fellow team mate Savic. Mancini commented, "I spoke about this with Kolo yesterday. He said he did not say anything about this. Kolo and I do not have any problem. He explained this to me and for me it is finished. It is okay now." When asked if he believed Toure, Mancini said: "Yes I did, I believe him. I did not read the article so I don't know what Kolo said, I can say only yesterday at training he told me about this interview. I don't know what he said or didn't say. Yesterday before training he said to me: 'Sorry boss but in the newspaper it will come out that I said this, this, this - but I did say nothing about this.' For me this is okay. In this moment, no. Kolo is part of our plans for this year. Kolo is a good player, a good guy and if he plays or not - because we have a lot of good players - he is part of our plans. Kolo is important for us because he is experienced. In the summer he told me he wants to leave because he wants to play. I have respect for him and we can talk about this, but not now."

My sources told me that City were seeking any evidence, whether a tape recoding or a transcript. Mancini had given his player the benefit of the doubt, but the City management are investigating the case. Stefan Savic insisted that there was no lingering issue with Kolo. "He has said to me that he didn't say anything," Savic said. "Straight after it came out in the newspapers he spoke with me and said he didn't tell them anything like that and I can only believe him." Savic had a few doubts – "I don't think he should say something like that." Usually a centre-half, Savic played at right-back because of injuries to Richards and Zabaleta, and justified his selection with a solid performance. "I'm happy because the manager picked me and I think I will play a lot of games for this club in the future," he said. "That was my first game in the Premier League from the start but I am getting used to this. I came from the Serbian league and I needed a little time but now I think everything is better and the time is in front of me. I have a lot of experience playing international football. I also played in the Champions League last year with Partizan Belgrade and when I am training with these good players I can only improve."

Tuesday, Dec 6, 2011

City gave AC Milan permission to speak to Tévez's representative, according to the Italian club's vice-president Adriano Galliani. Joorabchian said his player wanted to play for a "great club" and will stay in Europe. Milan would let Brazilian star Pato go to City if they relaxed their 'no loan policy' on Tévez. Mancini branded Tévez 'stupid' for the behaviour and reiterated that the club must get him off their books in January. "I don't know what the situation is with Carlos at this moment. I think that for us it is important to sell him. We can do this for him and for the club. If he has the chance to go to Italy, I am happy for him. Tévez behaved stupidly in the way a player shouldn't – especially a great player. I was really angry because I was not expecting that from him. I always had excellent relations with him. That's the first time I've seen that in such an important match when there was 40 minutes still left to play. Ten days after what happened in Munich, I invited him to come to my place to talk. I told him if he apologised to me, to the club, to the team, he could come back into the squad. I would have forgiven him but he replied that he didn't have to apologise to anyone."

City sources told me that no deal had been agreed with AC Milan, despite reports to the contrary, and that they would not sanction a loan deal. Milan offered to take Tévez on a free loan for the rest of the season with a view to buying him for a pre-arranged price of £20m. However, a loan offer would be rejected out of hand. My source insisted: "That will not happen. The club have made it clear that there is no loan option for Tévez, so nothing seems to have moved on."

The plot thickened as later that evening AC Milan vice-president Adriano Galliani revealed an agreement had been reached for a January loan move, although City had yet to accept the offer. "Between yesterday and today I laid a few bricks to reinforce an already formidable squad," Galliani said. "I've been in my office with Tévez's agent and the situation is clear: Milan have an agreement with the player and just now we sent a proposal to Manchester City – a free loan with right to buy at certain conditions." Asked why City should accept the bid, though, Galliani remarked, "He is not playing, he's a great player and if he does well with us then we'll buy him. The player is giving up a mountain of money. He had enormous bonuses with City for the Premiership and Champions League. I spoke to Carlitos and he wants to join us. Half the agreement is complete; now we await City's response. If Tévez arrives, it'd be a new champion for all of Italian football to enjoy. We are close. The player was fantastic for the economic sacrifices he made and his great desire to come to Milan. I hope City say yes, as I managed to beat away some threats from Italy and Europe, but I cannot tell you who. We are in pole position."

PSG were also linked with a move, and although Galliani claimed he was aware of interest from the Ligue 1 big spenders, he still hoped of success. "Yes it's true, PSG are also in the running although I haven't heard from (their sporting director) Leonardo. We know City's desire is to the sell the player, our proposal is to loan him and hope City say yes. I'm neither optimistic nor pessimistic. I can certainly say the player would prefer to be at Milan but you have to convince City to send him out on loan and that's not easy."

Galliani brushed aside rumours Pato or any other Rossineri player would be included in the deal to bring Tévez to the San Siro. "There is an offer sent to Manchester for Tévez," Galliani said. "However, we have not spoken about any of our players going to City or any other club. Our fans can be calm because this is the truth. We know that City's desire is to sell the player but our offer is to get the player on loan with an option to make that deal permanent. We hope that City says yes because our offer will not be modified. I am neither optimistic nor pessimistic. What I can certainly say is that the player would like to come to Milan, it would be his preferred destination. But we must convince City to loan the player out and that is not easy."

Mancini intended to confront Karl-Heinz Rummenigge over his persistent sniping at City, "I don't understand Rummenigge's behaviour against Manchester City. For six months he talks against us every time for Financial Fair Play and he continues to say he hopes Napoli go through to the second stage. I don't know what's different with us. I think Manchester City are working for this FFP for the next two years. But I don't understand what's happening with Rummenigge. Tomorrow I will ask him." Mancini believes it is unfair to single out City, even though their progress in the three years since Mansour bought the club has been remarkable, "I think every team is worried about Manchester City because Manchester City in the future could become one of the top clubs in the world. But you don't want to see that every time an important man like Rummenigge who is the Bayern Munich chief executive and a representative of a top club in the world, every time he says things against us. Because there are other teams in Europe that have a problem with Financial Fair Play, not only Manchester City."

Jerome Boateng had no regrets about leaving the club having spent a season with City before returning to his native Germany. Boateng was frustrated at being deployed at full-back by Mancini but the German insisted that was not the only reason he left. "There were other reasons too. Obviously I've played at full-back at Bayern too but centre-back is my favourite position. I've been asked this question a thousand times but I'm happy at the club, and it really doesn't bother me if I'm played at full-back or centre-back."

Boateng felt the club was making good progress under Mancini. "I wouldn't say they are much different (to last season) but obviously a couple of quality players have been brought in. Last season they won the FA Cup and this season they are in the running for the title, although they are not doing so well in the Champions League. I think their coach is doing a very good job and the fans will be satisfied with that."

Wednesday, Dec 7, 2011

David Silva and Yaya Toure scored as City produced a fine attacking display to secure the win they required but Napoli's defeat of Villarreal sent them tumbling out of the Champions League. A 2-0 win at Villarreal secured Napoli's passage to the knockout phase by a point from City, who ended Group A with 10, normally enough to secure qualification.

Mancini planned to return stronger, admitting winning the league was made harder by playing in the Europa League on Thursdays, but insisted life was "not over"…far from it. Mancini said: "We will be back and we hope for better next year. We are a good team and we are sorry for our supporters and my players who deserve to play in the Champions League. But we need to improve. We got the hardest group, we knew that before the start. Our lives aren't finished now, we will go into the Europa League and it is an important trophy for Manchester City. We need to win more trophies. Maybe now we think that the Europa League is not important but, if you arrive in the final, it is very important. I've never won the Europa League. Usually with 10 points you always go through, 99% of the time. It was a tough group and we made some mistakes but that can happen and the game in Naples did it. Congratulations to Napoli."

Both Manchester clubs crashed out in dramatic circumstances. United needed just a draw in Basle, but suffered a 2-1 defeat and were now set for the humiliation of playing in the Europa League. For City, with 10 points, one more than United, it seemed less a humiliation, more a huge disappointment. Vastly different for United, as Sir Alex looked grim faced with anger, while Mancini was resigned to wasting their chances against Naples, a shaky start he felt was understandable, but didn't produce in Naples, which he felt cost them qualification. Regarding United's shock exit, Mancini said: "It is strange for United to go out. We are not United or Bayern Munich or Real Madrid. For us to win the Europa League is an important trophy. It is clear we wanted to win the Champions League but this is not possible. The Europa League is now an important trophy. The Premier League is the priority – and the Europa League, Carling Cup, FA Cup. I think if we are lucky and we don't have a lot of injuries in the future, we have a team that can play all competitions."

Asked how the Manchester clubs being in the Europa League would affect them at home, Mancini said: "I think it doesn't change anything because we play both in the Europa League. The difference is that maybe the Europa League is more hard because we play Thursday and maybe we don't have a lot of time to recover for the games. Only this. We are disappointed, that is normal. We wanted to go into the second stage and now we can do nothing. It is my opinion next year, that if we play Champions League, we will do better. I am sure we will improve, but it is important to finish well this year. When I say finish well this year, I mean to maybe win two trophies. In the Champions League you know that every game is difficult. If you meet a team that is maybe not as strong as you, and if you don't play those games 100%, you concede goals. We can improve on this. I think we did well and I also think we were unlucky because in Naples we didn't deserve to lose. But this is football. You can play well but if you concede two goals you have to take more risks. In the Champions League you can't concede many goals, you must pay attention every game. You should arrive at the last game and it should depend on you – if you win you go through. We arrived in the last game depending on Naples and this is difficult."

Bayern coach Jupp Heynckes believes it will take City "years" to develop into a side who can compete at European level, "It takes a team years to develop at this level. City had a lot of new players in a short space of time but Roberto Mancini is slowly getting it together in terms of forming a good team. But in football today it takes time to develop. Good progress is being made but it will take experience and time."

Former Arsenal and Germany goalkeeper Jens Lehmann was very dismissive of Manchester City claiming that people "don't want to see" them in the Champions League. He commented, "Man City play very, very boring football. They just make their opponents fall asleep with lots of possession But to be honest, that is not tactically very demanding. The way they play here is the way any amateur team plays, only not on such good grass. They just pack men behind the ball, have five against two and just move the ball around. The goal then just comes from a fortunate circumstance." Lehmann, who played in the Champions League final for Arsenal against Barcelona in 2006, albeit for only 18 minutes before being sent off, was also unimpressed by the atmosphere at the Etihad Stadium. "There was no life in the stadium," he said. "It was dead. The fans are so quiet. You have got to say, though, that they have not got anything really to get excited about here. They had possession all of the time, albeit in their own half where nothing was happening. It is a shame because it is not typical English football. Napoli have heart and passion and I liked them. It is good that they have gone through. We don't want to see Manchester City in the Champions League."

Mancini responded diplomatically, "I don't know about this but I think we should respect every opinion. I remember him as a fantastic keeper in Italy, he was incredible."

Thursday, Dec 8, 2011

City acknowledged receipt of an offer from Milan for Tévez.

Richard Desmond's Channel 5 were licking their lips at the prospect of an advertising windfall with increased viewers expected when United and City joined the Europa League. The average viewing of last year's Europa matches was about 1.4m, should United and City reach the final, more than 6m would be expected to tune in, a record for 5's Europa coverage, and the most since the 2003 Liverpool versus Celtic quarter final tie. United or City should attract a 3m audience in the early part of the knockout phase, and 4-5m viewers if they make the semi-final.

Harry Redknapp suggested that being offered a place in the Europa League after failing in the elite competition is like being handed a Carling Cup semi-final spot as reward for being knocked out of the FA Cup.

Fri, Dec 9, 2011

Nigel de Jong insisted lifting the League trophy was always City's top target and the club are on course as City returned to domestic action on Monday night in a high-profile clash with a resurgent Chelsea at Stamford Bridge and the match should provide a good indicator of City's title-winning potential. David Silva and Juan Mata would be putting their friendship to one side. Chelsea hit a patch of form but were still 10 points off the title pace. "He's my friend. He's doing very well, playing for Man City and I will change my shirt with him," Mata said. "This season has been very, very good for him because he's showing his level. Man City are having a great Premier League. There are so many weeks until the Premier League finishes. We will keep going every week to win and to be closest to the leader." Asked whether Chelsea could still catch City at the top, Mata said: "I think it is not impossible for us. They have a big points advantage but I think it is not impossible. If we win against City we will have more confidence and the Premier League does not finish for another six months. Nothing is impossible. It will be very difficult for City to keep winning every game, so for us and the other teams, we just have to hope that they stop winning. So no, we do not have any fear of Manchester City, especially because we're playing at home in this match but we do have the ultimate respect for them because they're the league leaders. Fear, though? Not at all."

Petr Cech pin-pointed the brilliance of his City opposite number, "City's main strength is their midfield and attack, but they still concede chances and Joe Hart has been having a very good season. They do concede chances at the back – defending is not their strongest point. So far they have been converting chances but who knows whether they can keep scoring goals like this."

Cech challenged Daniel Sturridge to show City they were wrong to let him go to Stamford Bridge in 2009. Mancini's final act of last season was to seek out Sturridge in the tunnel at Bolton, where he was on loan, and ask him: "Why did you leave Manchester City?" Sturridge would not have been allowed to walk away from City had Mancini been in charge. "It was strange because Sturridge was developed in Manchester and someone let him go," said Mancini. "For sure he was one of the best young players at City. It was not difficult to see he was a good player. If Sturridge was here today, he'd be in the first team. I've watched him many times and know him well. When we played Bolton last year [where Sturridge was on loan from Chelsea], I asked him why he had left City. He said he didn't know. It would have been better for City to send him on loan to improve than let him leave altogether."

His uncle, Dean Sturridge, whose professional career included spells with Wolves and Leicester – where he briefly played alongside Mancini – says his nephew was not appreciated by senior figures at City, who were intoxicated by the millions coming in from Abu Dhabi. "I still think he has City in his heart and, in different circumstances, he may have ended up staying there," said Dean. "But City didn't value him as much as other clubs, and I mean in footballing terms. City were in transition at the time and he was not made to feel important in the big scheme of things." City had not missed Sturridge this season, averaging more than three goals per game in the league, with Agüero, Dzeko and Mario in top form. But Chelsea were still in the Champions League while City went out.

Samir Nasri was in no doubt where City's biggest challenge will come from in the coming months. "Man United are still the threat to us. I say that because they have more experience than any other team. It will be difficult when we play Chelsea, of course, but we knew it would also be difficult going to places like Spurs, Man United and Liverpool — and we had great results against those teams. So I don't know what we have to fear about Chelsea.'

He has become a more rounded player since he moved to City and although always grateful for Arsene Wenger's influence, under Mancini he felt he had improved, "I had six assists last year with Arsenal. I have already had the same number with City. I have learned new things tactically, you know? Tactically the Italians are very strong. The manager here is really into his tactics. He knows how he wants us to defend and so you always know where you have to be when we lose the ball. Mancini told me that I already knew how to attack because that's what I did with Arsenal. The important thing wasn't to work on what I did going forward but to show me what I had to do defensively. I still know that I have to improve that part of my game. But I am only 24, so I can improve a lot. Mancini is never happy with the result. Even when we won 5-1 he was angry because he wanted a clean sheet as well as three points. The players agree with him. We know that if we want to be one of the biggest teams in the world we need to defend as a unit. It doesn't matter whether I play, or it is David, James or Adam, we have to help our defenders."

Chelsea know from their own experience that large deficits can be overhauled. Mancini said: "Last year Chelsea had a big lead over Manchester United but in the end United won the title by seven or eight points plus. The Premier League is very difficult and in these two months, all the teams that play every three days will find it difficult. I think they can win it. They have 10 points less than us but we play two times against them and there are 24 games until the end of the season."

Mancini backed rival manager Andres Villas-Boas to deliver despite a rocky start since succeeding Mancini's compatriot Carlo Ancelotti in the summer, "I think that has shown in the last year he is a good manager. He did well at Porto, he won trophies. Chelsea did well to get him. Carlo Ancelotti is a fantastic manager and I was sorry for him when Chelsea decided to sack him, but I think Villas-Boas is a good manager for them."

Mancini took over almost two years ago and for a long time had to contend with speculation over his future. The supporters are behind him and exit from the Champions League has been met with pragmatism. Mancini said: "I think the City fans are fantastic. They are very positive about the team always, if we win in the Premier League or lose in the Champions League. This is an important situation between us and the supporters."

Mancini expects his players to learn from their Champions League disappointment. Mancini said: "I think every player thinks like me, and this is important. It is important to win and we need to be stronger in our mentality. In this moment when you have lost and you are disappointed, and there are some people who continue to criticise, it is important for us to work more.'

Saturday, Dec 10, 2011

Daniele De Rossi remained a top target for January with Mancini aware of the Roma midfield stars potential availability. City had no plans to replace Tévez until the end of the season when they will go for top target Arsenal's Robin van Persie. Mancini wanted a top-class centre-half but it was tough to find the right player in mid season. Mancini's main concern was that Yaya will potentially spend a month at the Africa Cup of Nations, which starts on 21 January, and that a difficult winter schedule on harder pitches could mean more injuries. So far, City had been fortunate in that respect, certainly more so than United, but Mancini did not want to leave anything to chance. De Rossi is a player Mancini coveted for a long time, and enquired about his availability in the summer, but was told a transfer was not possible.

City were also targeting young, up-and-coming players, Wilfried Zaha, the 19-year-old Crystal Palace forward. Mancini discussed the teenager behind the scenes, monitoring his progress closely. Zaha, an England Under-19 striker, caught the eye during Palace's Carling Cup win at United, and been watched by City on numerous occasions.

Reports that City agreed a £21 million deal to sell Tévez to Paris Saint-Germain were denied by the club. City knew Tévez wanted to join AC Milan, but City owner Sheik Mansour has a close relationship with the Qatari owners of the French club. My sources told me that City continued to demand a 'fair market price' for Tévez, or he would remain on the clubs books for the rest of the season even if he never kicks a ball again for them. That 'fair market price' was around 35 million euros, which made AC Milan's offer of 24 million euros well short of the likely threshold at which City would sell. Such was the incredible animosity behind the scenes that City dug their heels in. AC Milan emailed an offer to City to take Tévez on loan until the summer when a permanent transfer would kick in at 24m euros. That was instantly rejected on two accounts. Firstly, City were not contemplating any loan agreement, particularly AC Milan's loan deal without any fee attached, and then a permanent deal at the end of the season. Secondly the AC Milan valuation was well short. PSG were trying to lure Beckham, and backed by the wealthy Qatar owners also wanted Tévez, but so far there had not been a bid. City remained determined that Tévez's behaviour will not force the price down. A source close to the Tévez transfer action told me: "The club have not received a bid from PSG, let alone accepted a bid. The club are seeking a fair market price for Tévez, and as yet no one has made an offer that reflects the fair market value for the player. The club have all along made it clear, also, that it has no interest in any loan deal for Tévez, the manager has said it publicly and that is most definitely still the case."

Clarence Seedorf did not think Tévez would join AC Milan because he expected the striker to join the club which can "promise him the most money". With PSG offering Tévez a better salary than the Serie A side, Milan midfielder Seedorf admitted he was not expecting the Argentine to arrive at the San Siro in January. "Looking back at his career, his agents and every move he has ever made, I think Tévez will go where they can promise him the most money. Milan would be the first time in his life that he has chosen a club for his career rather than the money. We'll see what happens."

Reports in Italy claimed Milan were ready to offer Pato or Robinho to City as part of a swap deal. Galliani ruled out that possibility. "I reiterate that Pato and Robinho will not leave the club." Galliani added, "I know that there was a meeting between the player's agent and Manchester City this morning, but I don't know the outcome. We'll wait for Tévez until the last hour of the transfer window unless he signs for another club before then. Tévez is our first choice and you know what Milan's position is, that of the player and Manchester City. We know that the player wants to come – we just hope he doesn't agree terms with anyone else. We have up until 18:59 on January 31 to close the deal."

Mario Balotelli faced the wrath of Mancini after preparing for Monday night's crucial game with a late night curry that ended in the early hours of Sunday morning. Mario was out until at least 12.45am in Manchester city centre after a night out with friends. City declined to comment, but confirmed that first-team players are not expected to be socialising less than 48 hours before a game. Mancini has a more relaxed attitude than some managers, but he was unimpressed with another lapse in discipline from Mario, even though his player was not drinking alcohol in the Zouk Bar and Restaurant, and was happy to sign autographs and pose for pictures, described by one eye witness as behaving 'boisterously' with a group of friends. He is even reported to have staged a mock sword fight with a friend – using a rolling pin. City had their last training session before the clash in west London on Sunday morning, so Mario did not have had a full night's sleep beforehand. Mancini does not have a problem with players enjoying a mid-evening meal out in the run-up to a game. However, he views a night out that ends in the early hours as a step too far.

Mancini went to extraordinary lengths to accommodate the striker and there was times recently when he appeared to be listening. Although Mario's attitude improved, Mancini joked recently that it might be better for the striker to move in with him and live in the basement.

Monday, Dec 12, 2011

Roberto Mancini disagreed with two penalty decisions as City's 14-game unbeaten league run came to an end with a 2-1 defeat by Chelsea. City were in apparent command and leading 1-0 when they were denied a penalty after Silva was tripped while Lescott's handball allowed Chelsea to score a late winner. "The referee was too close to decide this and probably didn't see it," Mancini said of Silva's claim. "He saw very well their penalty, he was really sure. I don't agree with him." Bosingwa caught Silva just inside the penalty area as City's midfielder tried to skip past him but referee Mark Clattenburg, who was just a few yards away, waved play on. "It was probably because it was raining and cold that he didn't see the penalty because all the stadium saw the penalty, only he missed it," Mancini added. If the Silva penalty had been awarded, probably the game was finished. After the sending off it was a different match."

Frank Lampard came off the bench to earn Chelsea a vital win which puts them third, seven points behind Mancini's league leaders. Lampard scored after Lescott was penalised for handling the ball following Sturridge's shot. Before that, City were reduced to 10 men on the hour when Clichy received his second yellow card and they failed to hang onto a point after Raul Meireles equalised following Mario Ballotelli's brilliant second-minute opener.

Mancini bemoaned his side's inability to score more than one goal in a first half they dominated for long periods, and admitted that the sending off was the turning point. "I think we deserved to score two or three goals in the first half because we did a fantastic performance but in football if you don't score you can lose and after the sending off it was difficult to play. Chelsea played better when we had 10 players and before that they didn't take any risks. I think we are strong enough for the next game and I hope we can do another 14 games without defeat. December and January will be crucial months for us and it was important not to lose this game. The season is very long, and all the teams can play for the title."

Ashley Cole was accused of sparking a tunnel skirmish by hurling an aggressive 'Have That!' comment towards the visitors' dressing room, provoking an angry response from City's players after the final whistle. Cole mocked Mancini and his players with the chant: "Thursday night, Channel 5". Stamford Bridge had reverberated with fan chants of the same taunt. The jubilant Chelsea players formed a post-match huddle on the pitch before heading down the tunnel. There, they found Mancini and his backroom staff remonstrating with Clattenburg over two controversial penalty decisions. As the Chelsea players passed, eyewitnesses claim, Cole shouted: "F*****g have some of that" and "Thursday night, Channel 5". City players reacted and stewards had to step in to push players towards their respective dressing rooms.

Chelsea reached the knockout stages of the Champions League for the ninth successive year the previous week when they beat Valencia to win Group E. Cole was in the Old Trafford tunnel for Pizzagate in October 2004 – when his Arsenal side's 49-match unbeaten record was ended by United and Sir Alex was hit by a piece of pizza thrown during a post-match row.

'I don't know if Cole said something,' said Mancini. "I didn't understand it but if the Chelsea players are saying we are a top team, for us that's really important. They were lively because they beat a top team."

Frank Lampard blamed the tunnel clash on the emotion of a pulsating game. "Sometimes you get overheated. Big games, big players who want to win things on both sides, and there was a bit of frustration. I've been involved in that before but there's general respect from both teams to each other."

The result left City just two points clear of United, who would leapfrog their neighbours if they win at QPR on Sunday lunchtime, four hours before the Blues entertain Arsenal.

"It doesn't change anything for us, because we knew before this we should lose a game at some point," said Mancini. "It is unusual that a team comes to Chelsea and plays like we did in the first half because we dominated the game. We didn't deserve to lose but we did. The season is very long and very hard. Now we should prepare for another difficult game, against Arsenal." Mancini urged his players to 'stay strong' following their first Premier League defeat of the season. "At this moment, we should be very strong. It is at these moments that you become stronger, as players and a team. For this reason, the result is a lesson for us."

The immediate impact of Clichy's dismissal is to deprive the full-back of a meeting with his former club at the weekend. It also triggered yet another personnel switch in an area of the field where City struggled for continuity. It extended an unhappy run of red cards to three in six games. "We are disappointed but now it is in the past," said James Milner, "The positive side is that we have another game coming up. We will be back in tomorrow, working as hard as we can. If it was possible to give even more then we would. The hunger is still there. If anything, there is even more incentive to bounce back with an even bigger performance at the weekend."

Graham Poll argued, "Manchester City should have been awarded a penalty when David Silva was clearly tripped by Jose Bosingwa midway through the first half. Silva's trickery fooled the Portuguese defender and the contact was clear. Mark Clattenburg had a good, unobstructed view but waved aside City's appeals, perhaps unsure of the contact. Chelsea also benefited from Clattenburg not seeing a poor Meireles tackle on Silva which escaped an obvious yellow card. Meireles was later cautioned for a reckless tackle on Zabaleta. However, two rash challenges from Clichy on Sturridge both correctly resulted in yellow cards."

Tuesday, Dec 13, 2011

Mario Ballotelli's latest escapade involved pinching a pair of gloves belonging to Sergio Agüero during the Chelsea game. Balotelli was caught by the TV cameras, even if Kun was oblivious to it. He even bit out the label from inside one of the gloves. Mario was just 'warming up' ahead of City's Christmas party after the game - when he arrived dressed as a bandit. There was also Batman, Darth Vader and Where's Wally? They were among the stars of City's Xmas bash. The team put the defeat behind them by partying at a trendy London nightclub until the early hours of Tuesday morning. The guest list read like a who's who of the TV/Cartoon/film world; Avatar, The Mask, Kermit the Frog, Iron Man, a Roman Centurion, a pirate. Mario was dressed as a Wild West bandit. Mancini was nowhere to be seen as the players partied at Anaya nightclub in Mayfair as Mario was joined by Nasri, Yaya and Kolo, Hart, Agüero, Hargreaves, Zabaleta and de Jong. Lescott explains the Iron Man costume. "we had to draw a letter and go as a character with that letter, so obviously it was the letter I for me".

Yaya escaped FA punishment for his kick and slap aimed at Juan Mata that appeared to turn the tide of the match. Mark Clattenburg saw the first incident and decided to take no action and the FA declined to press charges after reviewing video evidence. Yaya started every league game this season, and, with a number of crucial matches in January, Mancini contacted the Ivory Coast manager Francois Zahoui to see if the player's departure could be delayed as he could be at the Cup of Nations in Equatorial Guinea and Gabon, which started in mid-January, for up to a month.

Yaya said: "The Africa Cup of Nations is a fantastic tournament but this is a crucial time of the season. The team, the club and the manager need me but I have to go away and play in a different competition. It's difficult as I am very focused for City. My country needs people like me and Didier Drogba at the moment. We have fantastic players at City who can take my place. I want to come back and help us win the league."

QPR launched an ambitious bid to sign Nigel de Jong on loan as he had not started a Premier League game for City since November, but did appear as a substitute in the defeat at Chelsea. De Jong's contract expired at the end of next season and wanted the club to offer him a new deal. But with Yaya off to the African Nations, Mancini would not let him leave.

Dennis Tueart remained optimistic despite the defeat, "I've got a good feeling this season but I'm fully aware there will be curveballs along the way. It's how we cope with them and handle whatever disruption we come up against. City fans can see that success is possible but, understandably, they won't believe it until it's actually there."

Wednesday, Dec 14, 2011

Chelsea denied Cole taunted City's players. "Contrary to reports, Ashley Cole did not say anything to the opposition in the tunnel after Monday's game," a Chelsea spokesman said. "Ashley has huge respect for the players and staff at Manchester City, many of whom he knows personally and calls friends." Andre Villas-Boas offered a swift denial of Cole's involvement, saying: "It's untrue and it's unfair. It really doesn't matter now."

Harry Redknapp wanted Carlos Tévez on loan, which was never going to happen, not even the Spurs boss believed it could happen, 'He is a special player, the type of player who could make the difference, but I wouldn't think that's a real possibility.' A French radio station claimed that the Argentina striker's representatives had met with PSG earlier. My City sources informed me that there was no approach from Tottenham, and they didn't expect one, and that PSG only made a tentative enquiry in the initial aftermath of the Bayern fall out, and had not been back with an official offer since. "French radio were reporting a meeting between the player's advisors and PSG on Monday night when nothing of the sort was going on, and in fact we were at the Chelsea game" a City insider told me. "There has been media speculation that City have agreed a fee with PSG - again, there is nothing going on."

Milan owner Silvio Berlusconi said his club was Tévez's only option, if he can forget about the lure of money for once. Berlusconi was scathing in his assessment of the situation, as he insisted it should not be about cash, but credibility. "Tévez has to choose between the prestige that AC Milan represents, or the money of the PSG, led by the Sheikh of Qatar. AC Milan is a solution of prestige, with the possibility of playing in one of the biggest clubs in the world. If he comes with us, he will win the Ballon d'Or award. Tévez has two options, one which regards prestige and the other one money. He must choose between one or the other." Juventus were in official talks with City, according to a report that Juve director Pavel Nedved was in direct phone contact with Mancini and that the Turin side proposed a £21m deal.

Tévez enjoyed his extended holiday taking to the stage at an Argentine night club for a duet with a Latin American Noddy Holder type as a YouTube video of him crooning with a Latin pop star showed. In the video, an animated Tévez joins Juan Carlos Jimenez Rufino on stage at the nightclub in Cordoba. Tévez is cheered as Jimenez talks about City. Carlos cracked up with laughter as a musician pal joked about City's Euro failure after inviting him on stage to sing. Tévez laughed loudest as crooner abused City by ranting, "Que se caguen!" ie "F★★★ them".

Thursday, Dec 15, 2011

Mario Balotelli was involved in a training-ground confrontation with Micah Richards, towards the end of a practice match. Witnesses reported words were exchanged before the two players squared up. Richards, aggrieved by what had been said, was restrained by other players as he sought to prolong the argument. The incident was described as "minor" behind the scenes at City, where it has been stressed that it was quickly forgotten once the players had returned to the dressing room. Richards and Mario get on well, and Richards later Tweeted: "Me & mario are all good! these things happen in training & we shook hands after. It shows passion!"

Mario was involved in other training ground clashes, lashing out at Boateng after reacting badly to a challenge, while Adebayor and Kolo were photographed rolling around the floor during another fight and, with Mario photographed clashing with Kompany in May.

The perception that Roberto Mancini has assembled one of the more combustible squads was refuted by City, who pointed out that these kinds of incidents happen at other clubs, the difference being photographers can get easier access at their Carrington base because of a public footpath that runs by the side of the pitches. The club were putting up new fences in an attempt to keep out the cameras.

Mario and Richards 'squared up' in the dressing room at their training ground to pose for a picture taken 24 hours before the pair had a real bust-up during training. Richards regularly works out in the boxing area of the gym on a punch bag. As for that Mario bust up, "There's always going to be arguments because we've 25 very good players and players aren't going to be happy when they don't play," said Richards, having paid a visit with Mario and other team-mates to Manchester Children's Hospital 24 hours before the high-profile row, "But our team spirit is unbelievable, probably one of the best I've experienced at City."

City's next opponents Arsenal were in inspired form since losing four of their opening seven Premier League matches, taking 22 points from a possible 24. Kompany, speaking after a visit to the Royal Manchester Children's Hospital, believed the defeat at Stamford Bridge would spur the league leaders on. "We want Sunday to come as quickly as possible because that's the kind of team we are. We don't like to lose and for a team playing away at Chelsea we showed a lot of courage, especially in the first half. We were unlucky not to be up by more at half-time. But that game has been played now and there is nothing we can do about it. I definitely have a lot of respect for Arsenal. The way they have picked themselves up after a difficult month has been incredible. They are a top team and will make a top game of it but at home we still feel as if we are a strong and difficult team to beat. Even when we haven't won this season we have looked the team that was more likely to win."

Mark Hughes paid big money for Joleon Lescott, but he had to prove himself all over again. "I was definitely looking over my shoulder for a while, when Roberto Mancini arrived. He brought in Jerome Boateng the summer after he arrived, and that was a real test for me. This time last season I wasn't in the team, and I couldn't argue because the team was playing well. There were Kolo Toure and Micah Richards vying for places as well in centre of defence and it didn't look great for me. But I always wanted to be there, and when the manager eventually gave me my opportunity I knew I had to grab it with both hands. Although the circumstances weren't great, because of Kolo's suspension, thankfully I took my chance."

Lescott added, "If teams like Chelsea are seeing us as a big scalp then it can only be good for us. We took it as a compliment – not as a sign of disrespect. We saw them go into a huddle [of celebration] on the pitch at the end and we had heard their manager say that if they didn't win then their title hopes were over. That's not the case now, but we're still top of the league and that's where we intend to stay. We could see it meant so much to them, and Chelsea, like the other teams, know if they do finish above us they are going to have a great chance of winning the league. And that is a massive compliment to us. They was supposed to have said something – I was already in the dressing room, so I didn't see what was going on in the tunnel, but I wouldn't be surprised. We are not fazed by that. We're going into that competition looking to win it and if we do win, then it's a major accomplishment for the club. But the title is what we are aiming at."

Lescott believes his boss has transformed the club. "There were always going to be doubters at first when the manager arrived. But he has been so professional with us and he has made the club progress. We won the FA Cup last year and we're doing well in the league this season and other competitions so it is a good time. He's very demanding. If he's not happy with what you are doing in games, he'll show it in training; he'll show where you're going wrong. We tend to do a lot of work in training on the tactical side so that when situations do occur in games we can deal with them. Even when we've won 5-1 he's not happy with the goal we conceded. He says it's a gift and that we like to give the other team a present, stuff like that. He has made us progress, and that is what the club needed."

Fri, Dec 16, 2011

City could begin Sunday's home game against Arsenal as the League's second-placed club. United play at QPR earlier and will go top if they win. Arsenal hadn't lost in the league since October 2 and a win would bring them within six points of City.

While Arsene Wenger has not won a trophy for six years, Mancini hailed the Frenchman as a great. "In Italy I think it would be impossible to go six years without winning anything. But here in England there is more respect for the manager. For a manager like Wenger who has won so many trophies for Arsenal it's different. In football, if you win you are great and if you don't you are not. Football is like this. But for me Wenger is still a great manager. You see how well the squad play. He lost a Champions League final against Barcelona and recently has been up against great Manchester United and Chelsea teams."

Mancini likes collecting Arsenal players and is increasingly determined to sign Van Persie next summer despite another battle to persuade Arsenal to sell, especially after the bitterness of the protracted and ultimately successful pursuit of Nasri. Mancini paid tribute to Van Persie's form, 23 goals in 25 appearances for club and country this season. Mancini said: "Van Persie is incredible. He is like Sergio Agüero here for us. At the moment he is fantastic. To score all those goals is incredible."

Mancini was forthright in his view of Nasri's unspectacular progress since his signing. "I think that, in my opinion, Nasri is a champion. He's a top player but I think that he needs to do more. He can do more. Maybe when I change the team it gives some players a problem. He didn't play against Manchester United or against Chelsea, for example. Maybe he doesn't understand the situation, I don't know. Sometimes this happens with players. I would like him to play better. I have spoken with him about it, I think it was after Naples. Maybe he finds it hard to understand the situation and I think at the moment his confidence is a bit low because he didn't play against Chelsea on Monday. But if he plays against Arsenal on Sunday he will have a chance to show the quality I know that he has."

Nasri began the season brightly, but endured a bad night during the 2-0 defeat at Bayern Munich in September, and was left out of Mancini's team for several crucial games. Mancini prefers Milner on the right of his midfield for more defensive security, the reason Milner was selected for the

6-1 win at United when he was his team's best player. Mancini said: "Nasri is an attacking player but he also has all the necessary things he needs to defend. When you play with two strikers and with David Silva, there are some situations in a game where the team need to defend. Over time, I do think Nasri will show his quality. I hope he can play more games because he is a top player."

Mancini was confident that his players can lift themselves after their first defeat at Chelsea, "I think that at these moments we should be strong. After one defeat, we can improve - we know what we can do, and in this moment we can become stronger. We have never had a problem bouncing back after a defeat, and I am sure we will do it again. We play Arsenal on Sunday and at the moment Arsenal are playing very well. It will be difficult but we need to start again. What is important is that we start to win again."

Mancini laughed off the latest Mario controversy, Mancini said, "I asked him, 'Why always you?' He said it was because he didn't pass the ball to him. It was a really stupid thing, it was nothing. After 10 minutes it was finished. When you play a match eight versus eight and you are passionate, it can happen with every team. Not every week, but often. Mario and Micah were boxing, but they are like twins. They are very good friends. These things happen but it is stupid. I used to always be involved in things like this when I was a player. Once (while at Sampdoria) with Trevor Francis. This has happened with Mario four times now - he is the king for this. But it has happened with other players. However, Mario should pay attention, not just about this, but in every situation. We are near Christmas, at the end of the year it is a very dangerous time for fireworks. It is better he stays in the hotel!"

The draw for the last-32 of the Europa League tied City with last year's winners FC Porto while Manchester United faced Ajax. Reflecting on City's Porto meeting, football administration officer Brian Marwood told Sky Sports News: "It's amazing, we've gone from the hardest group in the Champions League to getting the holders of the Europa League. It's a big game and we'll be looking forward to it. One thing we haven't had to endure is going through the early rounds where you play a lot of games. Porto are attractive opposition and the current champions. They are games we are looking forward to and are excited about."

Ashley Young revealed why he snubbed City to join United. He penned a five-year deal worth £130,000-a-week at the champions, after being offered even more cash to go to City. Asked about City's interest, Young replied: "That's true, but as soon as I heard about Manchester United there was no other club for me. It's Manchester United. They are the biggest club in the world, and I think if you ask anyone who they want to play for the majority will say: 'Man United.' The fan base, the team and what they have won in the past is [all] amazing. I want to be part of that – and be able to bring the title back to United again and make history with a 20th."

Young was hoping the festive fixtures enable United to turn up the heat on City, "I do believe we can win the title. We are this side of Christmas and have many games to play and points to play for. If we keep up the form we have shown from the start of the season, then I am sure we will be able to retain that title. There are going to be a lot of games to look forward to and we have to keep ourselves fresh and go into games confident. The manager instils that and we go out there and enjoy it."

Saturday, Dec 17, 2011

Arsene Wenger believed Arsenal would be right back in the title race if they beat leaders City, "We are on the way of recovery but we have a big, big test on Sunday. We have to get closer to Manchester City to be in it."

Ferguson indirectly 'insulted' City by suggesting spurs were playing the best football, "Tottenham have been the most impressive team. They were unlucky last Sunday at Stoke but if they win their game in hand they are still in there and for me, Spurs have been playing the best football in the Premier League for the last eight games. They look confident and dangerous and I have been very impressed with them. They have played some terrific football and they must be contenders now they are out of the Europa League, that will definitely help them. Tottenham will definitely be challenging and I also think that result Chelsea got the other night has given them a lift and also takes a wee bit of pressure off the situation, with all the rumours coming out of Stamford Bridge. If you want to win the league, you have to make sure you don't lose as many points as your rivals round about you. That's what the second half of the season will be about. We have a lot of tough games ahead – we have to go to Arsenal, Chelsea and City. Chelsea did the league a turn by beating City. It was a tough game for both teams and a draw might have been fairer, but it's always tough going to Chelsea. It was a wee bit of a bonus. Arsenal have been gathering pace the last few weeks and it's a big game for them at City. They will be able to do themselves a turn if they win. When you look at the start of the season you expect the four to be there – ourselves, Chelsea, City and Arsenal but now Spurs are right in there without a doubt."

Plans to fly City's jet over the Etihad Stadium were scrapped after it was realised it would be too dark for supporters to see the stunt. Etihad Airways, City's main sponsor, had planned a fly past. The plane stunt would have cost around £100,000 but the 4.10pm kick-off ensured Blue Moon Rising stayed on the ground. City had the plane since the summer but the Arsenal match was chosen to have a sly dig at the Gunners' sponsors Emirates, although City dismissed the claims. The A330-200 aircraft, emblazoned with the club's name and colours, was due to fly at about 2,500ft, directly over City's home and air traffic bosses had provisionally given it the go-ahead. Manchester Airport was also backing the fly past. But Etihad pulled the plug less than two weeks before the game. The fly past may go ahead later in the season when the days are a bit longer. An airport spokesman said: "With plenty of advance warning for local residents and permission from air traffic control, a fly-past of the Manchester City stadium could have been an eye-catching spectacle. But the likelihood of Manchester's low-lying, grey, December clouds combined with the nights drawing in risked lessening the impact, so the decision was made to postpone the idea for now." A City spokesman said: "The possibility of the branded City plane flying over the Etihad Stadium was explored for a Partnership event, not for the Arsenal or any other match fixture. It was shelved due to altitude limitations and the resulting reduced visibility."

Sunday, Dec 18, 2011

Following United's lunchtime win over QPR, City restored their two point advantage, ending Arsenal's unbeaten run of eight games while maintaining their 100% home record this season and unbeaten at the Etihad Stadium in 2011, having drawn just two of 28 games in the last year. David Silva pounced after Mario's shot was saved to score the only goal of the match. Sergio Agüero could have made the win more comfortable but fired over early on, while Zabaleta hit the post. Hart saved from Gervinho, Walcott and Ramsey. Van Persie could not find his 20th goal of the season, with a shot saved and a goal ruled out for offside.

Former Arsenal players Samir Nasri and Kolo Toure were named in the City line-up and Mancini took steps to secure the lead as the visitors looked for an equaliser and with the game entering the final stages. Mancini felt his players had come through a test of nerve after losing their unbeaten record at Chelsea, and knocked off the summit by United earlier in the day, 'I think we deserved to win this game. We had half a chance and Silva scored an important goal. We are on the top again. I am delighted for this because after Chelsea it was really important to beat Arsenal and go again to the top of the table, also because Arsenal are a really strong team at this moment.'

Mancini accepted City won't stay at the top permanently throughout the title race. "We know United are a really strong team and we can't think that we can win the title without fighting against United. We know it is possible we could go into the second position sometimes because when there are squads like us, United and Tottenham it can happen. But it is important we are there in the end."

When it was pointed out City could now be top at Christmas for the first time since 1929, Mancini said: "We want to stay at the top for a long time, not only Christmas."

Silva slid in his sixth goal of the season but Arsenal had a penalty appeal for handball against Richards turned down. Wenger said: "I haven't seen it, but Van Persie is adamant - 100 per cent penalty. It was a game where it could have gone both ways. It was very intense with both teams going for it. I felt we were a bit unlucky and their keeper had a good game."

The Gunners trailed City by 12 points. Wenger accepted it would be hard for Arsenal to get into title contention. "It will be difficult to close the gap on City, but we will try. This is a game we couldn't afford to lose and that's why it's difficult to take. Let's hope we can continue our progress and get closer to City."

Prior to the game there had been yet another rumour about Mario - that he was out in Manchester the night before dressed as Father Christmas, handing out money to passers-by. Mancini said: "I don't know - with Mario it is possible! We should ask him. It could be, I don't know. But he was in the hotel and it was forbidden to bring fireworks!"

Monday, Dec 19, 2011

Roberto Mancini hoped Wayne Bridge, who made only one appearance this season, would leave in January, "I don't understand why there are some players that have a chance to go and play, and don't. Wayne is a good guy but I hope he leaves in January." Bridge cost City £10m when he joined in 2007, but made just 40 league starts for the club. Mancini was keen to move him on as he was behind Clichy, Kolarov and Zabaleta. Bridge rejected a move to Celtic in the summer. "I don't know why you would want to stay at a club where you can't play," Mancini said. "He has a chance, maybe not in the Premier League but in the Championship. When we are young and start to play football we don't play for money, we play because we like football. Every player should have this target in mind - to play football. Wayne is a good guy, but he had two or three chances in the summer, including Celtic, who are an important team. He trains with us sometimes and sometimes with the young players but I hope, for him, he leaves in January because it's difficult for a player to stay training every day." Asked how Bridge spends his Saturdays now, Mancini said: "Golf?" A joke, maybe, but Wayne didn't see the amusing side.....

City revived interest in Lille's Eden Hazard. The 20-year-old, a long-term target for Arsenal, was watched by Vieira and reports out of France say City were willing to sign the Belgium midfielder in a £30m deal and loan him back, if need be. Mancini was concerned by Nasri's performances prior to last Sunday's game against his former club Arsenal. Real and Inter showed interest in Hazard, who wanted out of Lille, but Athletic Bilbao's Javi Martinez and Everton's Jack Rodwell, heavily linked to Chelsea, were also considered.

Mancini admitted he may be forced into the January transfer market on account of the loss of Kolo and Yaya, "I can say we can have a big problem for Kolo and Yaya, because we lose them for one month," Mancini said in response to whether he would look to boost his squad in January. Ahead of his side's clash with Stoke, he added: "In this month we play every difficult games. It is a crucial month."

Tuesday Dec 20, 2011

City have only lost once in the league, scoring 50 goals in 16 games, but United remained just two points behind despite an injury crisis and the loss for the rest of the season of captain Nemanja Vidic.

United complained to the FA about the number of tickets they were granted for next month's FA Cup tie at City. Under FA rules, United were entitled to an allocation equivalent to 15% of the ground capacity, which would be 7,100 tickets. Instead, City offered 5,500 – exactly the same as United were granted for the first leg of the Carling Cup semi-final two years ago. City refused on the grounds that it would constitute a safety risk, so the FA were asked to intervene. The issue came to light over discussions about the tie, and the potential for a replay. United would not offer City 15% of Old Trafford's capacity for that. However, they do have special dispensation from the FA due to the size of their stadium and City would be allocated 8,500 tickets – just over 11% of Old Trafford's 76,000 capacity. The row heighten the atmosphere around a tie which will see the pair – currently first and second in the Premier League – meet at City in the FA Cup for the first time since 1955.

Wednesday, Dec 21, 2011

On Mancini's anniversary of the second year in charge, City beat Stoke 3-0 to remain two points clear of United and ensure they are top at Christmas for the first time since 1929. Mancini set a target of 90 points to land the title, "We are happy. I am happy for our supporters. They can have a good Christmas Day. But as I said many times, it's important to stay top at the end of the season. For this, it is difficult. United continue to win every game, the other teams continue to win, Arsenal, Tottenham. But it is better to stay on the top than second. If we want to win the championship we should get 90 points because Manchester United keep winning."

United won their record 19th Premier League with 80 points and their 5-0 win at Fulham kept them within touching distance of the leaders. The last time the top flight was won with 90 points was in the 2008-09 season, when United finished four clear of Liverpool. Two goals from Agüero and a fine Johnson strike ensured City remained unbeaten at home in 2011. Mancini added, "January is an important month. We will have a lot of games and we lose two important players like Yaya Toure and Kolo Toure and I hope we are lucky and don't get any injuries."

Mancini believed City were singled out for the same special attention by rivals that United had been used to down the years, "It is the same thing that happens against Manchester United. All the teams that play against them play with fear. They don't attack because for a long time, United were a top team and it was very difficult. Probably now, also against us, some teams have a problem and play in a different way."

Stoke boss Tony Pulis felt City would live to regret their early Champions League exit, "They must be distraught they are out of the Champions League. I thought they would have run that very close this year, never mind the Premier League. They are real contenders for every competition they are in. The depth of their squad and the quality they have got is what you would expect after spending £240 million, or whatever it is.'

City had dropped only seven points since the season began and scored an impressive 53 goals in 17 games. Yet, United remained just two points behind and Barry admitted City could not afford to ease up. When asked if City were becoming the complete side, having also kept successive clean sheets, Barry said: "You hope so - but you make those quotes at the end of the season, hopefully with trophies"

Thursday, Dec 22, 2011

City were given the go-ahead to build a new multi-million pound football academy and training campus, the scope of which is unparalleled in British football based on an 80-acre brownfield site next to the Etihad Stadium in Openshaw, incorporating 17 pitches and a 7,000 capacity stadium for youth matches. Manchester City Council planning and highways committee passed the plans, allowing City to group all of their football functions in the same east Manchester location. Chief football operations officer, Brian Marwood, said: "It is important to also make clear that the development and recruitment of youth talent is at the heart of our long term strategy of building a successful and sustainable football club for the future." The development will include a home for around 400 youth players, allowing them to train with senior players and study at the same time. In addition to this, sleeping accommodation and classroom facilities for 40 young players will also be constructed. There will be a bridge linking the Etihad Stadium and the rest of the Etihad Campus, which will contain a dedicated media centre and staff offices, a new building for the first team with a gym, rehab centre, changing rooms and a refectory. Playing facilities will be more than adequately covered too – 11 full-size youth development pitches and one half-size one will form part of the development, alongside 4 full-size first team pitches and one half-size field. The development will be a tremendous boost for a club planning to make its mark on world football, and a massive triumph for youth development prospects at City.

Fri, Dec 23, 2011

Sir Alex Ferguson performed his predictable mind games, but everyone was wise to them. Fergie said: "Yes, money can buy success as we saw when Chelsea suddenly became cash rich and we are witnessing a similar surge by Manchester City under their wealthy owners. Their transfer clout has taken them to the top of the league and they are favourites to win the title. But, while recruiting some of the world's leading players can lift you into contention for honours, it doesn't necessarily take you all the way — as I hope we will be able to demonstrate before the end of the season as other factors come into play."

Mancini, though, had more practical problems to concern his mind with, a schedule that would test any club's resources, even with the wealth of options available, he faced tricky decisions. Yaya started all 17 league games this season while Kompany started 16, Silva and Agüero 15. Silva featured as a substitute in the two he missed, Agüero in one. All four played all six Champions League games. With trips to West Brom and Sunderland, both teams growing in confidence in recent games, Mancini was wary of tampering with this core of his team.

Mancini wanted Agüero to hit the 30 goal mark this season, "I hope Sergio can score 30 goals. He is very strong physically. He is not tall but his strength is amazing. Also, he has always scored goals in every championship. For this reason I don't think he has had any problems. He is still only young and maybe now his value is even more because he has scored 15 goals in three or four months. He has the confidence to score even more but what is important at the moment is that he has improved our team."

Spurs were still in the race, argued Emmanuel Adebayor, as he cast doubt on City's ability to last the pace. The 27-year-old striker was on a season-long loan from City to Spurs, who wanted him on a permanent deal but could hardly afford it. "Of course Tottenham are still in the race. Man City are top at the moment, but they have to play all the big clubs. We are only halfway through. Can they keep playing the way they are playing until the end of the season? We will have to wait and see. They have Kolo and Yaya Touré going to the African Cup of Nations, so we have to see how they cope. They have got a great team and great spirit and are playing great football. But if they get a couple of injuries as well, it could be difficult." City were still subsidising a large chunk of his £170,000-a-week wages. He scored in the previous week's 1-1 draw against Chelsea, an encounter which confirmed Spurs' top-four credentials and left them in third place — their highest position going into Christmas since 1984.

Yaya Toure was named the 2011 African footballer of the year, establishing himself as a key player in the City team. A statement on the Confederation of African Football's official website read: "The 28-year-old pipped Ghanaian midfielder Andre Ayew and Malian Seydou Keita to scoop the top-most honour at the awards gala on Thursday at the Banquet Hall, State House in Accra." He is only the second Ivorian to win the award since its inception in 1992, following in the footsteps of the Drogba. The award was voted for by the head coaches of the national teams in Africa.

Saturday, Dec 24, 2011

City were top at Christmas for the first time in 82 years, looking to maintain their advantage when they visit West Brom on Monday. Mancini told his players that they must be mentally prepared to fall behind United during the course of the title race if they were to succeed in deposing their rivals as champions. "I think we've got more chance if we have that attitude. I've told the guys that we can be second for three or four games, and go one or two points behind United. But it won't change anything. We know that United have to play many games away and we can recover points in those moments. I think we are strong enough to stay on the top. We also know we can go into second position at some time. There are more than 20 games until the end. But it's important we stay there and continue to play well and believe in ourselves. When you are a strong team and you have a difficult moment you pull together and use it to stay where you are. United are very strong like that. I'm sure we'll continue to do well but we know that if we want to win this league we need to play well to the end and beat them at home."

Mancini predictably was in no festive mood to lord it over United. "It's a good omen to be top at Christmas but it would be better if United lost three games," he joked. "I think we are strong enough to stay on top, but we know that can change. There are 20 games to the end. In Italy when you're on the top at Christmas then you usually win it, but here it's different.'

Mancini confirmed new players will only arrive in January if some of the dead wood is cleared first – "We need to sell two or three players and then we'll see" – but in the meantime he will need Dzeko, Johnson and de Jong to make important contributions, 'We want to sell and after that we may have time to buy someone if it's possible. But it's not easy. I ask the owner for Messi but it's not possible!'

Wayne Bridge retorted to acidic remarks from Mancini about playing golf, "Roberto Mancini obviously doesn't know me very well because I don't play golf. When I was at Chelsea I was playing for a team where Ashley Cole was the best in the world and I still got games. It won't happen at City. There has never been an explanation but it's obvious they don't want me. Mancini doesn't really speak to me, he doesn't really speak to any of the players. The only time I've known a player isolated like this was Winston Bogarde at Chelsea. Usually you still train with the first team, even when they want you out. I've never caused trouble, I'm not that kind of character. If I kicked up a fuss, I might have got out easier."

Mancini responded to Bridge's criticisms of his managerial techniques. "Bridge said I don't speak to him. That is not true. I told Wayne two years ago that he was not part of our plans and if he wanted to find a good solution he should go somewhere else."

Mancini said it was possible Tévez could leave the club within 10 days if Milan accepted they needed to buy rather than loan. "We hope Milan want to take him. It could be close in one week or 10 days, but I don't know if it is possible. We can close this situation but they cannot take him on loan."

Sunday Dec 25, 2011

The top team on Christmas Day have gone on to win the title eight times in 19 Premier League seasons. City were sure to enjoy another bash at the Champions League as only Aston Villa in 1998-99 missed out on a top four place after sitting on top at Christmas.

Billionaire owners Roman Abramovich and Sheikh Mansour are rivals on the pitch, but it spilled over onto the entertainment front with the two wealthy owners throwing the biggest and best New Years Eve parties. The Chelsea owner was holding his annual New Year's eve celebration at his £58m estate in the Caribbean island of St Barts, his guests rocking away from 10pm until 4am, at which time they will retired to a fleet of super-yachts to finish off their celebrations. The exclusive event featured a star studded guest list. Last year Demi Moore, Ellen DeGeneres and George Lucas attended the party. Not to be outdone, Sheikh Mansour threw a lavish event, but instead of New Year's Eve, he was celebrating his niece's 16th birthday, paying Jay Z and Kanye West just under £4m to perform for the girl, who is a daughter of an Arab billionaire, and other guests. The rappers played several songs at the shindig, which took place in Dubai just before Christmas.

Sergio Agüero took his family for a brief excursion in the French capital to enjoy Euro Disney. He visited the resort with wife Giannina, the daughter of Maradona, and son Benjamin, Agüero tweeted a picture of him and his young family alongside Disney characters Donald Duck and Daisy Duck.

Monday, Dec 26, 2011

A frustrating draw at West Brom saw City draw a blank for the first time this season with United now only behind on goal difference. City's superior goal difference was slashed from 17 to five in the final month of the year. Mancini admitted it was two points dropped, "It was frustrating that we didn't score because we had enough chances. We knew before the game that if we didn't score quickly it would be difficult but I still thought a goal would eventually come. We know that it's impossible to stay top for for all 38 games but we will try."

City could even start 2012 in second place with United taking on Blackburn at home on New Year's Eve before City play at Sunderland 24 hours later. Mancini said: "I think United will win the next game and it's more difficult for us against Sunderland away and then within 48 hours again, but I'm confident we can do a good job by the end. It's important to stay in with a chance of the title at the end. If you want to win the title, we have to try to play well against United. United have a strong team but we are strong enough to do this."

City lacked their usual bite but were unlucky as Mario hit the bar from distance and had a goal ruled out for offside. He also had a free-kick deflected wide while Silva side-footed a good chance over. West Brom deserved a point with Thomas hitting the post, Brunt shooting wide and Scharner testing Hart.

Mancini said: "Sometimes you don't win. We know that it's impossible to stay top for all 38 games. Every team has a plan but if we don't score in the first half it's difficult. We will probably have another eight or nine games in the next 20 days like this. West Bromwich played with all their players around the ball and you have to find a solution if you don't score quickly in the first half."

Baggies boss Roy Hodgson was proud of the effort of his players, "We have got to be pleased with that, we knew the magnitude of the task. We had to be at our best to try to keep them at bay. It was a very disciplined, hard-working performance defensively. It was one of those games when we deserved the point we got and we got it by playing in the right manner. We don't stop many sides scoring — we are not a great clean-sheet team — so it was great to do it against a side of Man City's calibre. It's a bit concerning when you're the opposing manager watching the likes of Dzeko and Johnson coming on, when already you are dealing with Agüero and Balotelli. You think you are doing OK then someone else comes on to cause you different problems."

United swallowed up City's five-point lead in the last fortnight and both Manchester clubs were at the top of the table on 45 points. United's 5-0 win over Wigan halved the goal difference after 18 games.

Kompany, though, was pleased it could come down to a straight shootout between the Manchester clubs. "I wouldn't want anyone else to be battling for the title with us than United. It's a good way to fight for the title for us. Hopefully it will make it even more special to bring that trophy home."

City completed an excellent 2011 on a disappointing note, but Kompany believed there are better things to look forward to in the New Year, "This year has been a great year. But we'll work hard for 2012 to be even better. Winning the FA Cup was historic but I try to put that out of my mind now. The ones that are coming are more important. For the future of the club though it was massive. There's no guarantee of silverware because other clubs are going for the same trophies. But we have self-belief and I hope that can take us as far as we want to go."

An inspired display from the Baggies shows how City are now viewed as a major scalp. Kompany says that has been the case since the Abu Dhabi takeover more than three years ago and is convinced they can cope. "We're used to it. Before it was because of the money, now it's because we're top of the league. But we've got the right weapons to respond so I prefer it now to a couple of years ago. You always encounter teams that on a good day can cause you a lot of trouble."

Joe Hart says City felt the pressure of United breathing down their necks, "Of course we feel the pressure. The league is not set up for us to win it. Every team has their own targets - if they're not challenging for the title they're challenging for Europe; if they're not challenging for Europe they want to stay above the relegation zone, so everyone has got their own agendas and that makes for a great league. You have got to earn this title. It's hard work. It was disappointing to draw at West Brom. They were brilliant. They set out for a point and they got it. We need to be winning those sorts of games but we haven't and now we have to move on. I'm sure a lot will be made of the fact that it was the first game we haven't scored in this season – but let people make a lot of what they want. We're top of the league, still playing well, still creating chances. We're the team to beat and we're enjoying that."

After scoring 53 goals in their first 17 games, City lost their way in front of goal at the Hawthorns. "We had the chances to score, but didn't have the killer instinct," said Kompany. "In the end it was a difficult game for us. It would have been perfect to score an early goal and that is what we set out to do. We probably missed the edge on our finishing - something we have been so good at. Their defending was brilliant. During the course of the season you always encounter teams who, on a good day, can cause you a lot of trouble. I am not bitter about it. Credit where credit is due and we had chances. But I still think for us there are some positives to take out of it. I don't think it was a bad performance. That's three clean sheets in a row and we are very confident we can go on and win the next games."

Mancini was smarting at the way the fixtures panned out, "I'm not happy with the situation. I know it's for TV but having to play twice in two days when others play every three days is not correct. To play twice in 48 hours will make a difference. But we just have to keep our concentration. We know January is important.

Tuesday, Dec 27, 2011

City were preparing a 30m euro bid for Hazard, according to the player's agent. The Belgium international's representative, Marc Fourmeux, was expecting Mancini to make the first move once the transfer window was re-opened in a move which will allow the playmaker to remain with his Ligue 1 club on loan until next season. "There is much talk of an offer of 30m from Manchester City, which will see him remain at Lille for the next six months," Fourmeux told AS. "His future is in any case destined for a big European club like Real Madrid, Barcelona, Chelsea, Manchester City, AC Milan, Inter or Juventus. For Hazard, the president of Lille wants to receive 40m while the player himself has declared that he wants to play for Madrid."

Mancini insisted a January swoop for Hazard was unlikely. "No, this is not true. He is a good player but at this moment we have not spoken about him." Mancini confirmed his interest in De Rossi, although he admitted it would be difficult to tempt him away from Italy, "De Rossi? He is a champion and he would be the perfect man to improve City. If we get the right signals, it is right that we try for him."

Wednesday, Dec 28, 2011

Mancini's management style has got the club heading in the right direction, according to Patrick Viera. "Why is Manchester City finally top in England? There has been stability here for three years, and also Roberto Mancini has arrived. Each year key players came and pushed the team up a level, just as Sergio Agüero, Samir Nasri and David Silva have done this year. In his first game against Tottenham, Samir was extraordinary. Then he took a little time to adapt. But recently, he was named man of the match against Arsenal. He brings us his technique, and he makes the team play.'

Vieira was expected to move behind the scenes at Arsenal after a nine-year spell, but he was pleased with his decision to join City. "I'm often asked why I stayed at Manchester City instead of getting involved at Arsenal. People may have difficulty understanding, but this is a continuation of what I did for two years here as a player. The club has opened its doors to me, shown me respect and taken into consideration all my experience. Since I left Arsenal, I always had a very good relationship with Arsene Wenger, but I never received a proposal from them. With City, it was done without pushing things and it was the proposal that I wanted.'

Patrice Evra believed United's versatile squad would help secure a 20th league title. Evra and Carrick were emergency centre-backs against Wigan on Monday yet they still romped to a 5-0 victory. "This is the United spirit - you can play everywhere," Evra said. "If you want to win, you have to accept it. I've said that from the beginning, in six years playing here, there is a Man United spirit. No other team has got that spirit. If we win and score goals and keep many clean sheets, like we did against Wigan, we're going to be at the top of the league at the end of the season. But I'm a little bit worried because we need everyone fit if we want to win the league."

Ryan Giggs felt his chances of securing a record 13th championship medal depended on which side kept their nerve best in the run-in, "The experience that the manager, the players and the coaching staff have of what's required in the second half of the season, as well as the overall hunger and desire to win competitions, will help us. Big players can't wait for big games and towards the end of the season the games just get bigger and bigger. You want that in the run-in, you want to be involved in big games and going for the title. That's why you become a footballer."

Thursday, Dec 29, 2011

Roberto Mancini wanted his players to sharpen up in front of goal after failing to score in a league game for the first time since April. The dressing room was desolate afterwards, but there was no inquest into why a side which couldn't stop scoring earlier suddenly stopped. Mancini accepted the end of that run of 23 games since they last failed to score with resignation. "Every team has its plan, but in the first half we had three or four chances to score and maybe we were too slow in ball possession. We should maybe be quicker. In the second half we also had a chance but in the end they had players behind the ball. We knew when we played this game it would be difficult. It was difficult on Monday and it will be difficult in the next game because we play against teams who get players behind the ball. If you don't score when you have the chance – like at West Brom in the first half – afterwards it can be difficult. Sometimes you have to take risks. I was thinking on the morning of the match, that we always score. But I was saying two months ago that there will be a moment when we can't score and we don't know why. We have good strikers and good players but sometimes we can't score."

Mancini was also happy to take the positives, "When you can't score and concede one or two counter-attacks like today you can lose concentration and lose the game. The clean sheet is positive but if we want to win the title we need to score. We can't score every game. I think we are on top, we are happy and we know that now we have another 20 games. They will be very difficult games."

Fri, Dec 30, 2011

Mario was refusing to give up smoking two packets of cigarettes a week. He was photographed with a cigarette in his hand and seen smoking when out with friends in Manchester. Mancini admitted he failed to persuade Mario to give up, 'Yeah, yeah, I know this. I know that he smokes. For me, it's not OK but I'm not his father or his mother. If he was my son I would give him a kick on the a★★ but he is not my son! I told him that it is better you don't smoke. I am against cigarettes always. For this reason my son doesn't smoke. There are players who smoke in Italy and I think also here. I don't think he smokes a lot – five or six a day. But I told him not to.'

Mancini was all smiles as he discussed his club's most newsworthy player and doesn't feel Mario's habit was having an impact on his performances on the field. World Cup winner Ossie Ardiles, Jimmy Greaves, Holland legend Johan Cruyff, former Nottingham Forest winger John Robertson and one-time Chelsea striker Gianluca Vialli all smoked regularly during hugely successful playing careers, while England striker Wayne Rooney has also been photographed with cigarettes, as has Chelsea's Ashley Cole.

City faced Sunderland at the Stadium of Light, a game City felt they must win if they are not to be left behind by United's resurgence. Perhaps Mario would light up the Stadium of Light! City would be knocked off the top of the table if United beat bottom club Blackburn at Old Trafford on Saturday lunchtime. Mancini said: "Up until now we got many, many points. It is difficult to keep that up. Until now us, United and Tottenham have had a fantastic season but if we want to win this title we will have to fight every game because United are very strong. They are used to being at the top for a long time. But I don't think for us it makes any difference whether we are on the top or behind by one point. I think we scored 53 goals in 18 games and we didn't score any goals against West Bromwich last week. There will be some moments when we don't score any goals. United won't score five goals every game like they have the last two or three weeks, either. This is normal. It's important that we've scored 53 goals so far and we will score many more in the next 20 games of this championship. United are strong. I never thought that this championship was finished because last year Chelsea had seven points more than United and didn't win. I think the situation can change in December and January but it is important to be on top at the end."

After weeks suggesting he wanted him, Harry Redknapp finally admitted he cannot afford Carlos Tévez. "I like him. He is a great player," Redknapp said. "He is fantastic - a battler, a real talent - but we are not going to be able to get him. It's not happening. We are not pursuing it. The chairman won't put the club in trouble for one player. His wages would be astronomical."

Liverpool were next in action when they travelled to City, with Steven Gerrard relishing the meeting, having seen his team earn a 1-1 draw with Mancini's men on Merseyside in November, the Reds denied victory late on following a fine save from Hart. "They are a fantastic team who have started the season really well but we've got nothing to fear. We showed against them here a couple of weeks ago that we more than matched them. It's at home that we haven't got the results our football has deserved but we will go to City full of confidence. We will give it our best shot and see where it takes us."

Saturday, Dec 31, 2011

If Sir Alex Ferguson planned to toast his 70th birthday by taking United above City at the top of the table with at least a point against bottom club Blackburn at Old Trafford on Saturday lunchtime, he was to be disappointed. While United and City held a seven-point lead over third-placed Spurs, who had a game in hand, Ferguson insisted that Redknapp's team emerged as a genuine threat. With Chelsea and Arsenal respectively 11 and 12 points adrift of the Manchester clubs, Ferguson felt his team were now in a three-way race for the title. "The difficulty for Arsenal and Chelsea is that they have to overtake three teams and, unless three teams collapse, there won't be an opportunity. Tottenham at the moment are the best team in the country. Their form at the moment is the best anywhere and they are definitely title contenders. We've had the stats which say we are five or six points ahead of previous years' form at this time of the year. But you have to say that City's form is equal to that. To have 45 points is an enormous total at this point of the year. It will be nip and tuck between the two clubs, but Tottenham are the best team in the country at the moment."

Despite the opportunity to move three points clear of City, Ferguson knew the title race would not be influenced by such movements until the spring. "The crucial period always is the end of March, if you drop points then, that can impact on your opponents and give them a boost and make their opportunities better. There will be points dropped when it gets harder in March and April and more difficult to catch up. A lot of things come into it. When they announce what the televised games are, when you're playing, that can make a difference, if you're playing first or second. Also, we're possibly playing Thursday-Sunday through the spring in terms of European football. City have that as well and Tottenham are not involved in that. A lot of things come into the equation in terms of how the league will pan out."

With so much international talent warming the City bench every week, there were often rumblings of discontent but new Sunderland boss O'Neill said: "City are a top-quality side with strength in depth which is very important these days. If you go to a club like that, you're obviously going to get paid an awful lot of money and I think the situation would be plain to see. You've either got to get in the team to play or you'll be rotated. Otherwise, you'll be a squad player or just disappear. You take that chance when you go and play for Manchester City. They have real quality throughout and more besides sitting around. You take that chance — and you shouldn't moan when you're not in the team."

In one of the shocks of the season United went down to a 3-2 home defeat by bottom club Blackburn. Ferguson said: "We never expected that. We've lost two terrible goals in the game, and we can't do that in a game like this." Ferguson praised a resilient Blackburn side, adding, "They've defended for their lives." The United manager said his players had struggled on a heavy pitch. "I think they found the speed of the pitch not so good. It was really heavy rain all week and it made the pitch really boggy." Ferguson said when United got back to 2-2 he thought they would take the victory. "I thought at that point we were set to win it. We've got injuries at the moment but we had to take a gamble on Anderson's fitness. He did his best. It is a disaster," he confessed.

It was widely reported that Wayne Rooney felt the full force of Sir Alex's fury when he was axed after a boozy Boxing Day night out with wife Coleen and two team-mates. Ferguson apparently ditched his star when he discovered that Rooney had gone out on the town to celebrate the 5-0 win over Wigan with Jonny Evans, Darren Gibson and their partners. The United boss took the decision despite being hit by an injury and illness crisis. Rooney was stunned to be told he was being dropped and that his sense of injustice deepened when he was informed he would also be hit with a club fine. United have a rule that players must not drink 48 hours before a game. United, though, dismissed reports that Rooney, along with Gibson and Evans, were involved in "a boozy night out" on Boxing Day. United insist Rooney was omitted for fitness reasons and the club's website continued to report the statement Ferguson made about his team selection to prior to kick off. "Wayne hasn't trained well this week, he's missed a few days and we're hoping that he trains today, tomorrow and, by Wednesday, he should be okay. It's little strains here and there."

JANUARY

*'I always hoped that one day in my life
I'd be in Sunderland on New Year's Eve!'*
ROBERTO MANCINI

Sunday, Jan 1, 2012

Roberto Mancini and his players saw in the New Year with a midnight toast at the team's hotel in the North-East, with the City manager happy to confirm his resolution for 2012 is to win the Premier League, with his side top dogs at the turn of the year. Contradicting his image as a disciplinarian party, Mancini allowed his players a drink to toast the new year.

"I always hoped that one day in my life I'd be in Sunderland on New Year's Eve!" joked Mancini.

In two years, Mancini transformed a club riddled with dressing-room division into genuine title contenders. Mancini's arrival after Mark Hughes caused outrage. No longer. 'My ambition for 2012 is to be on top when we finish this championship. We were there after we started the season and I think we deserve to be there. It usually takes three or four years to build a team like Manchester City. But we have done this very quickly. The players have been fantastic. I trust them. If they continue to give 100 per cent we can be champions and it's only our second full season.'

Half the players used by Mancini in his first game, a 2-0 win against Stoke City, have left — Robinho, Bellamy, Given, Petrov and Ireland among them. Tévez remained, though currently, frozen out. The high-risk strategy worked with City winning their first trophy since 1976, lifting the FA Cup in May and collected 45 points in 18 games to lead the league. "It was my job to make Manchester City a top team but it's not always easy to change a situation very quickly," added Mancini. "Sometimes you need time to change some players, to take good players. I remember two years ago when we were talking about players, it was difficult to sign Yaya Toure, David Silva, Samir Nasri, Sergio Agüero, all of these important players. Now they are here. That's the most important thing."

To win the title Mancini had to get the better of Sir Alex Ferguson's famed verbal jousting with opposition managers like Keegan, Dalglish, Wenger and Benitez. The more threatening a rival, the more likely Ferguson is to indulge in mind games. A supportive Fergie phone call to Blackburn manager Steve Kean just before Liverpool and United played them may have been coincidence but the ultra-cool Mancini, a veteran of three Serie A titles with Inter Milan, was unmoved. "We should only think about our game, not what Fergie or the other managers say. That is not important. We have respect for him, for United, for all the teams, but we are strong enough to just look for the title."

Just before kick off, Roberto Mancini announced six changes with Tuesday's game with Liverpool in mind. David Silva and Sergio Agüero on the bench, Edin Dzeko up front on his own. Mario Balotelli travelled but was not involved. Mancini remarked on United's defeat, "I think that it was a good result for us. It shows the Premier League is very strong and every game is difficult and today will be very hard. We start this game on the top and we want to stay there, but usually this game is very difficult because we have never won here." As for the big changes, he explained, "We made the changes to the team because we play two games in 48 hours, it's impossible to play with the same players. We don't have any injuries."

Mancini blamed missed chances for the 1-0 defeat, after Ji Dong-won's injury-time winner left City level with United on 45 points. Mancini said: "We missed a big opportunity because we had a chance to go three points up on United. We are in an unlucky moment because we keep missing these chances to score."

Mancini headed down the tunnel before the final whistle, "It's frustrating because we can't lose a game like today's. In the second half, we had I don't know how many chances to score. But football is this. Sometimes you can't win. Sometimes you score three or four goals in a game, sometimes you can't score even if you have 10 chances to score. I am disappointed that we conceded a goal because a strong team cannot concede a goal like this."

Richards and Dzeko hit the bar with Sunderland goalkeeper Simon Mignolet making several saves from Agüero and a Silva effort. As his team pressed for a winner, Mancini was disappointed to be outnumbered in defence in the build-up to the goal and said his team had to recognise when to settle for a draw. It marks the second season in a row where City lost to a 90th-minute winner at the Stadium of Light. "We deserved to win this game, it's incredible, but this is football," Mancini added. "Last year here was the same situation, I don't know how many chances we had, and we lose the game in the end on a penalty. And apparently the goal was offside. A team like us, we can't concede three of four counter-attacks at the end of the game. Sometimes when you are on the pitch you need to understand that there are some games when you can't score. At that moment, you should understand 'OK we stay' and one point is better than nil. Sometimes when you attack with seven players it's enough, because if not you can concede a counter-attack like we conceded. In the first half we didn't play very well, second half much better. We had to win this game. This moment is a strange situation."

Asked if that was good enough, Mancini replied: "No, not for a top team. In that situation, we attacked with eight players and the same players who attack need to come back and run quickly. I know football and for that reason in the last 15 minutes, I continued to call Vinny and Lescott to say, 'Stay there, stay there, don't leave the space', because that was dangerous. We continued to attack and sometimes we wanted to attack with 10 players. This is impossible. But that's it, it's finished. We have a game in 48 hours and we need to recover now."

City suffered their second defeat in the league, failing to win away in four games. It also marked the second consecutive game in which they had not scored. Mancini explained: "We played two teams defending with all their players in the box, but we are missing a lot of chances."

Meanwhile Mario Balotelli was named our man of the year on the ESPNsoccernet podcast. Davide Santon suggested Mario is unsure over where his future lies. Newcastle wing-back Santon plays alongside Mario on the international stage and was also his club team-mate at Inter Milan, before the latter joined City in 2010. "We often speak and sometimes we meet up. He doesn't have a proper smoking habit, he is just a quiet boy who wants to have fun. I do not know what he wants to do in the future because sometimes he says he wants to return to Italy and sometimes he says he wants to stay a long time with City."

Monday, Jan 2, 2012

Roberto Mancini wondered what impact City's slump over the festive period would have on his players. "I hope it isn't going to be difficult to pick the players up after the defeat. I hope they understand we are a top team and we can't concede goals in the last minute on the counter attack like we did at Sunderland. But it is finished and we have to think about the next game. I hope the players can have a positive reaction. We lost a big chance to go three points clear of Manchester United. It was an important game but we have to start thinking positively about the Liverpool game and the future. We have 45 points and we have scored 53 goals, these are things to be positive about."

City had not lost at home for a year but Mancini was concerned about his side's vulnerability on the counter-attack, which led to Sunderland's dramatic late winner, "I'm not worried about us not scoring in the last couple of games. What I'm worried about is having players on the pitch who understand the situation when we're vulnerable to a counter-attack. We need to improve in this situation. We had chances to score but sometimes, when you can't win a game, you must make sure you don't lose it. We seemed to want to attack with 10 players and to do that's impossible."

Despite setbacks in their past two games, City were on 45 points at the midway point of the season, halfway towards the target of 90 that Mancini believed would secure the title.

The commanding five-point lead over United was wiped out, though, along with a superior goal difference of 17 which was now down to five, "We've had a bit of bad luck, but things can soon change. The players understand we've missed an important opportunity, but it's vital they switch on for the next game now. We've got 45 points and scored 53 goals, and we need another 45 points in the second half of the season.'

Agüero and Silva were left on the bench, Balotelli was given time to recover from an ankle injury, but it backfired as City drew a blank for the second game running and lost to a last-gasp goal at the Stadium of Light. Mancini said: "I will have to think about making changes. We are playing two games in 48 hours and that is difficult. I changed six or seven players because I trust all my players to come in and do a good job. It's impossible to play with the same players all the time, especially when you play twice in 48 hours."

Balotelli, who did not make the squad for the Sunderland game, should be fit to face Liverpool. "Mario had a little problem with his ankle so for that reason we left him in the stands. I hope he's going to be okay for Liverpool. We don't have any other injury problems." Asked about potential new arrivals during this month's transfer window, Mancini remained coy. "At the moment we have to go with the players we have got for the next few games. Maybe after that we can do something."

Craig Bellamy left the Etihad in August after never seeing eye to eye with Mancini, "Bellamy is just one player but he is in good form. I hope my players can have a positive reaction, we lost a big chance to go clear of Manchester United."

Kenny Dalglish sympathised with Mancini having to play just 51 hours after their loss at Sunderland. He made the same complaint when the Reds had to play at Chelsea in the Carling Cup just two days after facing City. Dalglish feels the players' union should work closer with the Premier League to push for proper breaks between games. He understands the TV companies dictate, but the product will suffer if players are not given enough time to rest. "I think Roberto made a great point here after our game when he said the players' union should be the one canvassing for the players. If the games are coming up thick and fast, then what do the players' union think of it? I think TV has been massively helpful to many people in the Premier League, ourselves included. So we can't bite the hand that feeds us. There has, though, got to be a bit of common sense. I think a game on the first and the third is a bit unreasonable really. Nobody listened to us when we made the same point when we had our Carling Cup game just two days after playing a league game. It's not up to us. I think in general there's got to be a reasonable amount of time for the players to recover. I know people say Roberto has a massive squad and he's got enough to field two teams and all that, but you've still got to take the players into consideration because after all, they are the ones who are the attraction."

Dalglish says Mancini deserves credit for the success he has had with City, "We've got the utmost respect for what they have done. It's all very well and good, saying they have loads of money, but they've also got a good team. The money they've got, everyone would love to have, but unfortunately they don't. For us, we'll just go and play whatever 11 he puts on the pitch no matter what they cost. We will give our all for this football club and try and get a result."

The league clash at the Etihad was the first of three meetings between the sides over the next 22 days and Dalglish rejected talk that Liverpool could strike an early psychological blow by getting a good result.

Edin Dzeko had now played more than ten hours without a goal, but the big striker remained convinced he can fire City to the Premier League title. Dzeko was among those under fire for failing to provide a finishing touch to a host of spurned chances in the last two games. His latest dip in form was nothing compared to the misery he lived through in his first six months as the club's £27m misfit striker. "I have to admit it was very tough for me in the opening few months in Manchester because everything was so different and I wondered if I could ever adapt to what was expected of me. First there was the need to settle in a different city, begin to understand a new way of life and then the football was so different as well. Every game in England is a real battle, the pace of the game is tough to get used to, and my confidence was not there at the start. I also had to understand how the referees worked in this country, as they allowed much more physical contact than I was used to in Germany. You feel the need to prove yourself in a team full of so many stars and the attention is all on Manchester City right now. We are the team that everyone talks about for spending so much money and you don't want to be the guy who falls short in this story. So I decided to find some positives last summer. The way I looked at it was that I was a part of the first City team to win a trophy in 35 years and that was a sign that I must have contributed something to this club and this idea inspired me come back with a fresh attitude. Thankfully, the goals came for me and people could see why City worked so hard to get me at the club. Some of the football we have played this season has been fantastic and now we all believe we can win the big prizes."

Edin Dzeko was also a bit part player in the darkest moment of City's season when he reacted angrily to being substituted against Bayern, "What happened in the Bayern Munich game was just an example of me feeling frustrated on a night when things went against me and I didn't mean it to look like any mark of disrespect to the manager. You have to realise what that Bayern game meant to me. I made my name at Wolfsburg and wanted to make an impression as I returned to Germany for such a big match. It did not work out for me and I lost my cool when I was taken off. I apologised straight away for my reaction and can say now that I have nothing but respect for Mancini and all that he has given to me. He was the manager who made big efforts to let me realise my dream and play in the Premier League and hopefully I am beginning to repay him now. There is still more to come from me this season and even though the big wins at Tottenham and United were very special, we know that this Premier League always has another big battle just around the corner. You only have to see the effort every team puts in against us to realise this is a competition that does not have too many teams you can beat with any comfort, especially away from home. This league is so tough, so competitive. That's why the Premier League is so difficult to win."

Dzeko emerged as one of the favourites for the Premier League's leading marksman, yet he has failed to score since the 3-2 away win at QPR, his drought stretching back 11 games for club and country. "Part of the reason City can be successful this season is the depth of our squad and this means I will not play every week. I'm not the star of this team, no one is. The great thing is that we have players scoring goals from all areas of the team, so we are not relying on just one main scorer. Sergio Agüero has settled so quickly at City and then we have Samir Nasri, Adam Johnson, Mario Balotelli and David Silva scoring goals consistently as well. When you have so many attacking players, there has to be room for some changes in different games. This is why I say being top scorer in the Premier League was never an ambition for me this season. Maybe I will play some games and then sit out others, so I just have to try and score goals when my chance comes."

Tuesday, Jan 3, 2012

City once again put daylight between themselves and United. After one point and no goals from two matches, they emphasised how much they are a formidable force at home, extending their 100% home league record to 10 matches, 55 points out of a possible 57 in at the Etihad Stadium in the last year and three days with an emphatic 3-0 win despite going down to 10-men. It was only the second time this season Liverpool conceded more than one in a league match, their worst result since losing 4-0 at Tottenham in September.

Sergio Agüero and Yaya Toure did the damage in the first half after benefiting from defensive lapses and even after Barry was sent off for two bookable offenses, City added a third with Milner's penalty. City were fortunate to escape from Anfield with a 1-1 draw in November but this encounter was not even close as they recorded only their second win in 14 matches against the Merseysiders.

In a battle between the league's top scorers and the meanest defence, few would have predicted the usually reliable Reina would be at fault for the opening goal. Having already denied Dzeko at the foot of his right-hand post, Reina made a complete hash of judging Agüero's 25-yard dipping shot and the ball flew underneath his body. That was in contrast to Hart's reactions in denying Downing moments earlier when his England team-mate threatened to score having been played in by Henderson. Then Reina was left helpless by Yaya's powerful header off the underside of the crossbar from Silva's corner in the 34th minute.

Ten minutes into the second half Adam was replaced by Gerrard, who had been the catalyst for victory over Newcastle on Friday, and former City striker Bellamy came on for Kuyt. The substitutions produced the required lift but it remained a long way back for the Reds. Liverpool appeared to have gained the momentum when Barry, having been booked late in the first half, was sent off for a second caution after blocking Agger. But seconds later the result was wrapped up when they conceded possession inside City's half and Skrtel fouled Yaya on the breakaway to allow Milner to make it 3-0 from the spot. City almost added a fourth when substitute Johnson's shot beat Reina but rebounded off the post.

Mancini was criticised for waving an imaginary card after Skrtel brought down Yaya in the area. He explained, "Maybe I made a mistake but I was nervous. I didn't agree with the referee for the second yellow card for Gareth Barry. I didn't understand. I watched the games yesterday and there were a lot of tackles without yellow cards. You play one important game like this evening and we lose one player for nothing."

Mancini, who will watch United face Newcastle at St James' Park ahead of their FA Cup clash on Sunday, said: "We produced a good performance and that was just what we needed."

Mancini said that if his side were still top of the League this time next month they stood a good chance of the title, "I think United are a strong team but we should think only of trying to win every game if possible and at the end we will see what happens. Tottenham are also very close but I hope we stay there for a long time."

Brothers Yaya and Kolo Toure headed for the Africa Cup of Nations with Mancini saying, "I've looked in my squad for another Yaya and I can't find one."

Wednesday, Jan 4, 2012

Sir Alex Ferguson insisted there was no need to panic after his side's 3-0 loss to Newcastle, but admitted City were now in the box seat, three points ahead, "Advantage to them of course. They played yesterday and got the three points, and we played today and didn't manage to win - so of course they have the advantage. It's not a time to panic - we have the experience to cope with that. Losing a game at this time of the year, you don't want it, but it sometimes can happen - you have seen some of the results recently. But obviously, we need to get the show on the road in terms of the run-in, particularly in March and April."

City's players were in for training the day after the Liverpool victory because Roberto Mancini had still not forgiven them for Ji Dong-won's winner at the Stadium of Light. "We have done well this season, but we could do more. Even the best teams, there are times during the year when you cannot win, and you don't know why. Maybe you are unlucky, you make chances and you cannot score. Then there are other games, like at Chelsea, like at Sunderland, where if you are a top team you cannot win, but you must not lose."

"We need to understand this. A clever team would understand it. "OK," they would think, "the win will not happen, but, just as important, we must concede nothing". That is why I was so disappointed about Sunderland. We deserved to win 3-0, 4-0 maybe, but from there we had to be strong, very strong. The same in Naples. To draw there was important. Draw and we reach the Champions League knockout stage. One month ago, all the journalists were saying we could go the season unbeaten, like Arsenal. But I knew then that we would not. We are not Arsenal, we are not strong up here like that team. No matter how many strikers we have, I knew there would be a moment when we did not score and we arrived at Sunderland

and it happened and we lost. And I could see this coming. That is why I knew we would not win all the games. We have fantastic players but we are not used to staying at the top a long time. There will be difficult moments, big matches, but it is not just about winning in the big matches. You must make sure you also win when you have won five, six games in a row. That is when you have to be at your strongest. We can lose at Sunderland and win against Liverpool and everyone says you have recovered well; but lose against Sunderland late in April and there is no time to recover. Your chance has gone. Too bad, you were not strong, so you lost the championship. We must be realistic. We must know this. It is different for Manchester United and for Chelsea, they have done it before. We know they will arrive strong in that last month but we may not be the same. Losing to Sunderland could have created a big problem for us. What if we had then lost to Liverpool? It could have happened. The first big chance of the game was for Stewart Downing. If he had scored, maybe Liverpool would have won 3-0. We had played just 48 hours earlier. We could have been too tired to come back.'

Jermaine Defoe warned both Manchester clubs that Tottenham are thriving on the pressure of maintaining their outside chance for Premier League glory, three points behind United boasting a game in hand. "That result on Tuesday shows that we are well and truly in the title race. The lads showed so much character to keep going when West Brom made it so hard for us. City and United know we are a threat, and with every game that we keep on winning we can put pressure on them to keep winning. This is such a good opportunity for us. We want to take it with both hands."

Roberto Mancini believes Mario Balotelli has the ability to perform at the level of Ronaldo and Rooney, but it was up to him to fulfil his potential. "He is a strange man. A good man, a kind man, but I do not understand him. It feels as if I need my own special translator, just for Mario. He is an incredible player but he does not understand his strength, what he could achieve as a player. Maybe he needs more time. Wayne Rooney, Cristiano Ronaldo, these are the players whose talent is up there with Mario, but they are clever, they know the career is short and it is no use waiting until you are 40 before you realise how good you were. Mario first played when he was 16. He has, at most, 15 years as a top player and he is 21 now. He does not know how lucky he is at the moment. But he needs to arrive at that point soon. I just hope Mario can understand how much he will improve when he becomes a man. He could be so important for me."

Mancini could delve into the transfer market, "We need to sell three or four players and with Carlos we could close with a club in the next three or four days, and also possibly Wayne. Then maybe we can do something. We hope for us and for Carlos we can do a deal. There are two or three teams in Italy, a team in France, and another team involved – I hope for him he can start to play football. We could maybe bring someone in, but we need to sell. We have three strikers, plus Samir, David and Adam Johnson. Maybe we need one midfielder if we can do it."

City desperately wanted Yaya and Kolo to play the Cup encounter with United, the pair were due to report for African Nations Cup duty, but Mancini requested that they be allowed to miss a team meeting in Paris on Saturday, and the first part of a two-week training camp in Abu Dhabi that begins on Sunday. "We have asked the Ivory Coast manager because they have a meeting in Paris on Saturday. We have asked whether Kolo and Yaya can stay with us and then they can go to Abu Dhabi. We are waiting for an answer and I expect to know either today or tomorrow."

Ivory Coast coach Francois Zahoui rejected the club's request. Under FIFA rules, players can be called up to two weeks before the competition, which starts on January 21. Zahoui refused to relax his stance, insisting the pair report for duty in Paris on Saturday before the squad flies to Abu Dhabi for a two-week training camp on Sunday. "Clubs know the rules," Zahoui told the BBC. "I'm expecting them for the FIFA deadline." Kolo re-established his place in City's starting XI, while Yaya scored six goals in his last 13 matches.

Mancini may not have enough players to fill his substitutes bench; with Barry suspended, Hargreaves not considered fit enough, Balotelli troubled by an ankle injury that prevented him playing against both Sunderland and Liverpool. "We have 17 players," said Mancini. "I do not know how it is going to work."

Mancini admitted following City's 3-0 victory against Liverpool that Hargreaves could make the substitutes' bench against his former club. With Yaya off for at least a month and de Jong's contract stalemate beginning to impact on his appearances under Mancini, Hargreaves was now a key figure. Yaya started each of City's 20 Premier League games this season, with Barry appearing in 18. de Jong started just four. Having failed to lure de Rossi from Roma last summer, Mancini was urged by Franco Baldini, Fabio Capello's trusted right-hand man, to turn to Hargreaves as cover for Yaya, Barry and De Jong in the holding midfield role. Hargreaves, who attempted to prove his fitness last summer by posting video clips on YouTube of intensive training under the guidance of LA Lakers fitness specialist Alex McKechnie, was recruited to provide experienced, top-level back-up this month. But while the 42-times capped England midfielder marked his City debut in September with a stunning goal in a Carling Cup victory against Birmingham, a failure to convince Mancini of his fitness resulted in Hargreaves managing just 149 minutes over three games in the first team. He had not appeared since the Carling Cup victory at Arsenal on Nov 29. Mancini said, "I hope he can play in the next week because he is OK, but he is not ready to play 100 per cent in the Premier League. In the last week he worked with the team and didn't have any problem, but I hope he can play this month because, when we took him, we thought he would be ready 100 per cent for January. When there is a player who doesn't play for two years, though, maybe he is OK for one week and then there is a problem. Maybe his calf and his knee, there is a little problem. But I hope he is fit for January."

Hargreaves' decision to reject a move to West Brom in favour of City hinted at the reality that he was best able to target 15-20 games a season rather than face the challenge of regular first-team football at The Hawthorns. Moving to City was also supposed to help him return to England contention ahead of Euro 2012, but those hopes have evaporated.

Mancini, who called De Rossi "the perfect fit for Man City", expected De Rossi to stay at Roma despite the recent revelation he has been learning English. "De Rossi is a top player, but he plays for Roma, a top team, and he was born there," Mancini said, "I don't know if he will leave."

Joorabchian confirmed to me in a text message that he was in Rio de Janeiro talking terms with Milan. Inter's technical director, Marco Branca, travelled to England for talks with City, as Joorabchian was talking to Milan chief executive Adriano Galliani, who was on holiday in Brazil, as Tévez wanted to join the Rossoneri. "We're here (in Rio) to finalise with Milan. We haven't heard from Inter since August," Joorabchian said.

But according to my sources, Inter lodged a formal bid in an effort to steal him from under the noses of Milan. Both Milan clubs were in direct contact with City and a bidding process was finally underway after months of posturing. A source close to the transfer activity told me: "Both Milan clubs are now in the frame, and meetings have taken place. City have not accepted any offers as yet." Milan still wanted to take Tévez on loan but were prepared to include a cause that would make his purchase obligatory if he plays in more than 50% of the club's games in the remainder of the season. City were still looking to raise 35m from his sale and indicated that they would be prepared to hold onto Tévez rather than accept a derisory offer. Galliani spoke to City's acting chief executive John MacBeath, Inter technical director Marco Branca simultaneously held talks with his opposite number at City, Brian Marwood, in London.

Joorabchian said Tévez was currently only talking to Milan, denting hopes that City will be able to spark a bidding war. Tévez flew to Rio from

Buenos Aires to meet the San Siro powerbroker at his home in Ipanema. After the serious business of negotiations, the pair, along with Joorabchian, were later all smiles at the fashionable Gero restaurant nearby.

Joorabchian commented, 'We have great confidence in the successful outcome of negotiations between the two clubs. We had talks with Inter for months. We met in Sardinia. But in August there was no more contact. Now we are talking only with AC Milan and Manchester City also know this.' Inter were offering a similar deal and were now in contact with their former manager Mancini. Reports in Argentina said Tévez has already picked his new home: a luxury four-bedroom apartment close to the fashionable Piazza San Babila at a cost of £4,600 a month.

Inter moved to deny claims Sneijder could be the man to bolster the City midfield. Branca wrote on the club's official website: "In no way, and entirely down to our own wishes, did we discuss Sneijder in today's meeting in London with Manchester City directors."

A year ago, Mancini thought he couldn't do without Tévez. No longer. "I have never thought I won the battle," says Mancini. "My relationship with Carlos was not just good, but fantastic. I did everything I could for him in two years. And now we are in this position. I tried to speak with him. I said, "Just apologise" but I don't know what was in his mind by then. I don't know his reasons. All I know is the club must always come first; ahead of me, ahead of players. So there is no fight that has been won, just a sad moment really. I understand what people are saying. It was an important time for the club and for the game. It was important to set an example to the players here. And I knew from the start that we had to change the perception of Manchester City, because many thought we were lucky to have these players. We needed to show players should want to play for us, that we are like Manchester United or Chelsea. And we are getting there. It is a different situation from two years ago. We cannot have players that think they are favouring us by being here; maybe Carlos thought so, I do not know. But it is not like a win because it is sad if it ends this way."

Mancini wanted to bring in at least one new signing, ideally three, but City were unwilling to provide the necessary money, because their last financial figures called for restraint. Mancini was led to believe the club could buy as long as they sold first but that position altered and he was starting to fear that he may be denied funding despite his urgency for a midfield player and a striker if Tévez went. "For Sunday, we have 17 players and I don't think we will fill the bench," Mancini said. "In January — and I said this two months ago — we could have a big problem. We play four important league games, big games, without Yaya. If we have strikers injured then we need to buy another and at the moment I have only one striker [Agüero]. So I have one striker and only two [central] midfielders [Milner and de Jong]. We are losing two players for a month and if we lose another we are going to need more players."

Mancini still wanted to sign De Rossi, knowing that the Italian international may be available for as little as £5m because he will be out of contract in the summer. However, De Rossi's salary requirements were described as "Tévez-level" and Uefa's incoming financial fair play regulations put immense pressure on City to reduce their costs.

Asked if it had been made clear to him that he had no money to spend, he responded, "Yes, yes, this is the problem. But if we don't have the players, it's tough for us. We are not United. United and Chelsea have won trophies for many years. This could be our first championship for many years and we need to do everything we can to win it. We could take in one player. We have been at the top since the start of the season and deserve it, until now. But the season is long and it will be hard. We have a problem because Yaya is an important player for us. Kolo is different because we have eight defenders and if we are lucky and don't have injuries I don't think we will have a big problem. But in midfield we have a big problem and, for Sunday, we have only two players there."

Mancini's complaints about depleted resources were unlikely to find any sympathy at United, where Sir Alex was missing 15 players through injury or illness at one stage in the Christmas period. Mancini believed that the long list of absentees at Old Trafford reinforces his case that City need more players, arguing that his team would not be able to cope if they were to experience similar problems.

Mancini was determined not to lose the impetus. A year ago, City had 41 points and a plus 17 goal difference. This year, having played one game fewer, City have 48 points and a plus 40 differential.

Mario Balotelli was out and about in the city when he spotted Matt Sherrington, 21, hitting top scores on a punch ball machine at a bowling alley. He challenged the United supporter to a contest. Mario came off second best by some way, despite launching a number of blows at the machine. Mario took a run-up at the electronic amusement in order to land one of his hits. A spokesman for City said Balotelli is 'free to do whatever he wants in his own time'.

Mario asked 'Why always me?' Mancini had the answer. "I told him, "Always you, Mario, because whenever there is trouble, you are inside it". He said, "Mister (Mancini pronounces it Meester) it is not my fault". I said, "No, I suppose it is my fault". He said, "No, it is not your fault but I was asleep when it happened".

Could Mancini take the hard line that Sir Alex occasionally has with Rooney giving heavy fines or suspensions? "I don't fine players. We speak. OK, maybe after three or four times, there is a fine, but I have my own ways. Mario was on the bench for a month at the start of the season, he did not play for five or six games. That was disciplinary. He was not working well enough. He does not get it all his way but top players are often different men. I remember Paul Gascoigne at Lazio. You will always find these guys in football, but usually they are the best players, too."

Friday, Jan 6, 2012

David Platt will buy dinner before the United game because he picked up the tab prior to the Liverpool and the manager will not wish to break a fortunate streak. "We'll win 10 on the spin now, you watch," moans Platt, "It will cost me a fortune." Mancini has a superstition about dining table salt pots, which must not be passed from hand to hand, but moved across the table, like a chess piece, released and only then picked up by the receiver. Mancini will let his food go cold rather than take it from his hand. "His worst one is the wine," adds Platt, "If you spill wine, he has to stick his fingers in it and dab it behind his ears, like perfume. Apparently, that wards off the bad luck. So we're in his office after the Liverpool game and I knock over a glass. There's nothing in it, really, but a drop comes out and splashes on the table and he's over, from the other side of the room, finger in the wine, dab, dab. And not a word of explanation to anybody. I can see Kenny Dalglish and Steve Clarke looking at him as if he's mad."

Vincent Kompany recently joined Twitter and asked fans to send him their inspirational words for his pre-match rallying call as City aimed for three wins in a row against United. Kompany promised the winning words will be used to whip up the holders before they meet. "Tweet me what you would say on derby day to inspire the team and I will make sure that on the day it makes a difference." The winner's words will be put on to a poster, signed by the skipper and they will also receive his shirt and armband. Kompany explained his decision to start tweeting. "I just hope that by joining I can get closer to the people that are prepared to support me in the good and bad times. I want to give them an insight into what it means to be playing for the fastest-growing club in the world and a young, promising national team."

In his usual media interviews, Kompany reckoned City are superior to United in every department, "Now City are superior to United in each of the lines but we do not want any surprises in this match and we need to play with our heads. They will be very motivated for this game and their objective will be revenge – and that makes Manchester United more dangerous than ever. A match against United in these circumstances is the match of the year. It's life or death in the FA Cup and we want to repeat our victory last season. A derby requires us to give our biggest effort because we are in the game for many things but, principally, for the pride of our supporters. After the victory at Old Trafford, many people consider us as favourites but even though our last memories against United are positive that does not guarantee a victory this time. The victory at Old Trafford was one of the best moments of my life. It was historical and for many years people will talk about that day. To be part of that day was a huge motivation. I could see people in the ground going crazy. It was incredible, magnificent. Now I want another festival this time but I warn our fans it will be complicated and very tactical. City are the team to beat now, whereas before it was United or Chelsea."

James Milner expected a United backlash following their 6-1 defeat in October's derby at Old Trafford. "The defeat will have hurt them bad. Everyone, from the players to the management, will be more than up for it. As much enjoyment as we got from it, they probably felt three times as much pain. We have got to be aware of that and it is down to us to put another good performance and build on the win against Liverpool on Tuesday. There is no tougher game than against United and we know they are going to fly out of the traps. They will want to get one over us, so we need to make sure we match their determination and will to win."

Mancini urged fans of both clubs to celebrate the best of Manchester football as Greater Manchester Police launched a huge initiative aimed at preventing the kind of trouble that scarred recent derby clashes at the Etihad Stadium. Officers will wear riot gear, an alcohol ban will be in place and the 5,700 away fans will be kept in their places long after the final whistle to give the home supporters chance to get away from the ground, reducing the potential flash points. Mancini wanted to enjoy a game that matches any rivalry in the world. "It is important the fans come and watch the game. It is a big game between two important teams. For the city of Manchester, it is important to have two squads like this at this moment. In the past, there has only been one that has won everything. Now Manchester has two teams who are important, in Manchester, England and Europe. This is a good thing for the city."

Saturday Jan 7, 2012

Roberto Mancini fears that all City have to fear is fear itself. "A player gets to his big game against Roger Federer, goes two sets up and needs the third to win the tournament. He is a top player, this guy, but not the very top. And he cannot do it. Avere il braccetto. The arm becomes short. That is my worry for Manchester City sometimes."

Ferguson once said "not in my lifetime" when asked whether City would ever go into a derby as favourites. But the bookies were backing City after their 6-1 win at Old Trafford. Mancini said: "If we win the title Fergie will be forced to recognise us as United's biggest rivals. He wants to stay for another three years and I think he'll do that even if we become successful."

City were on the brink of a hat-trick of derby victories for the first time since 1969. Mancini, though, concedes it will take more than just recent triumphs for his club to match United's famous mental strength. "If you want my opinion, Manchester United are the best team in England. Maybe not now because they have six or seven important players injured. But they have a strong team with a strong mentality and they are at the top. We can't be like them in two years. They have had this mentality for 25 years. We can improve if we continue to win, if we win the championship or other cups. We started it last season. But in two years it is impossible."

It took Mancini a while to find the diplomatic response to the question how many United players would command a place in this City team. "[United] is a strong team with a strong mentality. They are a fantastic team and for me, now, they are top." Asked again, he replied: "I am happy with my players but if you ask me how many top players do United have I can list them. Nani, Rooney, Giggs, Ferdinand, Carrick, Valencia. Great players."

Yaya has the mentality of a winner, 'This is Manchester City. Barcelona are like Manchester United. Their players expect to win the league. It is different for us. If every year you win the league, the cup, the Champions League, your club gives the others fear. I see that when United play. Every team that faces United is afraid. It takes 20 years to create strength like that and it will take many more years of work here to get to where United are now. When I went to Inter Milan it was the same situation. They had not won the league for 19 years. They found it hard to even win three games in a row."

No one could have imagined United would visit City significant odds-against with every bookmaker in Britain. Mancini was well aware of the expectation that 6-1 scoreline brings. "They had a man sent off early in the second half. We still would have won, but not by six."

When United beat Arsenal 8-2, Ferguson said he wanted the scoring to stop because he did not like seeing the opposition humiliated. 'No,' says Mancini. 'This is Manchester United. Keep scoring, keep scoring, keep scoring. There was a match, they were 3-0 down, they won 5-3. We were winning 3-0, then Darren Fletcher scored and you never know how the game will finish from there. So, no, I never thought 6-1 was too much. In Italy, you get three or four goals, you go slow, you stop. Here it is different. Firstly, you can win the title by scoring one more goal in England, and, secondly, if you are playing Manchester United and you can score, you score. To stop, that would be disrespectful. It is the opposite of what you are saying, I think. You are there to score goals and doing so shows respect for your opponent, it demonstrates that you are taking him seriously. I saw Alex after the game. I went to his office. He was kind. He always has been with me. We have a different culture in Italy. If you lose a game your mind does not work very well for many hours. Here it is different. Final whistle, the game is finished. That is a good thing. It has changed me. When we lost at Sunderland, it was difficult to feel Italian, but then I went to Martin O'Neill's office and I felt English. Alex Ferguson is 70 and still on the touchline, and do you know why? It is easier to manage here. There is more respect for the job, more respect for the manager. In Italy you have a problem every three days, supporters are demonstrating, lose two games and you are out. In England, they are patient so you work better. I have improved my mentality a lot here. In Italy, everyone is talking about the referee for three days before the game – "We don't like him, he is no good". Here, I ask David Platt or Brian Kidd, "Who is the referee?" It is the day of the game, they do not know. They do not care, we find out when we are on the pitch."

Mancini rotates regularly but when it comes to picking a goalkeeper, he insists you must always have a No.1. While Sir Alex decides whether to pick De Gea or Lindegaard to face City, Mancini keeps faith in the keeper he recalled from a loan spell at Birmingham to replace Given as his first-choice. Hart has since made himself England's No 1. Mancini said: "For me, the goalkeeper's position has to be handled differently because he always needs to know that you have confidence in him. To help his own mentality, he needs to be sure he will always play. I decided to put my trust in Joe. He was young, he was strong. De Gea is another young keeper, but he is good. Every player can make mistakes, but it is much harder for a goalkeeper."

The 6-1 defeat left Sir Alex "shattered", reflecting on "our worst ever day", but he didn't want that to be the motivational factor before the cup tie. "I will not be mentioning it," Ferguson replied when reminded of the October afternoon United were subjected to their biggest derby defeat since 1926. It is a day to which Ferguson seldom, if ever, refers. He was reluctant to join in the chorus of praise for Mancini's team, three points clear at the top of the league. "They have a strong squad and an experienced squad so it is not unexpected where they are at the moment, but to my mind it is Tottenham who have been playing the best football in the country. A lot is going to happen between now and the end of the season but I can't see anyone outside the three top teams winning the league. Arsenal and Chelsea need all three teams to collapse and I don't think that will happen."

City scored 56 goals, compared to Tottenham's 36, albeit having played a game more. Ferguson's team go into the Cup tie on the back of two demoralising defeats, against Blackburn and Newcastle, conceding three in successive league matches for the first time since February 2004. The run of bad form means United were 5-2 underdogs, their longest odds in a Manchester derby in Ferguson's 25 years, and though Mancini spoke of struggling to fill his substitutes' bench, Dzeko was expected to be fit after treatment for a knee injury and Nasri recovered from illness.

Ferguson's problems were more acute, with eight players missing through injury or illness, arguing it could be considered a success that his team were only three points behind City. "We can say in some respects: 'Well done, to be there.' The advantage on Sunday is with City, in respect of it being a home draw. But it's a Cup tie, a derby and anything can happen in these games."

Sunday, Jan 8, 2012

Manchester United held off a dramatic and pulsating fight back from 10-man City to win a pulsating FA Cup derby. United led 3-0 after a remarkable first half in which Rooney headed the opening two goals, Welbeck added another and City captain Kompany was sent off. City hit back after the break with goals through Kolarov and Agüero, but United, for whom Scholes came out of retirement to make a substitute appearance, held on to end City's cup defence in the third round.

Mancini insisted his team emerged as moral victors and defeat would inspire them to the title. "I think that this is important for us for the league. I think now we can win the league. United is the top squad in England and if we can play like we did against them with 10 players with that same attitude and same strength in every game we will [win the league]. I am disappointed for the game, but I think today we took two steps forward because we have shown character. When United played with 10 men they lost 6-1 and played for 40 minutes with 10 players. We played for 80 minutes with 10 and didn't concede any chances in the second half."

Mancini's comments were echoed by Kompany, who tweeted after the game, "Every single person involved with Man City FC were incredible today. Definitely the moral winners of this game."

The game, played on a greasy surface in continual drizzle, more than lived up to all the pre-match hype. At one stage it seemed United were on course to avenge their 6-1 thrashing in the most incredible fashion but City's recovery left them to settle for a narrow win.

City suffered their first home defeat since December 2010, reminding them that United remained in the way of their bid for domestic dominance. But the manner of City's comeback was not lost on Mancini who felt it was perhaps more significant than it appeared at the time. The afternoon began unbelievably enough as United announced prior to kick-off that 37-year-old Paul Scholes had rejoined the playing staff to help them through their injury problems and would be on the bench, having retired at the end of last season. Yet what followed was even more dramatic as Rooney, after speculation over his own future, made an emphatic statement and United, initially, were ruthless in taking advantage of Kompany's dismissal.

United took the lead against the run of play in the 10th minute. Valencia found and delivered a cross for Rooney, who had laid the ball off to the winger, to power home a superb header off the underside of the bar. City were dealt an immediate blow as Kompany was sent off for a challenge on Nani. Kompany clearly won the ball but referee Chris Foy showed a straight red card for the offence of lunging forward with both feet. City were angry with the decision but recovered their composure. Nani was denied shooting space on the edge of the box but he fed the ball wide to Evra, who crossed low. Nasri attempted to clear but did not make firm contact and Welbeck hooked in his seventh goal of the season on the volley.

It got worse for City as they conceded a penalty six minutes before half-time when Kolarov brought down Welbeck. Pantilimon, with Hart rested, saved Rooney's spot-kick but was unable to deny the United forward as he followed up to head in the rebound.

It seemed the best City could achieve in the second half was damage limitation, but they gave themselves hope as Kolarov pulled one back after 48 minutes. Evra was booked for felling Richards outside the area and Kolarov stepped up to bend a superb free-kick around the wall and into the net.

Scholes came off the bench to make an unexpected 677th United appearance when he replaced Nani just before the hour. United wanted another penalty moments later when Valencia went over as Kolarov challenged him just inside the box but Foy gave nothing. City got themselves right back into the game after 65 minutes as Milner nicked the ball off Scholes following a throw-in and whipped the ball in for Agüero. The Argentinian shot straight at Lindegaard but the Dane could only parry and Agüero blasted in the loose ball.

City sent on former United midfielder Hargreaves in place of Nasri with eight minutes remaining. City appealed long, but in vain, for a penalty when a low ball from Kolarov took a ricochet and struck Jones' arm. City had United holding on, Kolarov tested Lindegaard with a free-kick in injury time but United, with victory in sight, scrambled the ball clear.

City intended to appeal Kompany's red card for a tackle on Nani. As the City captain had been sent off for a straight red card offence once this season, he faced a four-match ban unless he could overturn the suspension. "We will appeal," said Mancini. "I am sure we will win." Mancini opted not to criticise referee Chris Foy. However, he thinks little can be read into the defence offered almost immediately by former top-flight official Dermot Gallagher, who claimed Foy had got it right. "This is normal. If I talk about the players, I defend the player. The referee is the same. He defends the referee," said Mancini. "I don't want to talk about the referee because I want to stay on the bench for the next game. But I think it is impossible."

Mancini, vilified for waving an imaginary red card during the win over Liverpool, said: "When I did this against Liverpool, people told me not to do it. I said I was sorry and made a mistake." After the flash TV interviews, Mancini later accused Rooney of contributing to the dismissal, "It was not a red card. Rooney told him his decision." When asked to clarify if he felt Rooney had influenced the decision, Mancini added: "Yes, he was near the referee." He continued, "There is no way Vincent shouldn't play against Liverpool in the Carling Cup semi-final on Wednesday. It was 300% not a sending off."

However Mancini was up beat, while Sir Alex was growling. Mancini commented, "My feeling is good because we gave such a good performance. I am disappointed we lost but I'm happy with our performance and proud of my players. I am disappointed with this game but I think we took two steps forward. If we play this way against United with 10 men and with the same attitude and strength in every other game then I think we will win the title. We did not want to concede any more goals in the second half and did not give them any chances, which was very good. At this moment it is difficult because we have players injured, players away, and now I think it is incredible that Vincent cannot play against Liverpool."

Mancini was taken by surprise by Scholes comeback, "Paul Scholes is a fantastic player but yes, it was strange to see him on the bench again, I said to David Platt that he should be on our bench!"

Sir Alex pulled no punches, claiming it was the right decision and that Kompany has been guilty of similar transgressions before. "It was a sending-off. It was a two-footed tackle. I have seen him do it before. He has got off with it in the past. But if Nani gets caught, he has a problem. It was a real bad one."

Mario Balotelli met David Beckham at the game, and declared he was happy at City and not seeking a return to Italy. "The newspapers are saying that I want to get away from Manchester but I've never spoken to them. They can say what they want, but I'm in Manchester, I am under contract with City and until the right time, will not talk about a new contract. [The Premier League] has been a new experience, even if at first it was difficult, but if I have to tell the whole truth now then it is that I am feeling really good." Mario described his relationship with Mancini as "great".

Monday, Jan 10, 2012

City opened formal talks with Inter Milan, having held discussions with AC Milan but were frustrated with the Italian champions' insistence on a loan deal with an option to buy. Tévez's representatives had yet to hold discussions with Inter and no fee has been agreed. Inter president Massimo Moratti said: "If you do something you don't do it as a joke but because you think it can be a good operation. We've acquired information on how things are going, there's room to act, we'll see if we can do it or not. There are still three weeks left. It's not about being optimistic but rather seeing how things are."

Once again, Mancini hoped for a conclusion to the Tévez saga, 'I hope there will be a good result for him in January because he has not played for three months.'

Mario Balotelli's agent slapped a £60m price-tag on the striker and told any suitors from Serie A to forget about signing him because he is "too big for Italy". Mino Raiola also indicated that the 21-year-old was ready to sign a new deal at Eastlands. "Mario is well in Manchester and perhaps he'll extend his contract. My feeling is that it won't be easy for him to return to Serie A. He is too 'big' for Italy." Raiola says the struggle that both Milan clubs are having to try to land Tévez proves they cannot afford Mario, "If Inter and AC Milan have difficulties in finding £25m to invest on Tévez, how can they pay £50m or £60m for Balotelli? This is the value of Balotelli, he's No 1."

Tuesday, Jan 10, 2012

Mancini remained convinced it would be a travesty if Kompany failed to win his appeal, "My opinion has not changed. I am confident because Vinny only played 10 minutes. He was sent off for nothing. He has already missed one game. I don't think about this (being banned). It would be not correct if that happened." Mancini claimed he was right to point out that Rooney gestured to Foy for Kompany to be sent off, even though the United star claimed to only have been pointing out it was a two-footed tackle. "Yeah, I did it. All the people were saying, 'Apologise, apologise, because in England we don't do this', so I apologised. But this is normal because, five minutes before, there was a red card for Gareth Barry for nothing. In Italy, it's normal. We're different. I joked with Wayne Rooney. But he did it," said Mancini. "Nani was there. He didn't say anything."

Mancini accused referees of singling out City, "I watched three or four players in the Premier League last week do tackles worse than Vinnie, and with the same referee. He did nothing, no yellow card, nothing. In 30 years I have never seen a sending-off for a tackle like this. I can't understand it. Vinnie took the ball, he did nothing. If there was danger then Nani, who was the player nearest the ball, probably would have said something about this, especially to the referee. But he didn't say anything. It's strange because in England the referee makes incredible decisions. Sometimes, they send off for nothing. This is strange, I don't understand." City had Mario and Barry sent off against Liverpool, Clichy dismissed at Chelsea before Kompany became the latest of Mancini's players to get his marching orders.

If Kompany failed in his appeal, he would start his suspension by missing the Carling Cup semi-final first-leg with Liverpool, the return and, in between, crucial League games against Wigan and Tottenham, leaving Mancini without six senior players for Wednesday's game, including Kolo and Yaya. Dzeko and Mario were also major doubts, along with Silva, who was replaced at half-time on Sunday. Mancini defended his call for further investment in his team, reiterating he does not have a big squad. City did come up with seven replacements, although they included Abdul Razak and Denis Suarez, who have just six first-team appearances between them, all but two from the bench. Mancini considered involving 17-year-old Dutchman Karim Rekik. "All the people think we have a lot of players, but we have 19, plus keepers. It is not a big squad. If we are unlucky and we have three or four players injured, like at this moment, we can have a problem. The club knows this. I said four weeks ago that December and January would be crucial months. Until three weeks ago we didn't have any injuries. Now, we have a problem. We have players injured and others who went to the African Nations Cup at a crucial moment. I am not happy about this but we can't do anything about it. If we don't get the players back we will play with the young players. If we don't have a central defender we will play with Rekik."

Kompany's appeal was rejected by the FA. The suspension consisted of a statutory three-match suspension for Serious Foul Play plus one additional game given this is Kompany's second dismissal of the season. Kompany warned that there could be a flurry of red cards, "I appealed because I obviously completely disagreed with the interpretation of the officials on the day but that happens in football and we move on. I wonder though if we are now going to see an unprecedented wave of red cards on match days because we sanction "ifs" and "maybes"?"

Wednesday, Jan 11, 2012

City, having gone unbeaten at home in 2011, lost twice in cup competitions in four days, with Liverpool becoming the first away team to keep a clean sheet at Eastlands this season.

Roberto Mancini and Steven Gerrard became embroiled in a tunnel row as the Liverpool captain accused City's manager of double standards. Mancini was furious that a robust tackle from Glen Johnson on Lescott in injury time did not receive a red card. He felt it was 'worse' than the challenge for which Kompany was sent-off. Gerrard, who scored the only goal of the game from the penalty spot, felt his comments were inappropriate. "I'm surprised at Mancini," said Gerrard. "He had a go at Wayne Rooney trying to get one of his players sent off at the weekend, and now he is trying to get one of our players into trouble – I don't think that's right."

Mancini confirmed he had exchanged words with Gerrard afterwards. "Gerrard came to me and said, 'you said this,' but that's not important. Steven Gerrard can say what he wants, no problem. I said what I think. The tackle was worse than Vinny's." This was the first time since February 2008 that City lost back-to-back home games.

City dominated the second period but lacked a cutting edge. Dalglish was thrilled. 'Not too many teams have come here and not conceded, so it's a fantastic effort by us.' However Mancini bemoaned a lack of cutting edge without Silva and as Balotelli limped off with an ankle injury after 39 minutes. "The first half we didn't play well. After six months that can happen. But in the second half Liverpool did not pass the middle of the pitch. We had chances but didn't score but we knew before the game it would be difficult. It is difficult because we were without three or four players. The result is not right. For me it was a draw. We played two difficult games. I knew that was going to happen. January is going to be an important month but I think in both games we didn't deserve to lose. The second leg is going to be difficult. Liverpool are favourites because they won 1-0 away."

Savic gave away the penalty. He said: "It was a bad decision from me. To replace Vinny, everyone expects a lot from you because he's our captain and leader. But I think I can do it. It's not easy but I'm getting more confident and I can do better — try and do everything for the team. I feel OK. As I'm playing more games I'll get more experience and confidence. I think as time goes on I'll do better."

Harry Redknapp said that all the pressure was on City after Tottenham moved to within three points of the leaders with the two sides set to meet at the Etihad Stadium a week on Sunday. Redknapp commented, "You look at the money they've been able to spend – on wages and fees for the likes of Agüero and Dzeko and Nasri and they're going to be expected to be there and win the championship. City are where they are because of Sheikh Mansour and Chelsea thanks to Roman Abramovich. We have not done it that way and it makes me proud. You don't have to go out and spend fortunes to find good players. Spurs are not third in the Premier League because someone has walked through the door at White Hart Lane and slapped a bundle of money on my desk. City can pay players £200,000 a week, it's unbelievable. Man Utd wanted Samir Nasri but he blew them out for City. The people running Spurs have invested wisely. Certainly they or Man United are the hot favourites. We're just hanging in there. I've been saying all along it's not impossible to win the title but it's very, very hard. But we're in there, we've got a chance."

Redknapp was bullish after the 2-0 victory over Everton which lifted Spurs level on points with second-placed United. Toffees boss David Moyes said that he felt Spurs were title contenders. Van der Vaart said Tottenham were increasingly confident of toppling City, "Everybody knows Spurs have a great team and if we can keep playing like this, then we're also favourites to win the title. When we played Man City in August, they were too good but in the last few games they have not been as consistent and they lost last night, too. Maybe it's a little bit in their heads. They have invested so much money, so everyone expects they're going to win it but we're still there. Do we believe we can do it? Absolutely. It's a massive game and we're really looking forward to it but first we must beat Wolves on Saturday. City have so many good players that even when they're not playing well, they can decide a game, whereas we're more of a team. We played well there last season but lost 1-0, so we will go there with confidence and there is no reason why we can't win."

The FA wrote to City to seek their observations over an incident which resulted in a laser pen being shone in the face of Gerrard just before he was going to take his penalty.

Thursday, Jan 12, 2012

Mario Balotelli parked his Bentley outside Xaverian College, Manchester, on Thursday lunchtime. He used the toilet before talking to students in the canteen and walking into the teachers' staff room. A college spokesman commented, "Xaverian was delighted to receive a surprise visit from Mario who chatted to some of the students." Student Edward Gasson, 18, was sitting in the canteen with friends when Mario walked in. He commented: "Balotelli parked his Bentley outside then came in and was asking where the toilets were, then he went to the teachers' staff room. After that he was just walking round campus like he owned the place and everyone was following him around. I'm a City fan so it was amazing to see him but it was a bit ridiculous for him to come here – you would never expect it to happen.'

Mario fancied becoming a DJ, following a meeting with The Big Dawg, Tim Westwood. The pair spent some time together at an event in Manchester on Thursday where Mario outlined his ambition to control the decks. He is a fan of club music and has come to an agreement with Westwood about a series of lessons. The duo crossed paths when they both attended the pre-launch party for the new PlayStation Vita. Mario will invest in the best decks ahead of the lesson, in which he hopes to learn how to play his favourite tunes – described as 'club bangers' and 'party jamz'.

Milan's bid of 20m euros plus for Carlos Tévez was rejected by City as 'too low' according to my sources. Negotiations in London involved Milan vice-president Adriano Galliani, lawyer Lorenzo Cantamessa and City officials Brian Marwood and John MacBeath, plus Tévez's agent Joorabchian and FIFA agent Giuseppe Riso, with City insisting on 30m euros plus add-ons to 35m euros. My source close to the transfer action said, "Clearly clubs are appreciating that City mean business and there will be no loan. AC Milan have insisted all along it was a long and then a deal in the summer, but there is now recognition from AC Milan that it has to be a sale or no deal. Whether it is now dead is up to AC Milan, but the feeling is that if AC Milan want the layer, then they will have to increase their bid, and Inter and maybe even PSG are still lurking there and could out bid them." The eleventh hour breakdown of Pato's proposed £22m transfer to PSG prompted Milan to halt their negotiations with City. "Pato has decided to stay, so Tévez will not come," Galliani told Sky Sport Italia. "Those two deals were connected, if one player does not leave, then the other will not come." When asked if PSG or Inter were now favourites to sign Tévez, Galliani added: "I am not rooting for either club, I know what is happening, but I will keep it to myself. I do not talk about Inter." Earlier, Moratti appeared to concede defeat when asked if he believed Tévez would join AC rather than Inter, he told his club's official website: "I believe so. That's football." Not so later, when he heard the news of AC Milan's break down in talks. "We'll see next week," Moratti said. "There is certainly contact. We are in talks with clubs from all over the world and not just City and we know all about this Tévez situation, but there is the derby now. My thoughts are on Sunday's game."

PSG boss Carlo Ancelotti did little to quell speculation that the Ligue

1 side were lining up a bid. After missing out on Pato, the Parisiens boss turned his attention to Tévez. "Tévez is a player I really like, he is fantastic," Ancelotti said. "If we want to play at a high level, we must act well in the market, looking for players who can give us a hand." Milan had not given up on their pursuit. Joorabchian says the striker could still end up joining Milan. "Carlitos has a huge debt to Corinthians, but they must accept the fact that he wants to play for AC Milan. The conversations between AC Milan and Manchester City have not yet been completed: there will be other meetings, but we will have to wait and wait and wait." Platt diplomatically commented, "We haven't got into whether the rift can be repaired. The club are quite happy to accept offers but if it's not the right deal he will still be a Manchester City player."

While Tévez was teeing it up in exotic Argentina, Agüero was playing golf in the less exciting climes of Cheshire. Mancini wanted the resources to bring in a forward and defender as well as the versatile De Rossi, and had been monitoring Fiorentina's attacker Stevan Jovetic, although the 22-year-old Montenegrin is rated in the £25m bracket.

Fri, Jan 13, 2012

David Silva flew to Las Palmas just prior to the cup tie to have treatment but scans revealed there was no major damage, Platt was expecting him to be involved at the DW Stadium. After losing successive games for the first time since 2008, City had to bounce back to preserve their three-point advantage over United and Tottenham. 'No one expected us to continue winning games without having a difficult moment,' said Platt. 'We can't accelerate the season by four months to see how it is going to turn out. But we are still in the Carling Cup semi-final and our players are quite capable of turning the situation around, and 19 clubs would like to be where we are in the championship. It is not a bad position to be in – some crisis.'

Sir Alex paid tribute to City's phenomenal start to the league campaign, describing their results in the first half of the season as one of the best performances in a long, long time. United could go level on points by winning Saturday's home game against Bolton, as could Tottenham by beating Wolves at White Hart Lane, and Ferguson said it is good for football to see two new teams challenging for the title ahead of the usual threat from Chelsea and Arsenal. "The main difference I can see this season is that City have amassed a bigger points total than Chelsea or Arsenal would normally have managed by this stage. Their first half of the season was fantastic, and the way it's going we could be looking at something approaching 90 points to win this league. It could certainly be a number in the high 80s, and that is surprising really, because in recent seasons more teams have been taking points off each other. Points will be dropped along the way, I always say that. I am sure we will be dropping a few too, because we have got a hard programme of games away from home. We have still got to go to Arsenal, Chelsea, Tottenham and City, and those are all games that could see points shared or dropped. There's a long way to go yet."

Sir Alex saw off Chelsea and thought he would do the same with City, "How we handled the Chelsea situation will hopefully apply itself again.' City were not the only challengers after watching Tottenham's rise up the table continue. 'Tottenham are a threat,' he said. 'You can't dismiss them. They are playing fantastic football. Somewhere along the line one of those three teams are going to win the league."

Meanwhile David Platt responded to Redknapp's assessment that City are buying their way to the title. "There's one trophy," said Platt. "There's no trophy for spending money or not spending money. You get a trophy for being top of the pile. Harry's got a right to be proud of what he's done. But I don't know where the money comes into it. I think it's irrelevant. He should still be proud if he finishes second and a point behind us. But we'll be happy with that as well! Spurs are genuine title contenders. We have always felt that and I am glad everyone else is now recognising them as a threat. It feels like they have been under the radar for a while, but maybe that's just the view from Manchester. Three points from the top with 18 games to play is not a bad position to be in."

Platt has known Roberto for almost 20 years, so he is best to assess how he will cope with a run of four defeats in the last eight games. "I have no worries that this is somebody who loses his head. There's no way on earth he will go under. I think of all the people I have known or worked with, and he is right up there if not right at the top when it comes to having strong opinions and a strong mind. There is a desire to win. It's almost a drug. He just deals with things and there are no grudges. He will remain the same. It will be the perception of him that will change."

Mancini is driven, never satisfied, always searching for more trophies. "If we win the League this season, he will want to win it again next season. He wants to win every single thing. His idea is to continue winning. I know for a fact one of the things that floats his boat is the ability to come and change a club from not winning to winning – and not just once. He changed it as a player. He was involved very deeply with Sampdoria and had suitors right, left and centre to go to bigger clubs like Juventus, AC and Inter Milan, but he enjoyed the fact that he was helping build something. He has brought that doctrine to Manchester City. He's not your typical Italian manager. The way it is in Italy you coach for two years here, two years there. He is different to that. He likes to build an institution, to be at a club for a significant number of years. He didn't want to leave Inter Milan (where he won three successive league titles). They got rid of him. He would have stayed there and continued to win."

How does he react to two defeats on the bounce? "He reacts to a bad pass," Platt admitted. "He is a perfectionist, an absolute perfectionist. I have seen him getting angry when we've been winning 3-0. Does he lose his temper? Frequently. But he quickly puts all that away, and that's to the benefit of the next game." It's why there was a tunnel bust-up with Gerrard. Platt said: "The game has characters, it has personalities, people with opinions. In the overall swim of things this was something out of nothing. It won't be affecting Roberto and I'm sure it won't be affecting Steve. There's no grudge."

Nothing will dent the friendship between Platt and Mancini, forged two decades ago in Italy. "If I've got an opinion I will give it to him but you are not going to change the character of someone who has certain things in him when I first knew him at 26 or 27. I will say something to him. Whether he takes it on board depends on what mood you get him in. It's a case of just complementing each other. We now have to navigate our way through the next four months as best as we possibly can, as a group – players, managers and staff."

Saturday, Jan 14, 2012

Only Barcelona could cope with the huge number of absentees that the club had to deal with at present, according to Mancini, "Maybe Barcelona could. Manchester City no. In four or five years, Manchester City probably yes. But not now. When I said one month ago that December and January would be the crucial months it was because I know football. Every year in every squad you have one difficult moment. At the moment we are not strong and we have lost important players, so it is difficult."

United won 3-0 at home to Bolton to turn up the pressure on Mancini's men but Spurs blew their chance of joining them level on points with City with a draw at home to Wolves. Redknapp commented, "I've never said to anybody that we are going to win the league." He insisted that they were aiming for a top four spot, rather than a first league title since 1961. "I only answered the question of if it is possible, and, of course it is possible. Man City and Man United will be red hot favourites but, if we have a fantastic run in the second half like we have had in the first half of the season, it could happen."

Sunday, Jan 15, 2012

Inter president Moratti confirmed a 25m euro bid for Tévez, and would wait until the derby game with AC Milan before turning their attentions back to the pursuit of Tévez. "There are no secrets in football," Moratti told Controcampo. "The offer is 25 million euros. Now it is up to City whether they accept that bid or not. However, I do think that there are a number of other clubs who are interested in him. There are some English sides and also Paris St Germain."

Having seen his side beat Serie A champions Milan 1-0, Moratti continued: "At this moment in time it seems that we don't need Tévez, but football gives a different answer on a daily basis."

Milan pulled out of the latest round of negotiations, and Inter coach Claudio Ranieri was asked a succession of questions about Tévez in the post-match interviews: "Tévez? If the president wants to give the city of Milan a present... I'm used to working with what I've got."

Mark Hughes took charge at QPR and was immediately linked with Tévez, given the player and Hughes are represented by Joorabchian. In response to a question on whether they could sign Tévez, Hughes said: "Not in this window, absolutely not. Ideally I would love the chance to work with Carlos again but it is not going to happen any time soon."

Monday, Jan 16, 2012

Roberto Mancini refused to apologise for waving an imaginary red card once again as City beat Wigan to extend their lead at the top to three points. Mancini was merely copying Rooney in demanding the dismissal of Figueroa for deliberate handball and that his gesture was not as bad as Rooney's call for a red card for Kompany.

City recorded their first win in three matches courtesy of Dzeko's brilliantly headed goal and a fraught finale was encapsulated by the reaction of their bench when Figueroa deliberately handled substitute de Jong's through-ball to prevent Agüero going clear in the 88th minute from just inside the City half and Martin Atkinson's decision to issue only a yellow card prompted a furious reaction from Mancini and Platt, who both ran to the fourth official waving imaginary cards. Mancini apologised for an identical act when Skrtel tripped Yaya vowing never to do it again. He then condemned Rooney for urging Chris Foy to dismiss Kompany for a two-footed tackle on Nani and was involved in an exchange with Gerrard after saying Johnson deserved to be sent off.

The City manager's latest dispute prompted Rooney to say on Twitter: "Was manchini asking for a red card????" (sic)

Mancini, having initially refused to discuss the subject or apologise, responded: "I used to do this but I don't want to say anything. I did it because Wayne Rooney did this. It is normal with a chance like that to do it." Asked if he was therefore wrong to condemn Rooney for a similar response, Mancini said: "Yes, but I am on the bench. It's different. When you are a player very near to the referee you can have more of an influence. I am on the bench and the referee cannot see me."

Martínez believes Mancini should know such actions will be condemned, "I've been here long enough to understand that trying to influence the referee is not accepted in the British game. When a player tries to simulate or buy a decision from the referee that is regarded as cheating. I understand that in Italy, France and Spain it is acceptable to try and get a decision from the referee, but it is different here. I don't think it's a goalscoring opportunity. James McCarthy was coming back and Maynor wasn't even in his own half. I don't think it's a red card."

Mancini knew it was vital to get back to winning ways, "It was about the victory not the performance tonight. It was important to win. We had three or four chances to score in the second half. Wigan are a very good team with a fantastic manager and they are dangerous at home. At this moment it is important to take three points. This month it is important to take maximum points from every game. I was nervous when it was still 1-0 but that's normal, every player and manager is nervous."

Dzeko's first-half header ended an 11-match goal drought, taking his tally to 14. But there was one hilarious, almost comical, mix up in front of goal. Dzeko said: "I was waiting for him to shoot. In the end the ball came to me and he wanted to shoot, and I wanted to shoot, but it doesn't matter. We're happy now." Mancini hoped Dzeko can build on the goal, "I'm very happy for him because he deserved to score a goal. He scored this very important goal for us and I hope he continues it in the next game."

Tuesday, Jan 17, 2012

Harry Redknapp criticised Mancini for waving imaginary cards, "I don't like it. I wouldn't do it. I don't like to see it. I don't think there is any need for it. He has done a great job there and when I have met him I have found him a really good guy. We all do things we shouldn't do at different times. We get caught up in the game but it's not something I like to see." Mick McCarthy agreed, "None of us should do it. It is something I don't like. There is a cultural difference. Roberto is in this country now. It is a little blip on a really good career for him at Man City because he handles himself with such good dignity and grace."

Mancini found an unlikely ally in Wigan owner Dave Whelan, "Roberto Mancini is one of these managers who do tend to get excited - he gets excited when he is watching his team and I don't blame him because they play great football and they are going for the title. A few people have had a go at him but for me he is a total and utter gentleman. I spoke to him before the match and he wished us good luck for the rest of the season after which I appreciated. He is a total gentleman. And I've got nothing but good things to say about the way City is run. They have got quite a few of their ex-players who go around with them such as Mike Summerbee. They were in the boardroom and they represent Manchester City superbly well. It is going to be an exciting race for the Premier League title this year. But I'd go for City, especially when they get Yaya Toure back. They have supreme quality."

Vincent Kompany signed up to do a Masters degree. Kompany is recognised as one of the country's most intelligent footballers, having turned down moves to big clubs such as Manchester United in his teenage years in order to complete his university studies in Belgium. Now he has gained a place on a Business Administration course at Manchester business school, the three-year course begins at the start of the next academic year in September with much of his coursework done at home.

Wednesday, Jan 18, 2012

Emmanuel Adebayor was ruled out of the upcoming Spurs game as he was on loan from City as only third-placed Tottenham seemed capable of preventing the Manchester clubs from winning the title. Adebayor enjoyed a successful loan spell, scoring nine goals since his arrival in September, to help Spurs move up to third. He was keen to make his move to Tottenham permanent, but Redknapp warned he will have to take a pay cut. Redknapp said. "The other week, one of the lads told him that he had not paid his £50 fine for being the worst player in training on a Friday morning. One of the lads said to him: 'Bloody hell, Ade, you are on 200 grand a week and you can't afford to pay a £50 fine!' He replied: 'Don't insult me, it's 225!'." Redknapp added: "He certainly isn't getting that here."

City warned their players not to become embroiled in a Twitter feud with United rivals amid growing anger at the Etihad Stadium over City-related tweets by the likes of Rooney and Ferdinand. Several members of City's first-team squad are users of the social-networking site, with Kompany, Richards, Johnson, Zabaleta, Agüero, de Jong, Nasri and Lescott regularly updating their Twitter pages. Mancini's squad were advised by senior figures to steer clear of engaging in a potentially-distracting Twitter row with United. The City squad were urged by the club to avoid using social media to comment publicly in the aftermath of Kompany's red card and subsequent four-match suspension.

Rooney tweeted, "Funny how people think I got Kompany sent off. Im not ref. I didn't give red card. But it was a clear red card. 2 footed tackle." Ferdinand, prior to City's appeal, by tweeting, "By the way how can there be any debate about the red card yesterday?? You leave the ground with a £2footTackle = Red card £fact." Kompany was given permission to issue a statement on his Facebook site following the FA's decision to reject his appeal, noticeably focusing on his red card and subsequent appeal, rather than responding to comments from within the United camp.

United's position on their players' use of Twitter is relaxed, with an acceptance that high-profile sportsmen embracing social media is an unavoidable phenomenon.

United captain Nemanja Vidic, who is out for the season with a knee injury, insisted that Sir Alex's side were still the team to beat. 'If you look at our history and commitment, you know we like to win all trophies and I believe we are the team in Manchester who will keep doing that every year. Of course we are confident. We are challenging for the title and we are only three points behind City. We have had problems with injuries but I think against Arsenal this weekend we have a good chance. We have a few players back which will help the manager. We have a good squad – a good balance between experience and youth.'

Vidic said that it is 'healthy' to have two strong teams in Manchester. "It's good for the city to have two football teams doing well – there's a lot of talk and banter. It's always healthy to have competition and we don't mind it. It helps to improve ourselves."

Thursday, Jan 19, 2012

David Silva was mobbed at a supporters' club gathering in Stockport as City supporters braved a wet and windy night to see him in the flesh. "The real pressure would come with being in the chasing pack and not being able to afford any defeats," said the Spaniard, "We are right up there and we have a certain margin of error and we'll be doing our best not to throw that away. It's going to be a hard and difficult game because there's a lot at stake for both teams but I really think it will be an entertaining game. It would be nice to repeat the 5-1 win at Spurs earlier this season but I think it's unlikely." Silva was part of Spain's World Cup-winning squad in 2010 but featured for only five minutes after the shock opening-game defeat by Switzerland. "Winning the Premier League would be just as important to me as winning the Euros and the World Cup. It would be very important because coming to England has been a challenge for me. The English and Spanish leagues are the best two in the world but here you've probably got more teams battling it out for the title, whereas for the moment in Spain there are only two in contention, so it's more exciting here."

Meanwhile Kia Joorabchian travelled to France for talks with Ancelotti and PSG sporting director Leonardo. City stated that reports of an offer being accepted from PSG were wide of the mark, but the Ligue 1 leaders had since made contact. Ancelotti discussed the prospect of signing Tévez, "Everyone knows that we want a striker. Carlos Tévez – it's a great opportunity for us to have a great striker. Today Tévez isn't playing for Manchester City, but he wants to play. Today, nothing is done. We have to talk with the player, and with Manchester City. We hope to find a good solution." Ancelotti stayed out of negotiations, explaining: 'I haven't had him on the phone, not him or his agent. It's Leonardo who is looking after that. Tévez isn't a problem. He is a great player. In 15 days he could get back into great physical condition. If Tévez doesn't come, we have the possibility of buying another striker. In January it's harder to get players. And at the end of the month, the transfer window is over. I look forward to it ending, because I am very stressed.'

Tévez had yet another 'advisor', or rather his advisor Kia had hired a "media advisor' Paul McCarthy, formerly Sports Editor of the defunct News of the World, who told talkSport that he could confirm Joorabchian will hold talks with PSG but did not expect a conclusion to be sorted until the last day of the transfer window. "Initial talks are planned today between Kia Joorabchian and PSG," McCarthy told Keys & Gray. "I think it is going to go right down to the wire. I think everybody involved in it now believes it will go right down to the wire of the transfer window. PSG are obviously interested. They have made no official bid to Manchester City but there is enough in the background to suggest it would be foolish to say they are not in the picture. I do believe the two Milan clubs' interest is not dead and I don't think it is going to be sorted very quickly, but I think by the end of the window there will be some kind of conclusion."

Talks were delayed 24 hours because Joorabchian was central to Taiwo's loan move from AC Milan to QPR and had to remain in London to complete that deal. However Joorabchian spoke extensively on the telephone to Leonardo and the financial package proposed by PSG for Tévez was far greater than the offers that have been made by both Milan clubs. Tévez favoured Italy, and Milan more than Inter. Inter director Marco Branca insisted the club remained interested, "I think that Tévez is in reality close to Paris Saint-Germain, as his agent received a very good offer from the French club. In any case, I am not optimistic or pessimistic with regards to Tévez. We are still interested and will continue discussing matters with his agent. We are studying how to get back into the hunt for Carlos over the next few days. We are not running late in this race. I believe Carlos and his agent can wait a day or two, seeing as he hasn't played for Manchester City for several months. It's not as if the situation will change over the next 48 hours. Besides, the transfer window certainly doesn't close tonight or tomorrow." But it didn't look good for PSG. Leonardo commented, "We didn't get a deal with Tévez, maybe we never will."

It was a different story for Agüero, who looked beyond the notorious weather and a tricky language, but was disappointed he never got the chance to strike up a proper partnership with Tévez, "I'm still adapting myself to the Manchester way of life... but Manchester is a beautiful city. When I'm not at training sessions or playing, I try to visit new places as I find the city is very interesting. But Manchester does not have great meat, like Argentina has. Luckily my friend Pablo Zabaleta has found a place where the meat is really good. I've also been learning how to speak in English. At the beginning I took classes three days a week and it was like I was back in school. Now my team-mates help me with English and let me practice with them. It was a shame that Carlos and Mancini had this fight. I was so sorry about it – but you know, this is football and these things happen in football. I hope Carlos finds a solution for his situation as soon as possible. But I think that I and the other players who came to the club this year were really helpful for the team. We have a great team with great players. We have this hunger for glory. I don't know if the fans or even the journalists see it, but I assure you we are hungry for glory and we want to win the Premier League."

Agüero could not have done it without Mancini's help, "He always tells me, 'Sergio, you have to do your best all the time'. I really like him. He looks out for me. He knows what he wants and he knows how to give us his message. The boss is really good at his job. He talks to me all the time during the training sessions. He teaches me to improve my movement, my runs, for example. I have understood that I have to be focused all the time on the pitch. Also, you have to run much more in England, as football here is faster than in Argentina or even Spain. I'm becoming a more complete player. I'm sure I took the right decision when I left Atletico Madrid for City."

Fri, Jan 20, 2012

Roberto Mancini confessed he was desperate for a Tévez deal to be done. "I hope this will finish very quickly. I don't know. I think he has talked with PSG and Inter, but not Milan. I hope for him everything can finish very quickly." Speaking at a press conference to preview the clash with Tottenham, he said there was no way Tévez could return to City. "This is impossible. Carlos doesn't want to stay. It is important for him to start to play because he is a football player. It is now three months that he hasn't played and this is not good for him."

Nedum Onuoha edged closer to a move to QPR after he appeared as a substitute in the win at Wigan. Mancini said: "I don't know. They were talking yesterday. Maybe today or tomorrow, it is possible. Nedum deserves to play. He is a good guy and if he stays here he will maybe play one or two games. That is not enough for a young player."

Tottenham were on the receiving end of a 5-1 hiding from City in their second game on the season but had only lost once in their following 19 matches – something which leaves their manager confident of a shock victory on Sunday that would blow the title race wide open. 'They are not invincible,' Redknapp said. 'I think we can win. We will go there as a positive team. I wouldn't want to go there and sit back. We have people who can hurt them. We have good players here and they will be looking forward to it. I don't think about losing. I think about going there on Sunday and trying to win.'

Redknapp cranked up the pressure on Mancini, claiming failure to deliver trophies this season will probably cost him his job, "City are not throwing money around for fun. The sheikh and the club's supporters expect Mancini to deliver and if they don't win the Premier League title who is to say they won't sack him and bring in someone who can? Personally, I quite like Mancini and I certainly don't blame him for spending the money he has. I would if I was in his position. But you have to accept that with it comes pressure and rising expectations. City have come from nowhere in recent years after living in the shadows of their neighbours Manchester United but, when you suddenly find yourself with the spending power to outbid any club, the past counts for nothing and people don't want you to win things, they expect it."

Redknapp maintained he had a very strong squad to compete with City, but he wasn't deluded and said there were one or two players they had he wouldn't have minded signing, if Spurs had the financial power to compete, "I'd be a liar if I said I didn't like David Silva, Sergio Agüero and Carlos Tévez. They are fantastic players and with them in your side you would have to fancy your chances, wouldn't you."

Redknapp still felt Tottenham could cause an upset, "No, we will go there and attack City. I'm only interested in taking three points. If we get the chance we will try and rip their throats out. We went there two years ago and had to win to secure a top four finish and came away with a 1-0 victory. I would settle for that. It's not going to be easy but we have some very dangerous players in our side and we are more than capable of hurting them."

Mancini felt the August thumping of Spurs at White Hart Lane would have no bearing, because meeting as title rivals was different to playing each other at the start of a season when results can be strange. "It's better to lose one time 5-1 than five times 1-0. We played five months ago, it was totally different. When you start the season anything can happen because all the squad are not ready to play 100%. Every team needs four, five, six games to be confident."

Mancini joined the band of admirers of Tottenham's playing style but fell short of Ferguson's assessment that Redknapp's team were the best team to watch at the moment. "They play the best football probably – after us. For me, the best football is Swansea, they play very well."

Sunday, Jan 22, 2012

Harry Redknapp accused Mario Balotelli of deliberately kicking Scott Parker before scoring the decisive last minute penalty that gave City all three points in this pulsating encounter that put Spurs effectively out of the title race.

Mario's clash with Parker went unpunished by referee Howard Webb and came after he had already been booked since coming on as a substitute. "It was a double one on Scott," Redknapp insisted. "The first one could have been an accident, but on the second one he's back heeled him straight in the head. I don't even like talking about people kicking other people because it's not my game, but it's wrong. I don't like seeing people react like that to a challenge. It's not the first time he's done it and I'm sure it won't be the last." Redknapp's fury was increased when Mario scored the late penalty after he was fouled by Ledley King.

City had opened up a two-goal lead courtesy of Nasri and Lescott but Spurs responded through Defoe and Bale before Mario's decisive late intervention in the closing seconds. Redknapp felt Balotelli should not have been on the pitch to take the kick, adding: "He reacts like that at times to challenges. Scott has got a lovely cut on his head. It is up to their manager to deal with it. I have got my own opinions, but what I would say is that I don't like people kicking other people in the head on football pitches, and I don't think it's wrong to say that. Why you should back heel someone in the head when they are lying on the floor is beyond me. It's not a nice thing to do."

David Platt, standing in for Mancini at the post-match press conference due to a sore throat, said he had not seen the incident and could not comment until he had. "I never saw anything live and there was nothing from the players live either. Until we have seen it we cannot really comment. What we are aware of from the last month is that different TV angles can show different things."

Reacting to the incident on his official Twitter account, Blackburn striker and BBC Radio 5 live pundit Jason Roberts was in the minority when he commented: "Balotelli... not 100% either way! For what it's worth I don't think it's a sending off but I don't think you can be sure. Movement was not 'natural' but he was facing the other way, and never glanced backwards. Only he will know..." On Match of the Day, Lee Dixon gave him the benefit of the doubt, while Alan Hansen thought it deserved a red card.

In an interview with BBC Radio 5 live, former Premier League referee Graham Poll compared the Balotelli-Parker incident with a moment in the 2010 World Cup Final when Webb chose not to send off de Jong of the Netherlands for kicking out at Xavi Alonso of Spain. "I struggle with the fact that Howard Webb didn't see it but then he didn't see six studs land on someone's chest in the World Cup. I like Howard, I think he's a great referee but basic instructions to referees are that if two players clash and you cannot trust them then you shouldn't leave them on their own. You stop play – it's as simple as that." Asked about the FA's policy on punishments Poll added: "They are so inconsistent on what they charge and what they don't. What's the matter with transparency? Balotelli is certain to my mind to get a four-match ban whereas Joleon Lescott is free to play. I do not believe there's a bias in the FA but I do believe there's inconsistency."

Mario was left shell-shocked on Sunday evening after his Bentley GT was egged by United fans. His car was targeted while he enjoyed dinner at a Manchester restaurant. He was forced to rush back to his £120,000 car and drive it to a nearby multi-story car park. One eye-witness said, "He parked down a side street but unfortunately it was parked right next door to a well-known Man United pub, where loads of fans were in there watching the later Arsenal game and they must have come out and seen his car. They pelted his roof with eggs. The yolk was dripping down all one side. It was pretty disgusting." United won 2-1 at the Emirates to keep the pressure up at the top of the table.

Monday, Jan 23, 2012

Harry Redknapp went straight from an abortive title race to a court case having been accused of tax evasion. Redknapp, tipped as a future England manager, was accused of two counts of cheating the public revenue when he was manager of Portsmouth. He was accused alongside the then Portsmouth chairman Milan Mandaric.

Mario Balotelli was charged by the FA and following a dismissal earlier this season he faced a four-match ban, but any unsuccessful appeal could result in a longer suspension. Lescott would not be punished after a clash with Kaboul. Lescott caught Kaboul in the face with his forearm in a separate incident.

Platt intimated the club would not challenge the decision, with a failed appeal risking an extended ban. Platt said: "We are likely to be without a player for four games. We found out the information last night and we have not sat down as a group to discuss it. But I don't think anybody thought we would win an appeal with Vincent Kompany, even though the majority of people didn't feel he deserved a red card or a four-match ban. It shows the futility of an appeal sometimes. This looks poor when you slow it down."

Mario's agent called for Webb to be "banned for life". Webb did not see the incident, but, having reviewed the footage, the FA charged Mario with violent conduct. Mino Raiola was furious, questioning Webb in an interview with Italian radio station Radio Radio. "The referee saw everything, because he spoke to Mario after the action. So in my opinion, this referee must be banned for life because he didn't tell the truth. The TV images show that he is really close to the action, how can he say he didn't see it? What was he doing? He says he didn't see it, only to defend himself." Raiola suggested Mario could seek a move away from England if he continues to feel persecuted against, adding: "Mario can't be banned for four games. He wasn't balanced and there was also a push from Modric. It is not an intentional foul because Mario doesn't want to hurt anyone, he didn't see Parker, that's all. I want to be balanced but I'm worried because when English players are involved in more serious things, nothing happens, whereas when foreigners are involved, such as Balotelli or Kompany, they were treated harder. If I find that there is something strange against Balotelli, my duty is to protect and then take him away. In this case I would speak with City, I'd ask them Balotelli's price and would look for the best team for him, as there are only six or seven teams he can play for. I talked to Mario who said he is happy to stay in England, but he does not understand certain things and they sadden him."

"I have accepted the ban because I couldn't prove my innocence," said Mario. "But I'm not a villain or violent. I didn't try to [place my] heel [on] Parker."

Agüero insisted Mario is a 'lovely lad'. "Firstly we all know what a fantastic player he is. And off the pitch, everyone has their own path. But those of us who are really close to Mario know that off the field he's a really good lad. Like a lot of players he has his own idiosyncrasies here and there. Everyone knows him as a player from what you see on the field. But I know that off the field he's a lovely lad. He's a young lad, he takes care of himself and approaches his life as he wants."

His madcap antics help take the pressure off City ahead of big games, James Milner claimed, "Mario is good to have around the place. He scores important goals and hopefully can score a few more winners between now and the end of the season. Is it a welcome distraction? Maybe, as long as it is at the right time. You can always rely on Mario to set some fireworks off to get the headlines. He is just very confident in his own ability. He has lots of that. He is fun to have around the place. I don't think I have done an interview this season without being asked about him. It sums up what a character he is." Milner, who has also taken on spot-kick duties this season, says Mario is the undisputed penalty king at the Etihad, "I wouldn't have wanted anyone else but Mario to be in that position. He is definitely the best I have seen. He takes them like that in training. It doesn't matter whether there is any pressure on him or not. I have seen him take 60 or 70 penalties against Joe Hart, who is no slouch between the sticks. Joe has only saved one — and when he did he was jumping around because he had saved it. He just waits for the keeper and makes it impossible for him to save it. I had full confidence in him that he would put that away."

Agüero was 'not really' a Liverpool fan, he maintained, 'It's just that one of the players who was my idol when I was growing up was Michael Owen. He was quite small and had an eye for goal, just like me. It's since he scored against Argentina in 1998, although I wasn't too happy at the time.'

Sunderland took Enoch Balotelli, brother of the City striker, on trial. The 19 year old was put through his paces by the club's football development staff after failing to clinch a contract at Stoke. Enoch was living with his brother in Cheshire and was keen to show his talent.

Tuesday, Jan 24, 2012

"Tévez wants Milan? We also want Tévez," Galliani told Milan's official website. "We shall see, there are still seven days left until the end of the transfer window." "I see myself only in the red and black shirt, I am hoping for Milan," Tévez is quoted by m24digital in Argentina.

PSG's director of football Leonardo confirmed the Ligue 1 club ended negotiations, "There was an opportunity, we have studied it, we made a good offer but failed to agree a deal. We will not pay excessively so we stop. It's over."

Then came the bombshell, media release by City with a 10pm embargo, which I knew was coming, so could prepare my article for ESPNsoccernet.... enabling me to write: "Tévez fit of pique in Munich and disciplinary rebellion will cost the Argentine superstar a staggering £9.3m in fines and withdrawn loyalty payments.... the latest and most costly sanctions against the striker."

City chairman Khaldoon Al Mubarak warned Tévez he will stay at City for the next two-and-a-half years unless the club receive the offer they believe the player is worth. "He goes on City's terms or not at all," in an interview with the National in Abu Dhabi, the chairman said, "Carlos remains a player with contractual obligations to Manchester City for the next two and a half seasons. Unless we receive an offer that we deem appropriate the terms of his contract will be enforced. Inter Milan and Paris St Germain approached discussions with us in good faith and it is always a positive experience to deal with people with a professional approach. As things stand AC Milan isn't an option for Carlos Tévez. Mr. Galliani and his advisors have developed a misplaced sense of confidence from their premature discussions with Carlos and his advisors. If they want to be a consideration in this transfer window they would do better to stop congratulating one another and begin to look at how they would meet our terms."

Tévez was found guilty by a City tribunal and fined a total of £2.9m, with the club upholding the decision on appeal. Tévez can now take another appeal to the Premier League. This is how the fines are broken down; £1.2m for a six week maximum fine under the current rules, plus a two month fine totalling £1.7m for refusing to return from Argentina. Added to his first two week fine (which was reduced to the two weeks by the PFA after he was originally fined four weeks wages) the fines now total £3.3m for the player who earns a basic £198,000-a-week. In addition City withheld £6m worth of loyalty payments due to him under the terms of his contract. City do not believe Tévez warrants loyalty payments for such indiscipline and going on strike for two months! The disciplinary action against Tévez dates back to December 22nd with City finding him guilty of a charge of gross misconduct for going AWOL since November 7. Since that time City have been paying him, and continue to do so, but Tévez had until January 7th to lodge an appeal, which he duly did, and it went to a formal appeal to the City Board of Directors on January 11. The appeal was thrown out and the six week fine, and docking of two months pay was up held. Tévez had until the end of the month to take the appeal to the Premier League, which no doubt he will do.

The City chairman also made it clear that the chances of being railroaded into a deal with AC Milan because he has agreed personal terms will be vetoed unless the terms are correct, hitting the 30m euro mark.

City released a statement, "The club can confirm that Carlos Tévez was found guilty by a disciplinary hearing on 21 December of gross misconduct for serious breaches of contract and was fined six weeks' wages. Carlos elected to appeal the finding, which was dismissed by an appeal panel made up of club directors. He has until 30 January to make a final appeal to the Premier League."

The Tévez camp were quick to react, insisting the striker has never been motivated by the financial aspect of his career. "Carlos has said many times before that money has never been a motivation," said a spokesman for the player. "We reached an agreement with Manchester City in terms of his wages and he returned to Argentina and nothing has changed on that front. Now all Carlos wants to do is get back to playing football again."

Inter announced they are no longer interested. Board member Marco Tronchetti Provera told Ansa: "Now we're no longer interested in Tévez. He is following a different path. Tévez remains a great champion."

QPR agreed a £2.75m transfer for Onuoha which could rise to over £3m with the add-ons. Onuoha was paid around £60,000-a-week at City, which was a big problem for QPR and indeed other potential suitors.

Wednesday, Jan 25, 2012

Roberto Mancini could not hide his anger at the perceived refereeing conspiracy as City crashed out of the League Cup at Anfield. The Italian claims it was threatening to sabotage City's season. Replays showed the penalty awarded to Liverpool by Phil Dowd to be wrong, the ball having hit Richards on the leg before bouncing up and striking his arm. "On Monday, they decided to send Mario off, yet the referee had been there and seen everything. If it was correct, then send him off during the game. So maybe they will change this result tomorrow. The referee was there, 10 metres from the incident involving Mario. If he thought it was a red card, he should have sent Mario off there and then, not after watching a video. The referee was there he can't say he didn't see it, Mario can do nothing he can't play for four games now. Here, Liverpool's first goal was not a penalty. I do feel a sense of injustice. It was a stupid penalty."

Mancini's anger stems from Kompany's four-match ban for a two-footed tackle and red card against United. When Liverpool's Johnson produced a similar tackle on Lescott and escaped punishment, Mancini was incensed at what he saw as double standards. "In the last two months we have been very unlucky with referees. It was not a penalty for Liverpool, because the ball touched Micah's leg before his hands. I don't know how it's possible to concede a penalty like this and not get one for the foul on Edin Dzeko. I haven't spoken to the referee it is impossible to speak to him. I am tired of it after so many games. I think Phil Dowd is one of the best referees in

England. I am just giving my opinion and for me it was not a penalty."

Savic looked out of his depth deputising. Savic did not emerge after the break, following a torrid first-half, the £7m City paid for him looking like one of the most inflated fees they have paid. Kompany's enforced absence emphasised just what a pivotal figure he is, not just in terms of his own defensive ability, but in the calmness and assurance his presence and authority transmits to those defenders alongside him.

Thursday, Jan 26, 2012

QPR signed Onuoha on a four and a half year contract. "Nedum is a player I know well," commented Mark Hughes, "he did very well for me at Man City and played a number of games, probably more than under any other manager. He is very versatile. He can play centre-back or right-back and has good pace."

Milan vice-president Adriano Galliani said the club will make a final decision on signing Tévez on Friday.

Brian Marwood is secure in the role of director of football, even if the club appoint former Barcelona vice-president Ferran Soriano as the new chief executive despite speculation from Spain that Soriano will bring his former Barcelona colleague Txiki Beguiristain to head City's recruitment — the job Marwood carries out for Mancini. Marwood had a difficult working relationship with Hughes, who preferred the counsel of his close-knit group of assistants rather than a director of football. But Marwood and Mancini developed a partnership trusted by the Abu Dhabi owners, who recognise the value of Marwood's football contacts. The expected selection of Soriano was a drawn-out process: head-hunters Odgers had him as their prime candidate in November.

Mourinho would decide on his Real career in the summer, his potential availability inevitably leading to speculation about a potential move to City where Mancini was under pressure to land the title. Mourinho is City's No.1 choice to replace Mancini if they make a change. Mourinho was beginning to warm to the idea of taking over at City, having previously ruled out taking the job, instead waiting in the wings to land the United vacancy from Sir Alex when he decides to retire. But that stance has changed with Ferguson showing no signs of wishing to stand down.

Fri, Jan 27, 2012

Roberto Mancini claims decisions go against his club because referees can also get tired. ''I think playing a lot of games is also difficult for them. The refs sometimes are tired - to play every two or three days is difficult for the players, and for the referee. The referee is like me, like the players. They can be tired sometimes." Mancini did not think his team were victims of any conspiracy, only bad luck. "Yes, yes - in December and January, it is only this way."

City were shocked that Joorabchian suddenly pointed an accusing finger at Mancini as the reason for the breakdown of his clients relationship with his club. The latest row in a series of bust ups surfaced with Mancini becoming the unexpected target. Joorabchian, insisted the manager's handling of the situation has been generally poor. "The relationship with Mancini has never been good ever since Mancini came into the football club," he said. "After the explosion of that day, Mancini created an impossible situation. Carlos Tévez served his two-week suspension, he trained with the reserves. Once he had done that Mancini should have re-integrated him with the first team. For two years he was dedicated to the football club, he even went to Italy to get massive treatment on his knee to come back and play in the FA Cup final."

City pointed out that Tévez first asked for a transfer and nearly signed for Corinthians citing that he needed to be closer to his family. He has also given a reason for the fall out because of problems with the executives, rather than the manager. The goal posts moved on to Mancini's managerial methods and fall outs with other star players as well as himself. On occasions Tévez has even publicly declared that there had not been a fall out with his manager. Also, Mancini offered Tévez an olive branch inviting Tévez to his home and suggested that he apologised to him and the players and moved on. Tévez refused. Now Joorabchian claims Mancini was a divisive influence at the Etihad, with fall out with numerous other big name players.

"There was a point where Carlos was saying 'I can't get on here' and he's not the only one. Craig Bellamy, Emmanuel Adebayor and Shay Given have all left in an awkward way and Wayne Bridge is now not training with the first team. Mancini's done a good job at the club but there are not many managers in the world who can throw away the quality of Adebayor, Tévez and Bellamy. He's in a very fortunate position. When he was at Inter Milan, and now at Man City, the club was the highest spending team in the world. You look at the people who are running Manchester City and they are trying very hard to sort out some of the problems from the Bayern Munich match. These are situations where the manager needs to be managing the football club. Mancini has been very clear that he doesn't want him in the first team. Carlos is going to have to come back, pick up his money and play with the reserves. He's not that type of player who wants to walk around the club with that hanging over his head though."

City told me that in the extensive Tévez files you can find Tévez saying:

"Mancini and I have arguments and moments but it's not such a great matter to me. He's a great manager. Things happen in the heat of the moment, silly things that can happen when we are trying to do what's best for the team." When Tévez transfer request was first made public, City issued a statement in which they expressed their disappointment with the actions of the players representative.

"I can confirm I have handed a transfer request to the chairman of Manchester City Football Club," Tévez said in a statement. "Now I need to clear my head and think because this is an important part of my career. My feelings have not changed and it is regrettable that we have reached this situation. But it is something I have felt for some time and have spent many hours thinking this through." Tévez was unhappy about the insinuations that he was not making his own decisions and feels City cast doubt on his motives for leaving the Blues. "I hugely resent the management's suggestions that I have been unduly influenced by others," Tévez continued. "I wanted to leave in the summer, but was convinced to return to the club. Sadly, my feelings have not changed. I am disappointed that the management should now see fit to try to portray the situation in another light. My relationship with certain executives and individuals at the club has broken down and is now beyond repair. I do not wish to expand on this at this stage. They know, because I have told them." Tévez continued by saying that he bore no ill-will to manager Mancini, despite a touchline row during City's win over Bolton, while he also thanked owner Sheikh Mansour. "I wish to clarify that I have no personal issue with the manager Roberto Mancini," he said. "The owner has been very generous with what he has offered to me. I would like to thank Sheik Mansour for his understanding and support." Tévez appeared stuck at City until the summer after several potential transfers fell through.

Kia Joorabchian said: 'We've been in negotiations with three big clubs but I don't think they have reached the figures Manchester City want. Carlos will remain at Man City until the summer. They would like to move him on but only at a certain price.' AC Milan seemed the player's most likely suitors but the Italian champions were unable to come up with an offer to suit City. Joorabchian says a deal may now have to wait until the end of the season. 'This summer will open up a lot of markets. All of the big clubs are looking for players who can play in the Champions League. Carlos Tévez is cup-tied and that creates a big obstacle. You're spending a lot of money on the transfer and the salary and he can't play Champions League. You have three-and-a-half months and then you can restructure your team, and buy Carlos, in the summer. PSG want to build a long-term project and I think Carlos is six months too early for them. But there is a big chance he will go there in the summer.' Ancelotti said there was no chance of Tévez moving to the French capital before next week's transfer deadline, 'The player is a striker that we liked but there is ultimately no agreement. We respect the choice of each and PSG is a club that interests Tévez, but it will not be this winter.'

Kia Joorabchian played down suggestions that he had opened a Twitter account to discuss Tévez's future and insult the French league. "It is a fake Twitter account. I didn't tweet. Above all, Carlos has no problem with Le Championnat (Ligue 1). In England, Argentina or Brazil, Carlos won everything. He now needs a new challenge."

Milan abandoned their pursuit, and Tévez intended to report back for duty at City. Mancini made it clear that the only way Tévez will be allowed to return to first-team training is if he apologises. Joorabchian says that will not happen. "What is he apologising for? It's almost like a false 'I'm sorry'. He doesn't believe, deep down, that he did anything wrong." Joorabchian believed City were contractually bound to reintegrate Tévez. "Mancini has said it is impossible but he has to understand Carlos has a contract at City for the next two and a half years. Carlos has been on walkabout but he has come to terms with the fact he has to come back and live with Mancini."

"We were ever so close with City," Milan's managing director, Adriano Galliani revealed. "If someone had asked me at 1830 who would be coming, I would have said Tévez. But we've left things well with City and the misunderstandings have been overcome. The market opens again in four months, so perhaps it will be just a few months of separation with Carlitos. I did everything I could to bring him in. It was heart in the mouth stuff right up until the deadline." Joorabchian said Internazionale "had never been in the race" but added that a deal with PSG may be resurrected at the end of the season.

Joorabchian was again asked about the night Tévez refused to leave the bench. "There are always two sides to the story and, if cooler heads and maturity prevail, these things don't get out of hand. I think it's the responsibility of the older man, the manager, to control the players. The hierarchy at City have been excellent. If it was the hierarchy, the people running the club, they would have handled it in a different way and things wouldn't have exploded. The explosion of that day – the manager's comments [Mancini had described Tévez as "finished"] – was so bad it created an unsustainable. Carlos served a two-week suspension, then he was training on his own and then training with the reserves and at some point you have to say: 'He's served his suspension, now integrate him back.'.' But there was never any door to that, which is probably why he left. He could not see any daylight and Mancini has made it very clear he doesn't want him in the first team.

So what does he do? Does he stay in the reserves, collect his money and say 'Stuff you'? It has never been about money for him."

Media reports suggested Liverpool contacted City after the clubs met to ask whether they would be willing to contemplate a straight exchange with Carroll. My City sources confirmed that "tentative enquires" had indeed been made. Marwood rebuffed the idea, even though Carroll was a player Mancini admired when he was at Newcastle. But Carroll scored only six goals in 35 appearances since becoming the eighth most expensive footballer. His problems adapting on Merseyside left Liverpool willing to take a £10m loss, with Tévez valued at £25m. Carroll's longest run of starts this season was three games and Marwood's decision was made on the basis that he could no longer improve their team even though Mancini had a shortage of front players at a time when Tévez's strike was in its 11th week and Mario was serving a four-match suspension.

Mancini confirmed his admiration for Carroll, but cooled the prospect of signing him. Mancini was aware of the speculation, but was not party to any conversation. "There was no phone call to me. I don't know if Brian Marwood was involved. I just read it in the newspaper. I didn't speak to Marwood about this. Carroll is a good player, he is young and strong but it would be difficult and I don't think it is going to happen."

Saturday Jan 28, 2012

Vincent Kompany was sorely missed as Micah Richards said: "He has been an unbelievable miss. He has played well in the big games and is a leader so it will be amazing to have him back. He has still been coming in the changing room before games and saying how he feels we can improve, and what he would do if he was on the pitch, so he has still been an influence."

Sunday, Jan 29, 2012

"I think I can win the Golden Ball ... But Messi has to lower his level of play or I can not do it." Mario Balotelli remarked in Telefoot, in an interview with former team-mate Inter team-mate Olivier Dacourt. On his personal life Balotelli said, "I spend a little 'less time with my friends and a little' more with my girlfriend, even if in the end we always talk a lot about me. Even when I go out to eat with my girlfriend talking about me, not I know why, but Inter were so, perhaps because I do things that are not normal." He added that he had much improved tactically, "whereas before I was a disaster."

Asked to compare Mancini and Mourinho, "With the first I have a fantastic relationship with other things I've done some mistake, but he liked me too." For a comparison between Ibrahimovic, former team-mate and Cassano, who knows Balotelli from the national team. "As to those who look like madness? I'm crazy like them both even if I leave the title to Antonio."

He was following the fortunes of PSG. "I'm following because there's Carlo Ancelotti as coach and there is Leonardo – he admits – I think that within two to three years will be a great team in the world." As for his infamous escapades, "Someone should explain to adults and elderly people that I'm not the only rich, young footballer. I'm 21 and I've been living far from home for almost two years now. I adapted well, but I don't have real friends here."

Monday, Jan 30, 2012

Roberto Mancini felt the need to address comments made by Joorabchian who claimed Tévez's relationship with his manager had never been good and there had been "feuds" throughout their time together. This came as a surprise to Mancini, who has always got the impression he had a good working relationship with a player he made his skipper at the start of last season. "Carlos doesn't have any problem with me." Mancini had a tricky problem trying to reintegrate a player in his squad who had taken such an extreme stance. "Everyone should always answer for his behaviour. If a player is at one club and wants to go to another, it is an option for the player. Maybe for the club it is a big problem."

Managing director, Adriano Galliani, would spend the final day of the transfer window in his office in Milan's Via Turati attempting to salvage some kind of deal. Galliani said, "We are not expecting Tévez to join us now and we will probably take another look at him in the summer. But there could be a surprise, you never know, sometimes things develop very late but right now I would have to say nothing will happen." He had spent the afternoon in direct contact with City's chairman, Khaldoon al-Mubarak, by telephone and fax. The offer was a no-strings-attached loan until the end of the season, which would cost them £10m in wages and fees, with a guarantee of a permanent transfer of 30m euors. A deadline of 6.30pm was set. Khaldoon turned him down. The deadline proved flexible as City did not ruled out another offer on the final day of a transfer window.

It emerged City stopped paying Tévez at the end of November. Once he reported to their training ground, the club had difficulty withholding his weekly salary of £198,000. It was 63 days since he was last paid; 83 since he left England possibly for good; 126 since he refused to come on as a substitute at Bayern and 132 since he played his last game. Tévez appealed to the Premier League. Tévez first appealed against the punishment but that was thrown out on 7 January after a hearing involving two City directors, Marty Edelman and Mohamed al-Mazrouei. The Premier League were forced to schedule a hearing date.

City signed Roma's attacking Chilean midfielder David Pizarro on loan. Pizarro was also a target for Juventus. There was a £1m option to make the move permanent at the end of the season. Mancini, who coached Pizarro at Inter Milan, saw the 32-year-old's ability to play in central midfield or just behind the strikers. "I feel ready," said Pizarro, "I know the league in England is going to be different to Italy but I have a lot of experience at the highest level and whilst I know I need to adapt very quickly, I am confident I can." He was hoping for a better experience than his last trip to Manchester, when he was part of the Roma side hammered 7-1 by United in a Champions League quarter-final in 2007. "That was a massacre. All I saw of Cristiano Ronaldo was the back of his shirt."

Wayne Bridge headed to Sunderland. Bridge played just 78 minutes this season, his only appearance came in the Carling Cup third-round victory over Birmingham. Bridge joined City from Chelsea in a £12m move in January 2009, managing only 58 appearances in his three years. Reading also showed an interest, but the offer of Premier League football eased Sunderland ahead of the Royals.

Tuesday, Jan 31, 2012

Mancini blamed himself for not preparing his team properly as City slipped to a 1-0 defeat at Everton, to remain top only on goal difference after former Manchester United boo boy Darren Gibson scored the only goal, while United beat Stoke at Old Trafford, and the United fans sang the name of their former player.

Interviewed immediately afterwards Mancini commented, "Probably it's my fault because we didn't prepare very well for this game. I thought before the game it was going to be easier but it is never easy." Mancini later suggested he had made mistakes with the team in training. "The players put everything on the pitch but I made some mistakes during the last three days preparing for this game."

Mancini admitted his team struggled against a side who they had beaten only once in 14 trips to Goodison Park. "Everton at home is a strong team. Every time they play against us they play very well. This evening we had the chance and when we conceded a goal we didn't have more chances to score."

Other than a couple of Nasri efforts which hit the bar, City were restricted to two penalty appeals, when Agüero was brought down and then when substitute Kolarov's cross struck Phil Neville's arm. "The decisions are very unlucky against us at this moment," said Mancini, who has also had to do without Mario. "It's very important that we start to win next Saturday against Fulham. The season is long, we have 15 games and I hope we can recover all the players quickly. But it's important that we recover our strength this week." Mancini hoped new loan signing Pizarro would be important. "He is a good midfielder, he has experience and I know him very well."

A man was charged by police after the game was brought to a standstill when a supporter handcuffed himself to a goalpost. The incident occurred five minutes before the end of the first half forcing the referee to halt play for five minutes. Merseyside police said 46-year-old John Joseph Foley, of Southport, was charged with going on to the playing area during a football match, an offence under the Football Offences Act 1991.

Both managers used the pause to speak to their players as several police officers worked to remove the man from Hart's left-hand post. The man, who wore a T-shirt, jeans and baseball cap, was eventually led away. In a statement, Everton said: "Bolt-cutters were used to remove the offender, who was roundly booed as he was escorted from the ground. It transpired that the supporter is a known professional protester, allegedly protesting about an airline's recruitment policy. He was arrested by Merseyside police, who are now dealing with the matter."

FEBRUARY

Tévez branded his stand-off with the club as 'comical' blaming City for failing to find a buyer. However, he later attempted to retract the interview that appeared in German Kicker magazine. Tévez was reported to have said, "I just think the whole situation has become almost comical. I wanted to leave City and had offers from clubs in other leagues, both Italian and Spanish. But in the end it all collapsed because City wouldn't accept any of the offers. They say at City that I cost them a lot of money and so they don't want to give me away on the cheap. But they don't want to loan me out, either. I really have no idea what will happen in the coming months. I sent City a letter in which I told them why I wanted to go. In the last few days I've also contacted the Premier League to appeal against the fine which City have imposed on me. I'm waiting now for an answer from the Premier League. Going to the League is the only option I've got right now.

"There were offers from Milan, from Inter and from Paris Saint-Germain. But each time nothing came of them, but certainly there were interested people who wanted to see me playing football again. Everyone has to do what works for them. Barcelona are a fantastic club, and La Liga a fabulous championship. But what happened, happened. There is also a personal aspect to all this. I wanted to be closer to my family, above all my children who are and were in Argentina. And because I couldn't play any longer at City I took control of the situation myself." Tévez appeared open to a reconciliation with City, "That's [talking to Mancini] something I would have to discuss with City's directors. Let's see what happens. Of course, what I want is to be playing football. But the way things are I have to make do with playing golf or making appearances like this coming Saturday, at the farewell match of my old friend Martin Palermo."

A statement issued by his representative read: "Regarding an interview published in Kicker magazine today, Carlos Tévez categorically denies both speaking to any journalist about his situation at Manchester City and the quotes attributed to him in the interview." Tévez was named in City's revised 25-man Premier League squad, raising the possibility that he might play for the club again. Tévez remained in Argentina and with speculation he was about to return. Mancini said: "I hope for him he has been training in the last three months to help his condition. There is only one thing on my mind, the Barclays Premier League. But if he comes back – and he is fit – it is possible."

Owen Hargreaves was also included in the Premier League squad. Mancini commented, "Owen always has these little problems, when he came to us in the summer, we took a gamble, because he had not played for two years. We thought we could try and get him fit in two or three months and then he would be able to play. But, like any player who hasn't played for two years, when they start to train, every day there is a problem, with his knee or his hamstring. I hope for him he eventually is able to play all the time. He deserves to."

Just 24 hours after Darren Gibson's winner, Wayne Rooney enjoyed a night out with his former team-mate. The pair, along with Rooney's wife Coleen and Gibson's girlfriend, went to see the musical Oliver at the Palace Theatre, before heading to Chinese restaurant Wings. Sir Alex joked about Gibson's goal that "it was all part of the plan". Rooney was first to congratulate Gibson after the game, writing on Twitter: 'Yeeeeeeessssssssss gibbo. Love u kid.' followed up by Rio Ferdinand on Wednesday morning, who added:'Just organising a FREE meal at my restaurant @RossoRestaurant for Darron Gibson!!'

Giggs believed that if United came through their testing month, it could provide the impetus for another successful title challenge, "We know that it's a tough run. We are not quite at the make-or-break part of the season, but it is an important time, and we know that if we win those games, then we'll be in good shape and good form going into the run-in."

Thursday, Feb 2, 2012

Ivory Coast's quarter-final clash the host nation took place on the same day City would welcome Fulham to the Etihad Stadium, with their lead down to goal difference. Yaya insisted the team were not suffering because he and Kolo were away, "We have a great team and I know I am certainly not irreplaceable. Look at the amount of money the club has spent on talent and still tell me that 'there is only one Yaya'. I do not believe this. Somebody can still play in my place and help us win. By the time the African Cup of Nations finishes I hope we will still be on top of the league. Every single player wants to be in the first team, so we all work incredibly hard to be there. In fact, I am more worried about regaining my place when I return. For me, being in Africa is like being injured. I like to imagine that I've got an injury that will last four weeks. When I think like that, I can concentrate fully on my task with my country and not worry about missing games for my club."

Fri, Feb 3, 2012

The tough times Mancini experienced as Inter boss will see him handle the pressure of the title race as City, who led the table since October, were unable to shake off the challenge of United. After delivering three titles at Inter - including ending a 17-year Scudetto drought - Mancini insisted he was far from losing his nerve. "There doesn't exist a place like Inter Milan, where you can really be under pressure. After Inter Milan, you can manage every team. Inter Milan has a big history like United. When you are a manager there you have a pressure every day, every minute. After Inter Milan you can't have pressure. It was really important for me, the experience with Inter Milan. Inter are a top team and you need to do everything well every day, every game. All the journalists and all the newspapers say the manager has made mistakes every game. It is so different from here. So, for this reason, after that, you can't have pressure."

Mancini felt his side would be on course for the title if they emerged from their tough January programme unscathed. "We knew December and January would be crucial months because we were losing important players to the African Nations Cup and could have players injured. I didn't think we could have players banned for four games - but this can happen. I said if we are on the top after January we would win the title - but not without problems. It is not easy to beat United. It is important for us to stay on the top now for this difficult moment. If we are on top after this difficult moment, what has happened with us in January can probably happen to other teams. Every team has a difficult moment."

Saturday, Feb 4, 2012

Mancini recorded his 50th league win as City beat the snow as well as Fulham to open a three-point lead with United playing the next day, after a stuttering run of form in January, during which City won only three of their eight games in all competitions. "Maybe something can change after this because January was a difficult month. The most important thing is the clean sheet for the team and to win very quickly after the Everton defeat on Tuesday night. We know we are fighting against fantastic teams like Manchester United and Tottenham. Like us, they know if you want to win this league you have to win all your games and not think about other teams. I don't think United have more pressure. They are used to it because they always stay there."

With three wins in their last nine games, facing opposition that had lost just once in eight visits to the Etihad Stadium, City's 17th consecutive League home win, just two behind the record held by United. Agüero opened the scoring from the penalty spot after Johnson was tripped by Baird, his 18th of the season, smashing the ball high to Schwarzer's left. Johnson went down with minimal contact for the spot-kick from which Agüero opened the scoring in the 10th minute. City's lead doubled when Baird turned Johnson's cross-shot beyond his own keeper. Kolarov whipped in a cross from left which Agüero helped on with a deft flick, Johnson put the ball back across goal and Baird could only divert past Schwarzer from close range.

Mancini praised his players, "I think we played well. It's always good to be lucky and I'm very pleased with my players. It was not easy as Fulham is a good team with a fantastic manager. I'm happy because we scored three goals and didn't concede any chances." Having previously questioned the winger's commitment, Mancini praised Johnson's work ethic, "He took his chance very well. He can become even better, but he worked and had a very good game." This was only his third league start since Mancini's criticism, although he appeared eight times as a substitute. Mancini was happy with Johnson's hunger, "I am pleased for Adam today because he took his chance very well. We all know what a fantastic player he is."

Johnson insisted he did not take a dive, "I felt the contact. Sometimes in normal time, when you are in the moment, you anticipate contact. There is a fine line between diving and anticipating contact but I felt it and went down. These things happen."

Play was halted twice to allow ground staff to clear snow from the lines before Dzeko added a third after Agüero's dribble wrong footed the defence. At one point midway through the second half, the heavy snowfall posed a real threat to the fixture as referee Mike Dean twice stopped play to allow the lines around both penalty areas to be cleared with shovels. City's title rivals - and Fulham - would have been pleased with a postponement but, shortly after Dzeko's third goal, the weather improved and the game was able to conclude with Mancini's men maintaining their 100% home record.

Agüero showed great balance to keep his feet and skip past the injured Senderos and tee up Dzeko to drive in from close range. Dzeko hit his own post when he diverted Ruiz's corner past Hart and there was time for City to hand a debut to new loan signing Pizarro as Mancini saw his side record a 17th straight league win at home to put the pressure on city rivals United ahead of their Sunday trip to Chelsea.

Asked whether he would be cheering for Chelsea when the game kicks off at Stamford Bridge, Mancini replied: "Yes. I will watch the game but I only support Manchester City." United had not won at Stamford Bridge since 2002, but Mancini insisted that the defending champions have too much experience of title races to feel any additional pressure. "I don't think this puts pressure on United. They are used to always being there. But they are like us. We know, if we want to win this league, we should just try and win all the games and not think about other teams. Manchester United can win all their games, because they are strong like us. All the remaining games are difficult, you are playing against top squads. Some of them are at the bottom and are fighting relegation, so there are no easy games."

Sir Alex believed away wins in London were required to maintain United's position as top dogs in the League. Ferguson said: 'It's the expectation that you have to live with at this club. It's like climbing a mountain. I've climbed Ben Donald in Scotland and when you get up there it's fantastic and you want to stay there. It's a tribute to us really that we won our first title in 1992-93 and 20 years on we're still battling there and we've only been out of the top two once or twice. We had 10 years battling with Arsenal. They were a tough side and the games became pretty physical and controversial for a spell. Then came Chelsea and they got off to great starts under Mourinho and we weren't able to catch them. For that third season onwards we changed the whole process of the way we prepared for the season and we managed to get a decent start and win the League. But it's not easy. It's a tough League and we are finding that now with City. They have improved a lot and are still the favourites to win the League, but if we win our two away games against Chelsea and Spurs then we have a great chance."

Roy Keane and Patrick Vieira attended a charity auction for St Bede's School in Cheshire on Saturday night, where Keano bid £500 on a meal for 10 at Manchester's popular Yang Sing eaterie. Vieira responded with an offer of £510, and the former Arsenal and United captains then traded bids up to £800, neither looking at the other during the process. As Mrs Keane jokingly appealed to her husband to "leave it", the pair then raised the bidding in £50 increments before Vieira's final offer of £1,000. To which Keane, naturally, offered £2,000.

Sunday, Feb 5, 2012

United were two points adrift of City following their three goal comeback at Stamford Bridge. United trailed 3-0 but two penalties from Rooney and a late equaliser by Hernandez rescued a point. "We have shown that spirit so many times over the years and this point could win us the League," said Rooney. "At 3-0 down, a lot of teams would find it easy to let their heads drop and accept defeat but we carried on working hard and, thankfully, got something out of the game. We really had to dig in. Of course it's two points lost, we understand that, but after being 3-0 down all the City players at home won't have enjoyed watching the way we fought back and the spirit of our team. They know it will be a fight to the finish and we'll be there at the end."

Tévez was present at the Bombonera stadium in Buenos Aires for Palermo's farewell game, but instead of playing as he promised to do, he arrived on the field at half-time and waved to supporters. The fans responded by giving him a standing ovation, chanting: "Leave the English and come back here." Boca Juniors president Daniel Angelici had earlier said that the club would happily bring Tévez into their squad, "If Tévez arrives for free then we would be happy to have him. If Manchester City call us and say that they need him to play games, our doors are always open."

Monday, Feb 6, 2012

City postponed their friendly in Genoa against a combined Genoa and Sampdoria XI in aid of the city's flood victims because of the treacherous weather in northern Italy.

Tuesday, Feb 7, 2012

Euro Wind-Ups would feature Mario and some top footballing prankster playing jokes on their teammates and rivals alike, while hidden cameras capture the action. The ITV1 programme will coincide with the 2012 European Championships. Ferdinand, a mischief-maker in 2006's Rio's World Cup Wind-Ups, is expected to lead the team of pranksters.

Tim Westwood, speaking at the launch of the PlayStation Vita, said he still has Mario's phone number on the back of a Post-It note following an earlier meeting. The DJ said Mario asked him about lessons on the decks and he said he's still open to the idea. "He's a cool guy so if he wants some lessons I'll hit him up, baby. I'm doing it for free too. He's a nice guy. He hangs out, man.'

Thursday, Feb 9, 2012

Vieira accused referees of mounting a conspiracy against City to deny them title. "It felt like that anything that City will do will be amplified and we get punished, compared to the other teams and the other players. I don't want to think about it because I don't want to say everyone is against City or anything like that. But when you look at the last few decisions, you are asking yourself if something is wrong here, if people don't want us to win the league." Vieira cited Lampard's dangerous tackle on Wolves' Adam Hammill and Crouch's eye-gouging of West Brom's Jonas Olsson as examples of inconsistencies in refereeing decisions. Lampard, who admitted he was lucky not be sent off, was cautioned, while Kompany was shown a straight red card. Crouch, unlike Mario, escaped retrospective action despite there being clear video evidence. Vieira said: "Lampard's tackle looked dangerous compared to Vincent's. Crouch, when he put his finger in the eye of another player, looked bad as well. We try our best to win the league, we accept our punishment. But when you look what is happening to the other ones, that makes us as a football club really frustrated. It seems like if you have one referee you get one decision but if you have a different referee the decision may also be different. It's difficult to understand some decisions compared to the decisions we had. I think this is what brings the confusion. The confusion is dangerous for our game. Players are saying that they don't know what the rules mean and if they are likely to be sent off or not. Confusion is really dangerous, especially for the referee and the refereeing body. I believe that they're making the referees job more and more difficult. A good referee is someone who referees with his personality and with common sense, to make the decision he thinks is right at the moment, not because he's afraid of the consequences."

Vieira believes referees and their bosses are in danger of ruining English football and stripping the game of its unique passion with their zero tolerance policy towards tough tackling. "Mario didn't get sent off, but when you look at the position of the referee you say 'how couldn't he see it?' Of course there's going to be a debate, but he made his own decision which he thought was right or wrong. I think this is the danger of not letting the referee just be a referee. With Vinnie my feeling was that when he went for the tackle he went for the ball. For me, it wasn't a foul. I was quite surprised that the referee gave a foul. I was more surprised that he came out with a red card. Ten years ago the game was much more physical than it is now. If that was a red card there would have been a sending off in every game I played for Arsenal. It was one of the harshest decisions I've ever seen in the last few months. England is the only country in the world where fans in the stadium applaud the striker who has scored but also the defender who wins the ball with a tackle. You will not get that anywhere else in the world. Now it looks like you can't tackle anymore. The refereeing body has to be really careful to not kill the passion of the game."

Fri, Feb 10, 2012

Mancini identified Barry, who expected a hostile reception again when he returned to former club Villa, as one of City's most influential but underrated players, "Gareth is a very intelligent man, and on the pitch he is a very important player. He understands the situations for me and with England as well because he's a very intelligent player. He could be the England captain. He's played a lot of times for the national team. He's a good man, a clever man both outside and inside the pitch. He's a really good player. In every team, there are players that don't seem important, but in the end they prove to be one of the most important players. These players are quiet, but can play in every position. They help the manager and their team-mates and are always available. They fight for every ball. Gareth is the one player who is like this. He's very important for us."

Mancini told Micah Richards he must keep improving if he wants to win back his place in the national squad. Largely overlooked by Capello, he was offered fresh hope of an international recall following the Italian's resignation. "Micah has everything to become a top full-back. He's improved a lot in the last year but he can still do better. He can reach the top but maybe, at this moment the national team, Johnson and Walker are better. It doesn't mean Micah can't play for the national team. If he wants to he could be there always - if he continues to improve."

On his countryman Capello's departure, Mancini added: "I don't know the reasons for Fabio leaving but the national team have lost a top manager. With Fabio, they could have had a big chance to win the European Championship. I respect his decision, although I don't know much about what happened."

Richards shut down his Twitter account because of racist abuse. Police were called in to investigate after he was targeted on the social networking site. Twitter was used by racists to target players, including Djibril Cisse, Louis Saha, Frazier Campbell and pundit Stan Collymore. Police investigated abuse towards Richards in November.

Mancini did not rule out the possibility of the disaffected Tévez playing a part in the club's title bid. Mancini did not want to be seen to be forcing him out, "Everyone knows Carlos is a top player. If he was here and playing it would be better, because Carlos can change games. If he were to come back next week maybe he can still help us in the next three months. It depends on his condition, and when he returns. We have already played a lot of games with only one striker and against Everton in our last away game, we couldn't make any changes from the bench. But Carlos knows the situation. I talked to him before he left, to try to resolve this situation, and if he comes back we can talk again. I don't have any problem with that. If he wants to play, it could happen."

Meanwhile Diego Maradona launched a stinging attack on Mancini over his treatment of Tévez, "I don't understand, has he lost his place at Man City because of a silly fight with the coach? It's so unfair. There is a great injustice that's gone on. I know Mancini really well. I've known him a long time. I'm sure Carlos has reasons for his behaviour. Mancini was always a spoilt child. He was treated like a spoilt kid at Sampdoria, at Inter and it's the same at Man City. I'm not defending Carlos as he didn't want to play against Bayern Munich. But Mancini used to be a footballer. He had to show a little tact. You can't ask a star like Carlos to go on to the field like he did. If you have a star like Carlos, you have to call him earlier in the game - or don't call him at all. But we are talking about Mancini, a complicated man who didn't answer Massimo Moratti's phone-call just because he didn't want to. I would love to see Mancini if he says I don't want Carlos - and Man City don't go and sign Agüero, or Silva, or even James Milner. I have talked with Carlos a few times and I will definitely call him again. It hurts me when I see what is happening to him at Manchester City as he is a great guy. But he is also a great player. Come on, there are no players who are good enough to be idols of both Man United and Man City, and he did that."

Maradona's son-in-law filled the Tévez void with some dazzling displays. Maradona added: "Everybody knew what kind of player Agüero was, so I'm not surprised by the level he's playing at Manchester City. When he left Atletico Madrid, I knew that he was going to play for a bigger team. He could have played for Chelsea or Real Madrid. Mancini has a better CV thanks to Agüero. He is making the difference at a team like City, in which the cheapest player costs £40m."

Mario Balotelli served the last game of his suspension while the Touré brothers were back from the Africa Cup of Nations, "Mario is looking forward to playing again, we will have to assess the others when we meet up again. I spoke to Yaya Touré a few days ago and he told me he was very tired, after playing five game in 15 days. But when we come back from Porto we do not have a game, so there is time for everyone to recover. I intend to name a strong team for the Europa League because we want to go to the final. It will be difficult because Porto are a top team. But if we have all the players back without injury we can make a few changes. We want to do the best we can."

Having averaged three goals a game at the start of the season, City scored only three in their last six away games in the League. Their most consistent striker, Agüero, scored only once in his last six matches. Dzeko managed three goals in 16 games, while Mario had not scored from open play for two months. Mancini commented, "Villa is a very important match. If we have a good result, I don't think we have big problems after that. I said if we were top by the end of this period, we would win the title."

Mancini believed teams were running scared of City and that City's three defeats – at Chelsea, Sunderland and Everton were inflicted against the run of play. "When we go away from home now, the teams we play keep all their players behind the ball and so it is difficult. At the start of the season, it was different. Teams gave us more space and we took advantage. In the last two months, our opponents have approached games differently. That is normal because of the results we were getting. We have lost three games away from home and we didn't deserve to lose any of them. We played well at Chelsea, Sunderland and Everton but couldn't score. When that happens, the team has to be more careful to make sure that we take at least a point. We need to show more attention when we play away from home. It is impossible to play at 100 per cent for the whole year. There will always be moments during a season when you play well and other times when you have a problem. I hope that, if we have a good result against Villa, things will change away from home. Sometimes we need to be more Italian and make sure that, if we can't win, we don't lose."

Sunday, Feb 12, 2012

City began a match for the first time since October without leading the table, after United won 2-1 against Liverpool at Old Trafford the day before, but Mancini saw his side return to the top, regaining a two-point lead, with a 1-0 win over Villa thanks to a 63rd-minute goal from Lescott. Mancini said: "December and January were difficult months for us. We had players injured, players banned and players away. Now we're still at the top. To stay at the top with United and Tottenham behind means we are very strong. We have 13 games to the end and to win the league we have to win 11 or 12 games." Mancini hailed the effort throughout the season. "We were there from August because we deserved this. It was a difficult game. We knew this before the game but the guys played fantastic football."

Lescott pounced from a Milner corner for the winner, Hart made crucial saves late on to preserve the Blues' lead but Mancini insisted he was not the best in the world - yet. "He's very young and there are other keepers with more experience. He has many years in front but he could become one of the top keepers. Joleon played fantastically as well, we played fantastic football in the first half and we were missing only a goal."

Mancini indicated an apology remained the key to Tévez finding favour again. "My reaction is always the same. Carlos knows the situation, we are here and it depends on him. Carlos knows the situation from September, we don't have any problem." Asked if an apology was still what City were waiting for, he added: "Yes, it's possible. For now we should be happy for this game. For Carlos' situation, we know what can happen. Carlos is a Manchester City player. We are in Manchester, we are always there. We have not changed in these three months, we are there."

Tuesday, Feb 14, 2012

Tévez arrived at the Carrington training ground on Valentine's Day afternoon at about 4pm, just as his manager had left for the day, leaving the pair's dispute unresolved. Tévez was given a police escort when he flew into Manchester after more than three months AWOL. Tévez spent an hour with the club doctor, who assessed Tévez's fitness. There was no suggestion Mancini deliberately snubbed Tévez's long awaited return. "The manager would not have been expected to be at the training ground that late," a source told me. The pair may have spoken on the phone, or through third parties.

Tévez received text messages from several City players welcoming him back. Referring to the return of Tévez, plus Yaya and Kolo from international duty, Lescott said on Twitter: 'All our players are excited to have Carlos, Kolo and Yaya back to help achieve our goal.' Tévez and Mancini would meet up on Wednesday morning, before the manager leaves with the team for City's Europa League match with FC Porto. Tévez was back because after he and his advisors had agreed a deal with AC Milan, they assumed City would drop their price or loan him out. The collapse of that deal left Tévez without football, and without wages either. A highly-placed City source told me, "Tévez has nowhere to go and that is why he is back."

Wednesday, Feb 15, 2012

Mancini confronted Mario Balotelli over his discipline, "I have spoken to Mario two weeks ago. I said: "Please, we have 13 games to play as well as the Europa League – try to have good behaviour on the pitch and think to only play football. Mario is an important player for us, he has a good quality. He can play with Edin, with Sergio. I think if his head will be OK in the next two months, he will be an important player. It's difficult to find a good definition for him. We know that Mario is a fantastic player. He's young, sometimes he will do some mistakes but for this reason, if he can keep his composure for the next months, he will be an important player for us, in the Europa League and the Premier League. It's my opinion that at this moment all the players will be important. It's important for me to have all players between now and the end of the season. If we want to get to the final of the Europa League or win the Premier League, it's important to have all players ready and available for all games. Mario is one of them. Now we'll have three strikers for tomorrow, I think that's a good thing for me and for this game."

Yaya and Kolo flew to Portugal after competing in the African Cup of Nations final. Mancini was unsure whether the pair will take part in the Europa League encounter, "I don't know. Before I need to speak to them and tomorrow it will be decided. They arrived here this morning." He was keen to focus on the match but did address Tévez's recent comments. "I don't want to answer your question because the game is more important than this, but I answer this question and then no more, because we have this game. It is an important game against a top club like Porto. I totally disagree with Carlos, what he said, because I never treated him badly. Maybe the opposite, I treated him too well, always."

Yaya phoned Mancini before the African Nations Cup final to say he wanted to play for City on Thursday despite being away for six weeks, "I talked to the boss and said 'I want to play. The final was very important for my country and for me but now I have a chance of winning the Europa League and the Premier League."

Thursday, Feb 16, 2012

City won 2-1 at the Estadio do Drago against the Europa League holders but planned to complain to UEFA about racial abuse suffered by some of their players. Mario Balotelli complained to officials about chants from the stands although Mancini had heard nothing unusual.

In the 78th minute, when City substituted Mario, whistling and booing reached a crescendo. Mario told a club official that he was subjected to racial abuse. Mancini insisted that the chanting had not disturbed him. "I didn't hear, sorry. I was concentrating on the game. I think Mario Balotelli and Yaya Toure are too strong [to be affected]."

Porto categorically denied those reports: "What we can basically say is that nothing abnormal happened, no one noticed anything strange, not even the UEFA delegates that worked closely with Porto during the match," Porto spokesman Rui Cerqueira said. Porto, the Portuguese champions and Europa League holders, insisted that certain chants from both sets of supporters of their respective players Hulk and Agüero could have been mistaken for other sounds. "Kun, Kun, Kun; Hulk, Hulk, Hulk," he said, demonstrating the chants. "Those chants can be easily confused with racist chants. We are very proud of having a multi-racial team, with players from all backgrounds and to have achieved many titles with respect. Porto players have never felt the slightest hint of racism and we were very surprised with the accusations." Yaya "heard something". "That's why we like the Premier League because it never happens there ... maybe in a different country they don't expect black players," he said.

Mancini praised Mario's performance, "I think Mario did very well, he played very well. He was calm and it is important he continues like this. I think this provocation can happen every game. For this reason I spoke with

Mario before the game. I said, 'Mario, think and play, think what you should do during the game. Forget other things.' I think only this is important."

City trailed to Varela's close-range effort following a powerful run and cross by Hulk. Pereira deflected Yaya's cross into his own net off his shoulder and City sealed victory when Agüero tapped home following Yaya's cross. On a memorable night, Mancini's players did not look as though they felt sorry for themselves as they returned to the continental stage for the first time since being denied a place in the knockout stages of the Champions League.

The League remained City's priority but Mancini said on the eve of the tie that he was keen for City to make a strong impression in the Europa League. The manager named a strong side which included a recall for Balotelli. Younger Toure brother Yaya was in the side for the first time since 3 January. Mancini commented, "I think that we played a good game, we played very well. In the first half we had three or four goalscoring chances. We were really unlucky. In the second half we played very well. We played as we know. We had seven, eight chances to score and we didn't give any chances to Porto, which is important because Porto is a top team. I think we won the game very well. We had more chances to score than them."

Fri, Feb 17, 2012

City stars welcomed back Tévez. Yaya Toure said: "Carlos is a fantastic player and I hope he will continue with us because we need him. For me, it is no problem because he is a great player and everybody likes him. He knows what he has to say to the boss and the rest of the players. Me and the rest of the players will be happy if he comes back."

Saturday, Feb 18, 2012

Razak and Assulin joined Brighton on loan. Poyet had chased the duo for some time but Mancini was unwilling to let them leave while Yaya was away on international duty. Winger Razak, 19, signed a three-month loan deal while former Barcelona youngster Assulin, 20, sealed a one-month temporary switch which can be extended.

Sunday, Feb 19, 2012

Sir Alex reveals he could have signed Hart for £100,000 years before he eventually moved to the Blues from Shrewsbury in 2006 for £600,000 to become one of the world's top keepers.

Ferguson commented, 'I could have bought Joe Hart for £100,000 so we all make mistakes. I've no doubt [that Hart will be England goalkeeper for the next 10 years]. If you look at the England goalkeeper situation for the last 20 years, I would think he's easily the best.'

Monday, Feb 20, 2012

Tévez said he was treated "like a dog' and revealed how he almost had a punch-up with Mancini in October 2010. He also failed to deliver the apology that Mancini wanted. "I want to go back to Manchester and win over the City fans. People turned their back on me but it's normal. I didn't understand. I've decided to return to City. I know I have what it takes to revert the situation. I know it'll be hard, but it's a nice challenge."

On the incident in Munich, Tévez added: "I had warmed up during the first half. Then I went to the dressing room. For the second half I was ready. I didn't understand City fans burning my shirt. It hurt. It's normal they react like that because they read all sorts of thing. It was a delicate situation. I decided to say nothing about it during all this time. I decided not to talk to the media for the last four months. Last time I spoke was right after the Bayern Munich game. In that second half, Mancini decided to replace Edin Dzeko with Nigel de Jong. It was a defensive sub. I didn't understand. Dzeko argued with Mancini.

"I decided to sit. Mancini was upset for arguing with Dzeko. Dzeko was speaking Bosnian and Mancini was swearing at him in Italian, so it was a real mess. I go and sit down, but he doesn't see me because he is having this discussion. But then he turns around and sees me and you can imagine what happens. He is in the middle of an argument, so then he tells me to keep on warming up and treats me like a dog. When he spoke to me in that tone of voice, I said 'no, I'm not going out'. I was willing to play, but the coach was in such a foul mood because he had that argument with Dzeko, he started on me as well. He started swearing at me, so that was him, because I was very calm. I was just sitting on the bench and you can see from the footage that I was calm and just talking with Zabalata. Mancini said some horrible things to me. Mancini told me all sorts of things there. I don't know why. I was relaxed. I was talking to Pablo Zabaleta. I had no problems. I never refused to play. I refused to keep warming up. The club investigated and then they fined me. I was worried about my future after that two-week fine. That fine was OK. But I want people to know the truth. They didn't want to. The club statement protected the manager. I got a lot of heat from the media in England, Argentina, everywhere.

"Now that I have a cooler head, I understand City fans. Back in the heat of the moment I didn't. I did a lot of things for City. To be insulted by fans after what happened in Munich was something I didn't deserve. I was very upset by everything and maybe I wasn't seeing things clearly. That Bayern episode could have been avoided. They could have kicked me out of the club without saying all the things they said. Deal with the situation in a different way. I think that's where Mancini got things wrong. If we had a problem, we could have sorted it out in a different way. Mancini is a winner. And I'm a winner too. None of us like to lose."

Asked about his relationship with Mancini, he said, "Last season we almost exchanged punches! After the home game against Newcastle, we almost hit each other in the dressing room. But we spoke the following day."

He added, "If it's true that Mancini said he will welcome me back if I'm fit, then I like those quotes. But he also said I was never going to be playing for him again. So I don't know. I'll do my best to be available and play. Mancini's position got stronger when Kun Agüero arrived. I don't know if he would have done the things he did if this was last season. But he never said anything. He got a better team this season and felt like making the decision."

On his lack of match fitness, Tévez commented, "I have been training on my own. I know I can be back on the pitch in two weeks. I'm willing to play. It's tough to talk about City's title challenge now. I feel like I'm out the squad. I wish I can go back there and help them win."

To aid the situation Tévez would drop his appeal to the Premier League against a six-week club fine. Kia Joorabchian said: "He's saying he will get himself ready as the club have requested him to do, because the club have said Carlos coming back can only be an asset to them. I've spoken to the club today, I've spoken to the club regularly on a daily basis and I think everyone agrees that from a football point of view Carlos can only be an asset. Now him and Mancini have obviously managed to resolve issues. What he had explained in his interview is how he felt back then. I think that the club and Carlos are taking this in a very positive way. He has a lot of repairs to do with the fans and he realises that and he has said that he's ready to apologise if he's done something wrong. And he's said that he sincerely never felt that he was doing something wrong at the time, and he understands that his actions may not have implied that."

Tuesday, Feb 21, 2012

Paul McCarthy, spokesman for Tévez's adviser Joorabchian, announced a clear-the-air meeting aimed at getting the player back in action. The issue was complicated by Tévez's interview on Argentinian television, screened just before he returned to Manchester. "They will have a meeting this week and I think a lot will come out of that," said McCarthy. "Last week Roberto Mancini obviously had his mind on the game against Porto, and quite rightly. It's inevitable he will meet with Roberto Mancini and then it is up to Mancini to decide a course of action for the rest of the season."

It was later announced that Tévez apologised "sincerely and unreservedly" for his conduct seven days after the player finally flew back into Manchester. In a statement released by the player, Tévez said: "I wish to apologise sincerely and unreservedly to everybody I have let down and to whom my actions over the last few months have caused offence. My wish is to concentrate on playing football for Manchester City Football Club."

The club issued a statement of their own: "Carlos Tévez has today apologised to all concerned for his recent conduct. Carlos returned to the football club last Tuesday, following a three-month absence from duties, without permission. Carlos has also withdrawn his appeal against the club's finding of gross misconduct which was due to be heard by a Premier League panel in the coming days. He has since begun a training programme designed to return him to optimum fitness."

West Ham co-owner David Sullivan revealed the Championship club made moves to sign Torres and Tévez, "We tried to get Torres from Chelsea. Three times we asked [about Tévez]. Three times they said 'no chance'." Tévez had not played since September, Platt said: "He still has a bit of work to do in terms of preparations before he is ready to go on to the pitch. That is probably not what people want to hear. There will be a clamour for a Carlos Tévez story but that is not the important thing. The important thing is Manchester City. We have to try and temper the clamour. It will take its own course and its own action.'

Tévez could become a scapegoat should City lose the title race. Micah Richards suggested that Tévez's spat with Mancini could return to haunt him, 'With the fans, it's probably 50-50. The best thing he can do is come back and get his head down. If we do end up winning the league and he's played a massive part in that, then I'm sure everyone will forgive him. If we don't, then it could be the opposite. It's a mixed feeling really but, for me, I'm glad to have him back because he's an outstanding player. He was our captain and leader, not only on the ball but off the ball as well, working hard, closing people down. He was a real nightmare to play against and to have that back in our team would be a boost for us. He's got something that maybe the other strikers don't have. Not in terms of ability but just knowing what the Premier League is like.'

Sergio Agüero commented, "Tévez is a big footballer and nobody doubts it. The day he returns [to the team] will be a big day for us. I prefer things with him in the squad because he is a very important player for us. I spoke a few times with him while he was absent. He is a super professional and it was up to him to decide about his future. I am happy he is back. I think his return could be important for us in the decisive period of this season. He has been one of the best forwards in world football over the last few years. City need all the players we have to try and win titles.'

Many believed that the Manchester derby could be the title decider. It was switched from Saturday afternoon to Monday evening to be shown live on Sky Sports. The controversial move came after violence at recent matches and warnings from Greater Manchester Police they will crack down on any troublemakers. A move to Sunday was not an option with 8,000 runners due to compete in the Greater Manchester Marathon around the city. Mancini braced himself for a title-decider two weeks before the end of the season. "If you look at the table, that's probably the case, but football is strange and anything can happen. We are top, but we need to try to win every game. I don't know how many points will be enough to win the title. We need to do the maximum we can do and we want to try to win all the games."

Wednesday, Feb 22, 2012

Agüero struck again, this time after only 19 seconds. With 20 goals, Tévez was right that signing Agüero had empowered City to take a hardline stance against him. With a beleaguered Andre Villas-Boas in the stands watching the club he guided to victory in this competition last season, his successor Vitor Pereira had a point when he described the result as a 'great untruth'. Porto were a threat right up until Agüero put in Dzeko for the second goal 14 minutes from time, which gave them a 4-1 lead on aggregate and a one-man advantage because Rolando picked up a second yellow card for dissent in the aftermath.

Pizarro proved a capable replacement for Agüero, setting up Silva for the third on the night before claiming his first goal for City. Tévez and his belated apology still dominated the after-match proceedings. Mancini confirmed that he will meet his rebel striker for the first time since he returned and opened the door for a first-team return when he is fit. 'I accept his apology. I don't have any problem. I will meet him before training and after that he can begin to work with us. He needs maybe two or three weeks to find good form and after that, he will be OK. He can play, like the other players. We are on the top of the Premier League, but we know Carlos very well — he's a top striker. I think that it will be good if he can help us to do a good job in the next two months.'

A crowd of 39,538 was impressive considering the unusual kick-off time of five o'clock. Some arrived late and most of them will have missed Agüero's opening goal, the joint second-fastest in the brief history of this competition.

Defender Nicolas Otamendi lost possession straight from the kick-off, De Jong fed Yaya and he slipped the ball through for City's top scorer, who guided the ball past Helton.

'It was a good night,' said Mancini. 'It isn't easy to beat Porto. They're one of the top teams in Europe and they played very well. I'm very pleased.'

"You're not incredible," the home fans sang as Hulk, real name Givanildo Vieira de Souza, didn't see the funny side. The Portuguese club prepared an official complaint asking UEFA to open disciplinary charges denying it has anything to do with an apparent humour bypass. Rui Cerqueira, the club's spokesman, said the matter would be reported on the grounds that City's supporters had acted in an improper way. Hulk had also been targeted with chants of "cheat" because of the Brazilian's tendency to look for free-kicks and Porto will claim he was the victim of unsporting behaviour. The allegations were met with bewilderment at the Etihad Stadium where they could be forgiven for wondering if it is tit-for-tat retaliation after what happened when the two teams met at the Estádio do Dragão.

Fri, Feb 24, 2012

City could equal a 120-year top-flight record; not since Sunderland in 1892 had a side gone through the entire campaign having won every league game at home. They won all 13 of their games in the 1891-92 season on their way to becoming champions. Chelsea and United hold the Premier League record for the most home wins in a 38-game season. Under Mourinho, Chelsea won 18 of their 19 games in 2005-06, drawing one. United achieved the same feat in the 2010-11 campaign.

It was a year since City last dropped a point at home in the Premier League, a 1-1 draw with Fulham on February 27. Mancini's men were looking to extend that run of 17 straight home wins in the Premier League taking on relegation-threatened Blackburn. City could extend their lead to five points with United not in action at Norwich until Sunday.

Mancini warned against underestimating Blackburn, who pulled off a shock 3-2 win at United on New Year's Eve, 'It is impossible to be complacent. Every game is like a Champions League final and for this reason we need good concentration. Now we have a game against Blackburn on Saturday and I think every game from now until the end will be difficult. When you play against a squad playing against relegation, it can be more difficult. Blackburn won away against Manchester United and we know they are a good team, they are strong on the counter-attack. They have been playing very well in the last two or three weeks. They are playing to get away from the bottom.'

Yaya returned to feature in both legs of the Europa League win over Porto. During his absence, City went out of both domestic cup competitions and suffered a disappointing league defeat at Everton. Mancini said: 'Yaya is a high-quality player, he used to play for Barcelona and he is used to playing to win every game. I think his mentality is very strong and that can help all the team. But we have other important players and I think it is a good mix.'

David Platt insisted nobody at the club had been doubting their staying power. 'What belief do we need? After two thirds of the season we sit top of the league. We have a group of players and a staff that believe that we can continue to do what we have done for the first two thirds of the season. If we do that we will be hard to shift off the top. We feel in a good position with a good dressing room that is full of very important players. Hopefully everything will move forward in a positive way.' Platt was aware people will expect City to ease past Blackburn and their relegation rivals Bolton next week. Yet he was taking nothing for granted. 'We are getting to the business end of the season but so are Blackburn, so are Bolton. Every team in the Premier League has 13 games to go and all have something to play for. The business end counts for 20 clubs.'

Saturday Feb 25, 2012

Another home win, another Mario classic, another message. Platt hailed a mature performance from Mario Balotelli, who opened the scoring with a deft near post flick as City ran out 3-0 winners in a one-sided contest to move five points clear with Mario making his first league appearance for a month. Mario was in the mood for love, celebrating his opening goal by revealing a T-shirt emblazoned with the words: 'Raffaella Ti Amo' — I love you, Raffaella. It was a message to his model girlfriend. He even had her name stamped on his boot.

Platt said: "I actually thought he was very disciplined in his performance and his work rate was exceptional both on and off the ball. His temperament was good. He can be pleased with his afternoon's work." Platt was also pleased with the way he dealt with his treatment from the Blackburn defence. "When a team defends deep against you like that, and to open them up you have got to give the ball to people who are marked and closely guarded, there are going to be kicks like that, but you never once felt there was going to be any reaction today." As for Mario's latest message, Platt said: "All players flash T-shirts nowadays. There are a lot of players that want to take their shirts off and show messages. I don't think it is a case of flamboyance." Mario's strike gave City a 1-0 half-time lead. The outstanding Agüero added the second earlier in the second half before Dzeko came off the bench to head a third late on with virtually his first touch.

Platt played down the significance of the goals for the three leading strikers – who scored 52 between them – in the week Tévez was welcomed back to training. "All three strikers have scored all season. They are scoring goals but the team is creating them for them. In terms of possession you saw that we controlled the game. We knew we had to get off to a good start, not to let them settle into their game plan and we did that. We created chances and felt the goal was coming."

Mancini urged his team to finish the job off, "We had a good February, now we need a good March, April and half of May. We had to be patient, it was tough as they played with 10 behind the ball. If you don't score you have a problem. In the end we scored three and it was an important win. Sergio Agüero had a good performance. I'm happy as three strikers scored the goals." Edin Dzeko scored with his first touch after coming off the bench. Mancini said: "It was lucky! But I'm happy for him as he scored in the cup and then scored in this game."

Rovers boss Steve Kean commented, "You know how difficult it's going to be with the depth of the (City) squad. It was probably close to a £400 million squad with the lads on the pitch and on the bench, so they can rotate and add quality when they decide to rest people."

Sunday, Feb 26, 2012

Ryan Giggs marked his 900th appearance with a stoppage-time winner as valiant Norwich were beaten 2-1 at Carrow Road. Scholes had given the visitors an early lead with a close-range header.

Monday, Feb 27, 2012

Carlos Tévez prepared for his comeback in a reserve League Cup tie against Preston that has been specially tailored to his needs. The game was originally scheduled for Chorley's Victory Park on Wednesday, but City succeeded in changing the venue and date after identifying it as an ideal opportunity for easing him back into action. Concerned at the state of Chorley's pitch, and intense media interest, City requested the tie be brought forward 24 hours and played behind closed doors at their Carrington training complex. The 2pm kick off gave Mancini the chance to assess match sharpness and how much more fitness work was needed.

"It's not pressure, it's just that he can bring quality to the team," Dzeko said about Tévez return. "We are all one team trying to play together and it's good that we scored three because in the end goal difference could be the key." He admits it is frustrating not starting every week. "That is normal but it's good you have so many quality players around you, and that they are all getting better. Of course [it is frustrating to be on the bench], when you have scored so many goals. Sometimes you can play badly, but in the end it's the decision of the manager and I respect that. We won 3-0 so no-one has to say anything. My goals are talking for me, so I'm happy."

Tuesday Feb 28, 2012

Tévez managed 45 minutes in the reserves' against Preston and was unlucky to be denied by a fine saving tackle when sent clean through on the goalkeeper. Vieira and Marwood were there to oversee the action. Tévez was told that he would not be considered for this weekend's first-team fixture against Bolton, with the game against Swansea on March 10 a more likely target.

Mancini held talks with the forward and everything was now fine after they worked through their differences. Asked if the matter is now closed, Mancini said: "Yes. He did everything." Mancini said: "I think he needs another two weeks and in this two weeks we put two or three games with the reserves as he needs to play. For him it is like pre-season, after two months it is not easy to play. At this moment he can't play but in two weeks maybe he can play."

MARCH

"Why is it always him, when it isn't even him?"
Gary Lineker on an after match interview,
when a BBC reporter thought Roberto was Mario.

Thursday, March 1, 2012

With two months and nine games to go, Alex and Roberto had already seemingly pencilled in their teams' meeting at the end of April as the title decider. Fergie's champions were only two points behind with City at home to Bolton on Saturday, United at Tottenham on Sunday. As Mancini and Ferguson looked at the run-in, neither would complain about the fixtures they had between now and the end of the season.

The game on Monday, April 30, at the Etihad Stadium will turn into one of the most decisive in the 20-year history of the Premier League. 'It does look that way,' said Ferguson. 'It is going to be a massive game either way. You can't see City dropping a lot of points and you can't see us dropping a lot of points. If you look at the rest of the season you would certainly say that, building up to a game that could turn out to be the decider against Manchester City later in the season, Tottenham is our hardest away game, but we'll be looking to navigate it.'

Mancini felt his team will probably have to avoid defeat against United, 'It could be the one that decides it. I think United will win 11 games from now to the end and we need to do the same. I don't know what will happen in the nine games before we meet United, but I'm sure United will win a lot of games.'

David Silva will stay at the club for at least another two years, as the club were planning to tie down their brilliant midfielder for longer by making him their highest earner and offering him a two-year extension to his current deal, which expires in 2014. Silva, nicknamed 'Merlin' from his City team-mates, commented, 'Mancini has total confidence in me. That's important for a player and I'm happy, team-mates are adapting to my game and that's also very good for me. In England, football is enjoyed to the fullest.'

Fri, March 2, 2012

Diego Maradona urged Agüero to join Real Madrid, who were interested in signing the former Independiente striker before he made the switch to Eastlands, though he once claimed he would never play for a team starting with the letter 'R', in reference to Racing and Real Madrid, the two bitter rivals of the clubs he has played for so far in his career. Maradona believes his son-in-law should go back to La Liga with Real and thinks "he made a mistake" by choosing to sign for City. "Kun has to play for Real Madrid. If he signed for them, it would be his big break. Even though he is flying at City, the best thing would have been to sign for Madrid. He made a mistake."

Agüero was City's top scorer with 16 goals and the club would entertain any bids, but Al Wasl coach Maradona believed Real president Florentino Perez would be able to convince City to sell. "Now, as he is doing so well, it will be difficult to get him from City. They will want to keep him because Mancini has him very much in his plans. However, if Madrid want someone, they get them. Florentino has no limits. It's a question of convincing City, but not with money because they have plenty of that. If Kun was playing for Madrid they would close in further on Barcelona. We would be talking about Cristiano Ronaldo scoring 60 and more goals, because Kun would move the entire defence."

Wayne Rooney insisted United's experience of tight situations will see them home in the title race, while United legend Peter Schmeichel believed that Sir Alex's side were the favourites for the title. Schmeichel commented, 'What you need to understand, though, is that you can have bad results in March and April and still win the league. Players at United know that losing one game won't lose you the title. They know that's no reason to panic.'

Noel Gallagher turned up at Carrington to greet Mario Balotelli. Gallagher dedicated a song at his O2 Arena show in London to him and the pair hit it off as they met at City's training headquarters. Speaking last month, the songwriter and City fan said: 'OK, he's a footballer, but I bet if he picked up an instrument he'd be amazing. He restores your faith in human nature! I'm so proud he's playing for Man City. You see him when he's not in his football kit and you just think, 'He fucking looks cool as f**k! He's a total rock'n'roller.'

Mario was snapped leaving the 'X In The City' strip club in Liverpool at 2.45am. Mancini expects his players to be at home and in bed at that time with a first-team game less than 48 hours away. Mancini will be especially angry as he was relying on 13-goal Mario with both Dzeko and Agüero returning from internationals. There was no suggestion Mario was drunk as he is a tee-totaller.

Saturday, Mar 3, 2012

The BBC interviewer leaped straight into his first question. Mario: "Happy with this afternoon's work?"

The City manager looked rather perplexed. Roberto: "He's a bit younger than me! I'm Roberto"

Gary Linker observed on Match of the Day: "Why is it always him, when it isn't even him?"

Eventually a question was going to be about Mario and his disco dancing before the big game, but the interviewer got his tongue tied concerning the two Italians. Few similarities apart from both being Italian. It was no laughing matter when the question was finally put. Mancini was fuming with his strikers' unprofessional preparation, "Tomorrow I will speak with him. I am really disappointed about this. It is not correct, not only for me and the squad but for him, because he is a professional player. He can't stay outside the house two days before a game until two o'clock. If it is true we will do the maximum fine that we can. Mario played well, he had a lot of chances. Maybe next time if he goes to sleep early he can score three or four goals."

Mario netted in City's 2-0 win against Bolton, a record-equalling 19th in succession at home in the Premier League and leaving Bolton in relegation trouble. City became the first team since the 1907 Newcastle United side to win their first 14 home games. But Mario's goal was not going to spare him the wrath of his manager. Mancini was not aware of the incident until the afternoon, "We prepared the game with Mario, he was fresh, but the next time he will go in the stand." Mancini would fine Mario £250,000, exasperated by his off-field antics, Mancini imposed the maximum penalty of two weeks' wages. Mancini insisted his patience was not yet at breaking point, instead warned him he is jeopardising his future and urged him to try and find himself a wife. 'It could be that marriage would help him in that respect. That could be the answer, because I am sure he understands that he has made a mistake. Mario is like this, but there is nothing we can do if he does not eventually realise he cannot keep doing this. It seems anything can happen with him at any moment. He is his own worst enemy and it is 100 per cent that he should have learned by now. When you are a professional, you should know you cannot stay out until after two o'clock in the morning, so close to a game. He needs to understand this. Now he is young, but at 25 or 26 it will be different. If you do not have a good private life then, you will not be able to play at the top level. Sometimes I feel a bit let down.

These things will happen at his age, but after 100 times, I think he should understand what is going on around him. I am very kind with him but, like all the players, he knows he has to behave well to stay in the team. He was on the bench five or six times at the start of the season, because his behaviour was not good. I think he is just immature, but he will have to pay for it.

"Do I think he's more trouble than he's worth? No. I have a lot of patience with him," said Mancini. 'Probably he gets bored quickly. There is no malice. He just doesn't think that there is a game in two days, that players are away on international duty and that we prepare for him to be the main striker because he would be freshest. He doesn't think along those lines, but this has to change."

Mario might have been dropped. Mancini not only retained him in his starting line-up but deployed him as a lone striker while Agüero, Dzeko and Silva were left on the bench. Mario responded with a display of pace and vigour that might have yielded several goals before he finally struck. Mario might have had a hat-trick before City took the lead with a Steinsson own goal in the 23rd minute but made sure of victory in the 69th minute.

City suffered a blow when Zabaleta was forced off injured in the 19th minute and Kolo took his place at right-back. Mario deservedly got on the scoresheet with 21 minutes remaining. Johnson was the provider as he weaved through the defence to set up Mario from close range with a nifty back heel which squeezed between Bogdan and Wheater. Milner then came on for Nasri as City wound down the clock towards another victory. Hart kept his 16th clean sheet of the season, making a great save from Myaichi along the way.

"Today was important because we have taken three points and we need to keep winning because Manchester United are very good," said Mancini. "If we could win the next 10 games, we would win the title. We just need to keep playing the way we are and we will have a very good chance."

United could cut their lead back to two points at White Hart Lane and the City boss said: "I will probably watch it but I think we all know the result, don't we? I think United will win. I have always said to win the championship we need to win our next 10 games.'

Sunday, Mar 4, 2012

Sir Alex labelled his side's 3-1 victory at the Lane as "a massive result", though he admitted his side needed "a bit of luck" to secure the win. A first-half header from Rooney against the run of play and a brace from Young in the second period took them back to within two points of City with 11 games left. The Manchester derby increasingly looked ever more like the title decider. Fergie added: "We know exactly what we have to do. You can drop surprise points and I think both sides will, but the important thing is to drop less points than our opponents. A battling performance today tells you that we are up for it."

Monday, Mar 5, 2012

Mancini said Mario needs to mature, and in a BBC interview with Noel Gallagher, he agreed, "If Mancini says something, he's right." He added: "But I'm 21, so I'm still young. I think from last year, already I'm bigger in my head."

Mario rarely gives interviews but agreed to speak to Gallagher for Football Focus. He said Mancini, who coached him at Inter, was a major reason he decided to join City, "If Mancini wasn't here, I never come here, but now that I'm here, I'm OK, I'm happy. This year I have already scored 14 goals and a pair of penalties, and the intensity and effort I put into training this year, are not comparable to last season. I have grown up, I have understood certain things. The intensity and commitment that I have shown this year, even in training, is not comparable to a year ago. I have grown up. My father, Franco, always told me that he would come and see me play in England when I got my head straight. He has told me that moment has arrived.'

He was a "really private" person and could not understand why being seen about Manchester caused such excitement in the media. "I just walk in town like a normal guy," adding that he liked to go to the pub but "not to drink".

Gallagher commented, 'I asked him about the rumours, we listed them all. Unfortunately 90 per cent of them are b★★★★★★★, but there's a grain of truth in them all. I told him he was killing me, because we want them all to be true. We want a footballer to be going around giving £1,000 to a homeless person, because it's just cool. We don't want professional footballers to be like Michael Owen or Ashley Cole, people that think the world owes them something. We want to believe that this kid goes into petrol stations and buys everyone a full tank of petrol. Not because that's what they should do, but because footballers are young and they should behave young.

"My favourite Balotelli story is the magic tricks. One day he was wandering through the Trafford Centre minding his own business, as if he could do, like a modern-day Mr T. And there's a guy doing magic, and he asked if he could teach him some magic. The guy said, "No, I don't teach magic." So Mario went home, pondered it, and thought, "I'm not having that", so he went back to the Trafford Centre and said to the bloke, "teach me these magic tricks". The guy said, "No, there's too many people here." So

Mario took him in his car, back to his house for dinner, and the guy showed him magic over dinner. That's where he learnt the tricks.'

Gallagher dedicated a song to Mario every night on his tour and says the reception has been phenomenal: 'I've been on tour and I've been dedicating a song 'What a Life' to him every night. It's amazing the reaction that it gets, all around the world. People love him. It starts off with booing because he's a City player, but it turns into cheers because he's a modern day rock-star. And he'd heard of this and he said if he was going to do an interview he'd only do it with me. So they asked me to do it, and I cleared my schedule. Too right, I'll do that for a laugh.'

Mario told City's fans not to barrack Tévez when he returns, "I think the supporters have to be like they were before. They should not care because Carlos is here and, if they make pressure on Carlos, then they make pressure on all the team. So they should do nothing." Mario struggled in the media spotlight, 'I don't like when people talk about my business with my life. I'm really private. Maybe some people think I'm really arrogant. I don't care, they can say what they want. I'm a footballer so the most important moment is Sunday on the pitch. If I go in the street and one guy gets a picture, they say: "Mario was there". Someone calls the press and says: "Mario was there". They day after that they say: "Mario was there". Is that normal? I'm just walking in town like a normal guy or I go to the pub. I've been to the pub, yeah. Not to drink.'

His manager would like to see him get married to try and curb some of his antics, "Do I think to marry? For me it is not soon. When you find the right person, it may be the time. Raffaella is the best thing that ever happened to me. It gives me peace of mind, she understands me when I make a mess. How did she take my evening at the strip club? Well I'd have got angry if she went to a male strippers' club with her friends. I didn't do anything wrong. But if you really love a woman, you should spare her that. This was the first mistake. The second was to go two days before a game.'

Fico calmed talk of marriage and even gave Mario her blessing to visit strip clubs. 'It is too soon to get married, we are still very young,' said the 24-year-old model. 'He doesn't do things maliciously, but when you are young you do certain things without stopping to think whether they are right or wrong. For me, he can go to a strip club if he does nothing wrong, with friends, but I have to say that he always comes back to me, his favourite.'

Mario felt comfortable City will come through in the title race, if they stick together. "We are a big group of quality. If we remain united as a group until the end, then United will be left behind us."

Mario was reluctant to remove an item of clothing when challenged by security staff at his favourite shopping mall in Manchester. He chose to leave the Trafford Centre rather than take off his hood and risk being recognised after he was told he was breaking the rules by hiding his face from the CCTV cameras. Mario was trying to keep a low profile but The Trafford Centre's strict 'no hood' policy was explained to him first in English and then his native Italian before he left on amicable terms, joking with staff that he will return in disguise next time. The Mall commented, 'The gentleman decided that rather than take down his hood, he would prefer to leave the centre. He was polite and friendly throughout the encounter. The customer, who is believed to be a regular visitor to the Trafford Centre, then shook hands with our security staff and departed for his car.'

Tuesday Mar 6, 2012

At Ewen Fields in Hyde, Tévez put in a good night's work in his first match back in front of a crowd for the club's elite development squad in the relative obscurity of a Manchester Senior Cup tie, scoring against Bolton reserves. Watched by assistant manager Brian Kidd and football administrator Brian Marwood, Tévez looked trimmer and sharper than when he appeared in a behind-closed-doors friendly against Preston. He scored in the 51st minute, stealing in front of his marker to fire City's equaliser in a 3-1 win. Just as important was the positive reaction from a predominantly City crowd of 1,047, who cheered Tévez at the start and again when he was substituted, ironically, by Mancini's son Filippo in the 66th minute. Having earlier given his shirt to a fan at half-time, he apologised for not stopping to sign autographs as he left the pitch. Tévez was back in favour and back among the goals.

Joe Hart insisted Tévez will be no more culpable than anyone else in the squad if Mancini's side fail to clinch the title. "A lot of people will say that but, personally, I won't. If we don't win the league, it will be our own fault. That includes Carlos, myself – everyone. I'm not interested in what's perceived outside of the club. All I'm interested in is what's going on inside the club and how we can win the league. If that means Carlos coming back, scoring a hat-trick and everyone saying he's the greatest player in the world, so be it. I couldn't care less."

Wednesday, Mar 7, 2012

Roberto Mancini arrived in Lisbon for the tie with Sporting, but the talk was back in England and on Robin van Persie. City were linked with a move for the prolific Dutch striker but it is the first time Mancini went public with his desire to sign him. "We are interested in all good players. This is normal, but not only us. I think all the good teams are interested in Van Persie. I think

Van Persie at this moment is one of the best strikers in Europe with Messi, Ronaldo and with Sergio and Mario. I think he is a fantastic striker, but I think he will remain with Arsenal."

City acquired Nasri, Clichy, Kolo and Adebayor from Arsenal. Mancini added: "I think if there is a good player who wants to leave a club, then we are interested. But if this player wants to stay, we don't have any problem. In my opinion, Van Persie will stay at Arsenal. I think Robin van Persie will sign a new contract with Arsenal because if Arsenal lose also Van Persie, they will have a big problem."

Mancini insisted that it would be possible to win the final in Bucharest and see off the constant, draining challenge of United, "We have to be careful and not lose even one more match," said Agüero. "Even if we draw a game, they could catch us. The Premier League is so competitive and now the matches are harder for us."

In an interview with the Argentinian daily El Grafico, Agüero said: "Even if we don't win the title, the fans will still say we had a great season". Maybe, maybe not. Maradona, could not understand why Argentina celebrated their second place in the 1990 World Cup, commenting tartly to his team-mates: "You don't celebrate second place, tiger."

When Mancini arrived in the press room in the Jose Alvalade Stadium, it was to face questions that City did not respect Sporting. There was the suggestion that some members of the City squad could not name any of the opposition players. For once, the questions directed towards Mancini were not dominated by Tévez and Mario, as the absence of the suspended Yaya was more significant.

Asked why Mourinho does not believe in him Mario Balotelli said: "That's his problem. They say he wants to come here? But me, with Mourinho? He's a great manager but he didn't understand me so he said that nobody can understand me. But I think the only one that cannot understand me is him, so it's his problem."

Mario believes Mancini's side should win the title as the reward for playing the better football. "If you ask me if we deserve to win, if we keep playing like that then yes we deserve it. It's unlucky to say before that we will."

On the eve of the derby with United, which City won 6-1 and in which Mario scored twice, his colourful personal life had been illustrated when the fire brigade were called to his house. "It started like a joke. I was bored, I was with my friends, and one of them was limping so I got one bin, a metal one, to put fireworks inside. So I left the room and I left the fireworks but I didn't light them. I walked out and then my friends go in the room and they just start screaming: 'Blah blah blah'. And the fireworks were going off and they put the fireworks on the bed, not on the bed, sorry on the toilet. But just the curtain caught on fire. That's it, nothing else. The firemen came for the curtain and the toilet. Just the toilet was lost."

After scoring against United in that derby he revealed a T-shirt 'Why Always me?' Asked if he prepared this in anticipation of claiming a goal he said: "I thought I was going to score three. The T-shirt was just a message. It's not a question, that people do to me, it's a question that I do to them. It was to all the people that talk bad about me and say stuff not nice and they don't know me so asking: 'Why always me, like, why always me?'"

Ibrahimovic and the Brazilian Ronaldo were two of his favourite players but he had not heard of City before joining. "No, nothing. I didn't know nothing."

Meanwhile Eric Cantona criticised Mario's t-shirt messages, pointing out his own dramatic gestures, including the infamous kung-fu kick on a Crystal Palace fan, were spur-of-the-moment rather than pre-planned, "I dreamt of being a footballer, of doing great things, of crying and laughing after a victory, of exploding with joy. It is about spontaneity. I never had anything on a T-shirt, never calculated anything. Every action is unique, every reaction unique.'

On Mario, Lescott observed, 'Italians generally have style - but we've probably got the worst dressed Italian in the world. GQ chose him as the second best dressed person in the country and he believes it!'

Brian Marwood was focusing on City's title challenge but he says the aim is not just to win the title this season but to sustain the success over a number of years. 'It would be a huge achievement, but it's not about what we do just this year, it's about what we do for the next five to 10 years.'

Thursday, Mar 8, 2012

Vincent Kompany picked up a calf injury in the sixth minute of City's defeat in Lisbon. Roberto Mancini played a strong team. The inclusion of Kompany, replaced by Lescott five minutes after picking up his injury, presented Mancini with a worry ahead of the weekend.

The manager was concerned to see his team play poorly at such a critical stage. Sporting scored in the 51st minute. Yaya was penalised for a foul 25 yards out and, when Hart parried Schaars' low free-kick, centre back Xandao scored with a lovely backheel after Hart had saved his first follow-up. Mancini said: 'We wanted to win but perhaps didn't play as well as we would have hoped. We have to wait for Kompany. A calf is a bad position.' City rallied to dominate the final 20 minutes, a Kolarov cross hit the bar,

Silva diverted a cross from substitute Mario inches wide and, in the final moments, Balotelli headed against the post.

Fri, Mar 9, 2012

Rooney has four medals from topping the table in battles with Arsenal and Chelsea. When asked if winning the current showdown against their noisy neighbours would top the lot, Rooney said: "I imagine so. I don't want to speak too soon but, if we can win it and pip City, I'm sure it would be very sweet." United would overhaul City if they beat West Brom at home and City lose at Swansea. Rooney commented, "You can sense the excitement in the city amongst the players and fans. It is great. These are the times you want to be playing football, to be in a title race like this. Over the last six weeks, we have got some great results in the league but City have done well this season. They have been similar to us in that they have won games when they haven't been at their best. It is going to be a really tight last 11 games of the season for both teams."

United also lost on Thursday night in the first leg of their Europa League last-16 ties. For United it was a second successive home loss in the competition, the 3-2 defeat by Athletic Bilbao following a 2-1 reverse against Ajax. Facing West Brom provided United with a perfect opportunity to rid themselves of any negative thoughts

Saturday, Mar 10, 2012

David Silva will host a "mad festival" for his team-mates should they wrestle the title off the Red Devils. "There is only one fear in our squad – my promise that I will organise a mad festival if we win the Premier League. We have Sergio and his arrival this season has increased the 'Spanish' flavour. We also have the 'king of anecdotes' in Mario, who is so unpredictable both on the field and the street – and then we have plenty of controversy in Carlos. Actually we all know he is a big player and we are glad to have Carlos back. He really could help us in the decisive final stage of the season."

Brendan Rodgers hailed the "outstanding" job by Mancini this season but observed, "Manchester United have that experience and I just think their football nous is fantastic. The strides Roberto Mancini has made with Manchester City have been superb. Even though he has had all the money and all the resources, I think he has blended things very, very well. The way he has managed to do that has been outstanding, and City will obviously feel they can win the league. I am not sure how things will turn out. I think it will be really, really tight and it's going to be interesting watching the final part of the season."

Beaten 4-0 at City on the opening day of the season, Swansea can have their say in the title battle in the return fixture as Swansea have shown they can upset the odds already this term, particularly on their own patch. Swansea also faced a trip to Old Trafford on the penultimate weekend of the campaign, but they hoped by then to have achieved their goal of staying up.

Sunday Mar 11, 2012

City lost their championship lead for the first time in five months as unmarked substitute Luke Moore headed Swansea's winner inside the final seven minutes as he guided in Routledge's pin-point right-wing cross. City dropped a point behind United following the Red Devils' win over West Brom. City had won only two of their last eight League away games. The Welsh side's victory ranked alongside their January triumph over Arsenal as one of the most famous results in their 100-year history. As Swansea celebrated, Mancini's men squandered their top-of-the-table berth with a below-par performance, feeling the effects of their midweek Europa League defeat in Porto. Kolo was captain for the day in Kompany's absence.

Mancini went to the lengths of making a first-half tactical substitution, as Agüero was introduced in place of Barry in an effort to spark his side into life. Mancini dismissed suggestions of a rift with Barry, who exchanged angry words with Platt as he left the field after being replaced. "Gareth has had a problem for three weeks. Gareth has a problem, I don't know where. It is a small injury. They had a lot of possession in the opening 30 minutes and we needed another striker to press high, not because Barry played badly. When asked about Barry looking unhappy at being taken off, Mancini replied: "This is normal. I decide this. I'm the manager."

Asked about reports that striker Mario and Yaya had a bust-up in the tunnel at half-time, Mancini replied: "I don't know." A late Micah Richards goal was ruled out for offside in a dramatic final few minutes. Swansea could have won more comfortably, Hart saving Sinclair's early penalty, the first time Sinclair had missed a penalty in 14 attempts.

Mancini said before the game he wanted his side to break Chelsea's title-winning points record of 95 set in 2005. But they were restricted to half chances against a side that have also taken points off Arsenal, Chelsea and Tottenham at the Liberty Stadium this season. Mario summed up the visitors' frustrations as he tried his luck from virtually the halfway line with a wayward effort.

With 10 games to go, United were now favourites, victory taking them top for the first time since 15 October. "I hope it is a significant day," Fergie said. "I don't mind being top of the league at this stage. I think we've clawed it back from seven points behind to one point ahead. We've turned it around and credit to the players for that. They have shown great resilience and determination. We had a period of injuries but we have come through that now. We will keep on playing. It is good to see that type of temperament. The City defeat was a bonus I didn't expect but I am happy to be top because only a few weeks ago we were seven points behind them. That is credit to the players and the resilience of the squad because as everyone knows, we have had a lot of injuries. Wayne is on a hot streak. I thought his first goal might have been offside because he was so clear but when you see his timing of the run it was fantastic.' United's victory came courtesy of two goals from Rooney, 26 for the season, including 15 in his last 14 games, an ominous sign.

Mancini continued to believe the United showdown would be the decider. "Today was not critical. I think this championship will be decided with three games to go. We should fight against them until the end. We have another 10 games to finish this championship. The season is long and every week the situation could change. Now it is important we are very comfortable together. It is better to stay at the top but, now we are behind, it doesn't change our target. I'm still confident about winning the Premier League. We were top for months but it just so happens that we are second with 10 games to play. It is important that we are there around the top. We know United have gone top, like we were, but now we should be more strong and it is a test for our players. It has been a difficult last four days for me but football is like this. The season is long and what happened today can happen also to United."

Mancini believed his side deserved something out of the Swansea game, "We missed three or four chances on the counter attack. This is the problem at the moment and we conceded a stupid goal. I don't think we deserved to lose this game. Swansea played well in the first 30 minutes but in the second half we had control of the game.'

Monday, Mar 12, 2012

The fan tormented on message boards nationwide, claimed: "I wasn't crying, I was just frustrated and very tired". Moore's late winner sparked the tearful reaction from John Millington, who realised defeat had enabled United to claim top spot, his emotional outburst broadcast across the globe. A thread on the Bluemoon fans' forum was quickly almost 20 pages long and counting with many City fans claiming Millington had made the club and its supporters a laughing stock. Millington, though, jumped to his own defence, telling the Manchester Evening News: "I wasn't crying. There may have been a tear in my eye but I was just exhausted and frustrated. I've been watching City for 21 years and we've always been second best. I thought this was our year and it just went wrong and at the time I just thought our chance had gone."

Tuesday, Mar 13, 2012

Joe Hart will not face any action from the FA for 'sledging' Sinclair, even though the controversial tactic cost him a place in the European Under 21 Championship final. Hart confronted Sinclair after Swansea were awarded a penalty and continued shouting at him as he retreated back towards his goal-line. He tried to put Sinclair off by telling him repeatedly that he would not score. It worked as Hart saved the striker's weak penalty. Sledging can be deemed unsporting behaviour. Hart missed out on an appearance for England Under 21s in the 2009 Euro final against Germany after being booked for trying to put off Sweden players in a semi-final penalty shootout by talking to them and even blowing raspberries. England Under 21s won that shootout in Gothenburg 5-4, but lost 4-0 in the final to a strong Germany team that included Ozil and Khedira. FA sources indicated that no action will be taken on this occasion,

There was a similar incident at Old Trafford as United took over at the top of the table by beating West Brom 2-0. Rooney stared at Albion goalkeeper Ben Foster after scoring his second goal from the penalty spot because his former United team-mate had tried to put him off beforehand.

Wednesday, Mar 14, 2012

The City fan at Swansea might have shed a tear, but Mancini was determined that it would not all end in tears. Mancini observed, 'We lost both games against Sporting and Swansea but we can't cry. Now is the time to be strong and keep going because we're a top team and we have time to recover. We have 10 games and it's in our hands. We have a derby three games from the end. If we win all the games, we will win the title. We can't cry because we're one point behind Manchester United. We were very disappointed for our supporters after Swansea. I saw one of our supporters crying on the TV. For this guy and all the supporters we want to change things.'

Asked if United would have the edge if they go out in Bilbao and City stay in Europe, Mancini replied: 'Probably. For this reason, we hope that United will win tomorrow. But we don't want to lose a game because it could be a distraction for the Premier League. Now we're here for the Europa League and we want to go to the next stage. If we want to be a top team and change our mentality we have to always play to win.'

Tévez trained with the first-team squad in the morning, wearing a blue and white hat, but was not eligible to play in Europe having not been registered. Despite originally being pencilled in, Tévez did not feature for City's reserve team against Nijmegen in the Netherlands as the club stepped up his fitness regime

As United go to Wolves on Sunday, City could go into the match at Chelsea trailing by four points, so Mancini may welcome the presence of Tévez. Asked if Tévez could be available for that game, Mancini said: 'We will see in the next week. It depends on Carlo. If Carlo is okay then probably, but it depends on a lot of things.'

Barry was troubled by a back injury. Mancini said: 'Gareth has had a problem with his back for 20 days. He can't run well. When he went to the national team he had a problem. On Sunday he didn't play well but I think that is because he had a problem. We will see for him in the next days but probably he needs another two or three days' rest. These players are not like robots, they need to rest. Instead they go to the national team instead of resting for two or three days. It is impossible for these players to play for 10 months every three days.'

Thursday, Mar 15, 2012

Manager Mancini accepted blame for the Europa League exit. City were edged out on away goals against Sporting despite a thrilling late comeback at the Etihad Stadium which will be remembered for the final touch, a header by Hart that the keeper finger tipped inches around the post.

City trailed 3-0 on aggregate after conceding goals to Fernandez and van Wolfswinkel in an indisciplined first-half performance. Goals from Agüero and a typically cheeky Mario penalty, all inside the last half-hour, gave City hope of an unlikely victory which Hart was agonisingly close to completing in injury time.

Mancini said: "In the first half we didn't play, but I am the manager and it's not the players' fault, but mine – I probably made a mistake. The players did everything, and fought on the pitch. When a manager doesn't prepare well for the game, this happens. When I lose a game I think about why I lost and think about where I made mistakes. I understand we have big players but in football every game is difficult, and in the Europa League and Champions League it is more difficult, because every team plays to win. Sometimes we make mistakes, but the manager is the person who always prepares the game, and I probably made some mistakes for these two games."

Mancini's comments were similar to remarks he made after an unexpected League defeat at Everton in January, when he blamed poor preparation. City now only had their title challenge to concentrate on. Mancini said: "I am proud for the second half because we had a fantastic 45 minutes, but I am very sorry for the players and our supporters because they were fantastic in that second half. But I am disappointed in myself, not the players. For the second time this year, I hope I don't make mistakes against Chelsea."

Mancini believed the manner of his side's fight back will stand them in good stead for the weeks ahead. "If we have the same spirit as we had in the second half we can win the next game against Chelsea and I am confident for the Premier League because we stayed on top for seven months and now we are in second position, one point behind. I am very confident we can win the title. I think that now it will be a good fight until the end of the season because we have only the Premier League and we can put all of our strength into this. I think it will be good."

Mancini joked that City followed United out of the competition to focus on their title bid. "We were envious of United because they lost, so we wanted to lose this game!" City had extra time to recover with their next league game pushed back to Wednesday due to opponents Chelsea playing in the FA Cup on Sunday.

Fri, Mar 16, 2012

From being seven points clear, City were chasing United and could be four points adrift by the time they face a rejuvenated Chelsea at the Etihad Stadium. Lescott said, 'I saw their win against Napoli, very exciting. Drogba and Torres are both world-class. If we're four points behind on Wednesday there will be more pressure on us.'

Saturday, Mar, 17, 2012

United were lording it back at the summit as Rooney commented, "If we can win this league then I'm sure it will be very satisfying for all the players, fans and everyone connected to the club because there was one stage when we weren't expected to win the league, which is mad when you are talking about Man United. So it's great we are back on top and the aim is to stay there until the end of the season. There's still a long way to go of course, 10 games left, we know we have to stay focused for all of those game to stay top. We know what we have to do."

Rooney described the derby loss at Old Trafford as a "nightmare". "It dented our pride. We're all proud people and we don't want to lose like that, particularly at home and against your closest rivals. It was a nightmare game for us. It was important we came back well and strong from that. I think the next six games after that were 1-0 victories, so we put it out of our minds and looked forward rather than back. I hope we don't experience a day like that again.'

Sunday, Mar 18, 2012

Mancini, Platt and Marwood flew to France to watch Hazard score one goal and set up two more in Lille's 4-0 win over Valenciennes. United and Chelsea were interested and Fergie watched Hazard last weekend. City can outbid any of their rivals with a deal worth over £150,000-a-week. Hazard revealed: "I heard before the game that Mancini was there. For my part I always try and play the same way, whether Alex Ferguson's there or Mancini now. I try and forget about that when I'm on the pitch, I try to play my own game. No matter who's in the stands I just try to show what I can do. We'll see what happens, but for now I'm concentrating on finishing the season well with Lille."

Sir Alex was pleased to have lowered the goal difference after a 5-0 win at Wolves who had a player sent off when one down, a victory Ferguson described as far from comfortable. Sir Alex felt the title will not be decided until the very end of the season. "I expect it to go to the wire, always hope for the best and expect the worst. There are only nine games left now, it is just a matter of games getting cut off one by one and hopefully we achieve what we want to achieve.

What's significant today is it's reduced the goal difference by five goals and that's down to three now and it may make a difference at the end of the season." After the win at Molineux, Fergie challenged City to match their feat, suggesting Chelsea under interim boss Di Matteo would pose stiff opposition. "[City] have a big game on Wednesday," said Ferguson. "Chelsea are back to form. It will be really interesting."

Monday, Mar 19, 2012

Joe Hart believed his side were capable of gunning down leaders United. "It doesn't feel good," Hart said. "As soon as the whistle went at Swansea, we knew. We didn't need to check the results, we knew what would have gone on elsewhere. We were hurt and we'll show how hurt we are with our performance on Wednesday against Chelsea. Now we have to push on, we have a big game against Chelsea. We need to focus on what we're doing and we should be OK. One result can literally change everything. It's madness but it's great. Being four points behind won't have any bearing on how we play. I've never won [the league] so it's hard to know what a title-winning side feels like. But we've got a good spirit, good attitude. And I'm sure anyone who has won a title will tell you that's what is required. We have all the ingredients. All we're short of is the medal round our necks."

United's decision to recall Scholes was a sign that there is "a little bit of weakness" in the leaders' squad. Vieira, who played against Scholes for

Arsenal and City, was impressed with the former England international's impact, "Paul Scholes is a player that I really love and admire, one of the best English players of the last few years, and seeing him come back is good for him and for United, but for him to come back just shows a little bit of weakness in United, because they had to bring a player back who was 37. I think it shows that, in the next few years, it will be really difficult for United to cope with other teams because, with all the respect I have for Scholes, him coming back shows that they don't have talent in there to replace him. When you see United losing young players like Ravel Morrison and maybe Paul Pogba, they should be really worried because that wouldn't have happened in the past."

Tuesday, Mar 20, 2012

Mancini refused to panic despite falling four points behind United. The bookmakers making United favourites to lift the title; most pundits believed their experience of a pressurised run-in will prove crucial. Mancini rejected that, "We lost top place in the Premier League at Swansea, but this is not the end of the title race as some people are saying. Now it is very important we are very comfortable together as a squad and as a club. We must regroup and find our best form and the fans will play their part against Chelsea. There is no need for anyone to panic. Of course, it is better to stay at the top, but now we are behind, it doesn't change our target. Now we have to show we are strong physically and ready for the challenge. This is a test for our players. It has been a difficult few days in terms of getting results and some injuries to important players, but we all know football is like this. The season is long and what happened recently can happen to any team. Against Sporting Lisbon and Swansea, we missed three or four chances on the counter-attack. This is the problem at the moment and then we have conceded what from our point of view have been stupid goals. Every game is difficult and different. We try to play good football and sometimes we can, and sometimes we can't. Football is like this. Sometimes you lose when you deserve to win and sometimes you win when you are not the best team. It is an unpredictable season, but we know the season still has a long way to go and that we can still win a trophy. We have another ten games to finish this championship and that is a lot of points. That is nearly 25% of the season. The season is long and every week the situation could change. We will fight hard, and together, right until the end, to give ourselves the chance to win the title.

"We will win the title, we will win. We will do everything to win the title. We need to think positive always. Until now we have had a fantastic Premier League, we need to continue like this. We play one game a week, we can have more concentration about this. Ten games is nothing. We can't think about this, we need to think positive always. Until now we have had a fantastic Premier League campaign and we need to continue like this."

Mancini remained optimistic about the chances of stealing the title from Old Trafford. "I am confident because the players are very strong and they know we have a big chance to win this title. I also think we deserve this after being top for seven months. We were top until one week ago, so we don't want to lose this chance to win. It changes nothing to be one point behind at this moment, because we have another 10 games, including a derby. We have everything in our hands."

United do not play again until Monday when they face Fulham at Old Trafford. Before, City travel to Stoke so Mancini was conscious that Sir Alex's men could again go behind in the title race. "If we win our next two games, we go two points up. We need to go our way and can't think about United. I think we can do this – we did it when we started the season, in the first 10 games we won nine and drew one, away against Fulham."

Chelsea had won all four matches since sacking their manager. Mancini admitted that the possibility of facing them without his best two central defenders was a daunting prospect. "It could be a big problem," the manager said.

In Villas-Boas' final pre-match press conference before being sacked, he called City's playing pool "a lot better" than his own. Asked if he believed Chelsea were capable of taking City on, Di Matteo said: "Yes, I do."

Wednesday, Mar 21, 2012

Mancini made two pivotal decisions to inspire a stunning comeback from a goal down to turn it around against Chelsea! Bringing on Tévez was his second substitution. Hauling off Mario was a tactical one at half-time with the score at 0-0.

Mario was sacrificed having wasted a glorious chance to break the deadlock in the opening period when an error from Lampard sent him clean through on Cech. Mario took his shot too early, and Cech was able to palm it round the post. That miss was the low point in a lethargic showing from the notoriously unpredictable striker, and Mancini said: "I didn't like how he played, so I made a tactical sub."

City fell behind in the second period after Cahill's deflected strike, but recovered to win 2-1 following a penalty from Agüero and a winner from Nasri, who scored after running onto a pass from returning Tévez. Mancini was pleased with Tévez's cameo and paid tribute to his side's determination. Tévez came on in the 66th minute and made an important contribution to the game, supplying a neat reverse-pass to set-up Nasri for his late winner. "Carlos is not 100% but that is normal," said Mancini. "But he knows the football. That was important because he did an incredible assist for Samir. What happened with him finished one month ago when Carlos came back and everything was finished. I have spoken to Carlos every day in the last month. He knew he would be on the bench today and would probably play for 20 minutes. If he can find good form in 10 days that would be important for us. Now it is important for him to play some games, for us, him and his future. Samir did well but he can do better. He can improve. He is a top player. If he plays like this he can be like David Silva or Xavi if he plays. I don't think we have played well in the last three or four weeks. Until then we have played fantastic football. Afterwards it has been so-so. Maybe after tonight something can change."

Nasri also paid tribute to Tévez. "I am really happy for him. He has showed great spirit and today showed he can be really important until the end of the season. It's good that it was him who gave him the assist." Nasri hoped United win their next six matches, ensuring their meeting at Eastlands was effectively a title decider. "It would be fantastic for the fans, and for us as well. I know United will be there until the end. They have the experience and a manager who has won everything for 25 years. Even if I said I hope they lose, sometimes you have to be realistic, and I don't think they will lose too many games - firstly, because they don't have any really difficult games, and secondly because they have experience of that type of game. I think they will win, so we have to do the same and win all of our games. I don't think they'll lose seven of their last nine games!"

Richards admitted the victory was a huge result in their battle for the title, "It's a massive result for us. After we went 1-0 down heads could have dropped, but we kept on going and managed to get three points. We did have to win tonight, we gave everything and showed good character. The lads will be delighted with that."

Di Matteo had no complaints about the handball decision that went against Essien that allowed Agüero to equalise. Mancini's side were now one point behind United as he offered hope that City could have captain Kompany back in the side for the trip to Stoke, but had less encouraging news on defensive partner Lescott. Kolo and Richards filled in at centre-half but he and fellow back-up centre-half Savic failed to impress. When asked if either of his defensive rocks would return at Stoke, Mancini said: "Joleon I don't think but for Vinnie maybe he has some chance."

Mancini admitted that injuries at the back affected their form, but remains hopeful that beating the Blues will be a turning point. 'I don't think that we played well in the last three or four weeks. I think at times we have played fantastic football but in the last month maybe it has been so-so. I think that after maybe today something can change.'

Thursday, Mar 22, 2012

Adriano Galliani, vice-president of Serie A giants AC Milan, watched Tévez make his comeback and rues failing to bring the player to the San Siro, "I was in love with Tévez and yesterday I saw him returning to the field with Manchester City and I loved it so much. When he entered the game changed. He drives me crazy, but some trains have to be taken in the exact moment which they pass, while fate decided otherwise. However we are delighted with what Maxi Lopez is doing with our shirt."

Maradona told Tévez to put his differences with Mancini to one side and get back into the City fold. Maradona said: 'I told Tévez three months ago that he had to talk with Mancini as soon as possible. I said that because he was losing money — but also because he needed to play football again. I told Tévez, "you must go back now".' Maradona and Tévez became friends during the former's stint as Argentina manager, and spoke during the latter's spell in the country while in self-inflicted exile from Manchester.

John Guidetti, on loan at Feyenoord from City, had 18 goals in 17 starts for the Rotterdam club and was front-page news. Vieira had been across to Holland more than once to assure Guidetti that he was in Mancini's thoughts.

Bryan Robson was not sure City had the mental strength to win the title. "You do feel pressure. As soon as you slip up, that pressure is on you - 'It looks like it won't be your year. Certain players will have it in the back of their mind that they're never going to do it. Some will be really positive, but others won't have the same character." With two of City's next three games being trips to Stoke and Arsenal, Robson claimed, "City must be really disappointed. When you look at what they've achieved this season, normally they would be top of the league easily. But United have been grinding it out and have the advantage as it stands. City also have a tough fixture list. You wonder whether they can get maximum points out of that. It's going to be really hard, especially with their away form. They're fantastic at the Etihad and everybody will say the key issue is the game at Manchester City. If United win it, they'll win the league. That would be the season done and dusted. United won't slip up too many times. The other thing in their favour is that they've been there, seen it, done it, year-in, year-out for the last 20 years. The manager is so experienced, he knows how to handle it. If I was in control of either team, I'd want to be in control of United, because they're going to have to lose it rather than City winning it."

Robson claimed United boss Ferguson may be the difference "The manager does man-management really well and that can be the biggest difference. Another little downturn for City is the little bit of negative publicity – the Tévez saga, Mario Balotelli on a couple of nights out. Those little things, Sir Alex always keeps right on top of, and doesn't allow them to happen. The boss isn't interested in one individual. He's interested in the whole group. That's why he'll always clamp down."

Robson cited Fergie's decision to drop Rooney from the New Year's Eve home game with Blackburn – which they surprisingly lost 3-2 – for disciplinary reasons. "When you look at certain managers, you ask whether they would have left Wayne Rooney out. United had a million injuries in that game, he's fielding a depleted team and then he says, 'I'm not having this' and Wayne is left out. A lot of managers might have fined him but put him in, because it was an important game and they didn't want to slip up. But the boss saw the bigger picture – Does Wayne think he can get away with it because he's one of the top players in the world? The boss has shown that's not the case: 'It doesn't matter who you are. If you are in my team, you don't get away with that.'"

Fri, Mar 23, 2012

Sir Alex Ferguson launched an amazing attack on City and warned them he has "plenty of ammunition" if they want to engage in mind games. Vieira said the decision to bring Scholes out of retirement smacked of desperation; United won nine League games and drawn one with Scholes in the team, suggesting the move has worked. Ferguson hit back in a week when Tévez made his controversial return. 'If it's desperation bringing the best midfielder in Britain back for the last 20 years then I think we can accept that. I think he (Vieira) was programmed for that. Roberto had a wee dig a couple of weeks back. We're all going to play our hand that way. There will be plenty of ammunition for that. If you talk about desperation, they played a player the other night who refused to go on the pitch, the manager said he'd never play again and he takes a five-month holiday in Argentina. What is that? Could that come under the description of desperation?'

United faced Fulham at Old Trafford on Monday, victory will ensure they regain the leadership. 'Every game is must-win now," said Ferguson. 'That is no issue for me. I have been used to that for years. Hopefully we can keep the momentum going.' Rio ramped up the rivalry in Manchester by claiming City fans have 'come out of the woodwork'. 'Walking around in town, you see more and more blue shirts than you probably ever would have seen over the last 10 years. But success sometimes brings people out of the woodwork. So fingers crossed we can delay that and make sure that we get this title sewn up this season.'

Asked if Wednesday's victory had sent a message to United, Mancini said: 'I think that it's important to have a message for ourselves because in the last month we didn't play very well. In some moments of the season there are games that can change everything, like this one. In December when we lost our first game, in London, it changed something inside us. I think this game can change things again. It can make us positive again inside the mind.'

Mancini had his sights on reclaiming top spot, 'I don't know if it was a champions' performance but we gave a very good performance in a difficult game. I enjoyed it like the supporters. It was really important to win. It was difficult because we were playing against a top team but we want to go back to the top. We have a very difficult game on Saturday against Stoke and this game was important for the three points. I was frustrated in the first half when we had three or four incredible chances and didn't score.

In this moment, at this stage of the season, when you get chances you need to score because it is very important. But I think they gave a fantastic performance; they wanted to win and they deserved to win the game. We didn't deserve to lose. It was a big performance, we expended a lot of energy and now we need to recover very well.'

Mancini admitted recent form had been a concern. City won all 15 of their home matches in the league this season – and a Premier League record 20 in succession – but away results prevented them pulling away from United. 'I don't think we have played well in the last three or four weeks. At times we have played some fantastic football but in the last month we have been so-so. But after this hopefully something can change.'

Agüero was signed to replace Tévez, they started one game together, but Agüero equalised from the penalty spot against Chelsea in midweek and Tévez came off the bench after a six-month absence to set up a late winner. Agüero backed Tévez to have a big say in the title race. 'Carlos is a key player because he's got five years experience of playing in the Premier League. He will bring a lot to the party for what remains of the season. Through what happened and the situation that came about, I've not had much chance to play with him. He was bursting to get out there on the field on Wednesday. I'm not Roberto Mancini but we all know he's an important player for us. With the nine games remaining in the season I think he can bring a lot to the side. It's an important time for him to come back.'

Agüero insists the comeback against Chelsea proved City can handle the pressure, 'The title race is all about not giving up. We are fighting for the title, we have confidence. We're the sort of team who know that if we go behind we can come back and win the game. (Being second) is a different type of pressure really but it's difficult to judge which is the most. The key is we are in a position now where we can't afford to drop any points. For sure Manchester United are quite experienced in these title chases but we have to focus on ourselves. We have dropped a few points here and there along the way but that's in the past.'

Saturday, Mar 24, 2012

Roberto Mancini did not trust himself to speak to media after being angered by events during his side's 1-1 draw at Stoke. Although regaining top spot on goal difference, City dropped two potentially crucial points as they were forced to reply to a sensational Crouch long range volley at the Britannia Stadium when the ball didn't leave the ground after being cleared by the keeper, a contender for goal of the season.

Yaya struck a superb, albeit deflected, long range equaliser but Mancini was angered by Stoke's rugged approach and an incident in the first half when Whitehead elbowed Silva, drawing blood, and the little forward had to have his head bandaged, but referee Howard Webb did not book the player.

David Platt, addressing Mancini's failure to attend the press conference, said: "It's not a case of being too angry - he's just wary that he might say something that gets him in hot water. It's about the way the game unfolded. It is very difficult when you come here and sometimes you look for a bit of protection. It's a bit hot afterwards but once he's calmed down he'll be fine. You know what he is like and if he comes in and something goes out where it is lost in translation..."

Mancini did not shake Tony Pulis' hand after the game, such was his indignation. "Everybody gets invited in [for a drink after the game]," Pulis said of Mancini. "I can't force him. He's obviously very, very disappointed. The money they've spent, the players that they've got at their disposal, I think they are expecting to win [the title.] I can see why he's a little bit down... because now it's pressure time. If people want to shake my hand, fine; if they don't, that's up to them." Pulis did not give a conclusive answer when asked if Mancini had refused to shake his hand after the game. "He has got to do what he has got to do. It was a very competitive game, a good game. We were disappointed in the first half we never got a penalty - we thought Barry's challenge on Whelan was a definite penalty."

Platt did not see the Whitehead incident but said Stoke had been tough opponents, "You know it is going to be difficult when you come here, you know what to expect. It is a great goal, no doubt about it. It is route one from the goalkeeper, what you expect - but you know as soon as it has left his foot, if it is on target, it is going in the back of the goal."

Platt rubbished claims the Manchester clubs were becoming embroiled in mind games, "It doesn't matter what the ammunition is and what words are. It is all about amassing points. It is not about winning leagues because of mind games. It is about players going onto a pitch to play football and gain points. If we have more points than them at the end of the season everyone will perceive that Robbie has won the war of words. If it is the other way round, people will perceive Sir Alex has won it, but it is inconsequential really. It is about what both teams do on the pitch." He insisted City were not feeling the Fergie pressure, and actually enjoying it, "Well yeah – why not? I mean, you have to enjoy it. Of course you can enjoy it. I think any team would like a 10-point cushion, wouldn't they? But that's what you're in the game for. You get highs, you get lows. Deep down, it's enjoyable."

This conversation was tense at times, though. "No, no, no, no. That's you saying that. I haven't said that. I've tried to answer the questions in a truthful manner and if that's the way you choose to write it..." he said when it was put to him that the media were observing a pressure situation playing out.

Mancini made a pre-match claim that he could deal with Sir Alex's barbs because he was in possession of "a big helmet". Platt brushed away the barb made by Ferguson on Friday, that the redeployment of Tévez, not Scholes, was an act of desperation. "When you look at the quotes, Sir Alex hasn't necessarily said that. It seems it was a bit tongue in cheek and there was a bit of fun there. Robbie just laughed. It's not a problem to him. It's not about him and it's not about Sir Alex. It's about the two teams alone and apart."

Limited to just two league victories – at Wigan and Aston Villa – on the road since November, was a major concern. Keegan used the German word ideen to define their problem: ideas. Substitute Johnson was involved in a loud verbal exchange with his manager by the end. That public spat raised the question of whether Mancini's intensity will actually aid the pursuit of the title. "He's fine. He's beyond fine – seriously!" Platt said of his boss, also insisting that what he said about Mancini 12 months ago – "he sees the game peripherally, to him what a player has just unsuccessfully tried is alien" – no longer applied.

"We try not to speak too much about them," Barry said. "The aim is to keep it to no more than three points before we play them at the Etihad. If we manage to do that, then we fancy ourselves in that game."

Sunday, Mar 25, 2012

Sir Alex said you have to "admire" City, "Experience is important, no matter who you are. If you've been there before, it helps. It's not absolutely conclusive that it will apply this season because you've got to admire City. They've done exceptionally well and been top of the league for a long time. They've got us to go to the Etihad and they've not lost a game there. Individuals and teams can win games, but I think what is important now is how the temperament is - how they hold their nerve. What we've got to get used to and it's the same for every United and City fan is there's going to be big games involving the two teams for the next decade. It will be semi-finals and finals, whatever, because the two teams will be at the forefront."

Antonio Valencia feared Tévez could wreck United's title dreams in the Manchester derby, scoring to decide the match and title, 'If Carlos plays against us, I'm sure he'll be motivated. He's an excellent player, able to change a match in an instant. What he did against Chelsea was no surprise. But for Tévez to score the winner? I hope it doesn't happen. And for us to fail and lose the title will bring pain for months. But I'm confident in my team. There's a lot of pride in Manchester that our two clubs are the best in England. But now we are focused on Fulham because our challenge is to win all our matches and to arrive with an advantage over City on derby day. I'm not saying whether that game will decide the title but it's clear the winners will deliver a morale blow to the other club. So I expect a big battle and for us to avenge our 6-1 defeat at Old Trafford.'

Monday, Mar 26, 2012

Wayne Rooney's 29th goal of the season helped United move back to the top, opening up a three-point gap with eight games to go. Late on Fulham should have been awarded a penalty when Carrick tripped Murphy in the box. "I think everyone in the stadium expected a penalty to be honest," said Jol. "You have to be brave to give a penalty away at Manchester United. I thought it was a difficult decision. If he had given the penalty he would have had to send Michael Carrick off."

Sir Alex challenged his side to use their game in hand to pull away from City as well as reduce their goal-difference deficit, admitting it could be an "issue" at the end of the season. They won, but no where near enough goals to dent the difference.

Although both clubs insisted they would not be distracted by the other's results, Ferdinand admitted that seeing referee Michael Oliver turn down a strong penalty appeal from Fulham for Carrick's challenge on Murphy in the dying seconds could prey on City's minds.

Tuesday, Mar 27, 2012

Mario Balotelli gatecrashed the Inter press conference with his unexpected appearance as new manager Andrea Stramaccioni was being unveiled. He parked a red Ferrari outside the press briefing, burst in and for reasons still unknown simply shook hands with those behind the top table, wished the new manager luck, and left without so much as an explanation. Inter CEO Ernesto Paolillo said Mario's visit was unexpected but not unusual. 'He came to say hello to everybody at the training centre then left. We did not know he was coming but it's not the first time. It's typical of Mario. I see him sometimes when he comes to Milan. I did not see the Ferrari as I was inside the press conference unveiling our new coach Andrea. We kissed hello and he left. We had no time to speak. I've known him at Inter since he was a young boy.'

Back in Manchester, Mario had a message for his admirers; pictured in Cheshire wearing a t-shirt with the words: 'Not only am I perfect, I'm Italian too!' Mario and his team-mates were given a couple of days off by Mancini, who paid a visit to a village where Catholics say the Virgin Mary miraculously appeared to six schoolchildren. Mancini said he was there "as a pilgrim" after his father Aldo, 76, recovered from a heart attack, "I have been very religious since I was a young boy. But I would not say that God or the Virgin Mary help me in my career. They have more important stuff to do. But I believe Manchester City will win the league." Former altar boy Mancini also went to mass and visited a monastery on his two-day trip to Medjugorje in Bosnia-Herzegovina with wife Federica and daughter Camilla. The highlight was walking to the top of Apparition Hill where the six children — now know as "seers" — had their vision of Mary in 1981. Mancini met two of the seers but refused to say what they had talked about. His mother Marina — who missed the pilgrimage — said: "You don't go to a shrine to ask for help with football but for more serious matters such as health. You can't ask the Virgin Mary to help you win a football championship. That would not be right."

Mancini went to an Irish bar to see the Red Devils beat Fulham before flying home on a private jet.

Wednesday, Mar 28, 2012

Mario had Mancini's permission to fly to Milan and spared himself a reprimand for returning late by reporting for training in time for breakfast in the Carrington canteen. But Mancini's exasperation with Mario's efforts on the training pitch led to the exchange of words before coach Attilio Lombardo urged Mario to train elsewhere. City officials dismissed the spat as another example of Mancini's demand for high standards.

Patrick Vieira launched a second volley at United, claiming they get preferential treatment from referees after the failure to give Fulham a last-minute penalty at Old Trafford that could have denied United two crucial points, 'When United play at home they get some advantage that other teams don't get. When you go to United, Madrid, Barcelona, or Milan, it's always difficult for the referee to go against these kind of teams. This is the way it is. It's something the teams who are used to winning get all the time, so we need to win games so we have this advantage in the future.'

Vieira's comments drew an immediate response from Rio Ferdinand on Twitter. 'Why is Viera so concerned with Man Utd....2 comments in a week or so....'Monday maaaaaan let it go,' said the United defender.

Vieira reacted to the interpretation given to comments made to the BBC in an interview to publicise Football Against Hunger, a campaign to tackle starvation in Africa. Asked to comment on the 'penalty' incident, Vieira said he had not seen the game. However, he felt this had not been made clear in reporting of his interview, which concentrated on his assertion that United receive favourable decisions from officials. City released a statement announcing that the BBC's Dan Roan, who conducted the interview, had been banned from the club's facilities. "Patrick Vieira has expressed his disappointment and anger at what he feels is a serious and cynical misrepresentation of an interview he gave to the BBC," said the statement. "Manchester City's football development executive gave the interview at the annual SoccerEx exhibition at the GMEX Convention Centre on Wednesday afternoon. He was representing Football Against Hunger, a campaign to tackle starvation in Africa. An interview given to the BBC's Dan Roan contained what Patrick feels was a very leading line of questions regarding Manchester United supposedly receiving favourable treatment by referees. Patrick feels that his views have been deliberately taken out of context."

Vieira said: "I am very angry with Dan Roan. I feel he has misrepresented me. I made it clear in the interview twice that I wanted to avoid criticising United and even stated that I didn't watch the United game against Fulham and had not seen the incident to which the reporter referred. That part of the interview was ignored and my comments were taken completely out of context. I called the reporter twice to ask for a retraction and an apology which has not come. I feel Dan Roan and the BBC have shown a complete lack of respect for me, the 'Football Against Hunger' charity and Manchester City Football Club."

The statement continued: 'Manchester City support Patrick in his strong feelings on this matter and have confirmed to the BBC that the reporter will now be banned from all Manchester City media activity." Chief

Communications Officer, Vicky Kloss, said: "Despite the Charity arranging the interview with Dan Roan for the purposes of promoting the Football Against Hunger campaign, the reporter pursued a leading and aggressive line of questioning, through which Patrick was very careful to tread a diplomatic path. A misrepresentative article by Dan Roan appeared on the BBC's website a short time later which omitted significant comments of clarification and took the interview completely out of context. Manchester City promotes a positive and welcoming approach to media outlets, however it is felt, in the absence of any correction or apology that there is no option but to issue an immediate ban to Dan Roan from future media activity."

Carlos Tévez scored on a reserve team outing at Morecambe as Yaya revealed the striker promised to do everything in his power to help City get their noses back in front. "Everyone can make mistakes but Carlos is a really good man. When you meet him, he is always good fun and a nice guy, even if people may have a different image of him. He knew when he came back to the club he had made a very big mistake, but now everything is over and he is focused on winning the Premier League. He wants to do as much as possible to say sorry to the fans. He will be an important player for us as he wants to prove he is a top player. I am sure he will be fantastic for the rest of the season."

Thursday, Mar 29, 2012

Mario was back on the training ground the day after his spat with his boss, pictured emulating the famous 'Scorpion kick' made famous by Colombian goalkeeper Rene Higuita, and more crucially, snapped alongside a composed Mancini.

Kompany was on course to make his return after missing the last four games with a hamstring injury. "Just had my second training session with the team," he Tweeted. "If all goes to plan I will be available for the Sunderland game.'

Yaya insisted City's big-name players are at Eastlands to win trophies and not pocket huge wages. "Players like Sergio Agüero, David Siva and Mario Balotelli have come here with me to City for one thing. Not for money – but to win games and win trophies." Looking at the title race, he said: "We know Manchester United are a fantastically strong team with fantastic experience – more than any other team – so it will be very, very tough."

Harry Redknapp admitted that City's money could pose a problem in his side's quest to keep Modric. Mancini was quoted as saying: 'It is by no means easy to get him because he plays for a big club. Luka Modric is an outstanding footballer, definitely one of the best in the Premier League.'

Tottenham fought off competition from City, United and Chelsea to keep the Croat last year – but Modric looks set to be the subject of interest again this summer. City have the financial clout to more than quadruple Modric's £50,000-a-week. Redknapp admitted: 'Only Luka knows what he wants to do with his life. But if someone is going to offer £200,000-a-week it could probably turn his head.'

Fri, Mar 30, 2012

"No, I don't trust Mario. No-one trusts Mario," Mancini said. The manager did not know what to expect from the unpredictable Mario. "He is a top player. He can do everything. He can score two goals against Arsenal next week. But he can also take a red card. Until now he did well and in the last eight games he could be important for us. But trust him? Never." Mancini clarified his striker's presence at the Inter press conference, "At the press conference he was there like a journalist. It is better you ask him why but he had two days off. I can't put him in his house for two days. Probably the moment will arrive when he will know what he should do when he has two days off. I hope he will grow out of it because he needs to know this is his job. He needs to work and rest. But he is young."

Mancini disputed Sir Alex's view that bringing back Tévez was 'desperate'. "Patrick is a top man -- he knows what he says," said Mancini. "I think every person can say what they think. But I can't talk about these wars. It is not important what Alex said. I have big respect for him. I'm sure what I say is not important to him. I think the only thing that is important for him and for me is to win the championship. Carlos Tévez is a Manchester City player. He wanted to leave the club in January, but this was not possible. Now he is again a big player for us. Desperation for what? We were without Tévez for seven months and dominated this championship. I don't think so. He is a City player and maybe he can help us in the last six or seven games. I don't think he can start but I think he can have more time. It's normal, he is improving every week."

Mancini insisted experience can be key, but United are not the only ones who possess that advantage, "In Italy, I won one title with Inter in the last game -- we won in Parma, Rome did not win in Catania. The only difference between United and us is that United have won the championship 19 times, they are used to this every year. For us, it is different because it's the first time and probably we have more pressure than them, but it's not big pressure."

Ferguson's players were beginning a golfing mini-break, split between rounds at Gleneagles and St Andrews, while Mancini could hardly relax when informed about a weird incident involving his top scorer.

Mancini was fuming over an injury to Agüero, whose skin suffered a severe reaction to a chemical spray which was applied to a foot injury. It left his foot badly blistered and burnt. Mancini described the "stupid injury -- not his fault". City sources were unwilling to discuss the exact nature of the ailment and Mancini added: "I don't know what's happened with Sergio. It's better that we don't talk about this. Why? Because I prefer this -- I prefer I don't say nothing." When pressed, he confirmed that the problem had occurred at Carrington, "I'll tell you when the season is finished."

A red rag to a red top, so one decided to tell us all now, that Agüero damaged his foot on his child's mini-motocross bike while playing with his three-year-old son Benjamin at their Cheshire home. He then treated the injury repeatedly with an anaesthetic freeze spray, causing burns and blisters that left him unable to play or train. Mancini was furious at the player for failing to consult the club's medical staff and at the consequences at such a crucial stage of the season. Agüero missed last Saturday night's 1-1 draw at Stoke after suffering the injury the day before. This was a version of events soon to be hotly contested.

There was another big problem. By the manager's own admission, Silva was below his best. "David always plays here and now maybe he is here," Mancini said, lowering his hand.

At least some good news; Martin O'Neill suggested Mancini won't be derailed by Sir Alex's mind games, "It's nothing to do with Mancini and Ferguson, but more to do with City having not won the league since 1968. United have been there, seen it and done it with Sir Alex at the helm – and that's a big thing. Mancini will be more concerned about player for player than mind games. They're in a real fight. United won't give it up. You'd have thought this year could be City's season, with the team they have. The mind games make me laugh, they really do. You can read into the mind games whatever you want. It goes way back to Kevin Keegan. O'Neill thought the depth of City's squad was telling, 'So Mario Balotelli decides he's going to have another fire in his house on a Friday night and he doesn't play on Saturday. So what? They've got 15 other players, they've got the squad."

Jose Mourinho spoke out in his Friday press conference to deny claims in the Spanish media that he has agreed to join City on June 30. The claims emerged in journal Mundo Deportivo on Friday morning, with the news quickly spreading Europe-wide. Mourinho, who is contracted at Real Madrid until 2014 on his current deal, addressed the reports and gave a curt response. "I can deny any contact. I have no need to talk about the issue, I have two more years on my contract."

Saturday, Mar 31, 2012

Mancini thought about substituting Mario after just five minutes of the frustrating draw with Sunderland. The enigmatic Mario scored twice but Mancini was frustrated by his performance as City surrendered two vital points. United could move five points clear on Monday and the situation might have been worse had they not hit back from 3-1 down to draw 3-3 with two late goals.

It was another eventful week for Mario. When asked if he thought about taking Mario off, Mancini said: "I thought this after five minutes but in the end he scored two goals. He didn't play well. In a game like this the strikers should be the difference – but not in the last two minutes, in the minutes before. A player like Mario or Dzeko should score two or three goals in a game like this. In this moment we need Carlos, a striker who can do different. I want this."

Mario equalised from the penalty spot in the first half but later showed frustration when he argued with Kolarov over who should line up a free-kick with Tévez. Mario was booed by all four sections of the Etihad Stadium as he tussled with Kolarov. Mario grabbed Kolarov and tried to wrestle the ball from him. But he was shoved back by the Serbian and then dragged away by Kompany and de Jong. At the final whistle, Mario petulantly stormed off the pitch without shaking hands or looking at anyone.

Mancini said of the free kick fiasco, "On the ball it should be Mario and Ali – after they decide who shoots. But it can happen in a moment like today, things like this. It is the last time."

Tévez was still not fit enough to start and was again on the bench while Agüero was missing. Mancini again refused to elaborate on the nature of Agüero's problem, although he said some theories in Saturday's newspapers are "not true"'. He said: "We missed Agüero and for this reason I am disappointed. I hope he can recover for the next game." When asked if he had confidence in the medical staff, concerning Agüero, Mancini said: 'I only trust my personal doctor.'

Mancini insisted the title race was far from over. "I think on Monday United will probably do a draw and we are always three points behind. It is hard but we have another seven games. We have done some mistakes in the last games but also United can arrive in a difficult moment. It is important we are there. Before the derby it is important we recover two points."

Mancini described the Sunderland match as a "crazy game, very emotional". "I'm not pleased with the point. In the end, maybe yes because it was 3-1 to Sunderland. We did some mistakes, we didn't play very well. We took one point in the end but we didn't play very well as team in the first half. It was really important to play very well, play a good game. We defended very badly in two or three situations. I think it is the correct result, a draw, but we didn't do a good performance. I am happy only for the last 10 minutes, for the other 80 minutes I am unhappy because we didn't play very well. I don't know why. In the first half we were flat and in a game like this, that is very important for us, we can't be flat in the first half."

Sunderland had already beaten City once this season and O'Neill felt they deserved to do so again. "They have won 15 consecutive games here – and we are the first team to take some points off them – and they are also second in the league, so they are a very good team. They are never out of the match because they have so many match-winners. I think we got a little bit tired, maybe after the exertions and the disappointment of Tuesday night (losing to Everton in an FA Cup replay). We seemed to put that aside and performed excellently (at first) but it was a combination of both Manchester City fighting back and us getting tired."

Martin O'Neill was unimpressed with the award of a penalty against Gardner for a foul on Dzeko, "I thought initially the referee was going to book their player for diving – but I should have known better. Referees have a really difficult job but I spoke to the referee in the tunnel at the end, and I assume he must have seen it since, and he said it was definitely a penalty. That confused me a bit. I didn't think it was and the replays will show that."

Sunderland's players complained Dzeko dived to win the spot-kick but he was insistent he had been fouled by Gardner. 'It was a penalty – I still have pain in my leg,' said Dzeko, who became involved in an argument with Sunderland defender Phil Bardsley over the matter after a later stoppage in play. On that, Dzeko said: 'One guy pushed me away and said, "Why are you cheating?" So I asked him what he was talking about and said it was a penalty. That's why I was angry. He said I was cheating. He can say what he wants, but should never touch me. Mario told me to stay calm, but I was calm – they can't push me and touch me that way.'

When asked if City were still in contention, Mancini commented, "I think so because eight games is enough to do two draws. Until we have a point to win this league we will try 100%." The result left City second on 71 points with seven games left, while United lead on 73 points with eight to play. Mancini, who looked disgusted, angry and frustrated on the touchline throughout the game, admitted: 'It will be hard to win the title now.'

But the Red Devils had won only two of their last eight league visits to Ewood Park and Mancini predicted they will falter again. "They can do a draw on Monday, why not? Probably." Looking ahead to the trip to Arsenal, Mancini added: "I'm sure that we will do better than today."

It emerged that Mario and Yaya almost came to blows in a dressing-room clash, the pair had to be pulled apart at half-time as they trailed 2-1 by Yaya's brother Kolo as they squared up in front of stunned team-mates. Mario took exception to the midfielder's criticism about his behaviour during the match.

Alan Hansen reckoned Mario was much more hassle than he's worth and that City should get rid of him. In his column for the Telegraph, said: 'If Manchester City really are prepared to sell Mario Balotelli this summer, then it would absolutely be the right thing to do. He has become a damaging distraction at the Etihad Stadium and Roberto Mancini must shoulder the blame for allowing the situation to develop to the point where the player is beginning to affect the unity of the dressing room. When you are going for a title, Balotelli and everything that he brings with him goes against everything that you want down the final straight. If he performed like Lionel Messi, Cristiano Ronaldo or even Wayne Rooney, then the players would hold up their hands and let him get away with it. But Balotelli is not a world-beater, he is certainly not playing well at the moment and he is a huge distraction.'

APRIL

Mancini for the sack! Media speculation suggested that the manager's position was no longer as secure as it appeared to be until recently.

Sunday, April 1, 2012

Roberto Mancini admitted the title race will be over if United win their next two games. United can open up an eight-point lead with wins over Blackburn and QPR, before City next play.

Mancini, whose City side dropped points at home for the first time in 15 months against Sunderland, said such a margin would be too big to close. "If we go eight points behind then it is finished. It's clear we are disappointed. We have made some mistakes, me and the team. We have also been unlucky, like losing three or four key players at an important moment. But when you are a strong team you should be able to pass these difficult moments. Yet football can change in two or three games. I had an experience in Italy with Inter Milan when we were five points behind with five games to go yet we still went on to win the title."

Sir Alex Ferguson dropped Rooney for the last meeting of the clubs, on New Year's Eve, after the striker turned up for training showing the effects of a late night out. United lost that match at Old Trafford 3-2, but since then Rooney has atoned with a scoring spree that has taken his tally for the season to 28. United clinched last year's title with a nerve-jangling 1-1 draw at Ewood Park and Ferguson was wary before the potential decider at City four weeks tomorrow, "There could be a shock around the corner. We have done particularly well over the last few weeks to get into the position we are in and it's a matter of keeping our nerve and keeping on playing our game. This is definitely a big game at Blackburn. We never find it easy there and they've done well when they've scored first. So it's not going to be easy and the players are aware of that."

Wayne Rooney admits that winning the League this season would be extra special for beating City to the title. "Would it mean something extra because City are challenging? Yes, of course. It's the first time since I've been here and the first time for many years that United and City have been going head-to-head for the title. To win it would be great for the players, the fans and the club as a whole, and it would definitely be one of the best titles we've ever won, if we can do it."

Meanwhile, Paul McGrath believes City should have cruised to the title, but the ex-United legend claims they hit the rocks after Mancini's men got 'cocky' when they were five points clear. "With the team City have they should be walking the title now, especially given they were five points ahead at one stage. There's a cockiness that comes in, but as Sir Alex Ferguson knows, you've got to fight right until the finish line is crossed. There is an enormous pressure on them though, and in average games that they'd probably win nine times out of 10, they're suddenly at this time of the season so wound up knowing they can't lose a game that they're afraid to play. This means some players don't want the ball and they end up with draws instead of wins." McGrath thinks that if Ferguson won the title with the current crop, it would be an incredible achievement. "They have had some great results, that great Arsenal win for example, but I don't think United are half the team they were, honestly. Player wise, they've had teams in the past with magnificent players all over the park, now they've got kids they're training up and obviously a few will go on to be great, but they've thrown a few of them in a bit early. That's what makes Alex Ferguson so good coming into a title race. He could write the book on it."

Morten Gamst Pedersen is a regular at Manchester Italian eaterie San Carlos – a haunt of Roberto Mancini and Mario Balotelli. He said: "I do like to go out and I am friends with some of the City players. Maybe if we win I'll ask them to pay for my dinner!" Pedersen played in Blackburn's 3-2 win at Old Trafford on New Year's Eve and scored both goals in a 2-1 win at Old Trafford back in 2005, the season Rovers also beat United 4-3 at home, "You always have good memories when you beat teams like that. But we face a team who are doing well. They caught up loads of points on City so the machine is starting to roll."

Pedersen hoped a win would boost Rovers relegation fight, "Nobody wants to go down, you can see that with the kit man, people doing the pitches, me and the players. We are all Blackburn Rovers."

Monday, April 2, 2012

The day began with Mancini's future being widely discussed in the media, and ended with two late United goals to steal the three points at Blackburn. A dark day for city.

Although Mancini retained the support of the club's Abu Dhabi hierarchy, with chairman Khaldoon al-Mubarak designated to make the final decision on his future, media speculation suggested that the managers' position was no longer as secure as it appeared to be until recently. Al-Mubarak and the club's power-brokers accepted Mancini's abrasive style of management does not endear him to some members of his squad and, with City enjoying five months at the top, it was regarded as a contributory factor to the team's improvement this season. Despite concerns over disharmony within the squad, no decision had been made to part company with Mancini at the end of the season with reports in Spain last week that a deal had been agreed with Mourinho to replace Mancini were forcefully, if predictably, denied by the Real manager.

Mancini's £3.5m-a-year contract expires at the end of the 2012-13 season and no negotiations were under way to extend that deal, the remaining games of this campaign were sure to be decisive in terms of what happens next, ending the season empty-handed, 12 months after winning the FA Cup, would be regarded as a failure following an outlay of almost £80m on new players last summer. If results continued to disappoint and United pulled clear and win the league by a comfortable margin, the reasons for City's collapse might mean Mancini paying the price.

The day culminated in a 2-0 United win at Blackburn with late goals from Antonio Valencia and substitute Ashley Young as the United fans massed behind the goal sang "City are cracking up" in reference to the apparent in-fighting within the City camp.

Tuesday, April 3, 2012

UEFA fined Porto £16,700 after their supporters racially abused Mario. The European governing body confirmed the punishment following a meeting of their control and disciplinary body which took place last week. Nigel De Jong warned Mario Balotelli to stop behaving like a 'fool' with the club's title charge at risk, speaking to Dutch publication NUsport, commenting "Sometimes Mario is a fool and at other times he is a genius, there are two sides to him. Lots of people expect him to pull off crazy stunts and as a result he feels he must do something. People like that need to have upheaval in their lives in order to perform. He is happy in his personal relationship. That is important and it makes him more focused. But he knows that he has to become more serious-minded."

De Jong quashed the notion that Mancini lets the former Inter Milan star off the hook, "Luckily, we have a manager who has his say, otherwise Mario would have gone off the rails a long time ago. Problems also seem to come from the people who hang around with him."

When asked if he was prepared to give up on Mario, Mancini said: "No". He explained, "I am frustrated because sometimes I think it is not possible that a player with his class and his technique can play a game like this. I think he is young and I hope for him he can improve very quickly for his future. A player like Mario in the Premier League should score one or two goals every game." The striker was also involved in a hot-headed exchange with Kolorov. "This was a bad moment," Mancini said. "I think a professional player can't do what they did in that moment, when we were losing 3-1."

Despite relinquishing their advantage at the top, Mancini was determined to fight until the last game, "We should be strong, I believe always. The message is always the same - we will do everything to win this title." When asked what he said to the players after Saturday's game, Mancini added: "Nothing because they were so tired. I said only, 'believe in yourselves' because we have seven games - 21 points. I think with 92 points we will win the title."

The manager jokingly told Mario he might have punched him in the head every day if he was his team-mate. Mancini understood why his squad sometimes got frustrated with Mario, "I told him, if you played with me 10 years ago I would give you every day maybe one punch in your head. There are different ways to help a guy like Mario. I don't speak with him every day, otherwise I would need a psychologist, but I speak with him because I don't want him to lose his quality. If Mario is not one of the best players in the world it will be his fault, because he has everything. Mario can be one of the top players in Europe. I don't want him to lose his talent."

Yaya Toure was upset by "untrue" claims of a tunnel bust up with Mario, "They said I fought with Mario at Swansea and against Sunderland. That shocked me. My lawyers called me about this and it was the first I knew about it. It's just not true. It didn't happen. I am a footballer, not a boxer. People don't know my relationship with Mario. He's not my friend - he's my brother and I love him. To say we had a fight is very sad. It upset me and I feel sorry for Mario. He suffers most from these things. At half-time against Sunderland it was very difficult. We are trying to win the league and are losing 2-1. It's not good. But everybody was quiet. We were just looking at each other, trying to find a way to turn the result. But I didn't even talk to Mario. The next day he sent me a text message saying, 'Apparently we had a fight'. I just want to stop people writing and thinking that."

Mancini commented, "Yaya Toure - that is totally false. What happened with Kolarov on the pitch, that is a situation that can happen in difficult moments. It is not good but I can understand this situation can happen. After the game it was finished. I am not worried - it is important that after the game everything was okay." He also believes Mario's behaviour on and off the pitch is blown out of proportion, "There are some people who think bad things against other people, like Mario. Every time Mario does something, is like a war. There are other people on and off the pitch that do worse than

Mario and no-one says anything because maybe they play for an important team or are not like Mario."

The tabloids claimed that the Italian striker cheated on his model girlfriend by having sex with Rooney's threesome hooker Jennifer Thompson. Well, if you are going to hit the front pages of the tabloids, this is the way to do it, bedding the tart he once taunted over her 2010 romp with Rooney. According to the tabloids, Mario met former escort girl five times and had sex with her twice behind the back of gorgeous model Raffaella Fico. Jennifer became notorious in 2010 when it was revealed Rooney paid her and hooker pal Helen Wood £1,200 for a threesome in a hotel. Two days after bedding Jennifer, Mario lifted his City shirt when he scored against Blackburn to reveal a message reading "Raffaella Ti Amo" — meaning "Raffaella, I love you". Five days after that Mario was seen in a strip club. And the following day he met party girl Jennifer again, though they did not have sex on that occasion. Mario's agent Mino Raiola admitted the player had a "brief involvement" with Jennifer. He called Mario "young and impulsive", a target for girls who "chase" footballers. Raiola added: "Mario prefers to admit what has happened, has refused any means to try to keep the matter silent and will deal with any consequences his actions bring in the way of public attention."

Clearly Mancini would prefer it if his former Inter Milan protégé could find a way to keep his private life out of the news. "I would like Mario to play, score and finish the other situation. It is not maybe your [media's] fault - it is his fault because if he wants he can play and stay at home. Like this no people can ask about the other situation."

Mario commented, "I know I must still learn to keep my private life separate from my profession. It's not easy, but I have taken this step to free me from the weight of this story. Recently, I admit, I have been troubled - because of this story, but not only. My natural parents in some interviews have been disrespectful to my family."

Mario told his girlfriend and his adopted parents about the imminent story when they came to visit him in Manchester at the weekend. Fico has since spoken about marriage and the couple posed for their first photo shoot together for an Italian magazine that hit newsstands the previous Saturday. She said in an accompanying interview, "Mario is the man that I love. We are busy and very young. But if he asked me to get married, I would accept. I, like him, dream of a family."

Wednesday, April 4, 2012

Spanish newspaper *AS* reported Real were considering a swap deal that would involve Gonzalo Higuain plus £8.5m for Agüero. AS claimed Agüero discussed a potential move back to the Spanish capital with team-mates, and that there was a growing feeling a move will materialise this summer. Mourinho, though, dismissed the story, claiming that the country's media are trying to destabilise his team as they chased a domestic and European double, "Last week I had signed for City, Casillas was going to Schalke, Higuain to Malaga..." On the Higuain-Agüero story, he added: "The front cover of (newspaper) AS is false. If you want me to comment on false front covers then forget it." The report in AS added that a strong relationship between Real and City's owners - Perez and Sheikh Mansour - enhances the chances of a deal going through, while Mancini falters on his own prime target, Arsenal's Robin van Persie with resistance from Arsenal and the player's family.

Thursday, April 5, 2012

Mario Balotelli, who drives a Bentley, was in collision with another vehicle in Medlock Street, near Deansgate, in Manchester city centre. He was unhurt in the incident. A passenger from one of the cars was taken to hospital as a precaution. In a statement, Greater Manchester Police said: "Shortly after 3.15pm, police were called to Medlock Street, Manchester city centre to reports of a collision between two cars. The passenger of one of the cars was taken to hospital for precautionary measures. Inquiries are ongoing."

A City youth-team defender apologised for celebrating United's win over Blackburn. Sam Jones posted gleeful messages on Twitter. "Yeahhhhhhhhhhhh united united united", before following it up with: "yeahhhhhhhhhhhhhhhh what a goal!!!!!" He also said: "Game over! Ashley Young you king!" Blues fans were not impressed; City officials gave him a dressing down. Jones, from South Wales, now tweeted: "I am sorry for causing offence. I shouldn't have said those things. The club has reminded me of my responsibilities." City signed schoolboy Jones from Welsh side Cardiff last month.

Vincent Kompany insisted Roberto Mancini was not to blame for the team's loss of form, "He's very clear in what he brings across to the players, always positive. Ultimately he gives tactical advice, because we need to know where to stand. We didn't do too well [against Sunderland] but we need to play in a way we can dismantle the other team and usually it works well. When you play with great players like this, you feel there will always be a moment when they can make something happen. But the reality is that you have to work hard for it and for long parts we didn't do enough. The disappointment is there, but I'll be the first one back at the training ground to get their heads back up because we have to believe."

Meanwhile, Mancini was glad to have Sergio Agüero back. "In just three or four days he is fit," Mancini said. "He started to train for the first time and today and after that he will be fit."

Fri, April 6, 2012

Roberto Mancini insisted the title race was far from over and was convinced United can drop points. Mancini would congratulate United if they win their final seven games and clinch the title, but he feels twists and turns lie ahead. "If they win all their games, we will congratulate them as they deserve to win the title, but seven games to the end, I believe anything can happen. We lose four points in two games, so it is possible also for them. Maybe in this moment there are some that do not believe because it is difficult, but in football we can believe always. It is important we go to win our game and after that we see what happens. We then play a derby, which can be three points and there are six other games and in that they can lose points."

"I think City are fearing our reaction already," Young told the Match of the Day magazine. "A lot of people wrote us off earlier in the season with City being seven points clear. But we've just been going about our job quietly and now we've managed to claw it back. The pressure has always been on City - there aren't any nerves coming from our side. We don't play with fear and we haven't got any nervousness going into games. We've got the momentum going into the final stretch of the season."

Saturday, April 7, 2012

Mancini was perturbed about negative publicity. At United, it is rare for a dressing-room spat to filter out. "It's true," Mancini, "We need to improve in this way because the problems should stay always inside." City's Carrington training ground is traversed by a public footpath, meaning any disagreement is immediately public, whereas United's training ground is justifiably nicknamed Fort Colditz.

"United are a strong team in their mentality," said Mancini. "Probably if we play with our best 11 players against their best 11 players they are not better. But they are better in mentality. This is the difference. Now we finish our job to build a strong team. The difference (between City and United) is in the 20 players, not in the 11 players and because they are used to playing without problems, they don't have the pressure that we have, because they have won everything. I think when you play against a team like United, this is the difference. Not the players."

To make up ground quickly, the club imported high-quality players in

Mario and Tévez. Mourinho kicked Mario out of Inter, Sir Alex did the same at United to Tévez. "We expect unity here," said Ferguson, "It doesn't happen everywhere but you need unity if you are to win the League. We tend to take it for granted here. We have experience of that in players like Rio Ferdinand, Michael Carrick, Paul Scholes and Ryan Giggs, men who can ensure that."

When Inter blew an 11-point lead in February 2008 to go into the final game of the campaign just a point clear of Roma, Mancini's doubts reputedly transmitted themselves to the players and, as forward Zlatan Ibrahimovic recalled, "I heard Mancini and the other coaches talking. They were worried. The nervousness had spread through the squad and confidence had disappeared. From having been a winning machine, we now didn't even feel confident against the bottom teams. The atmosphere in the team was awful. It was like a switch had been flicked. The harmony and optimism had gone." An injury suffered by Ibrahimovic, which led to the tempestuous Swede returning to Scandinavia for treatment, caused a fallout between player and manager. Mancini urged him to help the team through their slump. A more damaging rift with Luis Figo, during which the pair barely spoke for six months, has similarities to the five-month stand-off with Tévez. During the Mancini-Figo rift, sparked by the manager's reluctance to select the forward, questions were raised over his ability to handle star players.

Senior figures at City spoke of Mancini constantly "challenging" his superiors - a trait regarded as a positive element rather than a negative one - in terms of improving the squad, the club and their mentality. But his frustration with what he regards as City's lack of a winning mentality, prompted Mancini to voice fears of the "arm becoming short".

Patrick Vieira, a member of Mancini's title-winning team at Inter, insisted Mancini remained in control of players and his emotions. "He has been through all of this with Inter. At Inter, the team was winning and we were strong because Roberto believed in himself. Roberto gives the club that belief. It comes from the manager."

Mancini lost his previous job at Inter Milan only days after they won their third consecutive Serie A title. He hoped club chairman Khaldoon al-Mubarak would acknowledge the huge progress the club had made since he replaced Hughes. "I hope so because of what's happened over the last two years, but I know football very well and I left Inter after seven trophies in four years. In football anything can happen. The same regarding my future. I don't have a problem with that."

Nevertheless, Mancini admitted that should United beat QPR on Sunday and his side lose to Arsenal leaving them eight points behind the title race would be over, "If we lose against Arsenal and they beat QPR, yes, but I can say I am proud of what the players have done in this championship. We were on the top for a long time and we have been fighting with United until now. I think we have improved as a team, in the Premier League title. I think we have improved a lot as a team but it is not finished now. I don't believe this championship is finished.'

Whatever happened he was proud of the way the team had progressed. "I started this job 2 ½ years ago and since that moment we have improved a lot as a team, players and a club. I've been in this world a long time and I know you can lose the title. But it's important to me that the squad have improved a lot. I don't decide this, I do the best for my job and after I don't decide the situation."

Whether Mancini survives or not City were losing their highly-rated technical director Mike Rigg, who agreed to join Hughes at QPR after successfully overhauling the scouting system since his arrival in June 2008.

Sunday, April 8, 2012

City's pursuit of the crown appeared to be over after a late goal from Mikel Arteta condemned them to defeat at the Emirates Stadium. Earlier in the day, United beat ten-man QPR 2-0. City were eight points with six games remaining following a 1-0 defeat at Arsenal. Arsenal returned to third place, five points clear of fifth-placed Chelsea. Surely, it was all over. Just as Mancini said it would be if the two results panned out for a 'no chance' scenario.

Mancini had said before the game that if United were to beat QPR and his side lost at Arsenal the title race would be over, but he insisted City would keep on fighting. When asked if the championship was gone: "No, it's not mathematically, but it's clear now that it's very difficult. We have a game in three days and we will try to win. Never say never in football. United, in the last 12 games, have won 11 with one draw. They've done incredibly in the last two months. But, in football, it can change. Ten days ago, we were one point behind. Today, we are eight points. This can change also for them. Clearly, they have more experience than us, so probably it's difficult, but until it's impossible, we need to hope."

Arsenal had the momentum heading into the match, with seven wins from their last eight league fixtures, and enjoyed the better of the opening exchanges as Yaya Toure limped off with a knee problem. City, looking low on confidence, threatened only on occasions, notably when Mario - who was lucky to be on the pitch, having earlier escaped punishment for a knee-high, studs-up tackle on Song - had a half-volley from six yards cleared off the line following an astute corner routine. Mikel Arteta's low drive beat

Hart from 20 yards, and City's misery compounded when Mario received a second yellow in the 90th minute.

United's breakthrough came courtesy of referee Lee Mason, who awarded a soft 15th-minute penalty and sent off Derry when the offside Young fell in the area. Rooney dispatched the spot-kick and, to compound QPR's misery, Derry was sent off. United later killed the game off through Scholes, whose 20-yard drive dipped under Kenny's right hand.

Mancini said he would "probably" sell Mario this summer, suggesting he would not play again for him this season, although the club later claimed he said that because he expected the FA to throw the book at him. Mario would serve a ban of at least three matches after his sending off, but Mancini expected the FA to take further action against for a knee-high challenge on Song that went unpunished. Asked for how long he could put up with Mario's antics, Mancini said: "I am finished. We have six games and he will not play in the next six games." Pushed further on whether he would try to sell him at the end of the season, Mancini replied: "Probably - but I don't know. It depends, because Balotelli is a fantastic player. I can continue to play with Mario on the pitch. Every time, we risk one sent off, like today. But he can score also in the last minute." Mancini admitted Mario created "big problems" for his team-mates but joked the media would be happy for him to stay in the Premier League. "If Mario leaves England, what will you do? You should be happy if Mario stays here. You can write one, two or three pages in your newspapers!"

Asked if the authorities should examine the incident with Song that referee Martin Atkinson and assistant Peter Kirkup took no action over, Mancini said "I hope so" and admitted the striker deserved a lengthy ban. Mancini kept Mario on the pitch because he did not see the tackle on Song until after the game and defended his decision not to substitute him even after he had been booked for another bad challenge on Sagna. Mancini added: "I love him as a guy, I love him as a player, because I know him. He's not a bad guy. He's a fantastic player. But, at this moment, I'm very sorry for him because he continues to lose his talent, his quality. I hope, for him, that he can understand that he's in a bad way for his future, and he can change his behaviour."

Arsene Wenger had every right to be as furious with the Mario challenge that could have broken Song's leg. "Fortunately, he didn't. If the referee had television, he would have given him a red card. I thought it was a bad tackle. I said to my physio, 'What happened to Song?' because he said he was touched at the knee. I thought maybe it was a red card but I didn't know until I saw it." Unlike Mancini, Wenger said he could sense Mario was on the edge. "He flirted with 'orange' a few times. I don't know him and it's not my job to do that. I don't want to interfere with Mancini's job. Everybody has his cases in his own camp and I have enough work."

Asked if the Gunners had ended City's title hopes, he said: "Not completely, no. They cannot afford to drop any points now. Once the team 'smelt the stable', it's difficult for them to drop points. In French, you say when a horse smells its stable, it's difficult to stop them."

Monday, April 9, 2012

Mario Ballotelli's agent was confident he will remain with the club next season. "In England, only tabloids write about Balotelli and I use them to clean my car," Mino Raiola said. "People expect always a lot from Mario so everything he does is amplified. Mario wants to do well for Mancini, who is a big friend of Balotelli. Mancini says Balotelli will be sold this summer? I don't think so. I will talk to the club and Mancini."

Raiola insists the striker felt remorse after being shown a second yellow card for sliding in on Song late in the game. "I spoke with Balotelli and he was very sorry for what happened today. I didn't see the incident but like Mancini said, things can happen. I don't want to discuss the chance that Balotelli can leave the Premier League. If Mario wanted to leave he didn't need to do it like this but simply to ask the club." Raiola, though, felt Mario would not play for City again this campaign, "Mario will receive a big suspension after this red card. At the end of the season I will speak with the club and we'll see," Mario said in a statement provided by his agent to Italian news agency Ansa. "I'm very sorry for what happened and for the disappointment caused to City."

Mario's apologies were directed "especially to Roberto Mancini, who I admire and wish well". Mario phoned Prandelli to apologise but the Italy coach told his player to publicly apologise. Mario said of his actions against Arsenal: "I didn't break the code of ethics. I already missed out on the national team for foolishness and I wouldn't do it a second time. I hope to be there at the training camp in April. Let's wait for the final verdict of the ban." Speaking two weeks before Italy's two-day training camp, Prandelli commented: "I'll evaluate from the videos of the sending off whether or not to apply the code of ethics for Balotelli."

Tuesday, April 10, 2012

Roberto Mancini believed City should be proud to finish second after seemingly throwing in the title race towel. "To arrive second position, I don't think that is a bad championship. I am proud of my players and I think all the supporters should be. I don't think it's been a bad season because we have improved a lot since last year we have 15 points more now than we did last year. We can be disappointed because we were at the top for six months. We need to improve but it is important that we stick together: the club, the players, the supporters. Now Manchester City is a top squad and it needs only to win whether it is this year or next year. We don't need to change. It's important that every year we improve."

City faced in-form West Brom at the Etihad Stadium knowing only a win could keep them in touch with United and stop them running away with the title. "It's not finished," Mancini added. "I think it will be very difficult but I anything in football can happen and for this reason it is important we continue and start to win. We also have the best defence in the league but it is clear we are not good at the moment. We have lost two or three key players to injury. At this moment it is clear it is difficult but I am proud of my players. It is important for the players to finish well in this championship because we need to do the maximum that we can do. We need to improve that when we are in a bad moment that we can improve."

Mancini offered encouragement for Mario, 'I love Mario like a guy, like a player, but he made another mistake and I said that he will not play because I think that he will take a three or four game ban for this reason. I hope for him that he can improve.'

Samir Nasri bet Piers Morgan £10,000 that he will get his hands on silverware before his former club Arsenal after he took exception to the former Daily Mirror editor's jibes on Twitter following the Gunners' win over City. Nasri hit back via his own social network page, advising Morgan and other Arsenal fans to 'move on' and 'support your team', rather than harbouring resentment towards him for making the switch to City. Morgan referencing Nasri's quotes about 'leaving Arsenal to win trophies'. Nasri responded, 'I'm aware what I said about titles I'm sure I will lift a trophy with Man City before AFC.' Morgan challenged him with a £10,000 wager, to which Nasri replied: 'No problem we bet and the winner gives the money to a charity.' The FA will have something to say about Nasri indulging in gambling, regardless of its light nature. Nigel De Jong tried to warn him off getting into a war of words with the serial Twitterer before he agreed to the bet, saying: 'Don't waste anymore tweets 2 Morgan @SamNasri19. Easy 2 sit behind your screen and give comments. Be a real man and say it their faces.'

Mario will only serve a three-match ban after the FA admitted they could not charge him over the tackle on Song, media predictions of a nine-match way off target. An FA statement read: "Retrospective action in relation to the incident involving Mario Balotelli of Manchester City and Alex Song of Arsenal, which occurred in the 20th minute of Sunday's game, will not be taken. Where at least one of the officials has seen the coming together of players retrospective action is not taken, regardless of whether they have seen the full extent of the challenge. Retrospective action can only be taken in scenarios where none of the match officials saw the players coming together. In agreement with FIFA, this is how 'not seen' incidents are dealt with retrospectively in England. It is a policy that is agreed with all football stakeholders."

"I thought Mario would be banned for six or seven games, that's why I said he wouldn't play again this season," Mancini said. "He only got three games so I'm pleased for this. He will be back for Manchester United. He will be ready."

An eight-year-old girl sent Mancini some of his favourite sweets, Fruit Pastilles. Megan Kinghorn felt the City boss needed cheering up after his team suffered a poor run of form. The young fan spotted Mancini chewing on the sweets in the dugout decided to send him a packet of the Rowntree treat. She said: "I sent them because I am a big City fan and I love Roberto and I wanted to send him something to cheer him up because he has a really tough job." Megan's mother Kirsty added: "We had a running joke in the house that whenever City were on the telly Mancini and his assistant Brian Kidd always seemed to be eating sweets. During one match we spotted what looked like a packet of Fruit Pastilles. Megan said she was going to buy some with her pocket money and sent them to him. We went to Asda, got a four-pack and she wrote a letter and sent it to him. She thinks he's wonderful." Mancini wrote a reply letter. It read, "Dear Megan, How surprised and happy I was to receive some Fruit Pastilles from you the other week. I am afraid Brian and I have eaten them all!! You also took the trouble to write me a beautiful letter which I have pinned up on my office notice board. I am sending you a picture of me which I hope you like and also a picture of the team. I am glad we have great supporters like you. I hope you enjoy the rest of the season." Megan's mother said the reply was 'lovely' considering how busy he is.

Wednesday, April 11, 2012

Mancini shocked the watching TV audience in his after match interview when he insisted his side cannot win the title despite narrowing the gap to five points as City thrashed West Brom 4-0 and United crashed 1-0 at Wigan in a night of yet more surprises, twists and turns. With five games to go including the clash of the two teams, Mancini flicked back his greying locks, "It is finished. Five points is too much. United have got fantastic spirit.

We don't have this spirit."

Yet, in his programme notes for the match, which City won with two goals from Agüero and one each from Tévez and Silva, Mancini suggested that "everything can happen". Mancini denied attempting mind games, that he was focused on ensuring his side ended the campaign positively. "I think it is important for us to finish the season well. This is our best season for 50 years and I am proud of the players." He thought United were actually playing Wigan on Thursday. "Only at the end of game did I realise they played tonight."

The win was an impressive return to form following the limp loss at Arsenal, which seemed to have ended their title hopes. Agüero was lethal in front of goal, Silva looked more lively than in a long time and Tévez scored his first goal in 11 months in his first start since 21 September last year. "I'm happy for [Tévez] and his performance," said Mancini. "He is not ready to play one game but he played 60 minutes and he can improve in the last five games. It was an important win because I think West Brom are a good team with a good manager."

Next up comes Norwich City at Carrow Road, with United hosting struggling Aston Villa the next day. Mancini said it would surprise him if United lost to Villa, but admitted: "I don't know. Football is very strange. When you think one thing then the opposite happens." Mancini knew the title would once more hinge on the two teams meeting, "It's important for us to beat United here, to beat them two times in a season. United are a fantastic team and I don't think they can lose five points. It is important that we finish this good season for us well. This is the best season since 1968 and this is important. I fight always, every day, and also my team but now I think it is too late. I think they have fantastic spirit, United. We don't have the same spirit and for this reason I think this is very difficult."

Sir Alex criticised referee Phil Dowd after United were denied a penalty. United were the beneficiaries of a generous decision in the first half when Wigan had a goal chalked off, correctly in the eyes of Ferguson. The champions then fell behind to Maloney's 50th-minute winner, which came from a corner that should not have been awarded according to Ferguson. United then saw strong penalty shouts for handball against Figueroa waved away, Sir Alex was not happy, "Phil Dowd had a disappointing game tonight, he never got to grips with it, but that doesn't take away from the performance of Wigan tonight – they deserved it. We were completely dominated by Wigan."

Thursday, April 12, 2012

Agüero insisted the title race was not yet over, "They dropped three points, which gives us more confidence to fight for the Premier League." Agüero praised the influence of Tévez, "Obviously Carlos is a fantastic player, like Edwin Dzeko and Mario Balotelli are, but we've played quite regularly together in Argentina. Because of that, he knows my movements and so we seem to do it quite well. The most important thing is we are all happy. We have done fairly well – myself, Edin and Mario – but I think it would be nice to have Carlos on board to add goals. Carlos is a key player as he has got a lot of experience of playing in the Premier League."

Manchester rapper R.I.O persuaded Mario and Rio to appear in his new video. The promotional clip for Can't Stop We has already proved an online hit, with more than 46,000 people viewing it on YouTube in just four days, thanks in part to it featuring the footballers. R.I.O, real name Rio Nelson, met Mario through his uncle and Mario agreed to perform some ball juggling tricks in a barber's shop for the video. "We were showing off to each other, seeing who could do the best. But I had to be careful when he went in for a tackle," said the rapper, who used to play for non-league Barrow. "Hanging out with him he is such a humble, down to earth, really nice guy." The shots of Ferdinand were taken when R.I.O supported US rap star Rick Ross at Manchester Academy.

United first-team coach Rene Meulensteen suggested Sir Alex would never sign a player like Mario. "City do not have a well-balanced team. They only have individuals who play for themselves. You can see that City lack the right team spirit. There is no chance of Balotelli playing for Manchester United. A player who gets up to the antics he does has no place at our club. I don't believe that Sir Alex would sign a player like Balotelli. We shouldn't get in people like him – they only bring frustration. United are accustomed to the pressure involved in going for the title. City are in a position to win the league for the first time in a long while but that is breaking them up. I thought they wouldn't hold out to the end."

Inter Milan will not look to re-sign Mario, but were interested in Kolarov, who made just nine Premier League starts this season after struggling to oust Clichy. "Kolarov is a player that interests us, it's true," Branca told FC Inter News. "We can move on this issue at the end of the season. Balotelli? He is good but not in our plans."

Mancini wanted to sign Luka Modric but thought it "unlikely" Spurs will sell, "Luka Modric is an outstanding footballer, a great player. He is definitely one of the best in the Premier League. It is by no means easy to get him because he plays for a big club, Tottenham. It is unlikely that they would let him leave. We are lucky to have another great player from these parts in Edin Dzeko. I have worked with quite a few players from these parts – not just Croatians, but Bosnians, Serbs and Montenegrins. I have many friends among them and I am very proud of it. They are really something special and they mostly play with invention and creativity." Dzeko would be happy if Modric was brought in to strengthen the midfield, "Everyone is after him, but I would love it if he came to City. He would be a great addition. Besides that, he would have everything at City – Champions league, fighting for the title, great wages. I am cheering for him to choose City."

Fri, April 13, 2012

Roberto Mancini claimed the trip to Norwich could be harder than the forthcoming derby against United. City would cut United's lead to two points if they win at Carrow Road, with the Red Devils not scheduled to play Aston Villa until Sunday afternoon, but Mancini was wary that the game comes just three days after the impressive win over West Brom. "United is easy," Mancini said. "We could lose or we could win but it is an easy game. Against United or Chelsea, our concentration will be 100%. Norwich will be really tough because we have only had two days to recover after West Brom." A playful Mancini bizarrely backed the comments of Meulensteen that the Red Devils have greater togetherness. "I agree with him. They have big experience and are a fantastic team. We are nothing. But sometimes the best team, or the team that has balance, doesn't win."

In a fresh phase of mind games, he sarcastically heaped praise on title rivals while dismissing his own side, "They are perfect and we are the opposite. They are not a team like us, who have players who only think about themselves." The wry smile indicated his comments were tongue-in-cheek, "United are fantastic, they have won everything for 20 years and we are here. We make mistakes. We are not on the moon, we are normal. Like normal people we can do mistakes."

Mancini went on to defend City's spending programme, "All the time, people say we have spent money. But it is only like the other teams. In the last seven or eight years, they have spent £400–£500m as well. We didn't buy Cristiano Ronaldo, Lionel Messi or Andres Iniesta. If we bought Messi, we should win. We would have a player who scored two goals in every game. But we bought young players who need to improve together."

City were without the suspended Mario but Mancini remarked, "I am happy if he wants to stay. If he does want to stay, he should change his mind-set. I spoke with Mario a couple of times about this, I don't think he can stay here with me for 10 years. But in two or three years he can change his behaviour. He must do that for the quality he has. He can lose all his quality with this attitude. It's important that he changes."

Mancini poured scorn on Uefa fining City £24,740 for being one minute late back on to the pitch in a Europa League tie, £8,000 more than Porto for their fans directing racist abuse at Mario and Yaya in the same competition, "Maybe Uefa needs some money at this moment. Italy needs money, Germany needs money. It's a difficult moment for everyone and maybe it's the same for Uefa."

Sir Alex Ferguson insisted that the title race is very much alive and that he will not be fooled by Mancini's mind games, "It is back on the race. They have a chance haven't they? They haven't been playing well but 4-0 is a good result at this time of the season." Responding to Mancini's assertion that the title race is over, Ferguson added: "I think he maybe picked the wrong time to say it. If you want to use it as mind games, you can do that but it didn't mean anything to us."

Saturday, April 14, 2012

Roberto Mancini continued with his mantra that title race was all over, despite a Carlos Tévez hat-trick and a 6-1 win at Norwich. City were eight points off the pace at the start of the week, Mancini was adamant "It's finished." When pointed out City now trailed by just two points, Mancini replied: "No. Five points." He did not expect any United slip-up at home.

Tévez's swerving effort beat Ruddy before he set up Agüero. Norwich replied when Surman blasted in after Hart's punch. A Tévez header and Agüero's solo effort added the gloss before Tévez rounded Ruddy to complete his hat-trick and Johnson slotted in from close range. Tévez celebrated his third strike with a golf swing, mocking those who questioned his desire during his leave of absence in his home country where he was pictured on the golf course.

Agüero, who scored two fine goals, came inches away from his own hat-trick when he hit the post late on as City recovered their fluency, but the scoreline was harsh on Norwich, who pressured the visitors early on, and tested them again after reducing the deficit to 2-1. Four goals in the last 17 minutes swept their challenge aside to give City their first away league win since 12 February.

Joleon Lescott cleared Holt's header off the line, as Pilkington blocked Hart. City players had already made their feelings known to referee Chris Foy when Tévez was booked for diving, after he appeared to be caught by Bennett. But soon after, Tévez's rehabilitation continued when he was fed down the right by a re-energised Silva and struck a swerving shot that beat

Ruddy at his near post. The second was a exquisite as Agüero supplied Tévez and then picked up his instant back heel to fire past Ruddy.

When Surman steered the ball in after Hart had punched Drury's cross clear, Mancini reacted, Yaya's arrival from the bench pivotal, three goals in seven minutes. Another substitute Johnson completed the rout. Lambert commented, "Their strike force is incredible, the first two goals were world class. Manchester City are a top-drawer team with top players. That second goal came from absolutely nowhere."

Mancini was impressed by Tévez, who was starting successive league games for the first time in 11 months. "I think now he is better. I think we did well this season also without Carlos for four, five months." When was asked what City might have achieved had Tévez been available all season. "I'm sure if we had Carlos with Agüero, Mario and Dzeko, we would have scored more goals." Mancini hinted it might not have made a difference, "Carlos did not play for us for six months but it is only in the last month that we have come off the top of the league. Everyone makes mistakes. It's important that when you do them you apologise. I am not frustrated because we lost Agüero for two games, Vincent Kompany for one match, and Joleon Lescott for four weeks too." United played twice before City were next in action, and Mancini was asked whether he felt Sir Alex's team would drop points in those games, against Villa and Everton. "It's not important now. We should continue like this. We should score, we should win if possible."

Carlos Tévez thanked Mancini for keeping faith with him and felt the title race was not over. "Of course we can still win the title. Obviously we have to put pressure on United. We just need to continue to play the way we are and we will arrive and the top. Mathematically it's not impossible. I am very happy that I played very well today but the most important thing is that I want to say thank you to my colleagues for all the support they have given me since I arrived. It wasn't easy coming back to training and to play but they have given me a lot of support and the technical staff have been very good to me too. I really appreciate everyone's help." Was that golf swing goal celebration a dig at Mancini? "It was an important goal, not just for me but it was important for the people, for the club and for the fans, for my colleagues, for Roberto. We all went through some difficult times. That's why I celebrated the way I did because I have my feet on the floor and I am happy for everyone."

Mancini was not confident Tévez will remain at City. When asked if Tévez would feature for City next campaign, Mancini said: "I don't know. I don't know this. It depends. Now I think it is important that we think about the next four games. After that, at the end of the season, we will see what can happen with all the players." Mancini insists that he and his players now have no issue with Tévez, "There is no problem. It is in the past."

Mancini wanted Rooney to recover form an ankle injury and face City, so that there will be no excuses from United if they lose the derby, "I think it is better if Rooney plays on Saturday. He's a fantastic player and has had an amazing season. He will be a danger, of course, but United have many fine players in their team, but we have beaten them once at home already and can do it again. I think it is best if both teams are full strength and then the side who takes the three points can truly say the best team won and there is no reason that cannot be us."

A veteran of Milan derby battles, Mancini believes there are many similarities between the two big city derbies, "Supporters live for these games and look forward to them more than any other match each year. It is about passion and desire and results do not always go to form. Of course, this isn't just a game about local pride: we want to finish in fourth place and every match from now until the last will be just as important. We need our fans to keep doing what they do each week and get right behind the team from the first minute to the last. They can inspire us to even greater heights and they have a huge role to play against United."

Sunday, April 15, 2012

As Mancini expected, United re-established a five-point lead with a comfortable 4-0 win over Aston Villa at Old Trafford. Ashley Young was at the centre of more penalty controversy seven days after facing accusations of diving against QPR as he went down under minimal contact once again. Rooney converted his 30th goal of the season from the spot-kick before Welbeck finished off from close range just before the break. Rooney added the third in the 73rd minute before Nani fired home in injury time as United put further daylight between themselves and City.

Despite moving further ahead, Ferguson denied his side were now favourites for the league title. "There could be twists and turns yet but the name of the game is to enjoy ourselves and play with expression like we did today. You can never be too confident. The name is the game is to not drop too many points."

Mario was "upset and speechless" by the death of Livorno midfielder Piermario Morosini. The 25-year-old, who was on loan from Udinese, suffered a cardiac arrest during Saturday's Serie B match at Pescara. Mario, who played for the Italy Under-21s at the same time as Morosini, commented, "He was a great lad. It's a terrible event and makes you reflect on your own existence. It teaches you to appreciate life and to live it with care and dignity.

I was upset and speechless when I heard of Morosini's death. I couldn't believe it and thought it was a terrible joke. He was a great lad, a really great lad."

Monday, April 16, 2012

Under Mancini, Mario thrived, "When I was at Inter Milan I called my mother to solve every little problem. Now I have to go it alone. First of all I need to improve as a player. I am lucky to work with Mancini. He's one of the best coaches in the world, maybe the best. After my red card against Arsenal he feared a long ban so he spoke about me with some harsh words. But we have explained things to each other. I know he believes in me, as he always has done." Psychiatric help has been suggested, but he felt misrepresented in the media, "A psychologist for me? I believe psychologists are important. Sometimes they can be very useful, but I don't need one of them. Every day there is an exaggeration about me and I would like it to stop. I want to be judged for what I do on the field. I am a shy and simple guy. I like to have fun with my friends and I always try not to bother anyone."

Tuesday, April 17, 2012

At the prospect that United could win the title on City's home turf, Joleon Lescott replied, "Yeah, of course. We're aware that they could win it at our ground. So no matter what happens in our games this weekend, we are going to be looking to win that game a week on Monday. Whether it's for the title race or just for the fans alone. We know how much derbies mean to people and those involved at a club. If they can clinch the title at our ground...well...all I can say is that we'll be doing everything in our power to stop that from happening. In fact, we're not going to let it happen, even though they're a great team. If they win the league at our place I think that would equal the pain for us that they must have felt in October. But again that's something that's not yet in our control. We've both got another massive game before then and I'll be an Everton fan even more so this weekend. Hopefully they can get a result at Old Trafford. There were doubters after the Arsenal defeat recently. The result wasn't great but what really let us down was the performance. We don't often play like that. But then last Saturday against Norwich it was more like the old Man City. We were playing really well at the start of the season but I understand that no team, no players can play well for the whole season. We're no different to that. Our bad spell came at the wrong end of the season but we've shown in the last two games what we're capable of."

Wednesday, April, 18, 2012

The City board continued to back Mancini, and both he and Platt had been on scouting missions in the past two weeks looking at summer transfer targets in Europe. City were expected to offer Mancini a new contract at the end of the season. His current deal had a year to run and the club hierarchy would review the situation at their quarterly board meeting at the end of the campaign.

There has been speculation that City would look to a new manager such as Mourinho. "I am confident that I will continue to do this job next year," Mancini said. "I don't think we have any problems because I think we have done a good job."

Thursday, April 19, 2012

James Milner made three starts in the past two months, an unused substitute for City's last two games. But he had no problem with being rotated by Mancini if the end result is City picking up silverware. "It's frustrating at times because you want to play every game and it's not going to happen. But that's your will to win and your drive as a footballer. It's about the team, not the individuals. It's about City winning trophies and the rest doesn't matter. You want to play with, and against, the best and become the best player you can be. Playing with the kind of players we have here will improve you. You need competition for places and I knew it would be difficult to play every single game. But you have to back your own ability to be a big figure in the dressing room, improve as a player and contribute as much as you can to the success of the team."

Fri, April 20, 2012

Roberto Mancini knew Tévez and Agüero were a good mix, scoring eight goals between them in two games since Tévez returned, where as Dzeko and Mario, signed for a combined £50m, are too similar to make a good partnership, 'Carlos can play with Mario, Sergio and Dzeko. The only players who can't play together are Mario and Dzeko because they are the same type of players. Technically they are different but they're the same player. For this, the two players can't play together. Only Mario and Dzeko can't play together because they have some problems. Dzeko didn't play very well against Arsenal but we made a big mistake when we conceded a goal three minutes from the end. If we'd drawn against Arsenal it was another point. But we can't do anything about it now.'

Asked again if the season would have turned out differently were it not for his dispute, Mancini said: 'It's normal that if you have another player like Carlos you can score more goals. The difference is clear but we did everything in November and December to try to keep Carlos here. We have good players and Carlos is one of them. In the end we'll decide.'

Mancini felt the Premier League was the same as Serie A when big clubs get big decisions. "I am frustrated. We have a saying, il tutto mondo e paese. Every place is the same. That means the rules are not the same for everyone. They are sometimes different. When I was in Italy I always thought here had the best referees. My ideas have changed, probably."

Mancini used the old Sir Alex trick, highlight referring decisions against you, to get the officials thinking, and here he highlighted decisions going in favour of United. Even Ferguson spoke to Young about going to ground too easily but defended him against allegations of cheating. Mancini said: "This is a situation that I don't like because the rules should be the same for everyone, not for us or United or West Bromwich. They can't change from one pitch to another. This is not good. The man on the pitch in a black shirt doesn't have a blue shirt or a red shirt or a white shirt." Replying to suggestions of bias towards United, Mancini said: "No, no, I don't want to say this. But when I watch some games there are situations I don't like. Everyone can make a mistake but not like this. I don't want to talk about United because they're a top team, a fantastic team. But I think that every team should play with 11 players." Asked if it even itself out, "No this is impossible because there are some moments in the season when the mistake is more important." Young won his penalty against Villa a day after Tévez was booked for a legitimate claim at Norwich. Mancini said wryly: "No, for me it was a red card for Tévez! Not yellow, red. And a five-match ban!" Mancini's humour did not disguise concerns that these decisions could cost City the title.

Ferguson responded by saying and the reaction against Young was "because it's Manchester United". Fergie argued, "We didn't get one against Wigan in the week and we didn't scream from the rooftops about it. You get bad decisions, you get good decisions and it evens itself out, believe me. I've had a word with Ashley. He understands where we come from and hopefully that makes a difference. How many penalty kicks has Ryan Giggs got for Manchester United? That's a good quiz question. Five in 20 years. There's some record. You know why? Because his balance is good and he never goes down. That's the amazing thing about him."

Sunday, April 22, 2012

A pivotal day in the title: Everton twice battled back from two goals down to snatch a remarkable 4-4 draw at Old Trafford, while later in the day City beat relegated Wolves 2-0, reducing the gap to three points with a superior goal difference of +6.

A United team minus Young were punished for a laboured start when Jelavic broke the deadlock with a looping header. The Toffees led for five minutes before Rooney, formerly of Everton, nodded in a terrific left-wing cross from Nani at close range. United made a similarly sluggish opening to the second period, yet a moment of magic from Welbeck just before the hour edged them ahead, curling the ball into the top corner. Welbeck had a say in United's third, flicking the ball into the path of Nani, who clipped over Howard. Everton somehow pulled one back when Fellaini volleyed in from ten yards. United restored a two-goal cushion: Welbeck passing through Jagielka's legs for Rooney to produce the easiest of finishes. Jelavic kept Everton alive, volleying in a flick-on from Fellaini, then the Belgian again turned provider to tee up Pienaar who slotted past De Gea.

City had to complete their job by beating Wolves to put them in a position to move back to the top if they beat United in eight days' later. They did just that, and improved their goal difference. Mancini maintaining that his side were not in the title race, despite starting the day only five points adrift, but he had to change his view after goals from Agüero and Nasri. Agüero scored with his third effort at goal, Clichy the provider with a fabulous pass that arced beyond the final defender. Finally, in the 74th minute Nasri converted after Tévez's slide-rule pass, with a quick thinking, quick free kick against him.

"Is it a good day? Not really," said Mancini, "You all wrote the title race was finished. Seven days ago, the race was finished. You wrote it. I congratulate Sir Alex Ferguson on a good season. After the derby we play Newcastle, who are fighting for the Champions League, and QPR who are fighting relegation. We can talk about the title next Monday night. It's impossible."

Sir Alex now labelled the derby as the most important in his entire career, a "title decider". United knew if they lost they would surrender the initiative completely. "Yes, definitely," said Ferguson, when asked if it was the most important derby he has known. "We've given them the initiative, there is no doubt about that. It makes the game at the Etihad a really important game. A decider really. There has been an expectancy from City that it could be their decider, but it's our decider too."

Ferguson was stunned by the collapse against Everton for a team that had kept six clear sheets in its previous seven games. "There were defensive lapses. Their goals were really soft. It was a real shock for us to defend like that. It was a travesty of a result in some ways but we made it difficult for ourselves and if you look at our history we keep doing that. We've thrown a game away that we should be coasting. But we didn't so we have given ourselves a difficult task. It was a throwaway, an absolute giveaway. We just needed to see the game out. It was a travesty because some of the football we played was fantastic and some of the goals we scored were great goals. To give away four goals away at Old Trafford in a game that was so important, I just couldn't believe it. We need a result at the Etihad, no question about that. We've got to get a result at Etihad Stadium now, it's a derby of amazing proportions – probably the most important derby game in my time. We have to go there, make sure we perform in the right way and not give away silly goals. There's no reason why we can't."

Mancini played down his side's title chances, "I am pleased with this form but now we have three very difficult games, it could not be more difficult. We are there – I think they have a bigger chance, more than us in this moment. But we have another chance." Asked who was in pole position, Mancini said, "United, always. They're top, three points ahead. After the derby they have two easy games. We don't have more chance to win."

Mancini suggested United's experience was key, "I don't think they have pressure because they are used to it every year. For us, it's different because it's the first time. At the moment, we don't have any pressure because we are not expected to win. But we want to finish well. It's important for our season. It was important to win this game. The performance is not important. We played well all season but now it only matters to win."

Of the performance at Molineux, Mancini was dissatisfied, "So-so. I don't think it was a good performance like against Norwich and West Brom, our performance was not perfect. We needed to win this game, maybe we thought before the game it was easy but I told them before it was difficult. We had more chances to score – for this I am unhappy. I think in the end it was important to win this game." He offered commiserations to Wolves, "I am sorry for them being relegated. They play very strong always, every game they have a strong mentality."

Yaya couldn't believe City had another chance: 'United's result was amazing. It was an unbelievable day for us with United dropping points at home. For me, it was strange. We found out about it on the bus on the way to Wolves. It was quite unbelievable and we now have to try and take advantage. We did the first part by beating Wolves but we have to settle down and continue to work hard because United still have three points more than us. We have to play them at home and, if you look at the record of United, they are very strong away and it will be a very difficult test for us. I think this year the club need to win the cup (title) and it will be difficult. But we need to win this derby because it will be one of the most important games the club have had."

City didn't cope with the pressure when they were leading in the title race early in March, Yaya was sure City's big players will ensure they cope better now. "People say we looked nervous at stages of the game and we have a lot of young players and not so many experienced ones. When your big rivals drop points at home, and you have to win your game, it is quite difficult. But with the players we have, it can make the difference all of the time with the likes of Agüero, Tévez and Nasri, and we did the job."

The destiny of the title didn't only depend on events at the Etihad. Yaya pointed out, They are very difficult games to come. We have United, then Newcastle who are playing well at home. These games will be very tough until the end of the season, and QPR are playing well as well. But, with the team we have, if we win something this year it will be fantastic for us."

In the United dressing room there was dismay at the Everton result, as Nani commented, "There is anger from the players, of course, because we wanted to win. We're disappointed to lose four goals. We have to keep believing in our qualities because we still have a great opportunity to win the title. It's a huge game – there will be a fantastic atmosphere there. It will be a difficult game, but if you want to win the league you cannot think about the atmosphere or the opponents, we must just think about the way we play and try to win the game." Asked if he was still confident United would win the title, Nani said: "Of course."

Monday, April 23, 2012

Tickets for the derby were selling for £1,300 online with police concerned rival fans sitting next to each other. A Greater Manchester Police spokesman said: "We'd warn fans that if they buy tickets online they could be fakes and if home fans end up in the away end or vice versa they'll be identified early on and ejected." A City spokesman said: "We'd always advise fans to only purchase match tickets through the official club channels." The cost of the online tickets equates to £14 per minute of football.

Andre Marriner was appointed to referee the showdown. Marriner dished out 83 yellow cards and five reds, though, he had yet to issue a single red to a home side this season. United had yet to lose with Marriner in the middle.

Tuesday, April 24, 2012

Sheikh Mansour hinted Mancini will remain manager even if they do not win the League. In a rare interview with Abu Dhabi TV, Mansour said: "The difference is three points and we do have a chance. But whatever happens and even if we don't win I am very happy and satisfied with the players, team and management. They have performed very well and have improved in their last few matches."

QPR appointed Mike Rigg as their Technical Director, leaving a similar role at City, which he held since June 2008, reuniting him with Mark Hughes, with whom he worked at the Etihad Stadium, as well as at Blackburn and the Welsh national team.

Pablo Zabaleta admitted that following the loss at Arsenal, he thought their opportunity had disappeared. "We've never stopped believing in ourselves but to be honest, after the Arsenal defeat, I thought our chance had probably gone. We've been five points clear before so we know how it feels, but United losing against Wigan and dropping points at home to Everton shows that in football you have to believe, because you just never know. If we have another chance for the title it's because we deserve it. We've kept going and we will continue to do that and see what happens." Regarding the 162nd derby he added: "We know how important this game is. United are the team we want to beat, especially because it gives us the chance to get back to the top.

Wednesday, April 25, 2012

Manchester United headed to the Etihad Stadium knowing they must avoid defeat if they are not to surrender top spot, far more significant than the suggested battle between the Establishment and nouveaux riche, "That's not really accurate," Ferguson commented. "I don't agree with that. It's true City became rich in a pretty incredible way, but it's not the fact there is a new owner and new ambitions which necessarily change things. The difference is perhaps that we're trying to build with youth."

Brendan Rodgers rejected Mancini's claim United's run-in is "easy". "He knows we will give Manchester United a difficult game. What Roberto said was probably a bit tongue in cheek in fairness. I think what we have shown over the course of the season is our competitive nature. We might be a way down the scale in terms of many things at this level, but one thing that's guaranteed is that when you play Swansea City it's going to be a competitive game and a difficult game. I'm sure Roberto knows that." Swansea were 12th losing 10 of their 18 away games this season.

Thursday, April 26, 2012

Sir Alex took his players to Cardiff to escape the pressure, a two-day stay at the Vale Resort, a golf and spa retreat in the Vale of Glamorgan. United were given access to Cardiff City's training facilities nearby, returning 24 hours before facing City. Ferguson organised a similar break at St Andrews before United's last Monday night game against Blackburn at the start of this month. He felt some of his younger players were feeling the pressure and was delighted with the outcome as United won at Ewood Park to go five points clear at the top. Sir Alex admitted, 'You would have to be a confirmed masochist to enjoy it. But we are looking forward to it and the players will be fully prepared for it.'

As Mancini continued to insist United had won the title, Ferguson recognised the mind games, "Maybe he is trying to take pressure off his own players. But it doesn't matter. It is not going to affect our approach or attitude to the game. We know the exact situation we are in here. We are in a better position than Manchester City. We can get two results, they can only get one. They have to win. We can draw or we can win, which is what we will be trying to do. It was inevitable I suppose, it is all down to this game. There will be a considerable number of countries watching it, so I hope it lives up to the billing. We have to get used to playing Manchester City in important games. They are not going away. The support they have means we are going to be playing them in a lot of big games. Finals maybe, we already have done in semi-finals, an important cup tie this season. If we are going to be contesting for league titles regularly - and I think we will be doing - it will become just as important as the Liverpool game. Maybe not in terms of emotion because the Liverpool - United games are emotional. But there is certainly an importance which, at this moment in time, supercedes the Liverpool games. They are our direct opponents now. Manchester City are up against us to win titles. That is what our focus is on, the team who can stop us winning."

More than 600 police - an increase on recent Manchester derbies - will be on duty for a potentially highly volatile game. With United's allocation limited to 2,600, a large number of fans were expected to gather in the city centre. Drinking would not be permitted in the street from mid-afternoon in an exclusion zone between the city centre and the stadium, and any fans under the influence will not be allowed into the game.

Mancini knew it would be much tighter than the 6-1, "The derby is always the game of the year and this one is no different, but we don't only have this one - there was another derby when we won 6-1 at Old Trafford. That was fantastic; a game that can happen only once every hundred years. For the supporters, a derby is always a different game to the others. But we must not forget that there are two more games after Monday. Two very tough games."

While, Sir Alex billed it the as the biggest derby in his 25-year reign, Mancini played down the importance, "The biggest match was the FA Cup final last season. This is a derby - but just one more game. The only important thing is to win. We have three points less than United. We need only to play football. We are calm because we know we don't have any chance to win this title. It is a football game and we should think only to play football. We are happy to be where we are, we have nine points more than we got last year and I am happy that we can finish the season well. This is the derby game of all derby games - whoever loses will be tinged with regret. It's in the blood of the supporters and I know lots of fans who would give everything to win this game. If one loses, they are going to be reflecting on what may have been. But then you look at the points totals that both teams are probably going to amass and you'll see that it's championship form. It means everything to the supporters. Going in to work next Tuesday morning will be the most important day of their lives, for both sets of fans."

Fri, April 27, 2012

Roberto Mancini claims he will deliver the title next season even if they fail in this run in, "I have one year left on my contract, but I am not worried about it. The chairman Khaldoon and the owner Sheikh Mansour are serious people. One victory or defeat is not going to change things. We have set a project in place and we respect that. After that, in football, anything can change, but I have an excellent relationship with Khaldoon and we speak several times a week. He likes to know all about the team, the players. We are improving. We have played very well and we were top for 28 games. If Manchester City do not win the league this season, we will win it next season and we will be successful in the future years."

Mancini had been involved in bigger games "This is not the most important match of my life. I have had other crucial games, like the last day of Serie A in the 2007-08 season, when I was coaching Inter. At half-time on that day, Roma were champions, but we won the title by scoring two goals in the second half to beat Parma. But yes, this match against United is very important. City have been waiting for a match like this since 1968. I don't know if my heart will beat faster, though, and yes, of course I will sleep well on Sunday night. I will sleep peacefully. There are more important things in life."

Mancini would sign Rooney and a 'younger' Giggs, and still insisted United were favourites, "In the league, we have made enormous progress over teams who have been in the Champions League for a long time. I think we can be proud of our work. A few weeks ago, we were eight points behind United. When you are so much behind in the table, you can give up, but it was not true in our case and this is very important. It shows that, beyond the technical qualities of this team, there is strength. Beating United 6-1 gave us strength for the future. For us, it was also a strong signal. Our victory over

United in the FA Cup semi-final last season was also important. That kind of game is a turning-point. Playing against United has helped our progression, it helped us to learn. We are nearer to them, but they are still even better than us. They have more experience and that team spirit that we are currently building, but even when we lost to them, we had interesting games. Against them, we always manage to excel. But for twenty years, the club [United] has won constantly. Even when they are behind in a game, or in the league, they know they can come back because they have this inner strength borne from all of their success."

Mancini wanted to land Hazard, Cavani, Modric, Bale, and van Persie, yet top of his wish list ahead of the title showdown with United was their talisman Wayne Rooney. "United, Liverpool and Arsenal have spent a lot more than City over the last 10 years," Asked which United player he would buy, he added: "Rooney. He's a champion. I'd take Ryan Giggs as well if he could play for five or six more years." City failed with an audacious bid to prise Rooney away from Old Trafford two years ago when the striker put in a transfer request after contract negotiations at Old Trafford broke down, before Rooney did a U-turn and signed a five-year deal until June 2015 and repaired his relationship with their fans by hitting a spectacular overhead kick to win the Manchester derby four months later. Now Rooney has hit 36 goals in 43 appearances in all competitions including two in each of his last two games. City hit 12 goals in their last three games.

City gave top summer transfer target Hazard a tour of the property market in the north-west as they look to keep him out of the clutches of neighbours United. Staff from City gave the young Belgian a tour of the Cheshire commuter belt as they try to get one over on rivals United, who are also in the race - along with Spurs - for Hazard's signature. Hazard would be at the Etihad Stadium on Monday night. Mancini watched Hazard when Lille played Valenciennes, "I like Hazard a lot. He's a good player, he's young and he would do great things in our team. Given his technical qualities City would be the perfect destination for him. I know him and have been following him for a long time. He's a player a lot of teams want." Mancini spoke to the City hierarchy about summer plans and Bale was on their list, "Gareth Bale is a fantastic player. But I don't think he will leave a big team like Tottenham."

Mancini has some big decisions to make on team selection, "All the players are available, but I will make my choice on Sunday. Despite doing some silly things, Balotelli has also made some important contributions, like his two goals at Old Trafford in October. He has many qualities. With him, anything is possible. He is young and still makes big errors that can put your team in trouble. But I still think he has great talent. Carlos? I have always had a good relationship with him. I had no problem in forgiving him. Bringing him back was a logical choice as he is a player of great quality, one of the best strikers in the world. I thought he could lend a hand. Mario is a player like the other players. He is available for Monday and after we decide. In one game Mario can do everything. He can score two or three goals if he decides this. This is the manager's problem." Mancini has previously said he cannot trust Balotelli but thinks he could in such a big game, saying: "I think in this game yes - only in this game!"

"I'm not nervous," he continued, "Why should we be worried? When is the squeaky-bum time? I don't know that phrase. We are at the top of the league and have been there since the start of the season. This is where we want to be. Of course, it's important to get on with your chairman and the owner. But the owners at Manchester City are intelligent and they understand that to create a winning team takes time. When you start to build any team, you need time to get to know them and for them to know you. I'm only interested in winning. To achieve that with a team like City is more of a challenge but the goal is the same. When I started, some of the players didn't share my mentality. After a while they began to understand what is expected of them. I think you have to have angels that sometimes become a son of a b★★★★."

Sir Alex Ferguson commented, "You have an interesting combination of teams - the one with the best home record and the one with the best away record. It's a shootout, isn't it? It means everything to the supporters. Going in to work next Tuesday morning will be the most important day of their lives. It's in the blood of these supporters and I know lots of them who would give everything to win this game on Monday. Our fans would look upon it as a special one because it's against their most bitter rivals. If you ask any of the fans then I know what they would say. For me, it's another league game. But if one loses they are going to be reflecting on what may have been. Whoever loses will be tinged with regret simply because it's a derby thing."

Sir Alex branded Mancini's decision to recall Tévez an act of desperation, but even Fergie could see it was paying off, "We have not watched the games a lot, but he scored a hat-trick. That is an impact. We will just have to wait and see what he does on Monday."

Martin O'Neill hit out at Mancini belittling the Sunderland fixture as 'easy' for United, "I don't have an email address for him but I really thought about sending him one to tell him to keep an eye on what he says, but I didn't. He had obviously forgotten to check the fixtures list properly. We have taken four points off, but they have actually lost five points against us this season. But I think you just have to shrug it off and remember it for the next four years. I don't know what his insinuation was to tell the truth. But if he had any idea about the league at all he would know that the integrity of the league is pretty good. It is hard for someone else to come in and tell who to play, or not to play, but there is still that feeling you want to win the matches."

Nominated skipper at the start of the season, Vincent Kompany would have the honour of lifting the trophy. Kompany was ideally placed to assess the merits of the potential match winners, "Carlos approaches every single game like it is the most important of his life. He did it against Wolves, before that at Norwich and he will do it against United. He is like a guaranteed performer – that's what you get from him. And Wayne Rooney is one of the best strikers in the world. He is quick, powerful and a goalscorer. He is also a leader for his team, and that makes him a special player. It's great to play against him. Hopefully we will be playing against each other for a long time because it's always a great battle."

Saturday, April 28, 2012

Harry Redknapp revealed his "dream" to sign Tévez failed, "I said to the chairman Daniel Levy 'Can you get me Tévez?' That was my dream and so in January that's what I asked. It wasn't possible but that was my dream. The chairman would have loved Tévez but it wasn't do-able because his wages are whatever they are, £200,000-a-week. Daniel made some enquiries about Tévez and if he could have done it, the chairman would have. It was me thinking 'Tévez ... he's not in the team, he's fallen out with Roberto Mancini'. You don't know unless you ask. It was just a little try."

Mancini foresaw Tévez striking the decisive blow to put City back on top, "I think Carlos is destined to score the most important goal in the history of this club. This is my belief." He then explained why winning the English title would rank as his finest moment as a manager. "If we beat United to the title it would be the biggest achievement of my career. That's because it's in England, it's the best championship in Europe. For an Italian manager to win the Premier League would make it better than anything else I have done in the game. Winning trophies is important everywhere, whether it is Barcelona, Real Madrid or Manchester City. But when you win with a club like City you change history as well and that would give me a greater sense of satisfaction. For over 40 years they haven't won the league, so if we can do it, it will be better than at a club that's used to winning titles. One of the things that attracted me to City was the chance to change their history.

This has always been the way in my football life – I like a challenge. Some managers go to a club that's already set up to win because it has top players. For me it's different. I've always gone to clubs who haven't won anything for a long time. It's important that we don't win just one championship. I want to leave a legacy. I want all the City supporters to remember me for winning many trophies and because I've worked well here. If you win the title there can be no debate about who is the No. 1 team in Manchester for this year at least. But United have a fantastic history and it's impossible to change that. Our targets should be to match the achievements of United, Barcelona and Real Madrid. I think that now we are set up to win many trophies in the future. People say it would be easier if your main title rivals were not from the same city. I don't agree. I think it's good to win the title against your neighbours, rather than a team from another part of the country. I had this in Milan with Inter. It's more satisfying to beat a local rival and it's important for Manchester to have two great teams."

Tévez had yet to complete a full 90 minutes, "Carlos is not 100%, because it is impossible for him to be 100% after six months without playing, but he has experience, he is a clever player. He has scored four or five goals and this is important. It is difficult for him to play after six months. For this reason he played only the last two or three games. I think he can find his best form next season, after pre-season." When asked if that meant Mancini wanted to keep Tévez, he commented, "I think he has a contract with Manchester City, but I don't think in this moment it is important to talk about the future for everyone."

Meanwhile Carlos Tévez performed a complete u-turn over his future, "This club has been building something special for the last few years. It was the project and the dream that made me come to City in the first place. I've been here since the start of that project and I share the same vision as Sheikh Mansour. He has always been brilliant with me and I want to repay his faith and stay here as long as it takes to make the project a success. I am an ambitious person. I want to work hard and win things with City. That's all that matters to me, as a player and a person."

Owen Hargreaves was on a pay-as-you-play contract, which ended at the close of the season, and would not be renewed. He was not currently involved in full training. His last action for the club was the 6-1 win over Morecambe reserves on 28 March, in which he completed the full 90 minutes.

Monday, April 30, 2012

An estimated television audience of 650 million watched the remarkable drama unfold as Sir Alex squared up to Mancini on the touch line and later accusing him of "badgering" the officials throughout United's 1-0 defeat to City that put the title within Mancini's hands once again with just two games left.

The volatile managers clashed in the second half after a tackle by substitute De Jong on Welbeck, for which the Dutchman was booked. "He was badgering the official the whole game - the fourth official and the linesman. As soon as I go out there, he's up again," Ferguson snapped. "He was complaining about referees the other week... he can't be complaining tonight, that's for sure."

Mancini's sarcastic retort. "Him? Me? Him? Who said this? Him, no? He doesn't talk with the referee or the fourth official? No, never. I didn't speak with him, he came towards me, but I can understand. I said nothing against him, only spoke to the fourth official. He told me some kind words and I don't know why. I answered him, but afterwards, it was finished. I can understand because at this moment, the tension is high. I told the fourth official it was a foul for us, not for them."

While Mancini and Ferguson shook hands after the game, Mancini aimed a swipe at Fergie, "What was the key? That we wanted to win and they wanted a draw. This is the difference, but this can happen. I think that every manager can choose his tactics and for them, it was important to play for a draw. With a draw, they knew the championship was finished. We played better and deserved to win, but it was difficult because they had so many men behind the ball."

United had now taken just four points from a possible 12 in their last four games. "Yes, I think they are in the driving seat now." Ferguson said. "They only need to win two games of football. I can't complain about the result. They were more threatening and it's damaging to us. But it is not over yet. As long as there are games to play it is not over, but they have an eight-goal advantage and that is a big advantage at this stage of the season. We didn't test their keeper enough really, we started brightly and for the first 15 minutes we dominated, but the longer the half went on we were looking for half-time and the goal came at a bad time for us.'

City overturned an eight-point deficit in three weeks to dislodge United from top spot, but Mancini warned, "Football is crazy, but it is important to believe in yourself when you have a bad moment. We were on top for 28 games and I think we deserve another chance. But it is not finished and if we think it is finished, it will be a big mistake. I don't know if, four weeks ago, we believe in this, but we have a big chance."

Vincent Kompany lost Smalling at a corner to head the winner, putting City top on goal difference, with only two games remaining. "It was competitive. Not many chances in the match. We're disappointed we never tested their goalkeeper," Ferguson said. "Our crossing was poor. They were more of a threat because they had the ball more around our box. If you lose a goal at a set-piece at this level, you've only got yourselves to blame for that. It was a bad time to concede because there was nothing really happening in that first half."

City must beat Newcastle and QPR to take the title, Ferguson pin-pointed the Everton game, when they tossed away a two-goal lead in the last ten minutes. "They're in the driving seat now with only two games of football left. It's not over, particularly as we've got the same number of points, but an eight-goal advantage is a significant advantage for them. I think we look at last Saturday as the worst, in the Everton game. We should never have thrown that away."

Kompany was "absolutely buzzing" after his match winner, 'We've been waiting for it. It's far from over and we know that, but to give our fans two wins over United this season... we have to finish it off and we have to do it over the next two games. Someone text me today and said he thought I was going to score the goal, and I thought he was a lunatic! For us to get this result, we wanted it so bad. It all comes down to the dream we had when we were children, and we all want it so much."

Mancini still named United the title favourites. "We are happy but next Sunday we have another very difficult game. We deserved to win, we had chances, we played well, we had chances to score a second goal. They had no chances to score. It was difficult, though, because United are a top team... It stayed risky until the end. It's important we play a good game against Newcastle because United play an easy game against Swansea. For now we are top of the league but United have a slight advantage. We have two strong games, against Newcastle and QPR, one is fighting for the Champions League and one for relegation. It is important that we are top now, but it is more important to be top on May 13. This changes nothing. We are top, but we need to win the next two games. Anything can happen and we still have big respect for United because we know they have a strong team."

Sky pundit Gary Neville says losing on goal difference would be Sir Alex's "worst nightmare". "I know – I've been in that changing room for 20 years – it's his worst nightmare. Losing a championship on goal difference is what he always talks about, every single season. In January, in February, in March, whatever month it is going for a championship, he will say if you're 1-0, 2-0 up, 'score three, score four'. You never know whether it's going to get to goal difference, and you look at games like Fulham at home 1-0, QPR at home 2-0, and it's these sort of things you look back at during a season and think, 'we could we have done more'. It is his worst nightmare. For Manchester City, they have one game. I think the QPR game at home, with respect to them, the way they played on Sunday against Chelsea, they're a non-entity. It's that game away at Newcastle. Win one match to win a championship and now all the pressure's back on City."

Liam Gallagher gatecrashed City's post-match press conference. Gallagher took the seat reserved for Mancini, saying: 'What do you want to know lads? Top of the league. Well done City.' He then joked: 'Ferguson must have been on the whisky,' before adding: 'I love Mancini, he is nearly as cool as me.' He left, hugging Kompany and declaring 'Viva La Belgium'. Gallagher posted a picture on Twitter of his meeting with Maradona, accompanied: 'Maradona shakes the hand of God!' Kompany tweeted: 'Liam Gallagher Ladies and gentlemen :-) He sat with my family through out the game and that's an explosive cocktail!'

MAY

WAS MANCINI WINNING THE MIND GAMES OVER FERGIE?

"Perhaps Roberto has deflected the pressure from us
by saying the title is over."
David Silva

Tuesday, May 1, 2012

A lip-reader revealed the contents of the finger-jabbing touch line confrontation. Ferguson was seen to gesture at Mancini and shouted "I've f------ had enough of this..." according to lip reader James Freestone. Mancini is then seen to mimic Fergie's 'talking' gesture and then shouts "You can f------ talk".

Mancini insisted that the two men shared a post-match glass of wine and that everything is "forgotten", but while he was happy to defuse tensions, Mancini stressed his team's winning character was a determination to match United toe to toe. "Only for United, and the FA Cup tie was really important in that when we lost 3-2 at home in January, not when we won 6-1, because that game was easy. When we lost 3-2, after going down to 10 players after 10 minutes, we recovered the game and had a chance to score a third goal. United didn't have a shot in the second half with 11 players and I think that game was important in changing our mentality against them. But football is strange and Newcastle will be more difficult than the derby. It will be harder to beat them than it was to beat United." Sir Alex reacted because of the pressure, as Mancini said, "I don't know what else it could be. But I understand it. It is difficult for me. If another manager says something against me without a reason then I think I have to stand where I am. I didn't say anything to Sir Alex. I only spoke to the fourth official and it had nothing to do with him. Maybe it was because of the game. In a derby like that I can understand."

David Silva believed Mancini's psychological warfare helped turn the title race and took the pressure off his players, and with four wins from four since his 'concession' of the title began, his methods proved effective, "It's an important moment for us psychologically as we knew we had to win. We did that and now it gives us the confidence we need for the last two games. There was never a point when we totally gave up on the league but we did get to a point when we knew it was very difficult. Perhaps Roberto has deflected the pressure from us by saying the title is over. It's been a very, very long season, very tough. It's very important that we finish the job now. We don't need to think about United. We've passed that mental stage now. We are ready to win the title. We don't concentrate on United. We concentrate on ourselves. We beat them there, we beat them here. Don't get me wrong, United are a great team, a fantastic team. They've been winning titles for a long time but, as I say, we beat them there, we beat them here."

Silva was still troubled by the ankle problem that caused a dip in his form after a fine start. "I've been quite unlucky in the second half of the season. I've been knocked and knocked and knocked on the same ankle that's caused me a lot of trouble. And just at the moment when I felt the worst physically we had a dip in form as a team. That seemed to show up even more what was happening with my ankle. But we're finishing strongly as a team and I'm concentrating on finishing this season. My ankle is feeling slightly better but the team is also playing better, which helps. I'm just having a lot of physical treatment, getting a lot of movement in my ankle. I had an operation in that ankle years ago and it's just a question of keeping the movement going."

Roberto Mancini expected City's game at Newcastle to be tougher than the derby, "Newcastle will be our hardest game – harder than United. It is strange but it is like this. They have had a fantastic season and are playing to get into the Champions League. Their manager is one of the best managers here and it will be a tough game. It is another Champions League final on Sunday. We have two – Newcastle and QPR. We have to keep a big concentration until May 13." Tévez could well remain at the club but Mancini said: "Why not? He has a contract, he is a good player, but now our concentration should be on Newcastle."

Shay Given believed it would be for the good of the game if City landed the title. "It's fantastic for the Premier League if, please God, Manchester City do win it, because Man United have won it enough times. I've got lots of friends at Manchester City and it would be fantastic if they could pick the trophy up, but they have got a tough game at my old club Newcastle at the weekend. I think they're in the driving seat and hopefully they can get across the line. Years ago I was at Blackburn and Jack Walker had a lot of money and he invested in the team and Blackburn Rovers won the league, and I think if you look at the recent success of Chelsea and Manchester United they have had lots of investment in the team too. It's just that Manchester City have done it over a shorter period than the bigger clubs. But it's part and parcel of modern-day football. I'm sure Mancini is on a high this morning. It's a great win but I'm sure he's not getting carried away, there are a few games left to go and he will be keeping the players really focused on the job in hand. It's in their hands now and it would be a shame if they threw it away."

Wednesday, May 2, 2012

After Newcastle's impressive 2-0 win at the Bridge, Pardew commented, "It'll be special on Sunday. A team challenging for the title against a team challenging for the Champions League. If someone had said that at the start of the season, we wouldn't have believed them."

Thursday, May 3, 2012

Roberto Mancini imposed a 9pm curfew at their Player of the Year awards. In a week when three Aston Villa players were disciplined for a fracas in the early hours of the morning following a boozy awards ceremony, Mancini was taking no chances when the players gathered at the Etihad Stadium for their tribute night. Agüero (Supporters' Player of the Year), Silva (Players' Player of the Year) and captain Kompany stayed teetotal. The approach also applied to an event attended by several City players in Manchester on Tuesday for Given's charity Fashion Kicks. Hart cancelled plans to model clothes on the catwalk to protect a foot injury sustained when a United player trod on it.

Mancini remarked, "I was there and, at 9pm, I pushed the players to go. They went home because I told them and I stayed until 10.30pm to represent them. It had been organised a month ago so it was difficult to change the date. The other thing was for charity, which is important."

Mancini expected Agüero to stay. "I don't think this is a big problem. I think that all of the players want to stay here because it's going well. The club are one of the top clubs in Europe and the feeling is good. Usually we only talk about Agüero, because he scores, Balotelli, because of his girlfriend. But we should think sometimes about the other players because they are important. We need players like Zaba, Micah, Nigel de Jong, Joleon Lescott. Just now, City have a high profile in the world. Maybe we need another two years, but this is normal because you can't change history in two or three years. It needs to be for five, six or 10 years. If we continue to work like this then we can improve our profile."

City fans were concerned over the appointment of Howard Webb for the game at Newcastle as he had a reputation for favouring United. Webb had not seen Mario's stamp on Parker and gave United two penalties as they came from 3-0 down to draw at Chelsea in February. Kevin Parker, secretary of the City supporters club, said, "History tells us he has generally favoured

United. City fans do feel that. We'll just have to hope that isn't reflected on Sunday as it's such a huge day for Manchester City."

Arsene Wenger criticised the current rules that a player can not be disciplined retrospectively if any of the match officials at that game saw the incident in question. That policy caused outrage when Mario's studs-up challenge on Song went unpunished after at least one of the four officials at the game saw the incident, but referee Martin Atkinson failed to act. "Basically we are in the position at the moment where if somebody takes a player's leg off, if the referee has seen it and misjudged it, the player gets away with it. For me that is not acceptable. If you love football you want justice to prevail. How can it be right that Shaun Derry is suspended and Mario Balotelli isn't?'

Mancini wanted to seize the chance to make history, shake off the under-achieving tag, but to do that City had to take one step further of being champions of Manchester, to become champions of England, "I don't think it's typical City now. In the last two or three years Manchester City have improved a lot but, I repeat, it changes nothing. We've showed we are a good team but, as I've always said, it's important to be top when the championship is finished. We are the best team in Manchester probably. To be the best in the country we have to win the next two games. We are here because we want to do this. It can be close but until it's in your hands you don't have it."

City were last crowned champions after beating Newcastle at St James' Park. They could effectively clinch the title on Tyneside again, unlikely when City lost first place after dropping seven points in three games but Mancini was confident they would not stumble again, "We had some important players injured. But I don't think that now. We have a big chance and it is because the guys worked hard."

Mancini said Sir Alex was right to suggest that a win for City at Newcastle would kill off United's title hopes. "I agree," Mancini said. "He has more experience than me and if he said it like that, I agree with him. I think Sunday will be really difficult because of the crowd and Newcastle are a good team. It will probably be a key game. We are here because we want to do this. We've known that for two years. It can be very close but until it's in your hands, you don't have it. So we should do only what we did last Monday if we want to stay at the top."

Mancini was 'disrespectful' for twice saying Swansea would roll over for United. "If you say it more than once it is," said Rodgers, reminding Mancini of his side's 1-0 home win over City in March. "We were the better side and that after Roberto spent about £235m. So I think he knows it won't be an easy game."

Fri, May 4, 2012

Newcastle lost twice at home this season, to Chelsea and West Brom and remain unbeaten there since December. Cissé, who was the Premier League most expensive January transfer, scored two breathtaking goals in the 2-0 win at Stamford Bridge in midweek, taking his tally to 13 goals in his first 12 games, breaking Alan Shearer's record for the best start by a striker in the Premier League. Magpies goalkeeper Tim Krul said: "It's going to be electric on Sunday at St James'. We've beaten Man United and Sunderland at home and I'm sure the fans will generate the same atmosphere as they did in those two games. That will make teams crumble hopefully. I wouldn't feel any guilt if we stopped City from winning the title. We're fighting for our position and to be where we are is an incredible achievement. We've beaten a lot of the top teams already this season and it's now a huge game on Sunday. City are challenging for the League and we're going for the Champions League. It's not going to be easy so we'll keep our feet firmly on the ground. Two games to go and one point off the top four, it's incredible." Gutiérrez planned to wreck the title dream of compatriots Tévez and Agüero.

City signed a six-year kit deal with Nike that could earn up to £12m-a-year. City secured a 10-year deal with Umbro, worth £6-a-year, in 2009. Umbro were now owned by Nike, so that agreement was re-negotiated to reflect City's success on the pitch and the club will now wear the Nike brand from the start of the 2013-14 season.

Saturday, May 5, 2012

Roberto Mancini knew United would fight to the very last second, "United have a stronger mentality than us because they are a club that has been winning for 20 years. They win, win, win, win. When that happens you become stronger. You change more when you win. What happened in the derby won't change them. But it will change us. When you have been winning for 20 years, your mentality doesn't change because you have lost one game."

City's changing mentality started, not in that six-goal drubbing, but actually in defeat, when United won the FA Cup tie in January, when it appeared United would exact maximum revenge but ended up clinging on for a 3-2 win. "Playing against United the FA Cup game in January when we lost 3-2 was really important," Mancini said. "It wasn't the 6-1. That game was easy. But in the FA Cup, we had to play with 10 men for 80 minutes and we were also 3-0 down. Although we lost, they didn't have a shot in the second half, even though they had 11 players and we had a chance to score the third. It changed our mentality against them." It will encourage players

*(Top) and (Middle)
Captain Vincent Kompany
finally gets his hands on the
Premier League trophy after a
day of twists and turns.*

*(Left) Mario Balotelli,
Samir Nasri and Gael
Clichy prepare to parade the
trophy before a bewildered yet
delighted Etihad.*

*Manager Roberto Mancini enjoys the moment with
one of his key players, David Silva (above) and his coaching staff (below).*

(ABOVE) *Carnage in the dressing room as Adam Johnson and Joleon Lescott spray the champers* (BELOW) *French internationals Nasri and Clichy join in the celebrations.*

*(ABOVE) T[...]
triumphant players [...]
ready to party abo[...]
City's parade bus bef[...]
(LEFT) an estima[...]
50,000 fans, includ[...]
(BELOW) a car ador[...]
with City's colours a[...]
club cr[...]*

*All
photographs
courtesy
of Sharon
Latham at
Manchester
City FC
except the one
of the City
car courtesy of
John Conway.*

to stay, others to come, as Mancini argued, 'Against United there were 650 million people watching the game all over the world. They were watching Manchester City. And that is important to the owners. I think City have a good profile around the world, but also that we need another two years to get even bigger. You can't change history in just two years. We need five, six or even 10 years. If we continue to work like this then we can become an important club."

Ferguson said: "It looks like we're going to lose the League on goal difference and you look at the three goals we lost to City in the last three minutes at Old Trafford. Then that crazy, absolutely stupid game against Everton when we threw it away. You can analyse where you think you lost it or won it, but it could come down to goal difference and Gary Neville may be right when he says that's the worst nightmare. The Everton game was the one that was a killer for us, it was an absolutely ridiculous performance in the last 10 minutes, carelessness, absolute carelessness, a stupid performance, It's all right saying the history of the club is to attack all the time that's put us on the back foot. We'll have to accept, if we lose the league, it was the Everton game that did it. No doubt about that. Newcastle is a tough game for City, there's no question about that. They know that, everyone knows that. But at the end of the day, we're on the back foot. We're not favourites, that's for sure."

Ferguson was disappointed his team failed to put Hart under any pressure, "We didn't test the goalkeeper, let's be honest. We started the game very well. They didn't make any chances. The goal at half-time was a killer for us. Scoring in injury time, they could set their stall out the way they did. Play a bit of counter attack, make sure they weren't going to lose a goal. That was a killer." De Jong's tackle put Welbeck out of the match against Swansea, provoking the nose-to-nose row with Mancini, "I thought it was a bad tackle. But I don't think it was a red card. When I saw it again I think a yellow card was sufficient."

Sir Alex blamed rivals City for the "insane" transfer market, "It's been an insane transfer market for a long time and I think clubs like City create that. They can buy all the players and put a marker on all the players and that makes it difficult for clubs then to be reasonable. There's no chance of that calming down and I don't see how the financial fair play can work. No-one can match City's financial power – no-one. We have to accept that, so we do it a different way. We'll try to look at young players with the potential to develop in the club, which we're good at, so we'll stay with that."

Sunday, May 6, 2012

A champagne moment in the history of Manchester City but no bubbly for the man who made it happen! On religious grounds, Yaya Toure handed the large bottle to Joleon Lescott. Yaya was the obvious choice for man of the match, scoring both goals in a 2-0 win at Newcastle which put City on the cusp of a first league title since 1968. But on receiving the champagne, he turned to Lescott and said: 'I don't drink because I am a Muslim, so you keep it.'

It was at St. James's Park on 11 May 1968 that City clinched their last league title; 44 years on, City moved to within three points of the prize that eluded them for so long. Mike Summerbee, who scored at St. James's when City last won the title sat alongside Patrick Vieira with a tear in his eye. Summerbee scored in a 4-3 win that brought City their last title under the guidance of Mercer and coach Malcolm Allison.

At a subdued Old Trafford, mike in hand on his usual end of season address to the fans, Sir Alex urged United supporters not to give up after both Manchester clubs won 2-0, Mancini's team ahead with an eight goal difference. United failed to score at all in the second half when they had the opportunity to substantially reduce that goal difference. Yet, Ferguson addressed the supporters after the win over Swansea, 'Hopefully next week will be the biggest celebration of our lives.' This was despite saying in a television interview before the game that City "probably" had 'two hands' on the trophy as he reasoned, "The crowd will be right behind them, and they will be into the referee as they were doing against us."

After the match, he joked: "It's an important day for QPR. I just wish Sparky was playing. City are obviously red-hot favourites." Fergie couldn't help himself stirring the pot, "The whole future of the club could be resting on the game and I only wish Sparky was playing. Mark knows his job all right. He was sacked by City in a very unethical way and he'll remember that. Mark Hughes' teams always fight but QPR players are fighting for survival. We've won the title on three occasions on the last day and we don't mind doing it again. City are red-hot favourites and will want to make sure they win the match. The expectation and responsibility of Manchester United players is to win the match. We'll go there optimistic. It won't be easy but we'll have a go."

Fergie smiled at the notion there could be a collapse as dramatic as Devon Loch in the 1956 Grand National. "There could be a Devon Loch. You never know. Stranger things have happened in this game of football."

United faced becoming the first team to lose the league on goal difference (the title was then decided on goal average) since they inflicted a similar fate on Leeds in 1965. "We did what we had to do, we won the match. There was optimism from our fans and ourselves about scoring a lot of goals but it was over-optimism. It wasn't too difficult to lift them before the game. They all knew their responsibility. They know the expectation of this club that whenever you play, wherever you play and whoever you play we are expected to win."

Carrick admitted that the players watched intently the events unfolding at St. James's Park with hoped lifted with no goals after 70 minutes, but the players went out completely deflated. "I'm satisfied with the enthusiasm of the players, they did well," insisted Ferguson. "It could easily have been one of those days where their heads were down a little bit but they did well with good professionalism. It's a decent result. Swansea just killed the game and it is very difficult to get the ball off them. If we had got an early chance in the second half I think it would maybe have fired the crowd up, fired our own players up, made Swansea doubt themselves a little bit, but we didn't get that early goal and the game just petered out after that."

Asked if City are now favourites, Mancini, at last changed his tune slightly, said: "Maybe, maybe yes because it depends on us. If we beat QPR, we will be the champions. But at this moment, we can't think about this. We need to prepare very well for the next game, only this. I am excited because we are on the top, but it's not enough. One week more and if we play like we did today, we have a lot of chance to win. I think for us it should be a normal week. We don't change nothing, QPR will be tough, they are fighting for relegation. Nothing changes. It is ours to lose. It doesn't depend on other teams anymore. Toure's first goal was special, like the one he scored in the FA Cup final for us last year. This one may be more important if we can finish the season off."

Roberto Mancini's decision to replace Nasri with holding midfielder de Jong with 28 minutes left, which initially was badly received by City fans, which ultimately swung the game with the realisation that Mancini is a tactical expert. Instead of the preconceived idea it was a negative switch, it was actually the game plan that ignited the goal spurt. The Dutchman's arrival allowed Yaya to push further up, and he needed just eight minutes before he thumped a swerving low effort past Krul and into the bottom corner. With just a minute remaining, Yaya turned Clichy's pass past Krul from close range to seal a precious win.

David Pleat observed the tactical simplicity but so effective for Mancini, "Finally, by introducing Micah Richards for Silva in order to defend aerial assaults from Newcastle, Mancini replicated his changes in the Manchester derby. The template has been set: release Yaya Touré, the most dynamic midfielder in the Premier League, and shore up the centre with De Jong and then Richards. It has proved a most successful recipe in this vital week, where it looks as though City have broken United's resolve."

Mancini said: "Yaya is an important player for us because he has experience. He won with Barca, he won trophies and he brought to us this experience for this reason. Yaya is a fantastic player, but I don't think you can win here because Yaya played well. We won here against Newcastle because all the team played really well and we deserved to win." Yet he also sounded a note of caution, "I hope, but I think that it is not. We have another game – a difficult one like today. Today was difficult because Newcastle are a good team. I think we deserved to win, but it was a difficult game. But I will only feel confident after QPR."

Alan Pardew commented, "You have to say Manchester City were brilliant today. When you can bring on one world star for another... that freshness just made the difference today. But it is never over in the race for the Premier League title, no matter who your opponents are."

Brendan Rodgers was certain United will be a formidable force next season. 'I have never been in the position City and United are in next week. It is so exciting. It is brilliant. You are talking about two great sides. The professionalism of Manchester United today was exemplary. They were probably watching the game beforehand and when Manchester City got those two late goals it could have really deflated them. Manchester United are serial winners. What makes them great winners is how they respond to not winning trophies. So if it is not for them this year, when you look at their history, they always come back the next year and win, so they will be there or thereabouts next season."

After the game, with City officials hugging each other in the stadium corridors, Lescott revealed Yaya's moment of prophecy, "It doesn't surprise me because big players do big things at vital times, and he had already scored in the FA Cup semi-final and final last season. In training on Saturday, he was saying it was going to be him. He had a normal expression, and he just said it would be his time to shine. He believed it, and when you speak to players like that, you think to yourself 'Yes, it just might be' because those types of players can do those types of things. It's a bit different to him. It means just as much to him as it does to us, but if you look at his CV it's nothing to faze him. He has won the Champions League and La Liga, and other trophies, and for him it was probably just another game. We have a number of players who can come up with something at any given time. Yesterday it was Yaya, last week it was Vinny, and in the past it has been Sergio, Carlos, David and Samir. You dream of these things. I never once thought, yeah, I'm bound to win the Premier League. But it was always in my mind. It will be crazy days if we win it. If we could close it out, it would be unreal."

Lescott conceded that only a month ago, the title was a distant hope. "It was out of our hands. We didn't believe in it — more hope — but it was a case that if they slipped up we had to capitalise. It would have been crazy to have given it up after the Arsenal game. That would have been silly. There was no chance of that happening. No other word for it, it would have been criminal. At this level of our careers we are not going to just give up when we get close to something like this. The lads I play with have a never-say-die attitude and it is there for all to see. We've been together all season and listened to everyone's opinion. We know how close we are as a unit and it has been great to be a part of that. It's still not over yet, though. There are the lads who have won big things and they won't get carried away. I'd say to the fans, keep a lid on it this week and let's not get carried away. If it happens next week, they can celebrate then. When we beat United, the talk straight after was of beating Newcastle. If we were not professional, the United win would have meant nothing." Despite all of the cash, Lescott knew a title challenge was never guaranteed, "When I first arrived here it was more hope that we could win the league, rather than real belief. We have developed, got more players in and we are all starting to believe. It has been developing over time."

The arrival at the Etihad of Hughes, who brought Lescott to City from Everton for £22m in 2009, provided a final twist. Lescott added: "Mark isn't going to be playing us thinking how important it is to stop City winning the league. He is only going to be thinking about the three points available to Rangers."

Hughes was City boss for 18 months before being callously replaced with Mancini in December 2009. Sparky said: "It would be just fantastic to go there and get something. They are going for the title and we're trying to stay in the league. When I took over at QPR, I looked at the fixtures and that one lurked ominously in the distant future. It does feel a little bit fated for them and for us." QPR won their last five home games, having beaten Stoke 1-0 on the day City won at Newcastle, to leave them on the brink of survival. Skipper Joey Barton, who started his career at City, believed his team can pull off the great escape. "People wrote us off 10 or 15 games out. They said our run-in was very difficult. Now we have one game to go and are masters of our own destiny. If you'd offered me that 10 games ago, I'd have snapped your hand off."

Djibril Cisse backed Hughes to take "sweet revenge". Cisse said, 'His main concern is to keep QPR up so, first, he will be thinking about getting a result, but it will be sweet for him, too, if he can keep us up and deny City the title." Cisse's late winner against Stoke left QPR needing a point to stay up, 'It's a tricky situation but I think we are going to go and grab something there. We are capable of getting a point. You know it's only a football game. It's 11 v 11. They have got two arms, two legs, just like us, so we are going to try to compete. They are going for the title and maybe they will be nervous but this is not our problem. Our problem is to stay up and we will be giving everything to do that."

Mancini believed City deserved the title, "The situation we are in is very different to a few weeks ago but it was also very different 10 weeks ago when we were on top. Football is like this – it can change every week. We did well all the season and we had some problems five or six weeks ago maybe and today we did well again. All the players until now have done a fantastic job but we still have one game, and one game can change things. "We will play at the Etihad Stadium but it changes nothing. We should keep our concentration like we have over the last few weeks."

Mancini was calm after the game, but underneath he was feeling the mounting sense of joy. "I am excited because we are at the top but that is not enough because there is one week more but if we play like we did against Newcastle then have a big chance of winning. Winning the league is important for everyone – the owner, the chairman our supporters, for us because we work hard – because together it is a good team but we need to do it for one game more."

A number of players hit the town on Saturday night in celebratory mood. Nasri, Lescott, Kolarov and Dzeko spent the evening at popular haunt Panacea for a night which is described on the club's website as one of 'exorcism, devilry and mayhem'. Mario opted for the more refined surroundings of the San Carlo restaurant with his brother and two pals.

Monday, May 7, 2012

Eden Hazard will "definitely" be wearing blue next season, telling Canal+ after Lille's 2-1 win over Paris St Germain: "I have already said that my wish is to go to the Premier League." When asked on whether he prefers red or blue - Lille's home kit is red - Hazard told Canal+ that he likes both colours but added: "It's the blue that I'll be wearing next season. Definitely the blue." Bosnia and Herzegovina boss Safet Susic believes Dzeko will leave City this summer. 'It seems that Manchester City will win the title, which means Roberto Mancini and his staff will remain, and I saw that City are planning to bring in even more attacking players."

Tuesday, May 8, 2012

Yaya Toure felt League glory will be the springboard to major success. "Always I have said this club can go far, this club can win something. Khaldoon and Mansour are doing incredibly well. They have signed big players and they want to make this club a great club, one of the best clubs in Europe, and they are going the right way. Last year, we won the FA Cup and we have to continue like that and next week try to win the game against QPR. We know it's going to be tough, but I believe in this team, I believe in the players we have. We have some fantastic players. That's why I came here, to help the team... to help the club go forward and make it bigger than any club in the world."

Was he feeling the pressure, "No, because I have a lot of experience. I have already won some important trophies. I wanted to come to the club to make a story and my decision was to come to City. Of course, some people make some speculation about other things, but, for me, when you are a football player, you always want to go where you can be loved and be the best player. At Barcelona, I was a good player but at City I am an important player for the team."

Yaya, who once had a trial with Arsenal, reiterated his desire to finish his career back at Barca as he spent three years there before moving to City for £24m in 2010, "I said two years ago that I would return. It's been the most important team for me and if they call you don't think twice. I love Barcelona. In the press conference I did when I left I said I would return, in life you never know what will happen tomorrow, it's been the team of my life and I would like to finish my sporting career here. If I could return, it would be great."

Wednesday, May 9, 2012

Mancini pulled Mario Balotelli to one side during the training session at Carrington. The pair held an animated 10-minute discussion with Mancini waving his finger at Mario. After he was sent off at Arsenal, Mancini initially warned Mario that would never play for the club again. Despite backtracking days later, Mario had yet to make an appearance since returning from a three-match ban – coinciding with the club overturning an eight-point gap from United. Despite his 13 goals in the league, Mario would have to settle for a place on the bench.

He wears Kun Agüero on his shirt, a childhood nickname given to him by his grandparents as he resembled a cartoon character of the same name. City's fans repeat his first name. The pronunciation amuses Agüero, "I like it, it's original. In Argentina it was 'Agüero, Agüero' and in Spain they chanted

'Kun, Kun, Kun'. Now it's 'Sergio, Sergio'. I know how the City fans say it. It's pronounced 'Sehr-hee-ho' in Spanish but it's fun to hear the Mancunians' 'Ser-gee-o'. I know the fans can come up with new songs on their own and I'll always welcome new ones. It's always gratifying to be considered an important member of the team by the fans and hearing your name being echoed around the stadium is quite a rush. It makes me want to give even more when I go out on the pitch. But being held in high regard is only useful if it's useful for the team, so that we can reach our goals every season. The backing our fans give to me gives me confidence and I try to pay it back by playing my best football. I want to win the title this season and then many more seasons with City after that. We have had a great season but there is so much more to come from this team.'

Thursday, May 10, 2012

Mancini put it succinctly, "two fingers on the trophy". "We don't have pressure. Leading up to the Newcastle game, maybe we had some. But not now. We have two fingers on the trophy. But it is not enough, because we still have one more game and it is a difficult one. My feeling is good after the Newcastle result and so is the feeling of the players. But we need to play the QPR game in the right mood."

Complacency was the enemy for City. Mancini demanded his players complete their task without changing their mentality, "We have managed to keep the players' feet on the ground. We did it before we played United. Then we did it last week before we played Newcastle. We won't change anything. If we don't keep our concentration and prepare well for the game, it will end up being very difficult. The players know they have everything there for them. They have worked hard and they fight every game for one year in a championship that is very hard. Now they have a big chance. Here, we haven't won the title for 50 years and we are in a city where our cousins win every year. That is very difficult for our supporters. So I hope I can change this. We have played for six months and played very well. We played the best football in the Premier League. It's impossible to play well every game for one year. Maybe after Sunday we still won't have the title but we will have played the best football." A cute riposte to Sir Alex's suggestion that Mancini still had an 'Italian mentality'. Mancini, though, cares more about his own supporters. "They are very happy at this moment and they want us to win one more game," he said, laughing. "They tell me I am a fantastic manager, the best manager."

Mancini was excited about the future but put all thoughts of that aside to concentrate on the present, "I said three or four weeks ago I think Manchester

City now are one of the top teams in England, in Europe. After Manchester City can win a title for three or four years - it is possible. I don't know this, but now it is important to win the first. The second after. If we win the title, then we can change history here. The first title is always the most important. After 44 years, the players can be a big part of the history of this club. But they can also become part of the history of English football. I did this with Inter. They had to wait for the championship for almost 20 years and, when it came, it arrived on the last day of the season. I hope the same happens with City. When we started to win with Inter, it began with the Italian Cup like the FA Cup with City. Then we really started to win championships. We won seven trophies in four years and, after I left, Mourinho continued. Once you win, the players begin to understand that if they work hard, improve and show a good mentality, then they can change history. It was good with Inter. But I hope we do even better with City. It is possible."

Mancini had faith in his players, "I trust them 100 per cent. They know they have everything in their hands. Only this. The other things around are not important. I think to talk about next season is too early now. It is better we talk only about the next two days - finished. Next season we have time to talk about everything."

City would become only the fifth club to win the Premier League since its inception in 1992. Mancini said: "I think sometimes if there are other teams, not the usual teams - Manchester United, Chelsea - not like in the last few years, it is good for the championship. This is the best championship in the world. It is the most difficult championship. For me, it will be my best success, if. We have worked hard for two years for this. Now we have a chance to win a title."

Mancini accepted there may be nerves in the final hours but there was no tension in training, "It is a normal week, without problem, without injury. We have worked well. The players are very well. I think maybe tomorrow, Saturday, we can have pressure - I don't know - because it is the last game, but it doesn't change our situation. We need to play another difficult game. We need only to have focus about the game."

Mancini's father Aldo will be present, fit again after a year of heart problems. So, too, will Garry Cook, six months after his sacking, ironically Onuoha will be playing for QPR.

Joey Barton warned of a "reality check" if City were already planning a victory party. Barton, who spent five years at City after coming through their youth system, said his new club were ready to capitalise on the pressure, "I can't wait for the game, I can't wait to go to Man City. They expect us to turn up and them to probably stuff us and go on and win the league. If that is their attitude, they will get a reality check. It's 11 men against 11 men, there is a lot of pressure out there – I can't wait for it. We have one game to go and we are masters of our own destiny."

Anton Ferdinand said: "Rio's been on the phone asking for a favour. But it's about us. I'm concentrating on QPR as we have a massive job to do for ourselves. We've got to go there and get a point, if not three. I have faith in my team-mates that we could possibly do that. If we do get a result and United and Rio go on to win the title, then I will be chuffed for him. If they don't win it but we stay up I will be very, very happy. City have so much riding on it but so have we. This game determines whether people keep jobs or not at our club. We have to make sure every single person keeps their job for next season."

Nedum Onuoha grew up supporting his local club, became a ball boy there, joined their Academy, and played more than a century of games for the first team, but having moved on to QPR he must now help to stop them winning the title. A win-win situation, QPR stay up, City win. Even if QPR lose providing Bolton don't win at Stoke, QPR stay up. "The Etihad Stadium could be the best place in the world this weekend if they win and we stay up but unfortunately that is only one of many scenarios. I don't think I'd be invited to their party if they win the League as I only played five minutes for them this season. On a personal level it will be emotional, though, going back to where I spent so many years. But to think they could win the League and we could stay up — it would be one of the best days of my career. I don't think the way it ended clouds my memories at City because I have so many good ones and most of the people I looked up to and respected are still there. It was a shame things ended the way they did but it allowed me to come here and play every week. I'm normally in contact with the likes of Joe Hart and Joleon Lescott most weeks but we haven't spoken for a fortnight now — I think we are waiting to see who will go first! Being a City fan I have spent many years getting all sorts of grief from United fans so it would be really good if they took a step towards being as successful as United.' Do City deserve to win the League? "Yes, they've been the most consistent team all season."

John O'Shea was annoyed as it was "disappointing" that Mancini labelled United's remaining matches against Swansea and Sunderland as "easy" in comparison to his side's game against Newcastle and QPR. O'Neill expressed that view, and O'Shea echoed his manager, pointing to his team's impressive showings against City this season, having drawn away and defeated them at home, "Believe me, the two times City have played against us this season, they knew it wasn't an easy game. We've taken four points off them, and it should have been six if we think about the game at their place. I think he is starting to enjoy his psychological games but, as the gaffer said, to call the integrity of the Premier League into question is disappointing. He's going for the title and he's going to try certain things. But he doesn't need to do that."

Fri, May 11, 2012

Sir Alex Ferguson hoped for "something stupid" to happen, "Everyone wants to win their last game of the season and we're no different. It's important for us, we'll try and do our best and win the match and hopefully something stupid will happen to City."

Ferguson compared QPR's clash with City with the one the Aberdeen side he managed 29 years ago had against Real Madrid. "Do you know what happened 29 years ago today? I took an Aberdeen team to beat Real Madrid in a European final. 11 players, home bred and the oldest player was 27. That is Queens Park Rangers' challenge, to do an Aberdeen. The odds are stacked against them. City are in good form, at home. On the face of it you expect City to win, but as long as humans are humans you hope something stupid to happen."

Sir Alex paid a surprising compliment to Mancini suggesting he had matched him in the mind games department just as Mourinho once did at Chelsea. "We had to contend with Jose's management style, which was very effective. He did a fantastic job. You knew you were competing against a very clever manager. You weren't just facing the money, you were facing a very united squad. They were hard to beat. City are very similar to Chelsea at that time. Some of their players have had outstanding seasons. When you win the league you need five or six players who are consistently good all the time. City have had that this year and the manager, for most of the part, has done well."

Fergie relished the prospect of meeting City head on next season, but warned the City players that they could ruin the club's future if they fail to beat QPR, "We are certainly not going away, that's for sure. We know that there's a challenge and we accept that. The disappointment of losing the game would be unbelievable. It's untold what effect it could have on them. A nervous situation could arise if, with 10 or 15 minutes to go, City weren't winning. The crowd could get a bit uneasy. City aren't going away. With the money they have to spend, they will obviously go out and buy more players. But you can only buy so many and you can only keep the balance for so long before it disrupts. We have our ideas about where we are going in the summer. And I think that we will be ready for the challenge next year.

Whether that is as champions or as runners-up, we will be ready for it. We have to do something about it, don't we?

"We are probably going to lose out this season but there's a lot of young players in the squad. We're not looking as though it's an end of an era. In many ways, it is the start for many of the young players here. The challenge is obvious. Of course he's had a big financial advantage but you still have to pick the right players. If you buy right there is not a problem but sometimes you don't buy right. It has happened to us, when we maybe bought a player who wasn't suited to us. But in the main, City have bought well. It keeps me going, absolutely. It has taken three years off me and I'm feeling younger already!"

Kia Joorabchian suggested Tévez was likely to stay. "Carlos has had his turbulent moments, but he is now back and 100% committed. He has settled his differences and his relationship with Roberto is now right. I personally hope he stays and goes on to achieve European glory next year. We will wait and see as in football you can never say 100% whether anyone will stay. Carlos has said he is happy at Manchester, he feels settled and what is more important is this Sunday and there is no-one else who wants to win it as much as Carlos."

Vincent Kompany was named Barclay Player of the Season, the first time a City player has ever received this recognition. Mancini's side kept 17 clean sheets. The captain also scored three times, most crucially the winner against United in what was dubbed the Premier League's 'biggest ever game'. Kompany admitted he was glad to kick off after a nerve-racking week. "If I could have played the game against Queens Park Rangers the day after the Newcastle game last Sunday, I would've done it. The build-up has been a whole week, it is very annoying. You just want to get it over with but, then again, it's part of what is going to make it so special, I hope."

Roberto Mancini's coaching team reminded him that he agreed to have the City crest tattooed on his left leg, if he landed the title. Mancini celebrated winning the Italian League with Sampdoria in 1991 by having a club emblem tattooed just above his right ankle. When asked about the tattoo, "I have another leg. If I win the Premier League with Manchester City, I might get one."

Saturday, May 12, 2012

Mario Balotelli left City's Carrington training ground clutching his passport. Mario had yet to make an appearance for City since returning from a three-match ban.

Meanwhile Mancini ignored al the hype about The Revenge of Mark

Hughes. "This is not important – on Sunday we play Manchester City against QPR. For me, they are a good team, they don't deserve to stay at the bottom. They want to do everything to stay in the Premier League and for this reason I think it will be a tough game. I don't know him very well but it is not Mancini against Hughes or Hughes against Mancini. It is City against QPR. One team plays for the title, the other plays relegation."

There was no revenge mission insisted Hughes, "People keep throwing that word up," Hughes said, "but it is not in my mind at all. We've got to try and get in a position where we can get those emotions and those doubts and those feelings of apprehension flowing through them. You do that by being in a position where you can still upset the party and stop the streamers being thrown. Get ourselves in that position, and who knows? City fans have had years of being disappointed. If we can get into a situation where our future is still in our own hands then maybe, just maybe, City might get nervous. Over the years, if something can go wrong it undoubtedly will go wrong to City. That's something City fans have dealt with over many, many years."

As a member of the United squad that finally ended the club's title drought in 1993, Hughes knows how hard it is to take that final stride, "They've got good players who have won championships, but they haven't won it as a group. If we can frustrate, and play on the little bit of apprehension that undoubtedly they'll have – and even if the players don't have it, the crowd will – we've got to try and play on those emotions."

Hughes stopped short of taking credit for City's recent successes, "I came in when Man City were basically a mid-table Premier League team. We got to a point where I felt we were on the cusp of something really special, and then for whatever reason I wasn't given the opportunity. They felt that I wasn't the right guy to take them forward. I will argue until I'm blue in the face that I was, but it doesn't matter now. I would have hoped that we wouldn't have been in this position because when I came into the job and saw the fixtures that lay ahead, we were hoping nothing would be riding on this game. It's the wrong scenario, really, but we are where we are. So let's go for it. It's in our own hands. We can affect our own destiny. It's going to be a big ask, but in the end we may well have to hope somebody else does us a favour."

"With Manchester City having a chance to win the title in front of their own fans, there won't be many people betting against them," a hopeful Bolton boss Owen Coyle said.

United planned an open-topped bus parade on Wednesday. A Manchester council source said: 'Both clubs needed to give a week's notice for a victory parade so the police and roads can be organised and both clubs have done that. They must be confident." City booked their open-topped bus tour for Monday evening.

THE FINAL DAY

THE GREATEST FINISH IN PREMIER LEAGUE HISTORY

The book is a day by day diary, but for the final day, it merits a minute by minute breakdown of an historic day City fans will never forget.

Sunday, May 13, 2012

City last won the league title from United, on May 11, 1968 - Louis Armstrong was at number one with 'Wonderful World.' Harold Wilson was Prime Minister, the Kray twins had just been arrested and Britain's first heart transplant was carried out. After City wrapped up that title, United went on to win the European Cup final at Wembley, with George Best inspiring a 4-1 win over Benfica. Would United end the season without a trophy for the first time since 2005, or it could be the day United win an unprecedented 20th league title?

Former City striker Shaun Goater, speaking from Bermuda on BBC Radio 5 live, said "I have to pinch myself. It's a quality team that Roberto Mancini's put together. The players, the club and the fans deserve a result today. It's live over here, but I have to record it because it's Mothers Day here today! So I've sent a message to all my friends not to call me with scores and the results, and I will watch it all later."

Opta Sports tweets: "Mark Hughes has never lost as a boss away at Man City in the Premier League (W1 D4)."

BBC chief football writer Phil McNulty: "Lots of early arrivals at the Etihad - suspect most just don't want to be bag of nerves at home and have come to join their fellow sufferers. Great overheard line from a jittery Man City fan outside the Etihad: 'I can't be doing with this sort of stress every 44 years'."

MOTD's Guy Mowbray at Etihad Stadium: "I can't help but think of 1996 when it comes to Manchester City and final-day drama. Coming back from two goals down to draw with Liverpool, and false reports of Coventry losing at home to Leeds, led to City's staff telling the players a draw was enough to stay in the Premier League. Instead of going for the win they tried for too long to play out time and drew - as did Coventry. City went down on goal difference. Going down with them that same season were QPR. If

Rangers' first return to the top flight since then is to last longer than one season then they might need to avoid defeat - possibly denying City the title in the process. Time to sit back and watch the drama unfold. Let's just not expect the expected. I know that doesn't really make sense - but this is Manchester City after all. Things rarely have with them."

McNulty: "The maths are simple at Manchester City. Barring a seismic shift in goal difference, victory will bring City their first title in 44 years. QPR have relegation business to attend to and will cast eyes towards Stoke City, where Bolton have to win to stay up. The sense of anticipation - and tension - around the Etihad is intense already."

Mowbray: "Sky blue in Manchester - with a few gloomy patches. Is that how the day will go? What a final day. Lots of fans already here, and excited. Spotted two smiling QPR fans too. Can they get what they need? Will they have to? Monsieur Gerard Houllier just entered Etihad Stadium wearing a Man City scarf. I suspect it was thrust upon him outside. The last time Manchester City won the league championship, Manchester United lost to Sunderland on the final day of the season. But with the title again in City's hands, Sir Alex Ferguson's team are relatively powerless and will focus on the only thing in their control: beating the Black Cats. Martin O'Neill's side will hope to finish the season on a high, though, having failed to win in their last eight games."

McNulty: "I remember being at Maine Road when Man City mistakenly started playing for a draw they thought would keep them up versus Liverpool. Times change. City are unchanged for their crunch game with QPR. So that sees birthday boy Yaya Toure starting in midfield alongside Gareth Barry, with Carlos Tévez and Sergio Agüero up top. Mad Mario Balotelli is on the bench though."

City assistant manager David Platt on BBC 5 live: "We always felt confident even after the Arsenal defeat that we could go on and win our games and do our job. The eight-point gap gave us a bit of freedom and enabled us to go on. We have to make sure our concentration levels don't drop whatever happens at the Stadium of Light or here at the Etihad."

Henry Winter, Daily Telegraph tweets: "Loads of Man City fans driving the wrong way down the M56 hard shoulder after police close road near M60, following incident on bridge..."

QPR manager Mark Hughes: "It will be a difficult task. City are an outstanding team who have been fantastic this year but we are here to do our best and to see if we can get a result. On the changes he has made to his team: "We have played a certain way away from home and it has not been working for us. Today is an opportunity to try something different and see where it takes us. We have got good ability on the pitch but we have got to make sure we are nice and solid."

Liam Gallagher: "I've been hungover since we beat United, then sat around at home waiting for today. Hopefully we can do it and get on it. If we can't beat QPR to win the league, at home, then we don't deserve it. But I think with the crowd and the players we've got then we will nail them."

Sir Alex: "the odds are stacked against us winning the title today, but the situation is not as black as it's being painted". In his programme notes, Martin O'Neill reminded fans that City, Arsenal and Liverpool have all been beaten here and says his team will be "desperately striving" for a win that could lift his team into the top 10.

Robbie Savage on BBC Final Score: "United threw it away, after Roberto Mancini's mind games. I think City, over the course of the season, have been the best team this season. I think they will win."

Martin Keown on Final Score: "At Etihad it could turn into a carnival or the worst day in Manchester City's history."

McNulty: "It's an easy decision for Roberto Mancini to name an unchanged Manchester City team after those outstanding victories against Manchester United and Newcastle United. QPR boss Mark Hughes makes a positive selection by bringing in Shaun Wright-Phillips and Djibril Cisse for Adel Taarabt and Akos Buzsaky."

Garth Crooks on Final Score "I give QPR a chance and I won't be surprised if they get a draw. They are playing for so much – Premier League survival."

McNulty: "Literally rocking at The Etihad as interviews are conducted with The Smiths' Johnny Marr and The Cult's mighty Billy Duffy. Both City fans."

Mark Pougatch on Radio 5 Live: "Roberto Mancini is looking so relaxed – posing for photographs and signing autographs for fans."

Roberto Mancini: "We worked, we want this and we are here. Now it depends on us. It will be a difficult game because QPR are a very good side and they are playing against relegation. We want to control the game and have the same attitude as the last four or five games. All the players could be nervous, ours and theirs. We haven't changed anything but it is a special day. After the match will be a special day if we do it. The fans are happy in this moment but we have another difficult 90 minutes. It's difficult for me, the players, everyone."

Sir Alex Ferguson : "We have a very difficult game here. People keep talking about QPR versus Manchester City and making predictions around that but they seem to forget we have got a very difficult game here." Will you be passing news from Etihad Stadium on to your players? "It is very important our players concentrate on our game because they can easily be put off. We have to concentrate on this game and see what happens elsewhere. We have got to perform very well to get the result we want. I think all the pressure is on City. I just hope we can perform to our level in the last match of the season, because we have fans all over the world watching us."

★

Vincent Kompany leads City out on to the pitch at a packed Etihad Stadium.

GOAL: Within minutes, QPR fans are celebrating a Stoke goal.

Danny Mills at the Etihad, Radio 5 summariser: "If QPR continue to play like this then surely Manchester City will score soon. They cannot play 90 minutes camped in their own half."

GOAL: After 20 minutes United take the lead at Sunderland. Phil Jones swings in a cross from the right, it evades two Sunderland defenders, Rooney stoops to nod in at close range at the back stick.

Garth Crooks: "Do City now start to get a little bit anxious? Do they up it and try to force the situation, or do they continue to play calmly?"

Alan Green, Radio 5 commentator at Etihad: "You do feel an increase in tension around the Etihad now. They know about that goal on Wearside do the Manchester City fans."

Djibril Cisse's low shot punched out by Hart. A nasty challenge from former United forward Frazier Campbell leaves Evra injured. Campbell booked.

Mills: "For the neutral the afternoon is working out perfectly. It's going to be really interesting. City have got to keep their composure. They will create chances but have got to take them when they arrive. City are just starting to get a little nervous. This really reminds me of the game between Barcelona and Chelsea at the Nou Camp. QPR are camped really deep in their own half and have no intention of attacking. City are finding it difficult to find space. As it stands then. Manchester United are winning the league, Spurs are finishing third ahead of Arsenal and Newcastle, while Bolton are relegated. It's all going off."

Giggs almost makes it 2-0, set up by Young but his first-time shot with the outside of his left boot is saved... Rooney curls a free-kick from 19 yards against the bar on the half-hour....Rooney misses a sitter....Yaya goes down holding the back of his knee, trying to continue... Fraizer Campbell is on the end of a cross in to the box but can't control his volley and hits it over.

John Murray, 5 commentator at Stadium of Light: "United have had so many chances they could already have an unassailable lead.'

City are dominating possession but can't unlock a stubborn defence... nerves jangling on the blue side of Manchester.

GOAL: Zabaketa, 39 mins

Jeff Stelling anchoring the Sky/Gillette Football panel had his first crisis. Iain Dowie – over in the Potteries – was suddenly frozen solid in his gantry, the screen turned black as Paul Merson announced a City goal with a burst of 'blue moon, you saw me standing alone'. Stelling's explanation for this loss of pictures was 'there's a lot of wind, I'm told. Not from Dowie, from Stoke', cue laughs guffaws from his quartet.

That was pretty much it for a scintillating first 45 – save for Merson saying Yaya Toure was so crocked he was 'moving like Tiss used to'. Of which Thommo pondered aloud, 'that quick?'

Keown: "Paddy Kenny really should be doing better with that. It's no more than a toe-poke from Zabaleta, but Kenny could do no more than just push it up and in."

Meanwhile Yaya Toure is seen struggling....

HALF-TIME

MOTD's Steve Wilson at Stadium of Light: (half time) "Manchester United have scored one and missed a few. Wayne Rooney netted with a stooping header and then missed a sitter. The fans here are checking to see what it all means, but they know Manchester City lead QPR by 1-0."

McNulty (half time at Etihad): "The mood is celebratory at the Etihad as Manchester City have the lead they need. Events elsewhere mean QPR boss Mark Hughes simply has to be more ambitious after the break."

Danny Mills: "Bolton's goal is not good news for Manchester City. QPR have got to change their formation and change their style in the second half. They're heading out of the Premier League."

The title is City's as it stands, Spurs third, QPR relegated.

McNulty: "Mark Hughes marches off an unhappy man at half-time as QPR resistance is broken and Man City lead 1-0. May need Plan B here – City will be the much happier. Paddy Kenny trending on Twitter. With lots of love from Man City fans, I suspect. Effort for Zabaleta's goal looked even worse on replays.

And a sub I should have brought to you - Yaya Toure eventually succumbed to that injury and was replaced Nigel de Jong.

Mills: "I think Mark Hughes has got to change his whole philosophy. They came here to play a containing game and, on the whole, it pretty much worked. They limited City's chances. But they're going to have to play different now. One goal will change everything."

Pat Nevin, Radio 5 summariser at Stadium of Light: "Manchester United have played very well - but it's not all over here. Sunderland certainly don't want them to win and have the attacking talent to get back into the game. But one more United goal and it will be all over."

SECOND HALF

Rooney is almost in on goal 30 seconds into the second half....Agüero is in at the near post, his shot saved...Giggs, Young combine to put Rooney through but Mignolet makes fine save.

GOAL: Cisse, 48 mins. QPR above Bolton at the bottom.

At 4.08, in the Sky studios the cry 'Goal! Goal! GOAL! The title race is back on again' went up, as QPR equalised. Jeff Stelling gave Charlie Nicholas an opportunity to describe the atmosphere at United's game, but no sooner had he begun, than Le Tissier was in again – hollering 'Oh my God, goal – shut up Charlie' as Arsenal took the lead and pushed themselves back into third place.

Keown: "We've seen so many defensive mistakes today. Lescott went for a ball that he had no chance of winning, and Cisse is on to it in a flash. He either scores or gets sent off. He's certainly made an impact."

United fans heard all about goal at City, in raptures.... United are 40 minutes away from a 20th league title.

Mills: "Unbelievable. I'm almost speechless. That was a goal out of absolutely nothing. Lescott got it completely wrong, he just flicked the ball into Cisse's path. QPR fans have gone delirious, City fans left silenced and dumbfounded."

Sunderland giving it a real go....Barton sent-off against his former club for an off-the-ball incident with Tévez....then Barton knees Agüero in the back of the leg.... a major melee...Barton tries to head butt Kompany.... tangles with subs Mario...surely a big ban awaits.... free-kick for City, Tévez takes it but the ball is cleared to Nasri, whose low shot is hacked away. QPR set for siege.

Merson proclaimed 'red card Joey Barton'. Stelling summed up the day so far: 'City-itis – will it strike again? But QPR are down to 10 men, with barely a player on the field (Barton) didn't assault'. Cue laughter from his four top pundits.

Savage: "What Joey Barton has just done there is an absolute disgrace. He's just leathered Sergio Agüero as he's going off."

Crooks: "QPR are staring down the trapdoor again. They'd pulled themselves into safety, but now it's almost curtains."

Great save....City think they've scored but Kenny somehow keeps out Agüero's effort from close range.

McNulty: "Chaotic scenes after Joey Barton's red card and now QPR look condemned to spend the next 25 minutes camped inside their own penalty area as Manchester City try to win the title."

GOAL: Disaster for City, QPR take the lead! Traore bursts clear down the left, picks out cross deep into the area, Mackie header back across Hart. 66 mins. Incredible scenes. City haven't lost at home all season, only dropped two points.....

Keown: "Man City fans look distraught in the crowd. People are crying. The City players have to take ownership of this game now and play with their heads."

Murray: "Manchester United supporters here cannot believe their ears. They've certainly let their players know QPR are leading."

Dzeko on for Barry....City need two goals in the next 20 minutes.... City piling on the pressure....corner after corner...Mario in place of Carlos.... United twice denied, Scholes hits the post from 20 yards, keeper tips Giggs effort over.

Keown: "If Manchester City don't do this today you wonder what sort of mental scar it will leave on those players. They just need that first victory. We've just not seen Agüero or Tévez on the ball..."

Heroic defending....11 minutes to score twice.... emotions running high, the camera picked out several fans in tears, Mancini in a state of panic...

Mike Ingham, 5 live commentator at Etihad: "All Joe Hart has had to do this afternoon is pick the ball out of the back of his net twice."

Chelsea at Barcelona all over again... City camped 20 yards from the QPR goal without looking like scoring....

Savage: "City just cannot play. They are just blasting balls over the bar. They're wild. Whereas, what do Manchester United do at this stage of the season? They win. They've been so professional today."

Crooks: "When you see the replay of what Joey Barton did to Carlos Tévez on Match of the Day tonight, he should get a six-month ban, for that incident alone."

Into the last five minutes, United set for another league title.... Mario comes close, header saved....

Savage: "I just cannot believe what's happened to City. This is madness! Losing Yaya Toure was a huge blow..."

GOAL: PLUS TWO MINS. Remarkable. Dzeko heads in from a corner in stoppage time.

United fans are cheering wildly, they think its all over....its all over, United think they've won, but they had three minutes of injury time, City kicked off slightly later and had more injury time. The United players look bewildered at the end. What has happened?

GOAL: PLUS FOUR. Agüero picks the ball up, runs through two men and thumps the ball past Paddy Kenny

'As long as I've been watching football, this is the most unbelievable thing I have ever seen', exclaimed Merson.

Sunderland fans cheer wildly, the game is up, United players troop off totally dejected QPR stay up, Bolton down...32 PL goals, a total of 1066, the most ever in a single 38-match season....none more important than Agüero's.

Savage: "This is the greatest climax to a league ever! Unbelievable!"

Cue a pitch invasion, wild scenes of undiluted joy, City fans had given up...United fans were sure it was there's...City are champions

POST-MATCH COMMENTS

Mancini: "The football was incredible. This is for our supporters, they deserve this. To win like this is incredible. I've never seen a climax like this. We didn't deserve to lose this game. We had a lot of chances. We deserve to win this Championship. After 44 years I dedicate this to all our supporters. This is incredible. It's been a crazy season and a crazy last few minutes."

McNulty: "If you are going to wait 44 years to win the title then that was a finish worth waiting for. Manchester City were in despair at the start of stoppage time and on the highest high when it finished. Pure Premier League theatre."

QPR assistant Mark Bowen: "At the end of the day myself and Mark have got an association with Manchester City as well. We gave it our all. We had to rely on another result in the end but we're delighted. What an afternoon of football. It's not often I'm lost for words, but I'm speechless. We laid the foundations here at City and good luck to them."

Kompany: "I want to say it is the best moment of my life but if I'm honest then I would say please never again this way. We have been so good at home all season but in the second half we just couldn't get through the QPR defence. Did I give up? No, I never stopped believing. When Edin Dzeko scored to make it 2-2, it reminded me of our late goals against Tottenham and Sunderland. We had done it before this season so I had no reason not to believe."

Mancini, wrapped in an Italian flag added, "This is an incredible moment.

We wanted this title and we deserve to win this title. This is for all our supporters, the club, the chairman and the owner. This is the perfect finale for a crazy season. We dominated this season for 28 games, but when we beat a team like United twice in one season we deserve this."

Savage: "To go to Old Trafford and win 6-1, then again beat United not so long ago, Mancini now goes down as an iconic figure in Manchester. Whereas United threw it away, losing the title on goal difference."

Title winners of 1968 out on the pitch, led out by Franny Lee.....Mike Summerbee and Tony Book bring out the trophy.....lovely touch again...... City stars wearing shirts with 'Champions 12' on the back........a hug between Roberto and Carlos.....players receive their medals...Kompany lifts the trophy.

Sir Alex: "Nobody expected that. Everybody expected City to win, but they did it against 10 men for half an hour and with five extra minutes to help them. But I congratulate City on winning the league. Anybody who wins it deserves it, because it's a long haul. At the end of our game our players didn't actually know the results. Now, they're really disappointed, I'm glad to say. There's no other way they should be. They conducted themselves brilliantly today. Their performance level was good. I'm pleased at our performance this season. 89 points would win most leagues. It wasn't our turn today."

Redknapp on Manchester City winning title: "That's what makes our league so great. That's football, you do not have a divine right to beat anyone."

MOTD's Alan Shearer on BBC Radio 5 live: "My heart was pounding, so goodness knows what Mancini's and Sir Alex's hearts were doing! I couldn't see City scoring, because nothing was happening for them. But I always felt that, if they got one, the crowd might just put them through. That was the case. You could hear the roar of the crowd, and it was an unbelievable afternoon of football. Now City can go on and dominate for a while. It is City's title and they deserve it."

Dzeko chases down Roberto and eventually catches up with his boss to soak him in champagne.

Pablo Zabaleta on the pitch: "When we were losing 2-1 I thought we were going to lose. But right now I'm dreaming and I don't want to wake up. Everyone deserves this and I'm so proud of these players. When you believe in yourself you win."

Gareth Barry speaking on BBC Radio 5 live: "I was fearing the worst with five minutes to go. It was a massive mountain to climb. It all fell perfectly, with QPR knowing they were safe and all of a sudden we were on a high!"

Joe Hart: "It was a crazy day. I'm proud to play for Manchester City and to play with these boys. This means the world for these fans. We need to do it again. Let's do it again."

Mario Balotelli speaking on the pitch: "This proves that we are the best. That's why we won. The season's been good, so we deserve to win. Personally, too many people talk and say bad things about me. Now, they just have to shut up. Man City is a great club and a great team, and I don't see my future far from here."

David Platt on BBC Radio 5 live: "It was a strange game. They were a tightly-packed defence. In the space of 20 minutes in the second half we were staring down the abyss. But football has astonished me today. It's been absolutely bizarre. I can't put my emotions into words. We now have the experience of winning something, and we'll enjoy it now. For Roberto Mancini, he'll enjoy it tonight but tomorrow this will be gone. We go again."

City confirmed a bus parade through the city centre on Monday night, starting in Albert Square at 18:00 BST.

The players hit the town on Sunday night. Lescott wore his winners medal around his neck, Owen Hargreaves and Stuart Taylor joined the celebrations, despite amassing just one Premier League appearance between them this season. Mario was snapped away from the City squad, dining at his favourite haunt San Carlo restaurant, where he was said to have been given a standing ovation. Kompany posed with life-long supporters' Liam Gallagher and Ricky Hatton, Gareth Barry was greeted by a man wearing a Bo Selecta mask as he sat in a bar. It was a late night as Vincent Kompany struggled to cope with his hangover, 'Struggling to remember what happened last night. Woke up with a medal around my neck. Been told the party was decent. Memo to myself: Next time you're Champion, drink less, dance more.' Clichy wrote: 'I'm feeling FRESH!!!!! What a night.'

Monday 14th May 2012

MANCHESTER CITY PARADE

Roberto Mancini and his players and staff gathered at Albert Square to be greeted by thousands of fans on a 1.8-mile journey through the city that ended in Corporation Street. Members of the victorious squad were invited to a private reception at Manchester town hall in the afternoon before taking to a stage to greet a huge crowd in the city's Albert Square. Kompany, Mancini, Hart and Dzeko addressed the crowd.

Responding to big cheers, Mancini, wearing his trademark club scarf, said: "I think we should be proud of these players because they did everything for you - they wanted to win this championship for you. We had the best and worst five minutes in our lives. I think it was an incredible moment after we scored the third goal, but before it was very hard."

Tévez was in attendance, as were fringe players like Stuart Taylor and Owen Hargreaves, but Mario Balotelli had flown back to Milan early on Monday, reporting for medical checks after being named in his country's provisional squad for Euro 2012. Chairman Khaldoon al-Mubarak commented, "Everyone will have their own experience of what happened yesterday. I don't think any league will be decided like that for many years to come. Maybe some people imagined it was 'typical City'. We are not typical City. We have destroyed that thought. This is not a team that is going to lie down. Now we want to forget about 'typical City'. This club wants to win more than anything and will fight for that until the last kick of the game."

The course of the season changed after a post-match chat with Mancini, immediately after City suffered a 1-0 defeat that left them eight points adrift of United with six matches left. Khaldoon explained, "We had two choices. We could either raise the white flag and sulk or pick ourselves up and fight until the last second of this championship. I remember going down to the dressing room thinking we were not giving up. Something inside me said there was more to it. I had a conversation with Roberto. We both looked at each other and decided to take the pressure off everyone. We felt if we could win all our games and have a bit of luck, we could still pull it off. What Roberto did magnificently was to take the pressure off the entire team."

Sheikh Mansour's City project would expand even more once construction begins on a massive new training and academy project a stone's throw away from the stadium. Sheikh Mansour remained at home in Abu Dhabi, although he watched every second on TV as City won the title. "He has not missed a single minute of football this club has played this season," said Khaldoon. "Even if the match is not on TV, he finds a way to watch it. Yesterday was a rollercoaster for him and the telephone conversation I had with him afterwards was one of the most ecstatic ever."

Yaya Toure already has his sights set on winning more silverware, "We have been unbelievable. I thank all but I think next year will be more and I hope City will become a great club in the world. I will think about the new season and I hope it will be more exciting than the last one. I think the fans may enjoy it more because now we have fantastic players, they are growing. They have fantastic talent and I think next year we will get more cups than this year. It was unbelievable. When we had 10 minutes left I was thinking we needed a goal to try to help us. With all this season, always doing well, to have lost the Premier League at home - it would have been a disaster, I think

I can say that. I am very happy. I think the team deserves it, the fans deserve it, the boss deserves it. I think all this club deserves it this year. That was the character of the team, the winning mentality. The team did fantastically well. We proved all the players on the pitch wanted to fight for this club, to win something for this club, to be part of history for this club."

David Silva was also hoping the team can move on to greater things, "We made the game very hard for ourselves but we kept battling until the end. We managed to pull it off and I am really happy. This team is just getting better and better and let's hope next season we'll be even better."

Sergio Agüero, who scored that last gasp winner to finish his first season with 30 goals, said, "The only thing I can say is I am really happy. The truth is we can hardly believe it ourselves. We thought the Premier League had gone. Thank God it all worked out for us. We got two goals in five minutes, it was absolutely unbelievable. It's all about City now, not United. What we've done there is manage to pull it out of the fire and win it at the very last minute and hopefully it's the start of big things for City in the future. It was almost lost but we managed to save ourselves in the last minutes. I'm really, really happy. Obviously, given that it's a massive thing winning the Premier League. It's a fantastic moment. It would have been a real body blow, but the main thing is to concentrate on the fact that we did win it, and the effect is opposite; the total opposite. It's going to be a real boost, a real positive effect on the side going into the future. I came here to win trophies. I think City have become a great side. I think you can say we are up there with the big boys with that victory and a league title. Let's hope it is the start of a run of trophies."

Of his decisive strike "In my career so far it's the most important goal. You score the goal in the last minute to win the title. You're not sure if that's ever going to happen in your career again. I wish I could tell you how I did it but I can't. I thought for all the world that Mario was going to have a go himself but he just moved it on one more and it fell at my feet and I just thought: 'Hit the target, hit it as hard as you can and hit the target.' And it went in.", Agüero hoped that strikers Dzeko and Mario Balotelli would stay, "In terms of what their personal decisions are, it's nothing to do with me. I hope they stay because both of them as individuals are great players and have brought a lot to the side during the season. Let's hope they do stay because it would be a good thing for City [with] the quality they bring to the club."

Carlos Tévez said: 'I am very, very happy. The game was out of this world. When you are putting an end to such a long run without winning a title, you are always going to have to do it the hard way. It was absolutely incredible. This club have got the players that can win lots of trophies, this is a real big step towards that. Let's hope we can win more and more trophies. I feel very happy at winning this league title." Mario Balotelli commented, "It was better to win like that than 6-0, when you are sure to win. United have suffered a little bit, it is better for us. When I was on the bench, warming up with Micah and they scored their second goal, Micah was upset but I said, "Don't worry, we will win". That's what we did. I thought it was really possible. I believed in it and I was right."

Well, it wouldn't be Carlos with out a touch of controversy displaying a provocative banner...."RIP Fergie". Perhaps one fans reference to Ferguson's famous response to a 2009 question as to whether or not United would ever be underdogs against City. "Not in my lifetime," he said.

City were forced to issue an apology to United's manager, "The creation of the tasteless material is in itself reprehensible and in accepting and brandishing it, Carlos has made a significant error of judgement. The club wishes to express its sincerest apologies to Sir Alex Ferguson and Manchester United Football Club for any offence or distress caused." Tévez explained, "I got carried away in the excitement of the moment and I certainly didn't mean any disrespect to Sir Alex Ferguson, who I admire as a man and a manager."

But in an interview back in Argentina, Tévez said: "It seems like Ferguson is the president of England. Every time he speaks badly about a player or says terrible things about me, nobody says that he has to apologise. When someone comes out with a joke or banter, you have to say sorry - but I don't say sorry."

"It's not difficult to manage Tévez," Mancini said. "He's a good guy. We had a good relationship always. I don't know why we had that situation in September but in the end he's a good guy and a fantastic player." His return helped tip the title race in City's favour. "No question he made a difference. Carlos is an incredible, top player. Mario is different, he's young, but an incredible talent. He's young, and for this reason sometimes he can have bad behaviour - it's normal. But it's important for him to understand he can lose his talent. He can play football for another 10 or 12 years. I hope that now, after this title, he can understand that it's better that he starts to work in a good way."

Mario, Carlos, and the endless problems to overcome, then all the drama in the final game perhaps it's fitting that the last word should with the manager when he joked, "I'm 47 - after the game, 97!"

EPILOGUE

I was having tea at my hotel in London with Harry Harris, the author of this book, and Glenn Hoddle, the former England manager. We were discussing the new football world order, the upcoming European Championships and England's prospects, and the like. This is when Harry told me that he is putting the finishing touches to this Manchester City book, and I didn't hesitate in supporting his project. Regardless of who would end of as champions a week later, the team that did would be approaching 90 points for the season - what will now, inevitably, be the new benchmark for success. Any team that can manage that deserves acclaim. And the extraordinary events of a week later meant that City's win will live long after many other football memories have faded.

I'm not a fan of any particular football team but I am a fan of football - and of great football matches. But allegiance to a team or not, any ordinary person who loves the game will have something inside which, when watching a great contest between teams that are giving everything they have, favours one side or the other. It is human nature, and it is the nature of sports.

I've lived half my life in the UAE now, so I have more complex allegiances and identity than when I was a young boy. So once Sheikh Mansour Bin Zayed Al Nayham bought Manchester City Football Club in 2008, I just knew that my inner Emirati would be unable to resist wishing this new team all the best.

On the 13th May, I was taking part in a 120km coast-to-coast walk in Devon, a beautiful county in the south west of England. I only made it to my hotel room in time to catch the last ten minutes of the Manchester City-QPR game - the final game of the season; the game which, with Manchester United winning at Sunderland, City had to win to take their first title in 44 years. And as I ran to turn on the TV, somehow, City were down 2-1 against the ten men of an almost relegated Rangers team that were defending as if their lives depended on it.

Those ten minutes - the final five of normal time, plus five of injury time - were like a microcosm of the club's last 44 years of history, with the supporters of a club that they used to think was cursed bracing themselves for the horror of having thrown it all away. Then Edin Dzeko scored and in the last minute, Sergio Aguero scored a schoolboy's dream goal; a goal that will live forever; a goal to win his club their first league title in English football since 1968.

Dr Ahmed Samerai
Chairman - The Sahara Group
www.thesaharagroup.ae

Stastistics

Manchester City 2011-12

Date	Opponent	Comp	Res	Score	Scorers	Att
Sun 07 Aug	Manchester United	CS	L	2-3	Lescott 38; Dzeko 45+1	77,169
Mon 15 Aug	SWANSEA CITY	Lge	W	4-0	Dzeko 57; Agüero 68, 90+1; Silva 71	46,802
Sun 21 Aug	Bolton Wanderers	Lge	W	3-2	Silva 26; Barry 37; Dzeko 47	24,273
Sun 28 Aug	Tottenham Hotspur	Lge	W	5-1	Dzeko 34, 41, 55, 90+3; Agüero 60	36,150
Sat 10 Sep	WIGAN	Lge	W	3-0	Agüero 13, 63, 69	46,509
Wed 14 Sep	NAPOLI	CL	D	1-1	Kolarov 74	44,026
Sun 18 Sep	Fulham	Lge	D	2-2	Agüero 18, 46	24,750
Wed 21 Sep	BIRMINGHAM C.	LC	W	2-0	Hargreaves 17; Balotelli 38	25,070
Sat 24 Sep	EVERTON	Lge	W	2-0	Balotelli 68; Milner 89	47,293
Tue 27 Sep	Bayern Munich	CL	L	0-2		65,000
Sat 01 Oct	Blackburn Rovers	Lge	W	4-0	Johnson 56; Balotelli 59; Nasri 73; Savic 87	24,760
Sat 15 Oct	ASTON VILLA	Lge	W	4-1	Balotelli 28; Johnson 47; Kompany 52; Milner 71	47,019
Tue 18 Oct	VILLARREAL	CL	W	2-1	Marchena 43 (og); Agüero 90+3	42,236
Sun 23 Oct	Manchester United	Lge	W	6-1	Balotelli 22, 60; Agüero 69; Dzeko 89, 90+3; Silva 90+1	75,487
Wed 26 Oct	Wolves	LC	W	5-2	Johnson 37; Nasri 39; Dzeko 40, 64; de Vries 50 (og)	12,436
Sat 29 Oct	WOLVES	Lge	W	3-1	Dzeko 52; Kolarov 67; Johnson 90+1	47,142
Wed 02 Nov	Villarreal	CL	W	3-0	Touré 30, 71; Balotelli 45+3 (pen)	24,235
Sat 05 Nov	QPR	Lge	W	3-2	Dzeko 43; Silva 52; Touré 74	18,076
Sat 19 Nov	NEWCASTLE UTD	Lge	W	3-1	Balotelli 41 (pen); Richards 44; Agüero 72 (pen)	47,408
Tue 22 Nov	Napoli	CL	L	1-2	Balotelli 33	53,000
Sun 27 Nov	Liverpool	Lge	D	1-1	Kompany 31	45,071
Tue 29 Nov	Arsenal	LC	W	1-0	Agüero 83	60,028
Sat 03 Dec	NORWICH C.	Lge	W	5-1	Agüero 32; Nasri 51; Touré 68; Balotelli 88; Johnson 90+1	47,201
Wed 07 Dec	BAY. MUNICH	CL	W	2-0	Silva 36; Touré 52	46,002
Mon 12 Dec	Chelsea	Lge	L	1-2	Balotelli 2	41,730
Sun 18 Dec	ARSENAL	Lge	W	1-0	Silva 53	47,303
Wed 21 Dec	STOKE CITY	Lge	W	3-0	Agüero 29, 54; Johnson 36	46,321
Mon 26 Dec	West Brom	Lge	D	0-0		25,938
Sun 01 Jan	Sunderland	Lge	L	0-1		40,625
Tue 03 Jan	LIVERPOOL	Lge	W	3-0	Agüero 10; Touré 33; Milner 75 (pen)	47,131
Sun 08 Jan	MAN UTD	FAC	L	2-3	Kolarov 48; Agüero 65	46,808
Wed 11 Jan	LIVERPOOL	LC	L	0-1		36,017
Mon 16 Jan	Wigan Athletic	Lge	W	1-0	Dzeko 22	16,026
Sun 22 Jan	TOTTENHAM H.	Lge	W	3-2	Nasri 56; Lescott 59; Balotelli 90+5 (pen)	47,422
Wed 25 Jan	Liverpool	LC	D	2-2	de Jong 31; Dzeko 67	44,590

Liverpool won 3-2 on aggregate

Tue 31 Jan	Everton	Lge L 0-1		29,856
Sat 04 Feb	FULHAM	Lge W 3-0	Agüero 10 (pen); Baird 30 (og); Dzeko 72	46,963
Sun 12 Feb	Aston Villa	Lge W 1-0	Lescott 63	35,132
Thu 16 Feb	FC Porto	EL W 2-1	Pereira 55 (og); Agüero 84	47,417
Wed 22 Feb	FC PORTO	EL W 4-0	Agüero 1; Dzeko 76; Silva 84; Pizarro 86	39,538

Manchester City won 6-1 on aggregate

Sat 25 Feb	BLACKBURN R.	Lge W 3-0	Balotelli 30; Agüero 52; Dzeko 81	46,782
Sat 03 Mar	BOLTON W.	Lge W 2-0	Steinsson 23 (og); Balotelli 69	47,219
Thu 08 Mar	Sporting Lisbon	EL L 0-1		34,371
Sun 11 Mar	Swansea City	Lge L 0-1		20,510
Thu 15 Mar	SP. LISBON	EL W 3-2	Agüero 60, 82; Balotelli 75 (pen)	38,021

3-3 on aggregate - Sporting won on away goals rule

Wed 21 Mar	CHELSEA	Lge W 2-1	Agüero 78 (pen); Nasri 85	46,324
Sat 24 Mar	Stoke City	Lge D 1-1	Touré 76	27,535
Sat 31 Mar	SUNDERLAND	Lge D 3-3	Balotelli 43 (pen), 85; Kolarov 86	47,007
Sun 08 Apr	Arsenal	Lge L 0-1		60,096
Wed 11 Apr	WBA	Lge W 4-0	Agüero 6, 54; Tévez 61; Silva 64	46,746
Sat 14 Apr	Norwich City	Lge W 6-1	Tévez 18, 73, 80; Agüero 27, 75; Johnson 90+3	26,812
Sun 22 Apr	Wolverhampton W.	Lge W 2-0	Agüero 27; Nasri 74	24,576
Mon 30 Apr	MAN UTD	Lge W 1-0	Kompany 45+1	47,259
Sun 06 May	Newcastle United	Lge W 2-0	Touré 70, 89	52,389
Sun 13 May	QPR	Lge W 3-2	Zabaleta 39; Dzeko 90+2; Agüero 90+4	48,000

Squad List

Player name	Position	Birthdate	Shirt No.	Apps	Goals
Richards, Micah	Defender	24 Jun 1988	2	31 (+6)	1
Kompany, Vincent	Defender	10 Apr 1986	4	42	3
Zabaleta, Pablo	Defender	16 Jan 1985	5	26 (+5)	1
Lescott, Joleon	Defender	16 Aug 1982	6	40 (+2)	3
Milner, James	Midfielder	04 Jan 1986	7	23 (+13)	3
Pizarro, David	Midfielder	09 Nov 1979	8	2 (+5)	1
Dzeko, Edin	Striker	17 Mar 1986	10	26 (+17)	19
Johnson, Adam	Midfielder	14 Jul 1987	11	16 (+21)	7
Taylor, Stuart	Goalkeeper	28 Nov 1980	12	0	0
Kolarov, Aleksandar	Defender	10 Nov 1985	13	20 (+7)	4
Savic, Stefan	Defender	08 Jan 1991	15	13 (+7)	1
Agüero, Sergio	Striker	02 Jun 1988	16	39 (+9)	30
Barry, Gareth	Midfielder	23 Feb 1981	18	39 (+5)	1
Nasri, Samir	Midfielder	26 Jun 1987	19	37 (+8)	6
Hargreaves, Owen	Midfielder	20 Jan 1981	20	2 (+2)	1
Silva, David	Midfielder	08 Jan 1986	21	46 (+3)	8
Clichy, Gaël	Defender	26 Jul 1985	22	35 (+2)	0
Hart, Joe	Goalkeeper	19 Apr 1987	25	51	0
Touré, Kolo	Defender	19 Mar 1981	28	14 (+6)	0
Pantilimon, Costel	Goalkeeper	01 Feb 1987	30	4	0
Tévez, Carlos	Striker	05 Feb 1984	32	8 (+7)	4
de Jong, Nigel	Midfielder	30 Nov 1984	34	23 (+13)	1
Suárez, Denis	Midfielder	06 Jan 1994	36	0 (+1)	0

Nielsen, Gunnar	Goalkeeper	07 Oct 1986	37	0	0
Touré, Yaya	Midfielder	13 May 1983	42	41 (+1)	9
Balotelli, Mario	Striker	12 Aug 1990	45	21 (+11)	17
Ibrahim, Abdisalam	Striker	01 May 1991	50	0	0
Mancini, Andrea	Midfielder	13 Aug 1992	52	0	0
Roman, Joan Angel	Midfielder	18 May 1993	64	0	0
Abu, Mohammed	Midfielder	14 Nov 1991	tbc	0	0
★ Bridge, Wayne	Defender	05 Aug 1980	3	1	0
★ Wright-Phillips, Shaun	Midfielder	25 Oct 1981	8	0	0
★ Adebayor, Emmanuel	Striker	26 Feb 1984	9	0	0
★ Santa Cruz, Roque	Striker	16 Aug 1981	14	0	0
★ Onuoha, Nedum	Defender	12 Nov 1986	24	2 (+1)	0
★ González, David	Goalkeeper	20 Jul 1982	26	0	0
★ Assulin, Gai	Midfielder	09 Apr 1991	31	0	0
★ Cunningham, Greg	Defender	31 Jan 1991	33	0	0
★ Boyata, Dedryck	Defender	28 Nov 1990	38	0	0
★ Bellamy, Craig	Striker	13 Jul 1979	39	0	0
★ Weiss, Vladimir	Midfielder	30 Nov 1989	40	0	0
★ Mee, Ben	Defender	23 Sep 1989	41	0	0
★ Nimely, Alex	Striker	11 May 1991	43	0	0
★ Rekik, Karim	Defender	02 Dec 1994	44	0 (+2)	0
★ Chantler, Chris	Midfielder	16 Dec 1990	53	0	0
★ Veseli, Frederic	Defender	20 Nov 1992	56	0	0
★ Wabara, Reece	Defender	28 Dec 1991	57	0	0
★ Guidetti, John	Striker	15 Apr 1992	60	0	0
★ Razak, Abdul	Midfielder	11 Nov 1992	62	2 (+2)	0
★ Scapuzzi, Luca	Striker	15 Apr 1991	66	1 (+1)	0
★ McGivern, Ryan	Defender	08 Jan 1990	tbc	0	0
★ Trippier, Kieran	Defender	19 Sep 1990	tbc	0	0

Final League Table

| | | | Home | | | | Away | | | | | |
POS	CLUB	P	W	D	L	F	A	W	D	L	F	A	Pts	GD
1	**[C] Manchester City**	38	18	1	0	55	12	10	4	5	38	17	89	+64
2	Manchester United	38	15	2	2	52	19	13	3	3	37	14	89	+56
3	Arsenal	38	12	4	3	39	17	9	3	7	35	32	70	+25
4	Tottenham Hotspur	38	13	3	3	39	17	7	6	6	27	24	69	+25
5	Newcastle United	38	11	5	3	29	17	8	3	8	27	34	65	+5
6	Chelsea	38	12	3	4	41	24	6	7	6	24	22	64	+19
7	Everton	38	10	3	6	28	15	5	8	6	22	25	56	+10
8	Liverpool	38	6	9	4	24	16	8	1	10	23	24	52	+7
9	Fulham	38	10	5	4	36	26	4	5	10	12	25	52	-3
10	West Bromwich Albion	38	6	3	10	21	22	7	5	7	24	30	47	-7
11	Swansea City	38	8	7	4	27	18	4	4	11	17	33	47	-7
12	Norwich City	38	7	6	6	28	30	5	5	9	24	36	47	-14
13	Sunderland	38	7	7	5	26	17	4	5	10	19	29	45	-1
14	Stoke City	38	7	8	4	25	20	4	4	11	11	33	45	-17
15	Wigan Athletic	38	5	7	7	22	27	6	3	10	20	35	43	-20
16	Aston Villa	38	4	7	8	20	25	3	10	6	17	28	38	-16
17	Queens Park Rangers	38	7	5	7	24	25	3	2	14	19	41	37	-23
18	[R] Bolton Wanderers	38	4	4	11	23	39	6	2	11	23	38	36	-31
19	[R] Blackburn Rovers	38	6	1	12	26	33	2	6	11	22	45	31	-30
20	[R] Wolverhampton W.	38	3	3	13	19	43	2	7	10	21	39	25	-42